Reconstructing the Commercial Republic

RECONSTRUCTING THE COMMERCIAL REPUBLIC

Constitutional Design after Madison

Stephen L. Elkin

The University of Chicago Press CHICAGO AND LONDON

STEPHEN L. ELKIN is a professor in the Department of Government and Politics at the
University of Maryland. His publications include the award-winning book *City and Regime in
the American Republic* (1987), also published by the University of Chicago Press.

The University of Chicago Press, Chicago 60637
The University of Chicago Press, Ltd., London
© 2006 by The University of Chicago
All rights reserved. Published 2006
Printed in the United States of America

15 14 13 12 11 10 09 08 07 06   1 2 3 4 5

ISBN: 0-226-20134-1 (cloth)

The University of Chicago Press gratefully acknowledges a subvention from the University
of Maryland in partial support of the costs of producing this volume.

Library of Congress Cataloging-in-Publication Data

Elkin Stephen L.
    Reconstructing the commercial republic : constitutional design after Madison / Stephen
L. Elkin.
        p.   cm.
    Includes bibliographical references and index.
    ISBN 0-226-20134-1 (cloth : alk. paper)
        1. Political science—United States—Philosophy.   2. United States—Politics and
government.   3. Republicanism—United States.   4. Public interest—United States.
5. Common good.   I. Title.
JA84.U5E55 2006
320.97301—dc22   2005033766

For ETH

Who got there first

The beginning is not merely half of the whole but reaches out towards its end.

POLYBIUS

If it had been found impracticable to have devised models of a more perfect structure, the enlightened friends to liberty would have been obliged to abandon the cause of that species of government as indefensible.

ALEXANDER HAMILTON

A state may change in two ways: either because the constitution is corrected or because it is corrupted. If it has kept its principles, and the constitution changes, that is it's being corrected. If it has lost its principles, when the constitution happens to change, that is it's being corrupted.

MONTESQUIEU

Enough men never agree to a new law that looks to a new order unless they are shown by necessity that they need to do it.

MACHIAVELLI

Give thy Kings law—leave not uncurbed the great.

JOHN KEATS

Republican peoples are able to give themselves the law that their forebears have bequeathed them.

ANON.

The evil they notice [is] due much more to the constitution of the country than to that of the electoral body.

ALEXIS DE TOCQUEVILLE

It is more easy to change an administration than to reform a people.

EDMUND BURKE

A practical man is a man who practices the errors of his ancestors.

BENJAMIN DISRAELI

[A] theoretical crisis does not necessarily lead to a practical crisis.

LEO STRAUSS

CONTENTS

PREFACE

It is said that Gandhi responded to the question "What do you think of Western civilization?" by replying that it would be nice to have. That is my view of the commercial republic: it would nice to have one. In this book I consider the kind of politics that would be necessary to realize it, a politics that directs lawmakers to give concrete meaning to the public interest. I also lay out the foundations necessary for that kind of politics to flourish, and the steps we can take to secure the elements of those foundations. The result of my account is a theory of the political constitution of an American commercial republic. The theory rests on the shoulders of James Madison, perhaps America's most astute political thinker, and certainly the most penetrating political mind of the founders of this Republic. My constitutional theory, then, is neo-Madisonian, but it departs from Madison's flawed account in significant ways.

Americans are perhaps the only people for whom a commercial republic remains a living ideal. This kind of political order—a popular limited self-government married to an economic system marked by a significant measure of private ownership—is the one about which Hamilton said, in the first *Federalist* paper, that it would be a "general misfortune" for humankind if we did not succeed in establishing it and making it work. This is still the case, I believe.

I write here then as a friend of the commercial republic, in the hope that it can be further realized than it is at present. I am aware that the world offers other versions of good political regimes, but it has fallen to us to see if a commercial republic with its promised fruits of self-government, equal liberty, and economic well-being can indeed be more or less fully realized. The arguments I present suggest that the journey to such a realization is not beyond our powers, but there are significant obstacles to even undertaking it, much less completing it.

The argument presented here is perhaps best understood as an exercise in Aristotelian/Montesquieuian/Madisonian/Tocquevillean political science that calls for a reconstruction of the American political order. It may even be an exercise in Machiavellian political science. With this in mind, it is worth pondering the detail of Ambrogio Lorenzetti's *Allegory of Good Government* depicted on the cover of this book. Might the figures of Justice and Wisdom be on the princely side? At any rate, this would not be the first time that such an American reconstruction has occurred. It has happened at least twice before, with Lincoln and the Civil War amendments to the Constitution and with Franklin Roosevelt and the New Deal. These instances of reconstruction are not as comforting as they otherwise might be, since the first required a bloody civil war to make the changes possible and the second required a worldwide depression. It remains to be seen whether it can be done again. In deciding whether we should make the effort, it is essential to understand both our present failings and the concrete remedies necessary to put something better in their place. Both require an understanding of how best to constitute a commercial republic.

MANY PEOPLE have had a part in bringing this book to fruition, so many that I have tried not to let each of them know about the others for fear they would tell me that, with so much other help, their own would not be needed. I did need their help, all of it. Various friends and colleagues read at least one version of the book manuscript and offered detailed comments. Bill Galston, Mark Graber, Steve Lenzner, Peter Levine, Joe Oppenheimer, Karol Soltan, Clarence Stone, and Mariah Zeisberg were all remarkably generous with their time and advice. Ed Haefele not only read multiple versions of the arguments advanced in the book, but conversations with him were crucial to developing the foundation on which the constitutional theory presented rests. It is for this and many other reasons that I dedicate this book to him.

Two anonymous reviewers for the University of Chicago Press were also instrumental in showing me how the book could be improved. I have tried to meet their criticisms since they are sympathetic to the argument I am making and perceptive about its weaknesses.

John Tryneski of the University of Chicago Press also took up his editorial pen. However valuable that effort, it is his patience and encouragement over many years (the writing of the book he reminded me spanned two millennia) that I most deeply appreciate. All slow writers should be blessed with such an editor (fast ones too).

Two University of Maryland undergraduates of extraordinary gifts as footnote checkers and bibliographers, Jacki Hunsicker and Shawn Fraistat, created order out of chaos. Jacki also read the book manuscript with minute attention, forcing me to eliminate confusions and infelicities. It is hard to imagine two better research assistants.

Finally, there is my wife, Diana Elkin. Perhaps it is enough to say that without her editorial and other kinds of assistance the book would have taken even longer to complete. Her editing skills remain a marvel to me, helping me to turn a long torturous manuscript into something approximating a book. Her persistent questioning of what I meant by various formulations pushed me to be clearer than is my habit. Throughout the writing of the book, not to mention before, her companionship has been a blessing for which I regularly give thanks.

A NUMBER of institutions and organizations provided support for the research and writing of this book. The University of Maryland named me a Distinguished Research Professor for a crucial year that enabled me to give the book my undivided attention. The chair of my department, Jon Wilkenfeld, helped in the ways only good chairs can do. The Research School of the Social Sciences at Australian National University twice provided a home and resources at crucial moments, including a vibrant intellectual environment. I am especially grateful to Bob Goodin for his help in arranging these visits. The Democracy Collaborative of the University of Maryland also provided financial support for the project.

The Committee on the Political Economy of the Good Society (PEGS) provided financial support for the publication of this book. This makes it the fourth of a series of books which PEGS has supported, including the first in the series, *A New Constitutionalism*, also published by the University of Chicago Press.

1

Thinking Constitutionally in Light of American Aspirations

AMERICANS NEED a theory of republican political constitution. This is true even for those sighing with political contentment, for like all members of political orders past and present they too must eventually confront the inevitable deterioration of our political institutions. It is doubtful whether any social arrangement can long withstand unaided the forces of inattention, corruption, and debilitating conflict. The contented must understand this deterioration and what may be done about it, at least if they wish to remain content. And it would help if they could do so before political ruin is imminent. To undertake this practical task, they need an account of the sort of political regime we are committed to realizing, the characteristic sources of its corruption and decline, and how to maintain it in good order. They need, that is, a theory of the political constitution of the American republic.

The contented will need such a theory for an additional reason: there will always be proposals for reform that result in—and perhaps have as their sole purpose—undermining the working constitution, which is the very source of their sense of satisfaction. It would thus be well if those busily expressing their contentment with our political order were also able to detect schemes for reform that can do us no good. Their songs of praise should have within them the strong beat of what is essential if republican government is to succeed—namely, a theory of republican political constitution.

Of course, those who are discontented with our present institutions and practices, but who are still committed to some version of what we now have, also need a theory of republican political constitution—at least if they are committed to a full realization of an American republic. A list of the sources of their discontent would include (1) the markedly unequal distribution of wealth and income, including the persistence of a significant degree of poverty; (2) the decline in civic and political involvement; (3) the inequality of political power; (4) the uneasy position of the middle class, caused in part by economic insecurity and cultural conflict; and (5) the weakening of families. A more institutionally focused list would include (1) a judiciary that regularly turns into legal matters the questions of how to organize the economy and how to define its relations to the polity; (2) a Congress with the propensity to turn most matters before it into a problem of how to distribute benefits among the constituents of its most powerful members; and (3) a presidency that, through administrative rulemaking, has come to wield legislative powers over a wide swath of the public's business.

But how should we assess such lists? Do they merely contain the kinds of incidental weaknesses that characterize any attractive political system— the more or less usual complaints, conflict, and mild disarray that is the common stuff of a vibrant democratic political order? Or do they reflect serious failures in our political constitution about which we can and should do something? Is the regime facing a crisis in which an all-out effort of some kind is called for, lest the political order devolve into something less attractive? If there are serious failings, where shall we direct our energies in an effort to repair the damage? Should we focus on reforming political parties? On revitalizing local political life? These are the kinds of questions critics of our present political practices must answer if they intend to pro- mote a more or less fully realized republican regime. If they, and indeed all of us, wish to do more than wring our hands or latch onto the panacea of the moment, we must first understand the sort of political order ours is meant to be and how it is meant to work.[1]

The more reflective among the contented and discontented should thus join hands. Both need a theory of American republican constitution. Indeed, all of us who are committed to some version of the political order that has dominated our political discussions for more than two hundred years[2] need to think constitutionally.[3] While there are always policy questions to be addressed—for example, what to do about social security—there are always constitutive problems as well, difficulties with how we have organized ourselves through political-economic institutions to carry on our collective affairs. Unfortunately for the contented, the discontented, and the mildly interested, we lack a compelling and comprehensive theory of republican political constitution and the inclination to develop one is not, to put it charitably, very widespread. We have pieces of the kind of theory needed, but they are not for the most part understood as such. There are far too many accounts of parts of the political order without systematic attention to the political whole: all arms and legs, we might say, but no body. Or what is worse—arms and legs, after all, being of vital importance—such studies as we have are the political equivalent of hair and eyebrows. Nice but not crucial.

As a consequence, our responses to proposals for institutional reform, and our assessment of evolutions in our practices and institutions, are too often bootless, off-the-cuff evaluations, lacking any deep roots in a comprehensive understanding of the political order we are supposed to be and what that entails. The essential point concerning the subject of constitutional thinking was made long ago by Bolingbrooke: that by "[c]onstitution we mean . . . that assemblage of laws, institutions and customs, derived from certain fixed principles of reason, directed to certain fixed objects of the public good, that compose the general system, according to which the community hath agreed to be governed."[4]

Much of the blame for the lack of systematic attention to a theory of political constitution in its normative and empirical aspects can be laid at the feet of contemporary American political science. If anywhere, it is there that normative inquiry rooted in the real possibilities of political action should flourish, along with empirical analysis tied to plausible normative principles. After all, political science was created by Aristotle for just these purposes. That legacy, however, has been dissipated. The concerns of American political science's two principal branches lie elsewhere: empirically minded exponents of positive theory concern themselves with explanations of how the political world works, and normative theorists ask what sort of enterprise politics is and how best to judge it. Practitioners of neither branch spend much time worrying about how to achieve good political orders, given humankind as it is and might reasonably become.

Our general political discussion does not help matters. Much of it is dominated by the "size of government" question that asks whether there is too much government or too little. There is, of course, some reason to worry about this matter: centralized bureaucracy and rulemaking can be oppressive, and the vulnerable do need direct help from government. But many citizens seem to sense that the real problem is not "how much government" but "what kind of government"—and this is precisely where our political discussion lacks depth. To make real progress in understanding the American political order, we need, if not a new political science, at least a reworked one where efforts at explanation and evaluation are tied to the question of good political regimes and how they may be secured and maintained. That is, we need to construct theories of political constitution.

The great teacher of how to think constitutionally is Aristotle. He argued that one of the principal tasks of political study is to identify the various types of political regimes, to examine how they worked, and to classify them as good or bad.[5] His focus was on the political-economic order as a whole, not just particular institutions and practices. Aristotle's conception of the task of political study should be familiar to most Americans. After all, we were founded in an act of political constitution. Moreover, it is natural for us to look for guidance from those who played a crucial role in showing how best to constitute ourselves as a republic. And we thus turn to the thought of James Madison, the most careful student of how the new republican regime could be made to work. Madison, we might say, is the great teacher of Americans on how a republican political constitution can be constructed, which institutions and practices are necessary for republican government, and how best to maintain them.

Both Aristotle and Madison, we should note, tell us that in thinking about a political constitution we must also think about an economic constitution. Thus, for Aristotle, the middle stratum or class was crucial to the mixed regime of aristocratic and democratic elements that was one of his good regimes.[6] For his part, Madison thought that a central purpose of republican government was to secure private property, and that the propertied were to play a central political role in the new regime.[7] Both offered a political sociology for the regimes that concerned them, a sociology rooted in the organization of economic life.[8] A more accurate description, then, for an account of how to create and maintain a republican political order is "a theory of republican political-economic constitution." That hardly comes tripping off the tongue, however, and so I simply refer to a theory of republican political constitution. But felicity of expression aside, it is important to emphasize the political side of things because we are, after all, concerned with creating—that is, constituting—good political regimes, and that is the quintessential political act. Even more important, both Aristotle and Madison suggest that our concern for the economic domain be in the service of constituting an attractive political regime. Our interest in how economic production is organized, they indicate, should focus largely on whether it makes more or less difficult the realization of a certain sort of political life. This is a rather different emphasis than one sees in contemporary economic discussion in Western democracies. But this is where a serious concern with political constitution leads us, not least because it is difficult to justify acquiring wealth and income as an end in itself. It is what they bring that is important, and virtually any account of what this is will take us beyond economic considerations.[9]

To realize republican government in the United States, then, Americans need an account of its political constitution. At the center of this constitution, I argue, is a self-limiting sovereign people. The idea that republican government is limited government—and that the people must limit themselves—is not a new one. It was understood by Madison, among others, who was plausibly the best theoretical mind among the American founders. Indeed, Madison's constitutional theory centered on a self-limiting people.

A fine formulation of why self-limitation is so central to republican government is given by Walter Lippmann. He noted that there is "nothing left but the irresistible power of the mass of men" once the claims of kings and aristocrats are disposed of. As a result, "the people must rule," but if it is to achieve its "own best interests" the people must subject themselves to a system that "define[s] in specific terms the manner in which [they] should rule."[10] As Harvey Mansfield puts it, in the formulations of the most insightful republican theorists, "no favored class with a greater sense of honor or a superior faculty of reasoning than theirs [the people's] is postulated and endowed with power to check the people's choice."[11] The essential problem of republican government, then, is to prevent free men and women from doing that which could destroy their own rule. There is no greater force than themselves to prevent this from happening. If there were, the people would be neither free nor sovereign, and a republican regime impossible.[12]

In this and the succeeding chapters I develop this essential idea of self-limitation not only by analyzing it further, but also by discussing other elements of a commercial republican political constitution that must be in place if republican government is to flourish. I begin by considering the constitutional theory of Madison. Although there are important failings in his arguments, his overall formulation is sufficiently powerful to provide a good foundation on which to build. I then consider some general features of constitutional theorizing—namely, the relation between values and institutions, and the components of constitutional reasoning itself. After that, I focus on the political constitution of self-limitation itself, at the heart of which is the way in which the institutional design, and the politics in which it is embedded, provide strong and regular incentives for lawmaking to give concrete meaning to the public interest. That is to say, if republican government is to succeed, the people cannot rule any way they please. Power must be subject to principle and, more generally, must be exercised in ways that give life to the public interest. It is worth adding that constituting a republican regime is not an exercise for the innocent or faint-hearted. It requires consideration not only of "good" motives and "good" political processes, but also of ambition, self-interest, the desire to subordinate others politically, and the political processes these engender. A republican constitution, moreover, must not only control such motives, it must also make use of them.

ASPIRATIONS AND THE BASIC CHARACTER OF A COMMERCIAL REPUBLIC

What are the grounds for my saying that Americans need a theory of republican political constitution, and why republican rather than some other kind? The question can be answered in a variety of ways, from saying that all peoples must devote themselves to realizing the political regime that a theory of universal justice calls for, to arguing that a people should seek the sort of political life on which they happen to agree. To argue directly for one kind of answer over another is to recapitulate the history of Western political thought from the ancient Greeks forward. For, in one version of that history, this has been its central question. It is, of course, not possible to review that history here.

I ask instead to what sort of regime can it be said that we, as Americans, aspire and to which we should devote our political energies.[13] This may be called an "aspirational view" of the American regime, and its attractions and difficulties will reveal themselves as the analysis unfolds. But constitutional thinking properly understood does not turn on any particular way of establishing which political regimes are desirable in general and for a particular people. All it needs to get started—at least if its practitioners are interested in actual peoples situated in particular places—is some account of what sort of political regime is appropriate to be realized by them with the help of a theory of political constitution.

What then are our aspirations as Americans? Since we are, and must be, situated somewhere, rather than nowhere,[14] and thus have inherited a set of political institutions and a language in which to discuss them, our aspirations reflect to some degree these inherited practices. Our aspirations thus are likely to stem, in part, from the thinking of those who have helped to set these practices in motion, the founders of the American Republic. We must start, therefore, with where we already are, relying heavily on the local stock of political ideas to express that for which we hope. In doing so, we enter into an ongoing "rhetorical community" where words and their meanings, and the argued-for purposes of our collective life, have taken on a life of their own. A variety of symbols and kinds of justifications are thus not only ready to hand, but in some sense recognizably "ours." Consider here these lines in Louis MacNeice's poem "Valediction":

> But I cannot deny my past
>   to which my self is wed
> The woven figure cannot
>   undo its thread

Given that they must to some degree reflect our present practices, a minimum account of our aspirations points to our desire to be a regime in which government is both popular and limited, and in which economic life is organized in significant part through markets and private control of productive assets.[15] We thus first want to be a regime that has its foundations in popular self-government, one in which office holders are chosen either through popular election or by those who are elected. Our aspiration is to realize a republican regime in the sense that the opinions of the governed are regularly consulted and constrain the actions of governors. Moreover, while government is to be popular, it is also to be limited with the aim of serving well-defined purposes and carried on through well-understood forms. Its powers are to be exercised according to law so that each of us can conduct our lives free from the arbitrary exercise of governmental power. More popular control is not always better. The real question for Americans who aspire to realize a republic[16] is not whether the people must be limited, just as kings and aristocrats must be, but what the content of those limits should be.[17]

The regime is also to be a commercial one in the sense that republican government is combined with a business enterprise system that has a substantial private component and that subjects these enterprises to the test of consumer desire through the marketplace. Our aspirations require that many of the decisions about how to use society's resources ought to be in the hands of private persons and groups who enter into a variety of cooperative and exchange relationships to deploy those resources. Such an economy, it is believed, brings all of us at least a modest level of material well-being. A private-enterprise, market-based economy is also thought to lend support to republican government, not least because the prosperity it is supposed to bring increases attachment to republican principles.[18] Commerce is thought to be useful for self-government, not a principal source of its subversion.[19]

In their most general form, our aspirations join us to many others over the last 350 years who have argued that the mass of people are capable of governing themselves according to law in a manner that is neither arbitrary nor ineffective. The idea of lawful government is much older than that of popular self-government, reaching back through the arguments of medieval thinkers to those of the ancient Greeks. These older thinkers for the most part doubted that a popular regime could be a lawful one, but at least since the first part of the seventeenth century there have been more than a few who have thought this aspiration to be both possible and worth struggling to realize.

The normative force of our aspirations thus lies to some degree in a continuation of this republican tradition of thought and practice. I take it as given, however, that to the degree we have a choice in the matter, we do not wish to be a certain kind of regime simply on the grounds that it is an inheritance that we must live with. Because the regime we aspire to is essentially the one the founders of this Republic hoped to bring into being, is there something about this aspect of our inheritance that points to the value of our aspirations?[20]

This commitment to a commercial republic is not the only account of what our aspirations should be. But it is the one of longest standing, the most elaborated, and the one that has been subject to the greatest degree of searching argument: it is the most reasoned about.[21] This reasoning has operated through the invitation that many Americans have extended to their fellow citizens over our history to consider whether the outline of the regime the founders commended to us ought to be widely accepted and efforts made to realize it fully. The invitation has been eagerly taken up and, as a result, the founders' gift is highly valued: among those willing and able to exchange reasons, the dominant view is that something much like the founders' vision of a commercial republic should guide us.[22] We thus are bound by what those who have come before us have decided about the constitution of government, not because they are "founders"—or because they "came before us" (which is to say, because they are dead)—but because they are at least partly right about how to create a commercial republic: their formulation has continued to hold up in the exchange of reasons to which I just alluded.[23] And because, like all constitutions, the American Constitution cannot be a complete guide to how to constitute a commercial republic, we, like the founders, require a broader theory of political constitution. Our allegiance to the Constitution must be both conditional and a part of a larger commitment to realize our aspirations.[24]

The normative force of our aspirations thus derives from the authority of the reasoning behind them, not simply from the numbers of people who have concluded that a commercial republic is what they wish for. These reasoners have been spread out over many generations and have been sufficiently free, willing, and able to exchange reasons about the regime that is worthy of us.[25] "We" who have aspirations, then, are not those who merely talk about the political right and good, nor those who are powerful.[26] Thus, the "we" that has these aspirations is a category that cannot be fixed beforehand.[27] If these really are aspirations, they are neither the product of a simple consensus where we count heads nor a result of elite control. Neither words themselves nor power can confer authority—and any account of our aspirations aspires to be authoritative.[28]

This process of multigenerational reasoning may be thought of as a kind of chain novel in which the first chapter was written by the founders, who also provided a rough outline of where the novel was to go next. Those reasoners who followed wrote the next chapters of the novel, building on what had come before. The authors of new chapters, in turn, are free to move the novel's characters in different directions, add new ones, and so forth. But to participate in the writing of this novel requires that authors first pay attention to what has come before them in the text.[29]

To attack the view that our aspirations give us normative guidance means attacking our ability—or at least the ability of a subset of us—to reason about what is worthy of us. It would seem to require a kind of radical skepticism that cannot be sustained, not least because its proponents' views are themselves something we may treat with skepticism.

Our aspirations then are a kind of halfway house between counting opinions as a guide to what is valuable—all norms are conventional—and foundational justifications. The exchange of reasons over time is the link to foundational justifications, since our aspirations are open to revision in light of more universal standards.[30] Yet they are rooted in opinion in the sense that they start with the present practices that are counted as valuable among us.[31]

But why should we think of our inheritance from the founders and our elaboration of it as our *aspirations*—that is, as our hopes not just for ourselves but, realistically, mostly for those who come after us?[32] Justice or fairness might dictate that, just as we think we deserve some things from those who came before us, we should attempt to provide the same or similar things to those who will come after us, passing on to following generations things of value. But this is not just a question of the correct distribution of valued goods, which is the principal concern underlying most accounts of justice and fairness. It is also a more fundamental matter, perhaps best expressed as a recognition of a fundamental human injunction: just as those who come before us have an obligation not to wantonly or cruelly make it harder for us the living to make our own way, so must we do the same for those who follow us.

Here then is Burke's partnership between the living and the dead and those yet to come.[33] The partnership depends on recognizing that we do not spring full-grown from our own wombs, so to speak. The kind of reasoning that I have said lies at the base of our aspirations is a dialogue of sorts among the living, the dead, and the unborn—a dialogue conducted perhaps with more rationality than Burke may have thought possible, but a conversation of sorts with just those interlocutors he thought were essential to political evaluation.

Our commitment to a commercial republic thus does not rest on the imposition of a particular philosophically anchored doctrine. Our agreement rests, that is, on the broadest of philosophical points: that a doctrine can claim our allegiance if people willing and able freely to exchange reasons agree on it.[34] Similarly, the idea of a republican regime is a capacious enough conception of a desirable political regime to secure agreement on it from those who count themselves legatees of both the Federalists and Anti-Federalists.[35] Adherents of both of these traditions typically have argued that free government depends on some sort of marriage between popular limited government and commerce.[36] This is a very broad commitment, which is why it is reasonable to think that it constitutes the heart of our aspirations.

In my account of our aspirations, I am not claiming that a commercial republican regime is, or is thought to be, the best regime.[37] Our aspirations point to something more limited—the best regime for the kind of people we are with our history and capacities.[38] But this is not to say that the reasoning I have described does not point to political goods above and beyond the realization of a commercial republic. We cannot be relativists in our aspirations, since to aim for a political regime of which we can be proud implies that we wish it to be the best of its kind. In the same vein, we are in fact committed to looking to other regimes that may be counted as the best of their kind. For if we aspire to making the regime to which our aspirations point the best of its kind, and this proves impossible, we are compelled to look to other regimes of similar stature. Thus, in defining our aspirations, we are drawn outside our own community of thought and practice. But such external reflections can only tutor local understandings, not replace them, since politics takes place only among particular peoples.[39] As aspirants, therefore, we naturally move back and forth between the municipal and the universal. In doing so, we are also likely to be drawn into considering how other peoples organize and guide their political lives to see if we can learn from them how to minimize our own halting and confused efforts. We are drawn, that is, outside our own history, our evaluations of it, and our thinking about the collective enterprise in which we are engaged.

Those who share in our aspiration to fully realize a commercial republic should think of themselves as friends of the American regime. Friendship allows for a certain critical distance and, with it, the capacity to reflect on whether the object of one's affections still merits the esteem in which it is held. Love, if not perhaps blind, is rightly impatient with distance—and in politics should be reserved for the simply best regime and political practices. To love something that is not the best is, in politics, a recipe for misery and an invitation to corruption and worse.

Starting with our aspirations is partly an exercise in prudence in the face of the enormous difficulty of grounding and giving specific content to universal moral-political standards. Most of us in the richer parts of the world are rarely in the situation where wholesale change is either possible or obviously desirable. We are, like the inhabitants of most broadly popular regimes, in the political retail business.[40]

In the end, the most convincing argument for starting with our aspirations, understood as freely given accounts of people able and willing to reason, comes in the form of a rhetorical question. Is it likely that a significant number of Americans would think a move toward a fuller realization of our aspirations in the form I have set them out a bad thing? Some no doubt would, including those who cannot imagine any regime being acceptable that has within it any private control of productive assets. Nor would racists or misogynists find a fuller realization of a commercial republic very attractive. But once we lay aside the demands of either complete agreement or of a dispositive rationality—assuming these are even plausible foundations—might not most of us actually say, after we bring to greater fruition a commercial republican regime, that we are better off? In any event, the experience of political reform efforts over the last two centuries tells us that it will be hard enough to move closer to the realization of our aspirations, no less to realize even very imperfectly something more demanding.

Of course, there is always the chance that I am wrong in all this—and in two ways. First, a great deal of evidence of the quality and content of the conversation over the generations that I have been describing would be needed to test my argument, and that evidence might show that my account is inaccurate.[41] I would simply say in reply that my argument in behalf of our aspirations is enough to start the discussion of a theory of republican political constitution. Second, it might be said that our aspirations are not in fact the product of reasoning, but mere cynically offered justifications by the powerful. They cannot be just that, however, for as Michael Walzer says, the principles of justification offered by the powerful are not ones they would "choose [to offer] if they were choosing *right now*." Having offered them at some earlier point, their actions are now likely to be criticized in light of them.[42]

LIBERALISM AND JUSTICE

To further characterize our aspirations for a full realization of a commercial republican regime, we can say that Americans aim to serve liberal justice. That is, a commercial republic, like all modern regimes born of the desire for mass well-being, seeks justice, as against virtue, honor, glorifying God, or racial glory. Moreover, to realize fully a commercial republic is to serve liberal justice. In particular, a well-ordered commercial republic is one in which its people stand in relation to one another as free and equal citizens engaged in the kind of self-government in which the exercise of political authority is limited.[43] As a liberal regime, a commercial republic is one of several kinds of good political regimes. I will not attempt to defend this statement here[44] but will only comment that, to the degree that this is so, our aspiration to be a commercial republic is not only worthy of us but can be defended on the basis of arguments that distinguish good from bad regimes.

While any serious account of the substance of liberal justice would go well beyond what most of those involved in reasoned argument will have said about the value of the commercial republic, it is possible to provide a brief account of what might emerge in such an exchange. Thus, a free people is one where citizens are secure in their person[45] and the free exercise of their powers. Mill goes a step further: "The only freedom which deserves the name is that of pursuing our own good in our own ways."[46] To be free is to "lead our life from the inside, in accordance with our beliefs about what gives value to life," and we are to "be free to question these beliefs."[47] This task of shaping our lives falls on us as individuals, not on a set of authorities. Of course, each of us is only free to live the life we choose if it does not restrict the same freedom for others. Given this concern for liberty, the power of government must be limited. It we are to pursue our own good in our own way, government authority can be used to facilitate our liberty but not abridge it, at least not without reasons that follow from the other elements of liberal justice—namely, equality and self-government.

Freedom understood in this fashion requires a substantial measure of privacy. If we are to look at our lives from the inside, we must have the space to do so, and we must be able to draw into our own circle those who we believe have something to tell us about the value of the path we have chosen. Again, this concern for what must be an expansive private life means government must be limited.

If we are an equal people, we are first and foremost *equal* in our freedom to live our own life in our own way. We are thus equal in our standing before the state and its law. However freedom is understood, in an equal people no one is allowed greater freedom than anyone else, even if they are of the highest virtue, the largest wealth, or the greatest goodness. Again, as Mill insisted, each is to count for one and no more than one.[48] The equality of freedom stems from the common fact of our humanity, and it is the great gift of a liberal regime that it posits this equality in the face of the obvious fact that in virtually all other important respects we are not equals. In much the same way, an equal people is one in which all have the minimum resources necessary to participate in the goods of life. No one is to be so bereft of resources as to be unable to participate in the free life of the political community and the rewards to which it leads. Still, there are limits on what a liberal government may do to ensure such equality, limits that stem from the commitment of a liberal regime to liberty.

A people capable of governing itself is one that supposes ordinary people have the capacity to choose their governors, to judge their behavior, and, if they so desire, to become governors themselves. A self-governing people recognizes that some are better equipped than others to govern, but that this ability is neither restricted to a few nor dependent on some particular social or economic characteristic on the part of those who wish to govern. Self-government requires a wide variety of talents and is carried on by many different office holders who seek to ensure that political authority is used to serve the concerns of ordinary people. It is also intrinsically valuable insofar as it affords many people the opportunity to take responsibility for the consequences of the mutual interdependence among members of a society, to see that this interdependence is not denied, that the costs of it do not become unmanageable, and that its potential benefits are realized. Still, as noted above, a self-governing people cannot rule just as it pleases; its rule must have limits that take the form of self-limits.

While liberalism is a political doctrine, a search for a political *modus vivendi*,[49] there are moral implications of a liberal conception of justice, as well as implications for what counts as a good way of life.[50] Liberalism has few pretensions about remaking the moral lives of the mass of humanity. The central claim of liberalism is that political life cannot do much about the most problematic aspects of human life: that we are simultaneously dependent on others for love and kindness and vulnerable to their actions; that we need their emotional support but wish to be responsible for our own lives; that we must live together in community with others if we wish to be whole human beings and yet those communities exact a price of conformity; and that we die without any assurance of any kind of transcendence. Liberalism only promises a significant measure of bodily security and ease, a wide range of free choice, and a minimum of being subject to the will of others. It offers the promise that ordinary people can live out their lives in this fashion, and that human reason is sufficient to fulfill this promise and thus to bring liberalism to life in political-economic institutions and their associated politics. This is, in fact, a great deal—and it is certainly a more plausible promise given the history of humankind as we know it than are the promises of liberalism's competitors.

Liberalism gives a central place to human agency and, as noted, to the private life that such agency requires. Any conception of freedom, whether as the absence of arbitrary restraint or the Millian conception of freedom as the full development of one's powers, must provide some room for the private. Neither conception can be built on a life that is lived only in public, a life defined by being a participant in the exercise of public authority. For human agency requires the capacity to reason; reasoning requires independence; and independence requires time and space to reflect on one's purposes. In short, human agency requires a private sphere that provides the possibility of informed reflection and choice—and the possibility of acting, if not unhindered, at least within a large and stable enough arena to make our choices meaningful.

The promise of a liberal regime is, most broadly, that we will not be treated arbitrarily or cruelly, both of which degrade and demoralize us by denying our dignity as autonomous persons able to shape our own lives.

This is why liberalism is so concerned with limiting government and with law and equality before the law. Liberalism is a wager that human beings can be satisfied with a life in which what is fundamentally human and of deepest value is not made the direct subject of politics.

What a liberal regime finally promises is that we will be free to face, however we can, the fact that we are all limited and finite creatures. Our lives cannot be fully free without dependence on others. Indeed, our flourishing as human beings requires that we find a way of living that mediates between a deep desire not to be encumbered by others and a deep desire for their help, interest, and affection, in addition to a deep need for identification with others. Similarly, liberal regimes allow us to face on our own terms that other great given of human existence: that our lives have an inevitable end point, our extinction, which raises the deepest question of all. A liberal regime is one that, in protecting a wide private sphere, allows the ultimate form of freedom: to face the prospect of our own death in our own way, especially, if we so wish it, without assistance or direction from those who have historically claimed the authority to pronounce on these matters.[51]

CONCLUSION

A commercial republic is one way in which three desirable elements of political rule are combined: popular self-government, limited government, and active government. The value of the first two is widely understood and has already been discussed. As for the last, which I discuss at length in later chapters, it is enough to say here that any attractive regime of popular rule must have a government that is active in its efforts to modify the vicissitudes of chance and coercion that are a part of the lives of its citizens. If government is not active in this sense, there is little reason for ordinary men and women to prefer self-government. Other kinds of regimes are at least as able to provide political stability and a calm life where the rules are well understood and not altered in arbitrary fashion. American aspirations are important, therefore, not only for Americans. The degree of our success in combining these three elements is of interest to the rest of the world, just as the founders of the Republic said it would be.[52] Other countries have tried, and continue to try, other methods for creating stable and attractive political orders—and a nontrivial number have succeeded in doing so. There are, for example, social democratic regimes that rest on what might be called a "party corporatist" base. In such regimes, public policy mostly arises out of negotiations between majority party leaders, senior civil servants, and the heads of peak organizations representing labor and capital. The civil service, with its strong collective sense of responsibility for the common-weal, and the high level of organization for labor and capital make the "corporatist" designation appropriate. In such regimes, disciplined parties are the principal vehicle for citizen representation, and the minority party is the primary means by which the government of the day is monitored. As a result of these constitutive arrangements, policymaking in social democracies is typically more coherent and far-reaching, particularly with regard to economic equality, than is likely in any but a fully developed commercial republic. Still, a commercial republic is a compelling alternative, and at any rate is the one that fortune and reflection have assigned to Americans for realization. If we fail in our efforts to realize more or less fully a commercial republic, the failure will not only be costly to us but will also instruct other peoples in the limited value of this regime.

To take seriously the question of how to realize more fully our aspirations to be a commercial republic is to face such questions as the following: how can we have a limited government if the idea of private property as a transpolitical limit on the state has proved unsustainable in liberal practice, and if the idea of the rule of law has not fared much better? In a similar vein, how are we to have a serious measure of popular control of authority given that in commercial societies the political role of the propertied, in particular those who control large productive assets, looms so large, and that particular interests threaten to displace the public interest? Since at the core of a republic regime is a government that is both popular and limited, what will foster a citizenry inclined to serve not only its own particular interests but broader public interests as well? And where are the limits on the people's rule to come from and how are they to be enforced? Finally, how is any of this to be done in a society where a market system based on private enterprise generates economic and thus political inequality? To answer these questions, and thus to think constitutionally, is to analyze how to prevent the deterioration and corruption of popular limited government as it is joined to an economic system with a significant measure of private property. It also means giving an account of what will strengthen a regime built on these two pillars.

Our present efforts to understand these and similar questions, and to realize more fully a commercial republic, while not abjectly failing, have not been notable for their success. Thus, the reach of the state has grown without a corresponding account of how this expansion is to be justified in a principled way. As a result, government is felt by many as an unacceptable imposition and the resulting disaffection makes it difficult to serve the purposes that arise from the natural and legitimate desire of the mass of ordinary men and women to make their lives a bit freer, safer, and more commodious. It doesn't help that there are those who argue that popular self-government should not be popular at all, that is to say, that most of what the people wish for through the action of government is illegitimate. However, this view of the illegitimacy of much of what popular self-government has undertaken is contrary to what most Americans intuitively know to be true: that they aren't less free now than when they were economically insecure and discriminated against. Here we have a tandem act that can only feed citizen disaffection: proponents of active government who are either too lazy or unable to explain the principles that justify it, and opponents of active government who appear to think that a people that does not understand and accept their criticisms is unable to govern itself, appearances to the contrary notwithstanding. Is it any wonder that a significant chunk of the American citizenry is confused, and turns from politics to entertainment? If they cannot get much help from those who shape opinion in the country, they do what any self-respecting citizenry does: they turn off their leaders and turn on their televisions.

There is likely to be resistance among academics and public intellectuals to thinking about an American political constitution. Many now argue that questions of culture, religious belief, public order, and family structure are of the greatest importance. However, even if our religious beliefs are strong, our families intact, and our culture life affirming, we would still need a well-ordered political constitution to help us collectively decide many things, including defining our responsibilities to one another, particularly those that should be backed by the force of law. More generally, we would still need to answer the question of what sort of people we are, characterized by what set of relationships. This last cannot be answered by political life alone, but it cannot be answered without it.

Those friends of liberalism who are unwilling to accept the kind of aspirational argument that I have set out here may substitute whatever alternative account of liberal political value they find compelling. If they accept that, for such values to be given life, a political-economic regime must be constituted, then the following chapters on constitutional thinking will be of interest to them. Moreover, it is plausible[53] that the political constitution of a commercial republic, whose essential features I will sketch, is compatible with a wide variety of liberalisms, in addition to one aimed at securing a free and equal people engaged in governing themselves. This includes an austere "liberalism of fear," a Millian developmental liberalism, a liberalism of rational liberty, and a liberalism rooted in equal concern and respect.[54] A commercial republican political constitution should have more than enough room for each of these to find a home, whether in combination or where one of them dominates—just as its conception of justice should be compatible with that of even the more demanding of this list of liberalisms. In this sense, at least, a commercial republic is neutral between various liberal ways of life. It is also a powerful starting point for those who wish—and need—to theorize about American political life.

I

Madison and Constitutional Thinking

2

The Madisonian
Commercial Republic

WHAT POLITICAL constitution will give life to the aspirations of Americans? What theory ought to guide us as we attempt to more fully realize a republican regime to which we are committed? Aspiring to realize a good regime orients us to the world of political practice. But such an aspiration by itself tells us little about some essential matters: how we should judge our present practices; which ones ought to be maintained and strengthened, and how to do so; and which new ones we should try to bring into being.

The best place to begin answering these questions is with James Madison's account in *The Federalist* where he presents his essential views on the problem of popular self-government.[1] Those who participate in the founding of some great undertaking—at least if it is successful—are particularly valuable guides to its underlying theory. In trying to bring about this new enterprise they must think in depth about its foundations. "What must be changed," they ask, "if we are to succeed?" In answering, they point not only to what must be different if the enterprise is to flourish, but also to the essential features of the undertaking on which everything else depends. Unlike those who come after, those present at beginnings have before them the old as a living presence, and the comparison with the new helps to bring clarity to their thinking. For those who come after, such comparisons can only be imagined.[2]

There is a second crucial reason to start with Madison's account of the theory of republican political constitution: it is simply the most comprehensive and compelling one we have.[3] It is also the most authoritative in that it is the one we most commonly turn to when seeking guidance about how the American regime is to work. Madison is both the leading architect of American political institutions and their most persuasive defender.[4] In particular, he discussed at length how securing rights and serving the permanent interests of the community might be combined with self-government in a properly designed regime. We should study Madison's thought, therefore, not because he is dead (and hence of historic interest), but because he may have been right—at least about America, and possibly about the character of what we have come to call "democratic capitalism." Indeed, he was correct about one essential point: the central concern of constitutional theory for a republic is how to constitute a politics whose defining feature is a self-limiting popular sovereign. This is what the discussion here and in later chapters will attempt to show. Another important reason for studying Madison's political theory is that his views are not the result of revolutionary enthusiasm, but of sober reflection after the Revolution.

Madison is best understood in *The Federalist* as not just defending the written Constitution, but as setting out its underlying theory of political constitution. He is first and foremost a theorist of a working political regime, not of a piece of paper. He was concerned, that is, with the American constitution in the larger Aristotelean sense, with the working rules and the political-economic institutions that constitute a people, that form it as a polity. The Constitution as document may play an important role here, but in the nature of the case it cannot define all of the rules and institutions at work.[5] For Madison, the central concern in designing the new American regime was both that it embody popular self-government and that such government be limited. The authority of the new regime was to stem from its creation by the people as constituent sovereign and from the people as a citizenry who would play the fundamental role in selecting those who would govern. Madison was a republican and, as he said, "no other form would be reconcilable with the genius of the people of America." Indeed, republican government was "the best, even the noblest, form of political rule."[6] For Madison, the various political institutions that were to give the regime its essential character "derive[d] their existence from the elective principle,"[7] and the people were "the ultimate arbiter" of constitutionality.[8]

This popular government, however, was also to be limited. The people and those who speak for them could not rule just as they please. Madison's views are nicely captured by Walter Lippmann's formulation that the "authors of the American Constitution . . . did not fall into the error of supposing that the unorganized populace *knew how* to rule. They recognized that the populace had the *power* to rule. They had acknowledged that it had the *right* to rule. They then knew that the problem was to *enable* the populace to rule."[9] Madison's fundamental purpose was to construct a political regime that would make it possible for the people to govern themselves in such a manner that their rule would continue. To do so required preventing unlimited and arbitrary government that would sink into chaos, and structuring a system of lawmaking that would secure the people's aspiration to govern itself. The scheme of government that Madison proposed was to secure the regime to which the mass of Americans gave and would continue to give their allegiance: popular, limited government, that is, a republic.

There are six essential features of the political constitution that Madison argued should characterize the American political order:

1. institutions designed to prevent factions—particularly majority factions—from controlling government, factional government being for Madison the principal disease of popular government;
2. laws that bind not only the citizenry[10] but those who make the laws;
3. institutions that are designed to encourage the kind of lawmaking that gives concrete meaning to a substantive conception of the public interest;
4. more specifically, institutions that are designed to promote deliberative ways of lawmaking, which are necessary to "refine"[11] the people's voice;
5. a citizenry capable of choosing lawmakers who are disposed to deliberate on the concrete meaning of the public interest; and
6. a social basis for the regime, which would help make all this possible— in particular, men of standing and property whose self-interest overlaps with the public interest, and who might be induced to take a large view of their interests, thus increasing the overlap.[12]

It is useful to discuss each of these in turn.[13] But before doing so I want to emphasize that these features indicate that Madison agreed with some of the central tenets of what has been called "civic" republican thought[14]— notably, its concern for citizen virtue and the common good—and assimilated them to a liberal political theory. It is this, among other things, that makes his political thought so penetrating. The effort to join these two required that Madison think widely and deeply about the essential problems of popular self-government.[15]

PREVENTING FACTION

Of the six features listed above, the first has received the greatest attention by students of Madison's thought. Indeed, for some, it is the whole of his theory. As indicated, Madison thought that the principal disease of republican government—government where the people rule through representatives— was faction. What was wanted, he said, was a "republican remedy for the diseases most incident to republican government."[16] By faction, Madison meant "a number of citizens, whether amounting to a majority or minority of the whole, who are united and actuated by some common impulse or passion, or of interest, adverse to the rights of other citizens, or to the permanent and aggregate interests of the community."[17] Factions under popular government are inevitable since "the causes are sown into the na- ture of man"[18]—and thus the potential for tyranny is always present and with it the inclination to deprive others of their civil, property, and political rights. It is the deprivation of rights that has concerned most commentators on Madison, but Madison also said that factions, whether by intention or through the effects of their action, can undercut the "public interest." This has concerned fewer commentators, but is at least equally important for republican government, as we shall see.

Madison was among the first to see that even when the people rule, there is no guarantee that individual rights and the public interest will be secure. He commented with some asperity that "there is no maxim in my opinion which is more liable to be misapplied . . . than the current one that the interest of the majority is the standard of right and wrong."[19] Controlling the majority is likely what Madison meant when he said that the first task of government is to control the people, the next to oblige the government to control itself.[20] Reining in majority factions would, in any case, contribute to such control.

Madison thus extended the traditional worry that government itself en- dangers individual liberty to include the idea that the people, when wielding political power, also present a danger. Not only may government by the one or the few be dangerous to liberty, but so may government of the many if it is badly designed.[21] John Stuart Mill made the essential point in such a fashion as to render it unforgettable: "The 'people' who exercise the power are not always the same people with those over whom it is exercised."[22] Madison thus brought together the two lines of thought about how to pro- tect liberty: "It is of great importance in a republic not only to guard the society against the oppression of its rulers, but to guard one part of the society against the injustice of the other part."[23] He argued that a popular regime would be especially vulnerable to the passions of majorities since such a regime must work according to majoritarian principles if it is to be the rule of the people. Majority factions, that is, could claim the cover of law for their actions. Conversely, minority factions would be less of a problem since majorities would be able to "defeat [their] sinister views by regular vote." The "republican principle" is enough to prevent factional rule by a minority.[24]

In Madison's view, it was likely that civil and political rights would be in less danger than property rights. Even though there could well be majorities bent on depriving minorities of civil and political rights, for the most part the mass of citizens could be expected to see that these rights protected them and thus would defend them. Even the propertied could be expected to support civil and political rights, Madison believed: although they might be able to rule without such rights being extended to all citizens, on balance the propertied would benefit enough from a system of citizenry-wide rights to support their continuation.[25] Most worrisome, Madison argued, was that a majority might be formed from those with little or no property who would seek to use public authority to weaken property rights.[26] In general, while the propertied were strong enough to subvert republican government,[27] they were not so strong that they could by themselves protect property rights—especially since their lack of numbers denied them any hope of dominating elections. Factional conflict around "the unequal distribution of property" was thus the most dangerous kind for republican government, Madison believed, and an essential task of constitutional design was to control the effects of such conflict.[28]

At the Constitutional Convention, Madison made clear the reasoning behind his formulation in *The Federalist*:

> [A]n increase in population will of necessity increase the proportion of those who will labour under all the hardships of life and secretly sigh for a more equal distribution of its blessings. These may in time outnumber those who are placed above the feelings of indigence. According to the equal laws of suffrage, the power will slide into the hands of the former.... How is this danger to be guarded against on republican principles?[29]

It helps in understanding Madison's thinking to interpret these and similar remarks not as an indictment of the propertyless, but as, at least in part, a dispassionate account of what is to be expected given the nature of humankind.[30] Madison was not in the business of subverting popular self-government in the interests of a propertied class, as some have argued.[31] Although he had a healthy regard for his own interests, his concern was to protect a system of rights, not of interests. Moreover, he sought to find a balance between property rights and self-government, and not to eviscerate one to accommodate the other.[32] Even those without property, Madison thought, should value an economic system built on property rights because it promotes stability and increases material well-being for all.[33] Like many of his contemporaries, he thought that a regime that could not protect private property was unlikely to protect any other rights.[34] Madison understood, then, that there were going to be class divisions that might sink republican government, but that *both* private property and republican government were valuable. Republican government could not survive a struggle between the haves and the have-nots, and somehow the issue had to be prevented from becoming the center of political conflict. As Madison said, if property rights were the subject of significant political conflict, "the most violent struggle [would] be generated between those interested in revising and those interested in new-modeling the former state of property."[35]

Madison was clear that factions could not be eliminated on grounds consistent with republican government. Factions could be prevented from forming by destroying liberty, but this remedy is "worse than the disease."[36] Madison argued that, instead of trying to eliminate faction, it is better to work to control its effects. And indeed, if factional interests could be multiplied, faction would actually indirectly help to create and maintain a well-ordered republican government by making it less likely that a single majority faction would emerge.

Thus Madison argued that the way to limit factional strife and control its effects is (1) to create a system of representation; (2) to divide political authority through a separation of powers and tie that division to ambition, so that ambition could be made to counter ambition; (3) to extend the sphere of the republic to encompass multiple interests; and (4) to stimulate commerce to create the multiple interests.[37] Representation and these "auxiliary precautions"[38] would not only prevent the propertyless majority from succeeding in factional designs, they would equally impede others— for example, those bent on undercutting political and civil rights. These devices are all well studied, and only brief comments on each are needed here.

Representation would cool passion by placing an agent between a people given to factions and factious assertions of interest and the content of the laws. Representatives would "refine and enlarge the public views" leading to laws "more consonant to the public good."[39] If the republic were a large one, and if the number of representatives were to be limited enough to make for a workable legislature, then representatives would be chosen in large districts. This, in turn, would mean that those elected would likely be men of independent means and "established character" who could resist the pressures of faction to sacrifice "the public good" to temporary or partial considerations.[40] However, representation would be no cure-all. It could, and more than likely would, produce as representatives some men of "factious" tempers given to "local prejudices."[41]

Thus, while a system of representation is crucial for securing republican government, it is insufficient if liberty is to be preserved and the permanent and aggregate interests of the community secured. There must also be additional constitutional precautions.[42] One such precaution, and the second way to control faction, is to divide the powers of government, thus reducing the chances that a majority faction could gain control. It is important, argued Madison, that each branch of government have the inclination and capacity to resist what it understands to be incursions of the other branches and of those who are attempting to wield factional power through controlling these other branches of government. What will provide the motivation to resist? Madison's answer: ambition. What will provide the capacity? His answer: the constitutional rights of the place. The harnessing of ambition is what makes the separation of powers work.[43] The result is a separation of powers that is not a mere "parchment barrier."[44]

Madison's third method for controlling faction stands in contrast to the older view that republican government could only succeed in a relatively small and homogeneous country where there is a commonality of interest.[45] Madison stood this argument on its head and argued that large size, an extended republic, is an *advantage* in this respect. It is precisely the multiplicity of interests accompanying large size that is useful for republican government. That is, size makes it harder for a single large faction to form because communication is costly and the resources required significant. Further, Madison argued, in an extended republic majorities "seldom take place on any other principles than those of justice and the common good."[46] Moreover, a large republic also means large constituencies if the number of representatives is to be small enough to prevent "the confusion of a multitude."[47] Such large districts will reduce the likelihood that the practice of "vicious arts" will decide elections, and will favor the election of men of "the most diffusive and established characters."[48]

Fourth, and as Martin Diamond has argued, Madison believed that multiplication in the number of economic interests would lessen the chance of a single major economic fault line forming between the propertied and the propertyless around which political conflict could organize. The vehicle for multiplying interests is a vibrant commercial society in which, for example, those who pursue their livelihood in shipping will have different interests from those who work in finance.[49] One way to understand Madison here is to contrast a commercial society to an agrarian society in which there is a small land-holding class and a mass of agricultural laborers who are dependent on the landed classes for work. This agrarian society is an inhospitable environment for popular self-government because the interests of the two classes conflict and define all other relationships, and because the laborers are too economically dependent to be the independent citizens that republican government requires. Madison clearly understood the value of multiple interests in controlling faction, commenting that "the society itself will be broken into so many parts, interests and classes of citizens, that rights of individuals or of the minority will be in little danger from interested combinations of citizens."[50] It is also possible to extend his argument. In a large commercial republic, the makeup of majorities will fluctuate, he thought: the same people will not always find themselves in the majority.

There will thus be a tendency for majorities to limit themselves, and in particular to avoid factional schemes.

Madison's view overall, then, was that auxiliary precautions would increase the number of interests, making it less likely that two factions opposed to one another would emerge, and that these precautions would divide governmental power, lessening the possibility that any faction could control the entire government. Representation would create a class of political leaders of independent character and outlook who would be accountable to the citizenry but sufficiently removed by distance and, in the case of the Senate, by indirect election. Such leaders would thus be relatively insulated from the passions that inevitably roil the citizenry from time to time and would be in a position to consider the public interest.[51] The regime would be popular but so arranged that any passionate majority would need to persist over long periods if it were to hold sway, and perhaps in the process become cooler in outlook. The mass of citizens (meaning the mass of white men) would have the rights associated with participating in choosing their governors, but their role in the regime would not extend much further.

It is worth emphasizing here that in recommending the harnessing of self-interest and ambition, Madison was not suggesting that these are the only motives of humankind. He was clear that we are also capable of concern with a larger good. The problem is that this sort of motive is neither strong nor widespread enough to be used as a building block for republican government. Something more reliable is called for, and Madison believed he had found it in the related motives of self-interest and ambition.[52]

Madison was not only concerned about factional control because it would endanger rights. Most commentators neglect to consider that he also defined a faction as a "number of citizens" who are "united and actuated" by an impulse that is "adverse to . . . the permanent and aggregate interests of the community."[53] In speaking of the permanent interests of the community,[54] Madison was talking about a violation of what we would call the "public interest":[55] to undercut it is as much factional behavior as working to subvert rights. We might thus interpret Madison to have been saying that those who work against the public interest act factionally, attempting to substitute private for public interest. If this is so, republican government is as much in danger from those who actively stand in the way of lawmaking that seeks to serve the public interest as it is from those who work to abrogate rights. Moreover, if the elements of the public interest are valuable enough for the design of government to prevent their subversion, then they are valuable enough to be served directly.[56]

Crucially, therefore, the existence of permanent and aggregate interests of the community suggests that the problem of republican government for

Madison was not only to *prevent* something from happening, but also to se-cure or promote whatever these permanent and aggregate interests might be. The essential problem of republican government was the difficulty of "combining the requisite stability and energy in government with the in-violable attachment due to liberty and to the republican form."[57] In short, Madison's constitutional theory provides a warrant for government active in the service of the public interest. In much the same fashion, in its concern to protect rights, Madison's theory not only points toward working to pre-vent their abrogation, it also raises the question of what actions government must take to secure rights for all citizens.[58]

In his discussion of faction, then, Madison asserted that without limits on private power, public power would be in the service of private interest, endangering the rights of the citizenry and rendering implausible any claim that lawmaking serves the interests of the community. Not only can the public subvert the private, but also the private can corrupt the public. Thus, if we follow Madison, not only is our ability to conduct our lives as we see fit vulnerable to public intrusion, our legitimate desire to use public authority to promote the public good is threatened by private power. As Michael Walzer elegantly puts it, pointing out a crucial feature of the whole problem, republican government cannot tolerate either "state capitalism" or a "capitalist state."[59]

In answering the question of which views and interests should play the central role in lawmaking, Madison distinguished between those that seek to serve the permanent and aggregate interests of the community (or at least don't seek to undercut them) and those that do not. Not all interests are factional nor all governments factious. As he said, "to secure the public good, and private right, against the danger of faction, and at the same time to preserve the spirit and form of popular government is then the great object to which our enquiries are directed."[60] The same constitution of the regime that would prevent faction would also create the active government necessary for securing rights and for securing the permanent and aggregate interests of the community. Thus, if Madison's concern was simply to pre-vent factional government, why defend an arrangement in which branches share powers, as he did? It would be more effective simply to give each branch wholly separate powers that would enable them to veto actions by other branches.[61] But Madison insisted that the branches were to share powers: he wanted them to *cooperate*, to *act* in ways that prevented the worst but also aimed at promoting the good. They were to be intimates, not sep-arate fortresses that could refuse to cooperate with one another. Sharing powers would allow for broad legislation, even encourage an "enlarged plan of public policy."[62]

It is perhaps already clear that controlling faction cannot be a precise exercise because the concrete meaning of rights and the permanent and aggregate interests of the community are a matter of interpretation. Therefore, the devices to control faction must be relatively crude, with the result that some good majorities will be impeded along with reprehensible ones. Indeed, those devices may be *too* crude, a matter to which we will return.

Madison's understanding of faction suggests, in a fashion that he himself did not perhaps recognize, that the problem of minority faction is not so easily solved as he believed.[63] While it may be the case that a majoritarian voting system is often able to "defeat the sinister views [of minorities] by regular vote" and thus prevent any abrogation of rights, if our concern is the permanent and aggregate interests of the community, prudence suggests less optimism. Majorities may not be as attached to the permanent interests of the community as they are to rights, since such interests are broad and the cost of not serving them diffuse and long term. The door is thus opened for determined minorities.[64]

THE RULE OF LAW

A basic premise of the Madisonian design is that law is to bind citizens and lawmakers alike. This, the rule of law, will have effects similar to controlling faction: it will prevent law from being used to grant special privileges or benefactions to some while not only denying them to others, but making it difficult for them to contest the denial because these valuable things are granted by law. Thus, in speaking of the House of Representatives, Madison said "that they can make no law which will not have its full operation on themselves." He continued that "this has always been deemed one of the strongest bonds by which human policy can connect the rulers and the people together," and that without it "every government degenerates into tyranny."[65]

The rule of law for Madison might be further understood as requiring that governmental decision occur through a well-defined public process of lawmaking. It is different from command in being a product of reasoned effort by a representative body publicly assembled,[66] by judges appointed by that body, or by those who are otherwise the people's agent. The regime is to be governed by laws, not men (and, later, women)—laws made by the institutions that are created by the constitutional design. In everything Madison wrote concerning the new constitutional design, there is a presumption that popular government would be a dangerous sham if lawmakers were not bound by the law, since the result would likely be an elective despotism, and later, very likely, just plain despotism. In a Madisonian regime, neither the people nor any of their agents can legitimately act just because they will something.[67]

What restrains lawmakers "from making legal discriminations in favor of themselves and a particular class of society?" Madison answered that it will be "the genius of the whole system" and, above all, "the vigilant and manly spirit which actuates the people of America," essential to which is a "nourishment" of freedom. If this spirit is debased "to tolerate a law not obligatory on the Legislature as well as on the people, the people will be prepared to tolerate anything but liberty."[68]

The power of Madison's argument will be clear if the connection between the rule of law and controlling faction is made explicit. If factional government is prevented, the likelihood that there will be the rule of law increases, since the point of factional rule is to use the law to create privileges for a specific group, including the lawmakers who speak for it. And under the rule of law, factional government is unlikely for the reverse reason. Lawmakers who cannot exempt themselves from the law or give themselves special privileges are unlikely to legislate these for a factional group: why give things of such value to others but deny them to oneself? Under the full-blown form of factional rule, the law protects some people's rights but not those of others, and only serves some people's definition of their own interests and the permanent interests of the community. This is what the Madisonian constitution is designed to prevent and this is what the violation of the rule of law brings in its wake.

The rule of law mostly looks back to the traditional definition of tyranny where the enemy is the state. Thus, a powerful device for preventing governmental tyranny is to require that the governors be bound by the same rules as the governed. But this device is also useful in attempting to prevent the tyranny of one group of people by another—the form of tyranny that mostly concerned Madison. Tyranny of this kind can be seen in some of the new African states where one ethnic group uses its control of government to pass laws that command certain actions on the part of the subordinate ethnic group while exempting itself and its lawmakers from the law's reach. Widespread agreement in these countries on the value of the rule of law would make tyranny more difficult.[69]

THE PUBLIC INTEREST

Because Madison believed that preventing faction is the prerequisite for securing rights and serving the permanent interests of the community, he did not aim at creating a form of government where lawmakers spend all their time either embroiled in factional schemes or working to prevent them. Such a sorry political order might come about, but few would wish to advocate it. For Madison there is a positive side of lawmaking concerned with serving such permanent interests, one that depends on the "cool and deliberate sense of the community."[70]

To understand what Madison meant by this "deliberate sense of the community," we should start by recognizing that he was no pluralist—at least not in the sense that he thought that law should arise from the clash of multiple interests.[71] If anything, he was uneasy about the multiple interests (especially factions) that then characterized American society. When Madison said that "the regulation of the various and interfering interests forms the principal task of modern legislation," he meant that—except for aggregative lawmaking, to which I later return—government is to control interests, not be controlled by them. Similarly, when he went on to say that this regulation "involves the spirit of party and faction in the necessary and ordinary operations of government," he again meant that this is, in part, the subject of lawmaking, not a description of how it should work.[72] If there is any doubt on the matter, consider Madison's comment that "from the expediency, in politics, of making natural parties mutual checks on each other, to infer the propriety of creating artificial parties is...absurd."[73] And in addition to its intrinsic value, controlling its effects also has the purpose of freeing lawmaking to serve the public interest. Madison meant what he said: republican lawmaking must concern itself with the permanent interests of the community and, in doing so, it must be deliberative in form.[74] He simply commented that "the public good, the real welfare of the body of the people is the supreme object to be pursued and that no form of government whatever has any other value than as it may be fitted for the attainment of this object."[75]

Madison, however, said surprisingly little about the content of the permanent interests of the community. This, quite possibly, is because he thought that little of a very precise nature *could* be said. The concrete meaning of the public interest at any given moment must reflect the circumstances of lawmaking. To attempt to spell out the public interest in detail would not only be impossible, because impossibly complex, but also unwise. Any such attempt would seek to bind lawmakers without regard to the circumstances in which lawmaking occurs, and such circumstances—whether they be the amount of resources available or the range of concrete matters pressing on the society or the condition of the people—ought to influence sharply just how the public interest should be interpreted.[76] Lawmakers must exercise practical reasoning. The real problem, Madison indicated, is to design a set of institutions such that those who operate them will regularly pay some attention to the dimensions of the public interest, and, as part of such an effort, give it concrete meaning.

Still, something must be said about the broad dimensions of the public interest because, if Madison was correct, we cannot rely on lawmakers to search them out.[77] Nor can the political institutions that induce lawmakers to pay attention to the public interest be designed unless its broad outlines are known. And if we assume that the citizens of a republic will need to judge the quality of their lawmakers, we must know something of the substance of the public interest in order to tell whether citizens are capable of so judging their representatives—and what, if anything, we can and should do to ensure that they have the requisite capabilities.

What, then, are the dimensions of the public interest? In answering, I will draw on Madison's discussion of the commercial republican constitution that he commended, isolating those features of the public interest suggested by his analysis, even he if did not expressly say in *The Federalist* that they were to be considered as such.

At various points, Madison wrote as if he would include the securing of rights as part of the public interest.[78] Thus, aside from their intrinsic value, Madison believed that a government that could not secure rights could not be stable. Violations of rights that are the result of factional conflict would lead to civil disorder, and whatever else republican government must do, it must provide for the security of its citizens. Creating civil order—a society in which individuals are secure in their persons and property—is a prime purpose of government. But securing rights and providing for stability is not simply a matter of subjecting government to strict limits, as if government itself were the enemy of the liberty that these rights define. To the contrary, the enemy of liberty is not government per se but tyrannical (or weak) government.[79] Thus, the problem for the public interest is to define the kinds of actions government must take to make rights a concrete reality, thereby securing stability.

We also can be reasonably certain that Madison agreed with Hamilton's judgment that lawmaking in the public interest must foster a commercial society. Commerce was to be the engine of prosperity that Hamilton thought was both valuable in itself and necessary for the stability of the republic.[80] Thus Madison said his concern was to create a government with the power to "encourage ships and seamen" and to "encourage manufactures."[81] More tellingly, on the eve of the Constitutional Convention, Madison noted the importance of having federal power "to act positively for the 'common interest' in such matters as grants of 'incorporation for national purposes, for canals and other works of general utility.' "[82] In *The Federalist* No. 46, he looked to a "more enlarged plan of policy" that included government promotion of "national prosperity." In *The Federalist* No. 14, Madison described the Constitution as a "guardian of our commerce" and the ground of "great intercourse" in the country that would be facilitated by "new improvements."[83] And he noted that "domestic commerce" "facilitates a general intercourse of sentiments" that helps form a genuine public opinion that "sets bounds to every government and is the real sovereign in every free one."[84] At a minimum, therefore, republican lawmaking, for Madison, should aim to promote economic prosperity through an organization of wealth production that has a significant role for private ownership of productive assets and for markets.

Madison, however, was no defender of great economic inequality. In considering the condition of the citizenry necessary for republican government and the means to combat a growing level of inequality he feared would threaten republican government, Madison listed a numbers of steps to take:

> 1. By establishing a political equality among all. 2. By withholding *unnecessary* opportunities from a few, to increase the inequality of property, by an immoderate, and especially an unmerited, accumulation of riches. 3. By the silent operation of laws, which, without violating the rights of property, reduce extreme wealth towards a state of mediocrity, and raise extreme indigence towards a state of comfort. 4. By abstaining from measures which operate differently on different interests, and particularly such as favor one interest at the expense of another.[85]

Elsewhere Madison said that "every new regulation concerning commerce" can be set up so that it benefits "the *few*" and not the many, who are "the great body of their fellow citizens" and who by their toils and cares created the wealth.[86] We may infer from this that an additional dimension of the public interest for Madison was to "reduce extreme wealth" and "raise indigence." Among the most important reasons for doing so is that "poverty and dependence will render [citizens] mercenary instruments of wealth."[87] Thus, while property must be protected and factional struggle over its distribution avoided, it might still be possible "by the silent operation of the laws" to prevent massive economic inequality. The cost of protecting property need not be large-scale economic inequality. Indeed, in 1820 Madison said that "to provide employment for the poor and support for the indigent is among the primary...cares of the public authority."[88]

Madison thus wished to protect property rights, *not* the particular property of particular groups of the propertied. He neither supported an oligarchy nor drafted a Constitution to enable a particular class to rule—at least not in the sense that particular sorts of property were to rule (although, as we shall see, he meant to give the landed interest an important political role). He was open to economic innovation and to changes in the substance and meaning of property, and was thus prepared for some kinds of property to rise and others to fall. In general, although Madison felt that commerce presented dangers to republican government, not least because it would create and exacerbate conflict between the propertied and propertyless, on balance[89] the dangers seemed to him to be manageable and commerce necessary to the success of republican government. It would generate the kind of prosperity that would increase attachment to republican government and help to multiply the interests of the citizenry that would counterbalance the tendencies toward factional conflict that commerce itself generated.

Madison thus had a complex view of the value of commerce for republican government. In its guise as a right, protecting property is one of the central purposes of republican government. In its guise as economic prosperity, it is a crucial support of republican government. But in its guise as a generator of a class of propertyless men, it is worrisome. In this, Madison's thought is more sophisticated than that of many who claim him as a teacher in these matters[90] and of those who see him as a shill for the propertied.[91]

It is also possible that Madison believed that the public interest consisted of securing what we would now call a "civil society": that is, a society in which individuals would join together through associations to solve common problems or otherwise take collective action. This was already a feature of American society, as Tocqueville's later account suggests.[92] Moreover, in a free society, organized action cannot be the sole province of the state. Madison certainly shared this view, and thus undoubtedly would have agreed that a flourishing civil society was crucial for republican government. Like other founders of the American Republic, he would also have understood that such private cooperation was facilitated by the common law, and thus it would be important that national legislation assume the continuance of that law and not try to supplant it.

To summarize, the central feature of republican government for Madison is that it is a regime of limited powers where limitation is understood as controlling faction and using government for defined purposes.

PROMOTING DELIBERATION

Madison is clear that republican lawmaking, to some degree, must concern itself with the "aggregate interests of the community." It should, in part, reflect a summation of the expressed interests of the various groups that compose the society. It could hardly be otherwise in a complex heterogeneous society that any commercial republic is likely to be. Moreover, the stability of the new regime required that a wide array of interests be satisfied. Indeed, the very idea of a republican regime includes that many kinds of private interests may be legitimately pursued and that governmental power should be used to protect that pursuit. Lawmaking in a commercial republic will proceed to some degree by the construction of what may be called bland enveloping coalitions where the clash of interests is modified by bargaining and compromise.[93]

Still, Madison was clear that more is required from republican lawmaking. Having the opinions of the mass of citizens "refined"[94] by their passage through governmental institutions was, to be sure, partly aimed at preventing factional government. Deliberation among lawmakers—for that is what refining citizen opinion comes down to—would tend to bring out the narrowness and self-interest of factional claims: the difficulty in giving a reasoned defense of those claims would expose them for what they are. But Madison had something more in mind concerning the value of deliberative lawmaking:

> No man is allowed to be a judge in his own cause; because his interest would certainly bias his judgment, and, not improbably, corrupt his integrity. With equal, nay with greater reason, a body of men are unfit to be both judges and parties at the same time; yet what are many of the most important acts of legislation, but so many judicial determinations, not indeed concerning the rights of single persons, but concerning the rights of large bodies of citizens?[95]

To paraphrase John Taylor, no interest should be able to cook others in the mode most delicious to its appetite.[96] Just as one party to a legal dispute should not be the judge of that dispute, so in the legislative case, Madison said, the parties to a struggle over public benefactions and public rules cannot justly settle these disputes among themselves or through legislators who speak for them. They, or those who speak for them, will be inclined to settle the matter at the expense of those not present or represented—namely, the rest of the citizenry. Following Madison's thinking, we might say that citizens must rely on the legislature to speak for them as a whole in these matters, with the hope that it will move beyond the particular interests being promoted and invoke the principles the citizens themselves would invoke if they had the time, resources, and skills. It is when lawmaking invokes such principles, when it induces those who only wish to say "I want" to offer reasons instead for their claims, that the citizenry as a whole might plausibly acquiesce to their requests. This is especially so because any given law is likely to be costly to particular groups of citizens. Their willingness to count law as legitimate depends, at least in part, on their belief that there are good reasons for its content, that the law is not merely the imposition of the preferences of some people on others.

Madison thus argued that the essential task of lawmaking in a fully realized commercial republic is to "refine and enlarge the public views" passing the people's "temporary or partial considerations" through the machinery of lawmaking.[97] Lawmaking would be the last stop on the road to a progressive refinement in understanding what "the comprehensive interests of the country" might be.[98] Lawmakers would discern "the permanent...interests of the community."[99] The majority necessary for passing legislation would issue from a consideration of what these permanent interests called for in the case at hand.[100] These majorities may be ad hoc, which is what Madison apparently preferred at the time of writing *The Federalist*, or they could be longer lived in the form of political parties.[101]

Madison thought, however, that it was too much to hope that by making factional schemes difficult to pursue successfully, lawmakers who might otherwise speak for various factions and particular interests would concern themselves with the permanent interests of the community. If republican government were to succeed, lawmakers must deliberate. But being free to deliberate is one thing; being disposed to do so is another. To put it differently, the public-regarding motives of lawmakers that would be set free to do their work once faction is controlled are not likely to be strong enough to produce deliberative lawmaking. The problem for Madison was how to induce lawmakers, who must have discretion in how they fashion the law, to turn their attentions to serving the permanent interests of the community.

The Madisonian constitutional design, therefore, provides incentives to draw lawmakers away from being the servant of narrow interests or pursuing the small but comfortable legislative life. The separation of powers, which is meant not only to prevent faction but also to promote public deliberation, is crucial here.[102] Each branch not only has controls over the others so that it may protect its independence,[103] but the separation of powers also sets up an institutional structure in which national lawmaking must revolve around the efforts of the branches to convince one another of the merits of its views. Each branch has the constitutional means to resist the blandishments of other branches: their cooperation thus can most easily be secured through persuasion. And given that a significant portion of this persuasion will take place publicly, arguments showing how the legislation at issue serves the public interest will be common. Such arguments will be attractive to the citizenry at large whose approbation is needed if the cooperation of other branches is to be gained. Moreover, since the officials of each branch reach office by different means, the efforts of each branch to convince the others will bring into play a larger range of opinions and interests than if the officials of the branches were selected in the same way.

It is important to note here that Madison thought that the separation of powers would do its work even with lawmakers who have only a modest concern for the public interest. They would need the cooperation of other branches than their own and thus would be drawn into public deliberation—at least if they were ambitious and desired fame. The

Madisonian design will lead them to think of how they gain the approbation of their fellow lawmakers and thus their countrymen, and, as a result, perhaps find their place in history.[104] Madison also believed that even lawmakers with only a passing desire to see the public interest served would, on occasion, be drawn by the separation of powers into public and principled discussion of various pieces of legislation. Their ambitions would sometimes make them at least go through the motions of publicly persuading other lawmakers. Political ambition in the Madisonian design is thus harnessed to the service of the permanent interests of the community.

Overall, it was Madison's view that only strong and lasting majorities—ones that could bring together the separate branches of government—should be able to use the power of law to secure substantial changes in the life of the society. The idea was to cool passion and induce reflection, prompted in part by the need to find allies. Madison's design was meant to halt factious majorities and encourage nonfactional public-spirited ones that would be a principal source of energy in the new government. Again, he was neither a pluralist in the modern sense nor an advocate of simple majority rule. He was a republican:

> The aim of every political constitution is or ought to be first to obtain for rulers, men who possess most wisdom to discern, and most virtue to pursue the common good of the society; and in the next place, to take the most effectual precautions for keeping them virtuous, whilst they continue to hold the public trust.[105]

Lawmaking in a complex heterogeneous republic, Madison believed, cannot only be aggregative, at least not if there is to be any possibility of serving the public interest. Bargaining and aggregating interests can only serve the public interest by chance. In Madison's view, a properly designed representative government—a republic—was the best hope for serving the permanent interests of the community.

A CAPABLE CITIZENRY

The citizens who are the authorizing agents for the whole republican enterprise and whose judgments and actions are inevitably crucial to its success must have certain qualities, according to Madison. They are, after all, the ones who are to elect lawmakers inclined to deliberate on the concrete meaning of the public interest:

> But I go on this great republican principle, that the people will have the virtue and intelligence to select men of virtue and wisdom. Is there no virtue among us? If there be not, we are in a wretched situation. No theoretical checks—no form of government can render us secure. To suppose that any

form of government will secure liberty or happiness without any virtue in the people, is a chimerical idea. If there be sufficient virtue and intelligence in the community, it will be exercised in the selection of these men. So that we not depend on their virtue, or put confidence in our rulers, but in the people who are to choose them.[106]

Those elected, Madison hoped, would be "individuals of extended views, and of national pride" who would govern "with a sole regard to justice and the public good."[107] The system of representation would "extract from the mass of society" those whose "enlightened views and virtuous sentiments [would] render them superior to local prejudices, and to schemes of injustice."[108]

Madison's constitutional design rested, as he put it, on "sufficient virtue and intelligence" among the citizenry for the tasks that lay ahead.[109] The large electoral districts that Madison favored, which would be inevitable in an extended republic with a legislature of workable size,[110] would give substantial political advantages to those of wide reputation, and possibly to those with a reputation for public service. Such men would frequently be substantial property holders and this in itself would be an advantage.[111] Madison supposed that enough citizens would know such men, or at least know of them, and vote for them on the basis of their reputation. Of course, for this to work properly, the citizenry would need to be able to distinguish those who were known for skullduggery from those who had some concern for the commonweal.[112] Thus, the kind and amount of "virtue" Madison thought was required is modest enough: an ability to identify the notables in one's electoral districts and to know something of their reputation, to choose, as Madison put it, "men who possess the most diffusive and established characters."[113] As has been suggested, Madison had great hopes for nonfactious public-spirited or "civic" majorities.[114] The combination of the effects of the design on retarding factions and a modest measure of public-spiritedness, thought Madison, would produce such majorities. As Harvey Mansfield puts it in commenting on *The Federalist* No. 63, lawmakers are to be "responsible on their [the people's] behalf: responsible politicians in this sense do for the people what they cannot do for themselves, but *can* form a judgment about."[115]

Madison, however, was worried that the likely division of the country into the propertied and propertyless, which he could see on the horizon and which already existed to some degree, might overwhelm such virtue.[116] But he probably did not quite see how the necessary character of the citizenry might be fostered without an intrusion into the lives of the citizens that the new republican regime was designed to prevent. The problem, we might say, is whether it is reasonable to rest republican government on virtues the citizenry is presumed to have in common, if significant economic inequality beckons with its attendant deep divisions in the society. The presence of public-spirited officials might, to some degree, make up for what was weak or absent in the citizenry, but Madison thought this was simply too risky a strategy.[117] In the end, he did not give sufficient attention to the question of what would ensure that citizens would choose the right leaders. We may suppose that it was also his ambivalence about the capacities of the people that made him hesitate. The people—or at least the various majorities that would come into being—would be passionate and inclined to faction. But they would also be virtuous.

FOR MADISON, then, the institutional design of the regime must accomplish at least two things: it must facilitate deliberation, that is, the exercise of practical political reason through which the public interest is given concrete meaning; and, in order to make that possible, it must prevent any breach of the rule of law and, more broadly, control faction. The two major tasks reinforce one another: when lawmakers turn away from factional schemes and efforts to breach the rule of law, they can turn to a consideration of broader interests.

THE SOCIAL BASIS OF THE REGIME

Madison believed that the fully realized commercial republic that he hoped the United States would become could not rest solely on institutional design. A constitutional theory concerns not just the framework of government and how its major institutions are to work; it also requires a political sociology,[118] a foundation in self-interest. This did not only mean that self-interest was to be checked by self-interest: competing interests would be drawn into the complex and divided machinery of government to check one another. Madison also believed that a regime is a set of institutions harnessed to a conception of justice consistent with the one held by the powerful social strata of the regime.[119]

Madison looked to the propertied class to provide the regime's foundation in self-interest. In particular, he thought the political energies of this class could be harnessed in a way that would increase the likelihood that the permanent interests of the regime would be given due attention.[120] The design of government should not only protect property rights, but should also ensure that men of property have political advantages in the struggle to define the content of the laws. Moreover, the design was to provide incentives for the propertied to broaden their conception of their own interests, thus increasing the overlap between their interests and the public interest. There were thus to be two principal sources of energy in this new government: nonfactional, "civic" majorities, and a propertied class with broad interests.

To start, men of property were to be given political advantages—political influence greater than their proportion in the population would call for—in order to increase the chance that they would be a significant portion of those elected to office. It was likely that they would predominate in those offices filled by indirect election: state legislatures would choose men they knew, and those with large public reputations would likely be men of means; much the same forces would be at work in the Electoral College's choice of president. Additionally, large electoral districts would mean that most of the people widely known in a given electoral district would be major property holders whose holdings would allow them to engage in civic and political affairs, and whose resources would allow them time to run for office.[121] Moreover, popular government itself confers an advantage on the propertied class. Those with economic resources are better able to get their views disseminated, and thus are often opinion leaders.

As already indicated, Madison believed that men of property would naturally be drawn to limited government as the best way to ensure respect for their property rights. They would also see the importance of commerce and the value of government promoting it. But Madison was also aware that men of property might be drawn to deeply flawed versions of such concerns, ones that simply took their immediate and narrowly defined self-interest as the proper way to interpret these purposes. Still, he believed that the protection of property rights was necessary for republican government, that limited government was its very essence, and that promotion of commerce was a part of the republican public interest. Thus, the leading propertied men of the republic were crucial to the success of Madison's constitutional scheme, even if there were some danger in relying on them. Madison argued that republican government could not depend on statesmen to run it. It would have to rely on cruder devices, among them men only modestly inclined to look beyond their own concerns.

Madison thus believed there to be a providential overlap between the interests of the propertied and the security of property rights, on the one hand, and on the other the permanent interests of the community. He suggested that men of property and substantial community position would have a deep attachment to the new country if it would secure their standing, and they would likely be less open than others to the blandishments of mere popularity and the benefactions offered by particular interests. Additionally, because a majority of the propertied were likely to be men of *landed* property,[122] and the character of the new regime would significantly affect the value of such property, they might be supposed to take a particularly great interest in the fate of their country and to have a broad view of the country's interests.[123] And if the new country was politically stable, its citizens would likely be content with the new arrangements. Large landholders, as the major beneficiaries of this stability and contentment, might then be encouraged to think about ways to secure stable government, thus increasing the overlap between the permanent interests of the community and their self-interest.[124]

Still, even if the interests of the propertied did overlap with the rights the regime was to secure and with the permanent interests of the community it was to serve, the overlap, without further attention, would unlikely be sufficient to ensure significant progress toward the realization of these purposes. Compounding the problem, the constitutional design gave political advantages to the propertied. These same advantages could be used to prevent the serving of other than property rights as well as aspects of the permanent interests of the community other than promoting commerce. If the political sociology of the regime was to do its job, its institutional design must increase the likelihood that the interests the propertied would promote were not narrowly construed. Here, however, and elsewhere with respect to the political role of the propertied generally, Madison is at his least explicit. If we are to appreciate his argument, we must elaborate it.

We can point to several forces in the Madisonian design that promote an enlargement of the interests of the propertied. The first is simply the impact of elections. After all, in seeking public office, men of property could not plausibly say to voters that politics is a business and they are in it to add to their bank accounts. Here the majoritarian nature of elections has an effect. Asserting a broad conception of the interests of the propertied is prudent; and at least showing how the public good requires that attention be given to what turns out to be the economic interests of the propertied is likely to commend itself to those who speak for them. As Madison more generally said, perhaps with more hope than justification, if political institutions are properly designed and the array of interests that compose society are large in number, majorities in general will seldom form "on any other principles than those of justice and the common good."[125] Moreover, once the public interest is said to be at issue, those who are elected to office, including men of property, will likely make some modest effort to serve it now and again—not least because the citizenry has been handed a standard by which to judge them. Regularly claiming something to be the case has an alarming tendency to alter one's beliefs.

The impact of deliberation in lawmaking would work in much the same fashion. While again Madison is not explicit, we know that he believed that lawmaking would "refine" the views and interests advocated in the process. We may assume that those who hold narrow economic interests will be unable to simply assert them if such a mode of lawmaking is at work; and, once again, they therefore would inevitably be drawn to formulations of their concerns that emphasize the broad nature of the benefits to be gained from serving them. This too would provide a standard by which to judge their views, and the habit of using the words of the public interest would also do their work.

This tendency for deliberation to broaden interests is likely to be reinforced by the separation of powers. In seeking political influence, different kinds of property holders would be drawn to different branches of government and be differently advantaged by the manner of selection that characterizes each branch. If this is so, then various sectors of the propertied class would be able to influence the use of governmental powers; therefore, seeking the sort of cooperation that the separation of powers prompts would incline them to seek common ground. This, in itself, would tend to broaden their interests. Moreover, the separation of powers would, as noted, force disagreements partly to be played out publicly. Again the need to address the citizenry is likely to broaden interests, and the penalty for nonchalance in such matters would be the most painful one for public officials: loss of office.

Behind the broadening of interests induced by the separation of powers and deliberative lawmaking there is a larger force at work: the dynamics of coalition building. If, as Madison hoped, a vibrant, commercial, and differentiated society came into being, those seeking to advance their interests would find it necessary to do more than look for a set of particular benefits large enough to induce others to come on board to create a majority. They would also find themselves discussing what they have in common in the effort to coordinate their efforts. Thus, coalitions would likely be formed to press for a broad version of the interests of property, and in doing so to broaden the purview of the propertied themselves. Madison implied as much in asserting that interests will only come together around schemes of justice.

How far might this broadening of the interests of the propertied go? Certainly, Madison supposed that the prominent men of the community—the propertied—might be induced to rise above, for example, their factional inclination to be indifferent to the fate of their propertyless fellow citizens. Moreover, the propertied could be induced to see that they had a substantial interest in the maintenance of republican government.

Madison seems to have believed, then, that the propertied class could be relied on to play a crucial role in giving concrete meaning to the public interest. Cooled-off civic or public-spirited majorities would give government some of the needed energy, but the concerns of whatever majorities that happened to form would be insufficient to direct lawmaking down the path of securing all rights and the permanent interests of the community. To so direct lawmaking, Madison relied heavily on the propertied, who could give direction to government by playing a pivotal role in the forming of majorities that, while self-interested, would have a broad view of those interests. Whether Madison also thought that the propertied might play a vital role in civic majorities is a tantalizing thought, but one for which there is insufficient evidence. If the propertied could do so, they would become the vital center of the regime. In any event, Madison believed in popular self-government and thought it could work *if* men of property had their interests broadened.

Of great importance for constructing a compelling theory of republican political constitution, Madison modified the way he regarded the propertied as the politics of the new Republic unfolded. Among other things, as a result of his conflict with Hamilton he came to talk less about men of property whose interests would be broadened and more about nonfactious majorities and political parties that would be the home of many of them. As Lance Banning makes clear, Madison never departed from his overall account of what was required for stable and attractive republican government, although at different points he emphasized different aspects of it, depending on the state of the political life of the country.[126] This being so, we may assume that Madison never dropped the idea that men of property with broad interests—and thus the self-interest of a class or stratum—is a crucial element of the political constitution of republican government.

For Madison the ideal republican regime has an electoral system in which those elected include a substantial number of men of property and standing with an inclination to broaden their self-interest and to engage in deliberative lawmaking concerned with the public interest. In this fashion, both public-spiritedness and self-interest would be at work in the same lawmaker. If this proved impossible, it would not be because individuals cannot be both public-spirited and self-interested. Most of us are. Rather, such an ideal requires a citizenry of such discriminating judgment that it can elect such a splendid set of lawmakers. Still, a mix of the two kinds of lawmakers might well be sufficient for serving the public interest. So long as some citizens choose men of property disposed to having their self-interest broadened and others choose those inclined to be public-spirited, the mix might be sufficient to ensure that the public interest commands at least modest attention.[127] At any rate, while republican government must have a foundation in self-interest, the task was to harness it to the achievement of larger ends. And thus it was, he thought, with the propertied.[128] For Madison to be very explicit about these matters—especially concerning the favored political role of the propertied—might well reduce the chance that the regime he was trying to bring into being would gain popular support. Here discretion was important, not just for the benefit of those who would come to govern, but also for the benefit of the mass of the citizenry who might not see the best path to serving their fundamental interests.

PULLING THE ELEMENTS TOGETHER

At its heart, Madison's constitutional design aims to prevent factions from undercutting rights and permanent interests or from blocking efforts to secure them, and thus to facilitate lawmaking that will actively serve these permanent interests and secure these rights. The Madisonian design is meant to produce a concrete definition of the limits on government, and it will be the workings of the institutions that compose that design that, when well ordered, give specific meaning to the idea of limited and active government. Government will be restrained from pursuing certain kinds of purposes or pursuing acceptable ones through any sort of means. At the same time, it will be active in pursuit of those purposes encompassed by the private rights and public interests.[129]

In short, Madison set out a design for a politics of self-limitation. The institutions he proposed would in themselves, and through the larger politics they engendered, induce those who speak for the people to give regular attention to the boundaries of the people's rule. More generally, the focus of Madison's efforts was to bring about a new constitutional order—a new political whole or regime. He did not view this effort as antithetical to politics or designed to constrain it. Rather he was committed to helping to create a new kind of politics.

Madison believed that this politics must have three features: it would be relatively free of faction and thus able to secure rights and the interests of the community; lawmaking would be deliberative, which would increase the possibility that the public interest could be given concrete meaning; and the interests of the propertied would be expanded, which, when added to the force of the civic majorities that might be expected to emerge, would provide the political energy needed to secure these larger public interests.[130] At the center of the regime would be a deliberative core capable of practical reasoning about the concrete meaning of the public interest.[131] Putting the matter in this way helps reveal the connection between the negative and positive aspects of Madison's thought. And by talking about giving concrete meaning to the public interest, two features of his thinking on the matter are emphasized. First, Madison had a substantive conception of the public interest but, second, its concrete meaning could only be decided in the context of actual efforts at lawmaking. His interest throughout was with creating *effective* government.

Madison's writings thus provide no handbook for an indictment of the people's capacity for self-government, even that of the propertyless mass. It is instead a complex assessment of what the people's role can and should be if republican government is to succeed. The aim of his constitutional design is not to allow the propertied to defend themselves against "the landless proletariat."[132] Madison understood that a crucial problem of securing republican government in the context of a commercial society is the inevitable division between the propertied and the propertyless. Yet, commerce was valuable, he thought; it multiplied interests and, with the economic well-being it generated, would increase the attachment of the people to republican government. Moreover, the private property at the base of such government would define one of the barriers to overbearing government action. It would also provide the economic independence necessary if the citizenry were to feel secure enough to criticize and, if necessary, remove their governors. Additionally, a commercial society offered the best hope for the have-nots.[133] The desideratum was republican government, the essential difficulty was class division. At bottom then, the problem was how to get the propertied to serve in a government that would not be an exercise in class rule, while at the same time getting the propertyless to accept a regime that was not constructed with the express intent of alleviating their distress.

It should now be clear that Madison cannot be recruited to the ranks of either pluralists or libertarian thinkers, and why—if he is our guide—such views are inconsistent with the best thinking about the constitutional design of the American regime. Madison shares little of the pluralists' thrill when they behold a multitude of interests competing to gain control of pieces of the governmental machinery. Self-interest, said Madison, cannot be eliminated if liberty is our aim. Indeed, the value of liberty is, in part, that it allows us to pursue our own interests, narrow or otherwise. We must live with self-interest, appreciate its value, and harness it when we can; but we should certainly not join together to sing its praises. In its worst form, self-interest brings the death of republican government and, in its more benign forms, it makes it harder to serve the permanent interests of the community. In both cases, interest groups are much like Matthew Arnold's "ignorant armies" clashing "on a darkling plain."[134] They cannot see ahead and probably do not even notice the absence of light. As for libertarians, the most sophisticated thinkers among them realize that assertions that there is a substantive public interest leads inexorably to active government. Unfortunately for those libertarians anxious to claim descent from Madison, that is precisely what Madison applauded—a public interest and a government active in its service. But neither can Madison be recruited to the ranks of those who believe that if there is a problem, government is the solution. Republican government is limited government, and its limits follow from its purposes— namely, securing rights and serving the public interest. At bottom, Madison argued that liberty depends on a well-ordered government. The enemies of liberty are tyrannical and ineffective government: the first aims to squash liberty, the second leaves it hostage to the propensity of the strong to

dominate the weak. At the beginning of the Republic, Edmund Pendle-
ton said it as well as anyone: "There is no quarrel between government and
liberty. The war is between government and licentiousness, faction, turbu-
lence and other violations of the rules of society, to preserve liberty."[135]

THE STRENGTHS OF MADISON'S THEORY

A wide variety of political and legal theorists have come to think that Madison's political theory is the best we have to guide the American Republic. As I
have said, there are pluralists who think that the Madisonian constitutional
design puts interest group bargaining at its center.[136] At the same time,
there are public choice theorists, also proclaiming inspiration by Madison,
who tout the wonders of preference aggregation.[137] Then there are those
who think the real teaching of Madison is that republican government must
revolve around deliberative ways of lawmaking, either to refine the less reflective views of the people or because this is the only way to serve justice.[138]
In a different vein, there are those who take their guidance from what they
believe to be Madison's unsentimental understanding of the political ways of
the people under popular government.[139] One cannot be too careful here,
they say, for at any moment popular passion and narrow interest can be
unleashed and republican government endangered. In general, these theorists say, we should not expect too much from the day-to-day politics of
the regime. But there are still other theorists who say that, if we are true
Madisonians, we should be suspicious of taking major decisions out of the
hands of the people's representatives and reserving them for a supposedly
nonpolitical court.[140]

It is the protean quality of Madison's thought that makes it possible
for these various theorists to claim him as their guide. I have provided
an account of Madison's thinking that shows in fact that it does contain
elements of each view. The power of his thinking stems precisely from its
capaciousness and the way in which he relates these elements to one another.
In the same vein, students of the seemingly endless controversy concerning
whether the founding generation were liberals or republicans will (perhaps)
be relieved to hear that we (and they) need not choose.[141] Of the founders,
Madison, at least, was both. He thought that public-spiritedness and an
effort to serve the public interest were necessary to good government, as
were the protection of rights, consent as a basis of government, and limits
on government. The problem, he thought, is how to combine these features
of political life, especially in the face of a society likely to be characterized
by significant and enduring divisions.

For Madison, good government is not first and foremost democratic government, one that maximizes popular control of government. It is instead

popular government that secures rights, aggregates private interests, and serves the permanent interests of the community. Americans are the inheritors of his view that government must be both popular and limited, but that any marriage between them is not likely to be a smooth one. Moreover, Madison is perhaps our greatest teacher of the fundamental proposition that, in popular self-government, our concern should not only be that the people shall rule but also *how* they are to do it. Popular authority provides no warrant, according to Madison, for the people to do as they please: it is not open to republican government to pursue any purpose in any way it pleases.[142] That is, republican government is first and foremost the politics of a self-limiting popular sovereign.[143]

As I have suggested, Madison teaches that there are two interconnected worries about the use of political authority. One is its impact on individuals as they come into contact with the state. Here the worry is about the state itself—that its officials will go about wreaking havoc on the lives of its inhabitants, taking their property, torturing them, and otherwise treating them as resources for those who control political power. Even when the rulers are the people themselves, as is the case in the United States, there are still the same sorts of dangers when the individual meets the functionaries of the state. Joined to this concern is Madison's second worry. Here the concern is with majorities who control political power and what they might do with it vis-à-vis minorities. The first is an unavoidable problem in any governmental system except possibly ones that require unanimous agreement of the citizenry. The second is specific to any majoritarian system where governmental action only requires the agreement of a majority. Madison convincingly moves the discussion of tyranny and arbitrary government from how to control the state to how to control the people, and shows how the two can be brought together in a single scheme of government. The common thread in his formulations is that arbitrariness must be avoided.[144] Government without limits cannot be anything but arbitrary since it is government without principles and justifications. Thus a central task of republican government is to provide these limits with content, to indicate what kinds of purposes can be pursued and what means of governing are acceptable. Republican government, Madison argues, is quintessentially limited government.[145]

Similarly, Madison thought that lawmaking should be in the service of justice. At its worst, he contended, lawmaking is an exercise in which "a predominant party ... trample[s] on the rules of justice."[146] But in pointing to the securing of rights and to serving the permanent interests of the community, Madison directs us beyond such conceptions of the rule of law that the content of the law must be considered in open forum and must apply to both governor and governed. He gives no apparent weight to its form; the common idea that law must be general is given what weight is needed by the requirement that lawmakers must not exempt themselves.[147] The crucial element in Madison's thinking about law is that it must serve certain purposes. This, as we shall see, points to a more attractive conception of the rule of law.[148]

Madison is also one of the first modern theorists to teach that government is part of the *solution* of the problem of arbitrary rule. If properly arranged, government can thwart tyranny and increase the probability that the public interest will be served. We might interpret Madison as saying that the central problem of representative government is so to organize ordinary politics that the fundamental question of the concrete meaning of rights and the permanent interests of the community—and thus the purposes Americans should pursue and the means for doing so—get regular reflective attention. Just as important, there will also be political forces at work to contain those that would push in other directions. It is notable here that Madison never argued for a division of labor in which a special agent or agents—a high court, for example—is charged with ensuring that the ordinary play of democratic politics does no violence to the rights and the permanent interests of the community. Nor does he argue for "law" to bind "politics," a high court as the custodian of a higher law binding ordinary politics. Nor, again, does he contend that a special constitutional level politics should be created to constrain ordinary politics. These are the mainstays of much contemporary discussion of limited government.[149] Madison's conception of republican government is more complex than any of these. He contemplated a regime where legislative lawmaking, the actions of judges, the day-to-day activities of ordinary citizens, and ordinary representatives going about their regular political rounds would prevent the people from unlimitedly expanding the reach of government, thus allowing political energy to be focused on securing rights and serving permanent community interests. It is a constitutional *politics* that is to limit the use of governmental power.

Madison also shows us that while we must be aware of the dangers of government, an active government is central to a well-functioning republican regime. At a minimum, liberty is not a function of the absence of government or of a government small in scope, but the product of a well-designed government. Leaving citizens to their own devices, allowing the free play of passion and self-interest, will signal a movement away from securing liberty. Moreover, to allow the regular workings of the society to undercut serving the public interest is just as bad as the active efforts by factions to subvert it. While Madison was not always as clear as he might have been about the central importance of active government to liberty, he certainly understood this better than the classical liberals who followed him and claim him as their teacher. Thus, although Madison thought that the Bill of Rights was an acceptable device to help create a sphere free from governmental intervention, he also thought it was unnecessary. Madison's deepest views were that it was the structure of government itself and the politics of which it is a part that guarantees individual freedom and the private life in which it is rooted. There was no need, he thought, to spell out a specific set of rights because nothing in the new constitution suggested that the people did not have such rights.[150]

Overall, Madison is an equal opportunity teacher: the dangers to republican government, he believed, do not come only from those who think government is the problem, not the solution. There are all too many people in our nation's public life who think that government is the solution and yet cannot seem to grasp that, if there are no boundaries on what purposes government can pursue, politics will turn into an elaborate game of what public choice theorists call "rent-seeking." In this game, each of us tries to use the tax system and other legislative means to get other people to provide the resources to serve our private interests. This is a wholly human and understandable desire, but not one on which we should build our politics. Indeed, the problem is worse than this: if it is widely understood that government is no more than a giant benefaction dispenser and that those who get there early and well organized receive the lion's share of the goodies, then many will conclude—as many contemporary Americans no doubt already have—that law is simply another name for foisting some people's preferences on other people. This is not a recipe for constructing a regime that has a strong hold on its citizen's affections. Madison teaches the crucial lesson here. In the absence of a widespread sense that there is a substantive public interest, we can expect nothing but rancor and dark suspicions that government is something to avoid.

Moreover, and perhaps unnervingly in the current political climate, Madison teaches that a citizenry with aspirations to realize a republican government, one that secures liberty, must place a good deal of faith in its political leaders—as long as there is good reason to suppose that such leaders will be prevented from factional schemes and will be induced to look beyond narrow interests. Equally unnerving, Madison suggests that even a well-ordered republican regime must have its foundations in the self-interest of a particular class or stratum of the society. Republican government, he contends, cannot flourish if it depends more or less completely on "higher" motives, avoids taking account of the conflict among various powerful interests, and does not look to the overlap between public and private interests.

Madison also shows that the genius of republican government is that it can combine serving transpolitical rights (rights that do not depend on government recognition for their claims on us) and the permanent interest of the community, on the one hand, and self-government on the other. The key to doing so, he indicates, is getting the people to rule not as they please, but with due regard to these rights and permanent interests. Madison, unlike many later theorists, does not let the creative tension between popular government and rights and permanent interests be pulled apart. For him, there is not just popular self-government or the protection of rights or the serving of the public interest—all three are crucial and the central constitutional problem is how to combine them. If we are successful in doing so, we will have a government that is both limited and active—active in the pursuit of its limited purposes. In the same vein, Madison indicates that we should not pretend that we can achieve republican government by *telling* lawmakers what to do, as if that is sufficient incentive for them to do the right thing.[151] Rather, Madison placed his hopes for republican government in the acceptance by the citizenry of a constitutional design. If they accepted the design, the governmental "machine" would, if not "go of itself,"[152] at least produce incentives that dispose lawmakers to pay attention to securing rights, serving the permanent interests of the community, and facilitating private interest aggregation.

In addition to his teaching about limited government, Madison, probably without intending to do so, invites us to distinguish between the value of private property and a commercial society, on the one hand, and the attractions of the propertied class as the sociological foundation of a republican regime on the other. While the first two have at least in part an intrinsic value, the propertied are simply an instrument to achieve these important ends. It might thus be possible to construct a constitutional design that would allow us to defend private property and promote a commercial society while working to create a favored but limited political role for the propertied class. This is a matter of the first importance for a successful constitutional design of a commercial republic.

Perhaps most important of all, the Madisonian theory is an account of a whole political regime that contains the central pieces of many of the various political and legal theories constructed after he wrote. As noted, it has room for self-interest and private-regarding preferences, as well as for deliberation and the public interest. It is unsentimental—not looking for great feats of statesmanship, but resting instead on the more reliable extensions of self-interest. Yet at the same time, Madison realized that a substantial part of the burden of making the regime work must fall on the citizenry. He was perhaps too ambivalent and evasive for comfort about whether lawmakers and citizens were equipped or could come to be equipped to govern themselves. His astringent view of the *demos* and his strictures about a republic needing ambition to counter ambition do not sit easily with his concern for a regime that would select lawmakers capable of rising above their narrow interests.

But he did at least see that there are two sides to the problem: to prevent the worst and to induce, if not the best, at least the good enough. Madison's is a theory of the regime that is an exemplar of constitutional thinking. It is the kind of constitutional theory that we desperately need—one that enables us to understand the dangers to republican government from all over the political spectrum. And in its comprehensiveness—its delineation of the crucial interconnections of the parts of a republican regime—it is a powerful antidote to those who have forgotten or have never learned that to secure a whole political way of life is not a matter of getting right this or that political piece. If matters were that simple, we would have long since solved the problem of republican government—and Madison, and those who attempt to understand and embroider his complex teaching, would take their place in the large army of theorists who have wasted their own and other people's time.

Madison thought that while the people cannot rule directly, they could choose to be ruled moderately and with a concern for rights and permanent interests, if, that is, they would accept a constitutional design that harnessed their self-interest and gave full scope to their broadest interests. Madison's most profound teaching is that the same people who are the source of the fundamental problem of republican government are, if government is properly arranged, also its solution.

3

Flaws in the Madisonian Theory

JAMES MADISON is a great teacher of the theory and practice of popular self-government, but his work is not without blemish.[1] The place to begin an account of the flaws in his constitutional theory is the part of it that has received the greatest attention—the prevention of majority tyranny. Even here, where many have claimed the design a success, there are worries. The case can be made that Madison did not believe that his constitutional design alone would put an end to the subjugation of black people through slavery. The governmental structure was not expressly meant to protect the rights of those not included in the political order.[2] If this is accepted, it would also be inappropriate to criticize Madison for not seeing that the constitutional design allowed the continued deprivation of the political and civil rights of women. Such a defense might conclude with the argument that if black people and women had possessed full civil and political rights, the design would have protected them. More to the point, it is a reasonable argument that it was the Madisonian design—especially the centrality of the language of rights—that made the ending of the subjugation of black people and the winning of full equality for women possible. Still, with regard to black people specifically, we must ask whether the Civil War signaled the breakdown of the Madisonian system, and thus revealed it to be incapable of ending racial subjugation. There is also the not so small problem that, in political regimes different from the one at work in the United States, women were granted full political equality before we managed it.[3]

A strong case can also be made that the Madisonian design has not pre-vented periods of majority tyranny directed at those on the political left.[4] Starting in the late nineteenth century with the International Workers of the World (IWW), extending to socialists in the first part of the twentieth century, communists later yet in that century, and more recently with black nationalist groups and those who might be counted as part of the New Left, our treatment of these citizens has been marred by the disregard of their civil liberties. Is this the work of a small subset of law enforcement officials? It seems unlikely, for it is hard to believe that the abrogation of basic civil liberties could have been as extensive as it was without popular distaste for anarchists, pinkoes, black power advocates, and lefties. While our actual practices themselves cannot be used to impeach Madison's arguments— after all, our working constitution did not spring full-grown from his mind, mirroring completely his design—there remains sufficient resemblance between his design and that working constitution to give pause.

With these significant exceptions notwithstanding, however, the regime's record of preventing majority factions from subverting basic civil and political rights has been a good one. Gainfully employed white people of moderate political outlook have usually been spared any severe deprivation of rights. Of course, it might be argued that they are the majority and thus unlikely in any case to find themselves at the short end of the governmental stick; at least in this respect Madison would agree. He thought that the majority of citizens, either propertied or otherwise, would be inclined to defend their rights. We could simply say on Madison's behalf, then, that his design made it possible for such majorities to defend their rights successfully. Still, protecting the liberties of centrists and others well within the political pale is an altogether easier job than protecting the rights of dissidents and those left out of day-to-day politics. Moreover, the liberty of those in the political mainstream has been protected at least as well by many other Western regimes. A plausible conclusion here is that we, and Madison, could have done better in the hard cases while we have done well in the easier ones.

THE PROPERTIED, RIGHTS, AND THE PERMANENT INTERESTS OF THE COMMUNITY

Madison's constitutional thinking has other weaknesses than those concerned with controlling faction. To show this, we will need to consider further how the pieces of the Madisonian constitutional design are supposed to fit together. That design rests on Madison's belief that the citizenry had sufficient virtue to choose enough lawmakers to secure rights and serve the permanent and aggregate interests of the community. In particular, they would regularly elect men of property and standing. If the propertied were kept from succumbing to factional designs, and if their self-interest was broadened so that there was significant overlap between it and the public interest, then a politics of self-interest would reinforce what a public interest politics could provide. But for all this to happen, thought Madison, the propertied would need political advantages enabling them to have a significant place in the councils of government.

We might go further here, beyond what Madison could easily have foreseen, but consistent with his views. In the commercial society that Madison favored, men of property whose interests are confined to amassing capital might well find it more attractive to direct their energies to the marketplace than to elective office. If so, the way would be open for other members of the propertied class with less insistently narrow concerns to stand for public office. Moreover, these latter property holders would likely be receptive to the incentives built into the Madisonian design aimed at broadening their interests—or at least more receptive than the propertied whose principal aim is to acquire greater wealth. To extend Madison's argument even further, if there were nonfactional, public-spirited majorities at work, men of property running for public office might be expected to try to show how serving the interests of property coincides with the broad concerns of such majorities. Of course, it is also possible that some men of property and standing will be public-spirited to begin with.

If all this were to work as Madison hoped it would, then the constitutional design would be a success, in this respect at least. The rights of the propertied would be protected, and at least some of the energies of government would be directed at serving significant portions of the permanent interests of the community. This energy would be added to that provided by nonfactional, public-spirited majorities. The political advantages given to the propertied would be legitimated by the overlap of their own and the broad public interests. More generally, Madison's design is a very attractive solution to the problem of how, in a regime where the people are to rule, property rights can be protected, other rights secured, and the permanent interests of the community served. Even if men of property and standing proved to be as self-interested as the ordinary run of men, if their self-interest could be broadened and citizens regularly elected them to office, then lawmaking would still aim at serving at least some rights and some of the community's permanent interests. Private interest would still be harnessed to public interest.

However, by taking seriously the need to find a way to protect property rights and, similarly, to see that a thriving commercial society was achieved, both of which Madison thought would be of primary concern only to a minority, he was led to a series of problematic formulations. To see why, we need an outline of some crucial features of what I have called the "working constitution" of contemporary American democratic capitalism.

With the rise of large-scale capitalism, there have been significant changes in our political economy that distinguish it from the one Madison knew: (1) the nature of private property has altered; (2) there is now widespread agreement that the national government is responsible for promoting high levels of economic performance; (3) what might be termed the "administrative state" has come into being. Joining these facets of our political economy to features of the Madisonian design that have been put into practice—notably, the impediments to strong nonfactional and public-spirited (indeed to all) majorities forming and governing, and the absence of institutional forms to foster a public-spirited citizenry—has resulted in a working constitution that is badly flawed. It may even be failing where, on Madisonian terms, it must succeed—namely, in controlling faction, particularly minority faction, which Madison thought to be the worst disease of republican government.[5] Is that, in fact, our condition?

THE CHANGE IN PROPERTY

Madison's men of landed property and standing have turned into capitalists. They are no longer the respectable men of affairs who might plausibly have a broad view of the interests of the country, be receptive to having their interests further broadened, and have a serious interest in public matters generally. The new men of property have a narrower view and their concerns are likely to be more narrowly economic: those who control corporate assets are frequently advocates of "special interests."[6] Private productive property is now socialized in the guise of the assets of a legal entity, the business corporation, whose principal concern is to make a profit. Property is now "capital" and is looked on as something to invest in with an eye to a profitable return.[7] Those who control capital, whether as owners of it or persons hired to manage it, thus have a relatively narrow set of interests, not least because the law requires it. They are the fiduciaries of stock holders. This shift from individuals' owning the means of productive property to their being owned by the business corporation has, moreover, itself produced a narrowing of the interests of property: a corporation is not a person. A person will have multiple, complex interests and thus can have a broad view of his or her interests. But to be a corporation *means* to have narrower interests.

BUSINESS–STATE RELATIONS AND THE PROMOTION OF ECONOMIC PERFORMANCE

To the change in the character of private property has been added an increase in the powers of the state and the growth of mass communications. Together, they have made the idea of improving mass economic well-being not only more attractive than it has hitherto been, but more practical. These changes, in turn, have shaped business–state relations such that governmental promotion of economic growth is the centerpiece of the relationship.

Humankind may always have hankered to live above the level of the beasts of the field, but the economic and political means to do so were not available before the development of a fully fledged capitalism—especially one that is married to a system of popular government, which has made it likely that elected officials will search for ways to secure mass economic well-being.[8] When productive life consists largely of farming, there is little prospect of a high level of economic well-being for any but a few. Industrial capitalism unleashed enormous productive energies and, with them, the real possibility of a social surplus that can be devoted to mass consumption. If governmental power can be directed to facilitating the release of such energies—as we shall see, it must actually induce them—then mass economic well-being is possible. And if advertising via mass media and the evocation of the lifestyles of the well-off are added to the mixture, a significant majority of citizens will find economic well-being even more attractive than did their predecessors. They will also believe that it can be achieved. Moreover, those seeking high office will either share these views or act as if they do. All of this has, in fact, occurred, and it has made possible a particular form of the relation between those who control significant productive assets and public officials.

In the United States, the relationship between large-scale business and government is particularly clear and close.[9] This clarity and closeness has many sources, including the relative weakness of the American labor movement and the weakness of political parties. The core of the relation between large-scale business and public officials at the national level is the privileged political position enjoyed by these asset controllers.[10] Business privilege means that businessmen have special access to public officials. This is because (1) the fact of property rights means that the state cannot command[11] property holders to do its bidding; (2) controllers of productive assets need discretion if there is to be economic prosperity: it is unlikely that government officials possess the requisite information or skill to direct economic decisions;[12] (3) the political calculus of public officials includes that they will be penalized for poor economic performance and rewarded for good performance;[13] and (4) most businessmen, having discretion in how they will deploy their assets, will not make the kinds of long-term significant investments that are needed for high levels of economic performance without being induced to do so.

The inducement process is the central component of the privileged position of large asset-controllers. To induce significant investment, public officials attempt to reduce its risk and provide government programs to encourage it—for example, tax breaks, subsidies, and various kinds of legal permissions. Even more important are inducements that take the form of silence on the part of public officials, so that they do not raise issues that deeply affect what might be called the "prerogatives of property," except in the most pressing circumstances. Three prerogatives are of the greatest

importance: (1) the large returns in the form of profits and salaries to controlling productive property, and, concomitantly, the significantly unequal
distribution of wealth and income; (2) the power to move capital from one
locality to another at will; and (3) substantial control of productive assets
remaining in private hands as presently understood, that is, in the form of
the standard joint stock business corporation.

At the most general level, business privilege means that leading businessmen are consulted by senior public officials as a matter of course on all
major economic issues, and more so than any other interest. It is, after all,
the investment activity of businessmen that promotes the productivity and
economic growth that public officials need if they are to succeed politically.
If businessmen have a common view on a policy matter—or, at least, if a
large number of them do—their views will carry special weight in these discussions with public officials. Moreover, at any given juncture, a seemingly
unrelated issue such as health care can come to be understood as bearing
directly on economic performance, and in such cases business privilege is
also likely to be found at work.

In discussions between business and government, public officials have
their own views about how to promote economic performance. Moreover,
large-scale businessmen do not always have a common view of the matter
under discussion, divided as they are into economic sectors and lacking
time to work out a common program. To the extent they do not speak with
one voice, the degree of business privilege is reduced. But because public
officials are not ciphers, they will disagree among themselves about how
best to promote economic well-being, which strengthens the hand of businessmen. Still, because of electoral considerations, most officials recognize
the need to induce economic performance, even officials whose strongest
base of support is among those who control no productive assets and whose
economic situation is precarious. The efforts of such political leaders to ease
the economic situation of the least well-off is most often filtered through
a more fundamental concern to induce controllers of productive assets to
use them in the ways that foster high levels of economic performance, since
this is the easiest way to improve the economic lot of the poor.

This special political access by controllers of productive assets does not
depend on their organization as a powerful interest group, one that is better organized and has greater resources than its competitors. Large-scale
businessmen indeed have such organization and resources, but their greater
access depends on the privileged position itself.[14] Still, that such businessmen are well-organized and possess weighty political resources does ensure
that they will win many battles over law and policy, especially if the various
economic sectors that compose the business community share a common
view on the matter at hand. However, even with these two advantages—a

privileged position and significant political resources—businessmen will, of course, not win all battles. The degree of mobilization of other interests, the extent of prosperity, and the presence or absence of major political-economic crises such as wars and depressions affect whether business will carry the day. Thus, in acute economic crises, public officials are likely to be viewed as speaking for public interests, businessmen for particular ones. In periods of prolonged prosperity, officials may press businessmen to accept various forms of regulation under the supposition they are less likely to resist when profits are high. More generally, in conflicts with businessmen, public officials have the resources of law and popular will to set against the former's control of capital and substantial political resources.

In general, businessmen and public officials need one another. Each has interests that can only be served by depending on the other: officials wish to get elected, and businessmen wish to reap profits and increase their economic well-being. In its depth and breadth, this symbiotic relationship between politics and business is unique. It produces an extensive pattern of informal contacts, mostly centered on the executive branch, where, more so than in the Congress, the discussion can be carried out largely shielded from public view. This is especially true because many of the needs of businessmen in particular industries can be met by new regulations or in-terpretations of existing ones.

This coziness between public officials and businessmen has several sources in addition to political privilege itself. Most obviously, few public officials or businessmen have any incentive to publicize their conversations. Political officials prefer to avoid extensive public discussions of the size and kind of inducements they feel they must offer businessmen; the revelations that will follow in the wake of such discussions are likely to result in exten-sive criticism of the inducement process and its results. Business leaders are no less anxious than public officials about this sort of publicity and its con-sequences. Moreover, as noted, much of the discussion between business and public officials takes place within the executive branch, in administra-tive settings well shielded from outside view. Also, business organizations have extensive resources with which to tout the wonders of the free enterprise system, the businessman as cultural hero, and the importance of large-scale rewards if those heroes are to mobilize the full range of their talents. With the help of other agents of cultural transmission, business organizations induce a disinclination on the part of the citizenry to tamper with the business enterprise system. Citizens need not actively support its essential features; they need only lack any sustained interest in criticizing it and arguing for its reform. Charles Lindblom calls this shaping of opinion a process of "circularity," whereby public officials hear back from citizens much the same thing they hear from leading businessmen.[15] The result of all this interaction between politics and business is that the inducement process—with the notable exceptions of periods of war, long economic booms, and economic crashes—moves smoothly along.

Important American public figures have formulated the relation between business and the state in ways similar to the one presented here. John Kennedy, for example, said: "This country cannot prosper unless business prospers.... So there is no long-run hostility between business and government. There cannot be. We cannot succeed unless they succeed."[16] Herbert Hoover observed: "The sole function of government is to bring about a condition of affairs favorable to the beneficial development of private enterprise."[17] The relationship has also been well understood by business leaders. Richard Whitney, the president of the New York Stock Exchange during the New Deal period said, after the Exchange had reformed itself, that it was a "perfect institution" and that if the government proposed unreasonable regulations he threatened a "strike of capital."[18]

A particularly clear aspect of the business–state relation is found in the financial sector of the economy. The national debt has created a class of financial interests whose opinions and concerns *must* be attended to by the administration in office: if they flee from federal bonds and bills, it is in serious economic and political trouble. The importance of the debt in creating a "monied interest" and the manner in which it would tie the political regime to that interest, and simultaneously give finance capital political leverage, was understood as early as the seventeenth century in England and was clear to at least some eighteenth-century statesmen.[19] One need only consider in this regard the Clinton administration's deep concern with the bond market.[20] Equally informative is the worried response by those with strong ties to the financial sector when it was proposed that the large budget surplus predicted for the decade following 1998–99 might make the elimination of the national debt possible.

Much of what we need to know about business–state relations can be captured in the following formulation: controllers of large-scale productive assets will, must, and ought to have substantial discretion in how these assets are to be employed. They *will* have such discretion because, given their control over vital resources, they can, if necessary, take it. They *must* have it if there are to be reasonable levels of economic efficiency and high economic performance. Even if their actions could be carefully controlled—which they cannot—it would be counterproductive to do so. Controllers of productive assets *ought* to have such discretion because, given the reasonable concern of citizens for at least moderately high levels of economic well-being, there appears to be no other way to secure it other than giving asset controllers considerable discretion. The result of this discretion is also inevitable: the privileged political voice of large-scale controllers of capital.[21] In more concrete terms, policymakers, partly as a result of business privilege, typically consider only a limited range of ways to secure widespread prosperity. Their deliberations are restricted because of that privilege—which is to say that their worries about what businessmen will accept, and their regular interactions with them, mean that they tend to have views about how to promote prosperity similar to those of businessmen. Still, that business privilege is inevitable does not entail that the privileged voice be a very loud one. Nothing said so far bears on how extensive such privilege must or should be.

To summarize, business–state relations cannot be captured by either of these simplicities: (1) public officials are wholly autonomous and public policy has no built-in bias toward the interests of any group, strata, or class; or (2) public officials are controlled by capitalists and public policy reflects that control. The heart of the relation is a process of mutual control between business leaders and public officials that puts at the center of our political life the question of inducing controllers of productive assets to use those assets in a manner that will bring satisfactory economic performance.

THE ADMINISTRATIVE STATE

The rise of lawmaking that confers regulatory powers on the national government, the creation of administrative agencies of all kinds that must have substantial discretion in interpreting the laws they are to administer, and the explicit grant of such discretion on many occasions have all worked to produce an administrative state. This is the third aspect of the difference between our political economy and the one Madison knew. Its outlines are well understood. Administrative agencies, especially those with regulatory powers, have become virtually a fourth branch of government that combines legislative, executive, and judicial power. The agencies exercise something akin to legislative power in defining the content of governmental regulations: this is especially obvious when Congress has provided little guidance regarding the substantive mission of the agency. Regulatory agencies and others with large grants of discretionary power also execute the law, carrying it out, in some instances, by levying penalties for noncompliance. And finally, such agencies exercise a kind of judicial power through administrative hearings and similar procedures.

The crucial point for the present discussion is that the growth of such executive agencies has opened up the possibility, eagerly taken up, for businessmen with narrow interests to gain the benefactions they seek. This is especially obvious in the case of businessmen seeking favors for their own company or industry. These benefactions may take a variety of forms including subsidies, regulatory permissions, and waivers of rules. Such a narrow-interest politics would be difficult to sustain if it were subjected to vigorous scrutiny by members of Congress, prompted by their own concerns or those of their constituents. The low-visibility nature of the process, however, means that citizen pressure can only be intermittent at best, even if public interest groups, who claim to speak for the citizenry, are regularly paying attention. There is too much going on and too few resources to do much more than slow things down and achieve an occasional success. If, moreover, these citizen organizations found a ready welcome for their views from legislative subcommittees exercising appropriation and oversight functions, they would be more successful. They do, of course, find some allies, but the same business interests that find a home in the bureaucracy are often able to induce a sympathetic hearing from members of the relevant congressional subcommittees. These are the "iron triangles" of interest group politics much studied by political scientists,[22] sustained in significant measure by campaign contributions from business groups. In general, we can say that the rise of the administrative state has erected additional barriers to the Madisonian impediments to majoritarian government, with the result that the political role of civic majorities is further retarded.

THE POLITICAL ROLE OF THE PROPERTIED AND THE FAILURE OF THE MADISONIAN DESIGN

To discover whether the Madisonian constitution as it now works invites minority faction, it is necessary to further elaborate Madison's design for broadening the interests of the propertied. In addition to protecting property rights, Madison hoped to induce the propertied to focus their political energies on securing the "commercial elements" of the permanent interests of the community. We may assume that Madison wanted a capacious conception of what was entailed here—namely, governmental activity in the service of the kind of commerce that would bolster republican government. How was the broadening of interest to occur? The separation of powers was to play a crucial role. If the propertied and those who speak for them were distributed among the various branches, and if the interests of property were attacked, the various interests that compose the propertied class would likely find themselves discussing in public how to develop a common response. The propertied would lack the concentrated governmental power to negotiate this out of the view of the citizenry, and the need to negotiate would itself broaden their interests.

Even if everything worked as Madison hoped it would, it is important to realize that all this would still be a delicate operation. If my general account of Madison's constitutional theory is correct, he did not want such basic questions on the public agenda as whether there were to *be* property rights. Thus, the Madisonian design requires conflict concerning economic questions of the right kind—for example, over how to interpret property rights or other basic features of a commercial society, not over whether they are acceptable. The political advantages that the constitutional design confers on the propertied would be sufficient, Madison hoped, to dissuade dangerous attacks on property and commerce themselves. But the design is also meant to encourage public discussion and decision concerning other important aspects of a commercial society.

If Madison's constitutional design is to work as intended, three requirements must be met. First, the propertied must be distributed throughout the various branches of government in greater degree than their numbers merit—and they must be numerous enough to provide political energy and to draw in other officials in the various branches of government. That is to say, the Madisonian political advantages for the propertied must actually work. Second, the interests of the propertied would have to be challenged. More importantly, the challenges must be serious enough to cause the propertied to respond. This would require a citizenry sufficiently engaged in political life and attentive enough to the permanent interests of the community to induce the various propertied interests to formulate their common interests in ways that they otherwise might not find convenient—that is, in a form the broader citizenry finds attractive. After all, as Madison claimed, the most powerful device for preventing minority factions and other very narrow interests from controlling government is the majoritarian character of the system, which is to say the citizenry in its guise as majorities. The separation of powers is only likely to broaden interests if it is relatively easy for vocal, especially civic majorities to form. Finally, there would need to be among the propertied those who have a broad view of the proper role and concerns of property in a commercial republic: there must be something like Madison's men of landed property.

The Madisonian design as it has come to work has indeed continued to produce a significant number of public officials in all branches of government that either are themselves men of significant property or who, out of conviction or a sense of political advantage, are willing to speak for them. The political advantages that Madison hoped would produce this result are successfully at work. However, the rise of a politically privileged position for businessmen, the weakness of civic or public-spirited majorities, and the changes in the nature of productive property have short-circuited the broadening process to which Madison looked.

Consider that the privileged political position of business undercuts both the need for public discussion among business interests concerning their common interests as well as the reformulation of these interests in response to public criticism. While it may be the case that business interests need to discuss among themselves the kind of inducements they want, the discussion need not be a public one. Nor, if discussion occurs, need it be very strenuous. Many business leaders will conclude that if they are going to be the recipients of various kinds of inducements anyway, without much or indeed any exertion on their part—public officials will offer them for their own, political, reasons—it will not be worth their time to talk about whether the inducements offered are satisfactory. The inducements are almost free, and thus the costs incurred by seeking something better are unlikely to outweigh the benefits. More importantly, owing to business privilege and the circularity of opinion that supports it, business interests are not usually under significant attack. There is thus little need for businessmen in government and those who speak for them to reach out for political support to other officials in the several branches of government. Similarly, there is little incentive for businessmen to broaden their appeals, and thus the definition of their interests, so that they may effectively resist proposals that will curb their prerogatives or that are otherwise costly. Nor, concomitantly, must they work hard to promote more attractive proposals. In short, in this matter at least, the separation of powers does not have the effects Madison hoped for.

When the Madisonian impediments to easy formation of majorities are added to the effects of business privilege such as those just noted, the result is very limited pressures on businessmen to formulate their interests in a manner attractive to the mass of citizens. Moreover, even if business leaders and those who speak for them are engaged in public discussion aimed at developing a common position on a public matter, they are unlikely to face a citizenry that, in the form of civic majorities, will force them to think in terms of the permanent interests of the community and of a conception of property rights that will facilitate republican government. It is important to emphasize here that the fault is only partly Madison's. He, at least, looked to the formation of civic, public-spirited majorities as a source of republican political energy, although, to be sure, his proposals of how this might be fostered were sketchy. What has lived on as actual practice, by contrast, does not even stimulate much talk about public-spiritedness, no less make provision for facilitating majorities with such a disposition. Instead, there are barriers to the formation of strong majorities. Institutional contrivances that work to cool passion and encourage deliberation do something to promote civic majorities, but by themselves they are insufficient.

Finally, the change in the nature of private property and the elimination of landed property as a crucial element in the propertied class has meant the loss of a voice in the arguments among the propertied for a broad view of their common interests. While there are businessmen-statesmen to be found, they seem to have much less influence in shaping the business agenda than Madison and his colleagues had on the agenda of the propertied in their era.

Altogether, then, the privileged political position of business and the change in the character of productive property, when coupled with the Madisonian political advantages given to the propertied, mean that the controllers of capital are not, and plausibly cannot be, a principal source of political energy in the service of the kind of property rights that a commercial republic needs and of its permanent interests. Yes, businessmen work to protect property rights and to ensure that there is a functioning market economy with high profits and large rewards for those who control large productive assets. But they are inclined toward narrow versions of these things, and thus the overlap between the interests they seek to serve and the permanent interests of the community is rather less than Madison hoped for.

The political activities of businessmen not only impede a broad understanding of property rights and the commercial elements of the permanent interests of the community. They have similar effects with regard to rights and the permanent interests more generally. It is plausible, I have said, that the permanent community interests include securing a measure of economic equality, such that no group of people is without the resources to participate in the exercise of self-government. To this element we may add another: because a capable citizenry is crucial for republican government, creating the conditions to foster one that is politically engaged and has a measure of concern for the permanent interest of the community is itself a permanent interest.[23] Moreover, among the rights to be secured by republican government is almost certainly the right to self-government.[24] There is, however, little in the political actions of large-scale controllers of productive assets that promotes discussion of the substance of this right and these interests nor that gives them life. Indeed, there is much to suggest that large-scale businessmen are either indifferent to such matters or work, wittingly or otherwise, to exclude them from public consideration. The very substantial inequalities of wealth and income that controllers of productive assets demand, and the ease with which capital can move in and out of communities—both of which are crucial inducements to large-scale investment—undercut the rights and permanent interests just mentioned. Very large economic inequality will likely mean that some groups will find themselves excluded from the political life of the society, and concomitantly, will leave many individuals without the wherewithal to exercise their right to self-government. Similarly, stable self-governing communities are a source of the skills and outlook of a politically engaged, public-spirited citizenry.[25] The easy mobility of capital makes it difficult to create and maintain such communities.

If my foregoing argument is in large measure correct, the Madisonian design has, at the least, permitted a relation between propertied interests and government that hinders the realization of a commercial republican regime. It has done so by making it more difficult to secure some of its essential features—namely, those encompassed by the idea of rights and the permanent interests of the community. It is also likely that the design has facilitated putting into place an additional set of business advantages— those that have been termed the "privileged position" of business—which have made securing these features even less likely.

The story, unsettling as it already is for friends of republican government, is not quite over. For the rise of the administrative state has also undercut the separation of powers. For a whole range of purposes, governmental power is now concentrated in such a way that it hinders the inducement to the broadening of interests that dividing governmental powers would bring. With the rise of the administrative state, we may benefit from the political energy produced by the propertied, but it is in the service of narrow interests.

All of this turns us back to the question: does the Madisonian design, as it has come to work—especially with the addition of the privileged political position of business and the rise of the administrative state—open the door to minority factional rule? No firm answer is possible until we say more about just what rights we have and what the permanent interests of the community are.[26] Still, enough has been said to indicate that our working constitution does not broaden the interests of the propertied and that it allows large-scale businessmen to express narrow versions of their interests when they must engage in political struggle; that it allows a narrow view of these interests to be served in the inducement process; and that it impedes adequate consideration of other elements of the permanent interests of the community and of the substance of civil and political rights. This narrowness is reinforced by the interest group politics that has arisen with the creation of the administrative state, particularly the flourishing of narrow-gauge business groups. As that other great founder of the American Republic, Adam Smith, said in raising doubts about the political role of the propertied:

> The proposal of any new law or regulation of commerce which comes from this order [merchants and manufacturers] ought always to be...examined...with the most scrupulous [and] suspicious attention. It comes from an order of men whose interest is never exactly the same with that of the public, and who generally [have] an interest to deceive and even oppress the public.[27]

Madison's design, as it has operated in the context of a political economy different from the one he knew, has not served us well in avoiding the dangers to which Smith points. It is ironic that his design, which rests on the assumption that minority faction is not a great problem for republican government, has significantly contributed to a working constitution that opens the door to just such factional government.

THE CHARACTER OF THE CITIZENRY

The broadening of the interests of the propertied, which is a crucial part of the Madisonian constitutional design, requires a citizenry that is sufficiently attentive and critical to foster in the propertied class a concern for giving a broad account of their interests. As Madison put it, the citizenry needs to be "virtuous." In more modern terms, it must be "public-spirited." Madison, however, had little more to say about the matter, perhaps because he was unsure how to proceed beyond pointing to the need for citizen virtue. It is not easy to foster the citizen character necessary for republican government without employing the kind of intrusions into the lives of the citizenry that republican government is designed to prevent. To this might be added that Madison was, in fact, ambivalent about the capabilities of the citizenry. On the one hand, they have "sufficient virtue," while on the other they are given to "unfriendly passions" and "violent conflicts," and not inclined to judgments "consonant to the public good."[28] There are ways to reconcile these conflicting characterizations, but it is possible Madison did not see just how this might be done.[29]

The absence of a considered discussion of public-spiritedness leaves a substantial hole at the center of Madison's constitutional theory.[30] If public-spiritedness is in short supply, how can the citizens be relied on to choose the right lawmakers? In particular, how can citizens choose lawmakers disposed toward deliberative ways of lawmaking, ones who are also concerned with securing rights and giving concrete meaning to the permanent interests of the community, if they themselves lack the experience enabling them to make such judgments? The absence of any substantial account of how citizen virtue is to be fostered, moreover, weakens Madison's analysis of how the opinions of the citizenry must be "refined and enlarged" through the legislative process. A body of lawmakers not given to deliberative ways of lawmaking but inclined toward bargaining around narrow interests, means that the opinions brought to the legislative process will remain coarse and narrow. Similarly, if the citizenry lacks public-spiritedness, what will provide the incentives sufficient for the propertied to enlarge their understanding of the meaning of property rights and of the fundamentals of a commercial society suited to a republican form of government? To all this we may add that it is no longer the case, if it ever was, that it is too costly to "corrupt" whole electoral districts, or even the whole nation: the combination of mass media and the amount of cash available to pay for it means that majorities can be formed on some other basis than "justice and the common good."[31] The combination of money and media means that those who are merely rich or merely famous now have a substantial political advantage over those with public standing. As a result, a public-spirited citizenry is even more important if the right kind of republican lawmakers are to be elected.

A useful working proposition with regard to public-spiritedness is that in a highly commercial society like ours, which daily teaches the value of individual interest and the ways to serve it, the kind of citizen virtue that Madison thought necessary will be in short supply unless specific provision is made to foster it. I have said, however, that Madison may have had a more modest view of the kind of character the citizens would need:[32] if they could be relied on simply to choose established men of property, we might consider that to be sufficient. But, in fact, this would not solve the problem. For it is either the case that not all such men regularly rise above a narrow conception of their interests, and citizens therefore need to be able to judge which ones can do so, or that any man of property is as good as any other with regard to the broadness of his conception of the propertied's interests.

The first possibility simply takes us back to the qualities necessary for citizens to judge their lawmakers, for they cannot rely on wealth as a guide. As for the second, in addition to what has already been said about the political role of the propertied, the entire radical critique of popular government has argued that owners of large-scale productive assets regularly display the narrowest kind of self-interest. The burden of this whole literature, confirmed by much empirical analysis, is that across a whole range of issues, from the distribution of wealth and income to regulation of markets, those who control productive property cannot be relied on either to take a broad view of their self-interest or to resist an easy identification of their own immediate well-being with the future of republican government.[33] This view of the matter, moreover, is not confined to the left side of the political spectrum. It can also be found on the right. Here we have the panoply of arguments about rent-seeking and the use of public authority by some people to take other people's money raised through taxation in order to make their own lives more comfortable.[34] We are thus entitled to wonder about the degree to which the owners of productive assets have risen above a relatively narrow conception of their interests—not to mention whether they have been custodians of republican government.

Taken together, all this means that a well-ordered republican regime needs a different sort of citizen virtue than Madison may have supposed, and a good deal of it. Being able to pick out men of established property isn't enough for the job. A republican regime needs a reliable means for picking lawmakers who are disposed to secure the full range of rights and who wish to give the permanent interests of the community concrete meaning. There must, then, be a means of fostering public-spiritedness. Majoritarian controls can prevent faction but do not necessarily broaden interests in a significant way. They inevitably will do so to *some* degree since the propertied, for instance, cannot win elections by saying that they mainly wish to be elected in order to enrich themselves and their constituents. But whether majoritarian controls can do anything significant depends on whether there are institutional forms and other devices at work to foster a citizenry able to organize itself into public-spirited majorities. In the end, the Madisonian design requires such majorities if it is to work. If they are intermittently present, we can limp along, perhaps much as we seem to do so now.

Madison's design, therefore—and it would seem any successful commercial republican design—must not prevent or significantly retard *all* majorities from forming. The design must not be simply majoritarian but must allow other than factional majorities to form more or less easily if it is to increase the odds that the public interest will be served. Here, the Madisonian design is weak. It has insufficient provisions for fostering public-spiritedness. To this we may now add that it too strongly retards nonfactional majorities. In practice, such majorities have formed in the Madisonian-shaped political world we have inherited. We can point to the New Deal and the coalition on which it rested, and to civil rights and environmental legislation. But the Madisonian design has almost certainly made it difficult for other public-spirited majorities to form, and without question has made it even more difficult for them to be effective. Consider health care, where for some time there has been strong majority sentiment for some form of universal provision.

It is possible that Madison would have thought more deeply about the character of the citizenry if he had a more fully developed conception of rights and of the permanent interests of the community—which, together, we might call the "public interest." Had he done so, Madison would likely have concluded that the kind of deliberative, public-interest lawmaking that he thought a republic needed requires a citizenry capable of knowing something about the public interest. In failing to be more specific about the content of the public interest, Madison found it easier than he should have to believe that lawmakers chosen under his design would indeed work to serve it.

Madison is convincing in that we cannot rely on lawmakers on their own to search out the broad dimensions of the public interest. Few lawmakers are also statesmen[35]—and so we must rely on institutional design to ensure that the basic elements of the public interest are regularly brought to their attention. But to design the institutions properly, we must know what the elements of the public interest are; otherwise we will not know what kinds of pressures are needed to focus lawmakers' attention on the right questions. In the absence of such pressures, lawmaking will be bootless or, what is worse, destructive of the public interest. And crucial to those pressures is a citizenry that knows enough to distinguish time-serving hacks interested in the diversions of legislative life from those who are at least disposed to take on the heavy burden of giving the public interest concrete meaning.

CONCLUSION

Madison is compelling on the need for a social basis for a republican regime, and for an important role for the propertied in its political foundations. We may also count as Madisonian successes that his design has produced secure property rights and has helped to ensure that there has been little of the society-rending conflict over the distribution of property that so worried him. We might wonder, however, whether property rights and the distribution of property have presented (or will present) the kind of factional danger that Madison supposed they would.

Such a counterfactual question is difficult to answer. Socialism may never have been an option for the United States, but it is hard to see precisely what role the Madisonian design played in making us so different in this regard from other Western countries. In assessing the claim for a Madisonian success it is worth considering that a majority of Americans have been able to own some combination of small-scale productive property, shares of large-scale property, and consumption property. This was particularly important in the first decades of the Republic, which laid the groundwork for an ideology proclaiming that all citizens could own property if they work hard and, therefore, it would be a bad thing for ordinary people if property rights were curtailed. Moreover, since it remains true that a majority of Americans own property of the kinds described[36]—although fewer of them now own productive assets than has been true for most of the Republic's life—the ideology thus found receptive ears. Of course, it might be argued that this is Madison's handiwork. Widespread home ownership, for example, might simply be the result of the vibrant property rights respecting society that Madison envisioned.

On the other side of the ledger, there are the shortcomings in Madison's account of the political role of the propertied. The propertied, he said, must be induced to develop a broad conception of their interests, one that finds widespread acceptance among a citizenry capable of judging the matter. The Madisonian "political advantages" for the propertied can only be justified, that is, if this broadening process works. Otherwise, we are well down the road to factional rule.

A case can be made, I have argued, that the privileged political position of businessmen that has come in the wake of a developed capitalism has indeed led us down this factional road. It has short-circuited the need for those who control large-scale productive property to struggle publicly to find a broadly acceptable version of their common interests. Is this short-circuiting, in any sense, a result of Madison's failings as a constitutional thinker? Again, there is little doubt that there must be a privileged position for business. It simply follows from the fact that those who control capital need discretion, that large-scale investment is risky, and that the process of inducement might well not succeed if it has to be carried on entirely in public.[37] So, any successful theory of republican political constitution must accommodate business privilege. We cannot in all justice, however, tax Madison with being shortsighted here. The full-blown capitalism that is at the heart of the business privilege was too far into the future for him to register in any full way its effect on his constitutional scheme. What we can say is that the Madisonian design made it easier than it otherwise would have been to establish a low-visibility relationship between business and the state, resulting in what is probably an overgenerous set of inducements to business. That is, it is entirely possible that the size of the inducements to large-scale business, such as allowing the fruits of economic success to issue in very large wealth holdings and thus in substantial economic inequality, could be smaller—and large-scale investment still occur. The United States has one of the highest levels of economic inequality in the industrialized world, and although our growth rate has been high recently, that has not always been so. We might be as prosperous or nearly as prosperous with less inequality. In short, we may be paying too much for our economic performance, or, what amounts to the same thing, the price is too high as measured in steps down the road to factional rule. It would be nice if the propertied had to knock on the door of government at least some of the time, instead of having the door more or less permanently open to them.

Again, we cannot simply lay at the feet of Madison or any single thinker whatever failures there are in this domain. The problem of the political role of the propertied is an extraordinarily complex one for modern republican constitutional design. It encompasses: reducing the extent of business privilege and the size of inducements to business that issue from it, especially ones that impede serving the public interest; keeping that level of privilege necessary for large-scale economic investment; keeping the Madisonian political advantages that result in a substantial representation for the propertied in the councils of government, which, in turn, is necessary for broadening the interests of the propertied; and combining these two sets of political advantages, one of which requires a substantial degree of open political struggle (Madison's), the other a fair degree of

behind-the-scenes discussion (the privileged position of business). At a minimum, when it comes to those aspects of the public interest that have a
substantial economic aspect, lawmaking in a commercial republic cannot
and ought not to be characterized by "political equality." By political equality here we can use the rough and ready definition that every interest will
have an equal chance to be heard and the rules of the political game are
neutral with regard to conferring political advantage.[38] To argue for such
equality in the economic domain is to not understand the fundamental features of a commercial republic, and Madison is in this respect a compelling
teacher even though his solution to the problem is flawed. In general, we
may take as settled that the propertied will have political advantages in
a commercial republic. But how many, of what type, and for what purposes are more difficult questions to answer and we will need to return to
them.

What judgment, then, should we render about Madison as a constitutional thinker in the domain of political economy? He was less clear than he
might have been about the danger the propertied posed for republican government. Although he was a more sophisticated constitutional thinker than
his contemporary Gouverneur Morris, Morris was clearer than Madison
that, having the propertied represented in the councils of government, although necessary, was a dangerous business. According to Madison, Morris
said at the Constitutional Convention:

> The rich will strive to establish their dominion and enslave the rest. They
> always did. They always will. The proper security against them is to form
> them into a separate interest. The two forces will then control each other.
> Let the rich mix with the poor and in a commercial country, they will establish
> an oligarchy. Take away commerce, and the democracy will triumph.[39]

Morris wasn't the only one at the time of the founding who was clear eyed.
The Anti-Federalist "A Farmer" remarked:

> In time, in all governments by *representation or delegation of power*, where prop-
> erty is secured by fixed and permanent laws, from the rage of the populace
> on one side, and the tyranny of the despot on the other, the aristocracy will
> and must rule; that is a number of the wealthiest individuals, and the heads
> of the great families:—The perfection of all political wisdom is so to temper
> this aristocracy as to prevent oppression.[40]

Similarly, a bit later, John Taylor said:

> If wealth is accumulated in the hands of a few, either by feudal or stock
> monopoly, it carries power also; and a government becomes as certainly aris-
> tocratical by a monopoly of wealth as by a monopoly of arms.[41]

We can go further in our assessment of Madison. A compelling theory of political constitution would show how constraining and broadening the interests of the propertied must be joined to the deliberative lawmaking that is necessary if the public interest is to be served. This, along with the more general effort to prevent factional government, is the foundation of good republican constitutional design. An attentive and critical citizenry—one characterized by public-spiritedness—is likely the key here. However, Madison is less helpful in all this than he might have been. There are deep tensions in his proposed design between a politically advantaged propertied class and the other vehicles by which rights and the permanent interests of the community are to be secured. For there is a strong likelihood that, unless something is done, the propertied will act to frustrate efforts to serve these purposes.

The curious thing in all this is that Madison implicitly conceded[42] that the propertied could be just as much a faction as the propertyless. Still, whatever his belief, he had too little to say about how to reconcile the potentially factional behavior of the propertied with the need to allow them an important place in government councils. Moreover, by putting the conflict between the propertied and the propertyless at the center of his constitutional design, Madison made it difficult to think expansively about republican citizenship, and unduly increased his wariness of majorities even as his plan of government required them.[43] These last two points are related, since a principal vehicle by which a public-spirited citizenry will act is through a majoritarian electoral politics. Curbing majorities thus will curb public-spiritedness. It is entirely possible that it was his ambivalence concerning a majoritarian politics that led Madison to look to what virtue citizens might have rather than considering how more might be engendered.

In the end, the price that the Madisonian design exacts, as it has come to be overlaid by great changes in the political economy, is a high one. This is an especially poignant conclusion since it seems likely that we need not pay it, that we do not need the extent of political privilege for the propertied we now have. Nor do we need to live with a politics like the one we have, with its very modest degree of public-spiritedness. Moreover, it seems doubtful that were we to do something about business privilege and limited public-spiritedness, property rights would be in any danger. Nor, similarly, would the high level of economic performance that the large mass of Americans wants from its economy and government likely be at significant risk. We might echo Madison here and wonder whether his cure for the vulnerability of property rights and for a possible lack of political energy in republican government is worse than the disease.

The claim of a commercial republic is that it serves the fundamental concern of all its citizens to be secure in their rights, to govern themselves, to be moderately prosperous, and to be free to pursue their own conception of a good life. A vibrant commercial society is essential to all of this—and promoting it is thus part of the public interest. But such necessary forms of economic activity are not coeval with what either controllers of productive assets ask for or what government officials give them. Nor, again, is it likely that asset controllers must receive very large political privileges and advantages if we are to ensure that the commercial aspects of the public interest are served. Living in the midst of a modern industrial economy and in a society where most citizens wish for at least modest levels of prosperity and hold government accountable for its production, we likely already give controllers of productive assets more than they need to serve the public interest. To add this sort of privilege to Madisonian advantages is to more or less ensure an outcome that Madison found offensive: a republic in which, if it does not quite rule, a minority with narrow concerns is at least uncomfortably strong in the councils of government. It is the *restraint* of the propertied now, as perhaps it was not in Madison's time, to which our constitutional energies must be directed.

It might be worth asking what Madison would say if he were faced with a working constitution that looked to have an unnecessarily politically privileged role for business, less in the way of deliberative approaches to lawmaking and less of a virtuous citizenry than he thought desirable. In particular, would he rethink his theory of republican political constitution? His concern, after all, was not with securing the interests of the propertied as they themselves might define them. And he did believe there was a substantive public interest, and that popular self-government was of great value. This all being so, he might have set to work on a neo-Madisonian theory of republican political constitution.[44] Barring a miracle, however, if there is to be such a theory, we, his successors, must create it.

This is an especially important task because one way to sum up the results of the Madisonian design is that we have fallen well short of creating a politics of self-limitation, which I have argued is the central concern of a constitutional theory of republican government. The larger-than-necessary inducements and political access extended to business point to a degree of factional rule by a minority—and factional rule is, by definition, unlimited. To this might be added the episodes of majority factional rule in the areas of civil and political rights already mentioned. These shortfalls cannot be attributed, of course, solely to Madison. But neither is he blameless. He was after all designing a constitution, something meant to last beyond the vicissitudes of the times in which he wrote.

The key to an improved constitutional design is an account of the commercial republican public interest. Once we have that, we can move on to other crucial features of a republican political constitution. We would be able to specify to what degree controllers of productive assets need political privilege, how to prevent this privilege from turning into minority factional rule, the degree to which the interests of asset controllers overlap with the public interest, and how the overlap can be increased by broadening those interests. We would also be able to specify just what it means for a citizenry to be public-spirited and how that might be fostered. We could, moreover, define other features of a constitutional politics that would promote the deliberative way of lawmaking that is required to give the public interest life. We could, as well, consider further how the Madisonian formula for the foundation of a commercial republic in the self-interest of the propertied might be amended.

4

Political Regimes and Political Rationality

THE FOREGOING critique of James Madison's theory of a republican constitution indicates a number of its crucial features: a republican regime has a public interest; faction is a real danger; a significant part of republican lawmaking must be deliberative in form; the Madisonian design when joined with advanced capitalism gives the propertied a worrisome set of political advantages; a public-spirited citizenry is an important element in republican government; and majorities are crucial sources of political energy. But to develop the theory of republican political constitution any further—and to start doing so by providing an account of the public interest—we need to consider the character of constitutional thinking.

Madison provides a first clue insofar as he understood his task to be that of bringing into being a whole political order. While he did not use the term "regime," which he may not even have recognized, it nevertheless characterizes the goal of his efforts. The term is classical in origin and was used by Aristotle, for example, to connote a political order constituted by a series of political institutions with roots in a pattern of class rule. Such modern practitioners of regime analysis as Tocqueville, Montesquieu, and Madison added as constitutive parts of a regime its social mores, pattern of leadership, and political sociology. A regime, we may say, is a pattern of constitutional politics that makes a political whole, that is, constitutes it.

Madison provides a further clue to the nature of constitutional thinking. One of the most striking aspects for contemporary readers of his constitutional theory is the absence of legal language. While Madison sought to create a government bound by law, he did not think that the way to achieve it was by making the high court the center of the political order or the principal custodian of that law. Nor did he think that the security of rights was a matter of law, even the law embodied in the Bill of Rights. The security of rights depended, Madison thought, on the design of the *whole* political order. His reasoning and its results—constitutional theory—are an exercise in political rationality.

One further prefatory comment is necessary. To whom is the constitutional theory being offered here addressed? Unlike Madison, we have no constitutional convention to convince nor ratification process to influence. Madison, however, not only addressed those with the authority to decide constitutional matters, he also directed his arguments to the prospective citizens of the new Republic. His concern was that they should understand just what kind of political order had been put into place and how to maintain it. Moreover, we may presume that he even more insistently addressed the opinion leaders of this new Republic—its teachers, thinkers, and public men—because they would have a great effect on the citizenry's understanding of the new political undertaking. We need do no more than follow Madison's lead.

With these clues as to its nature in mind, I now turn to defining in some detail what a political regime is and what kind of reasoning should inform efforts to constitute good ones, especially republics.

VALUES AND POLITICAL INSTITUTIONS

When seeking to uncover the precise nature of a political regime, it helps to consider some of the ways in which the relationship between political-moral value and political institutions has been discussed. For whatever else a political regime is, it is also some combination of valued purposes and institutional arrangements.[1]

Most of the contemporary discussion concerning the relation between political-moral value and political institutions is marked by a style of political and moral philosophy in which theorists appear to believe that they have acquitted themselves nicely if they have simply set out the meaning of and the justification for a particular value or set of values. The implication of such discussions is that the design of political institutions to serve these values can be taken up later, probably by someone else. Values and institutional form are two separate matters, it is implied, which can be treated through a division of labor. The underlying idea in this approach is that political institutions are means for achieving valued ends and that we should first settle precisely what those ends are—for example, by giving an account of distributive justice, individual autonomy, or some other value. Consider here the remarks of Phillipe van Parijs, who describes his book *Real Freedom for All* as an effort "to find an optimal fit between a consistent set of principles and one's considered judgments."[2] Unless consistency here means that a crucial part of one's "considered judgments" concerns how various political-economic institutions can plausibly be made to work—which is not, in fact, a central concern of his book—the implication is that this question can be put aside. We may, that is, later address whether there are institutions that can effectively give life to the principles.

In this context, it is important to note that talking about a *policy*—for example, one that will provide a guaranteed income to all, which is van Parijs's major concern—is *not* sufficient. Without an account of whether political institutions can work in the necessary ways, including whether there can be consistent political support for their appropriate operation, talking about policy adds little to the discussion. It is akin to saying that giving people a guaranteed income is a good way to serve equality. That tells us something. But it is far from settling the question whether this conception of equality is worth pursuing, given that we do not know whether there are institutions capable of defining the policy in detail and carrying it out at a cost worth bearing. Similarly, in defending a conception of rights against the charge that it is too indeterminate to be of much use, it is commonly said that this criticism is "more of a practical than a theoretical objection."[3] Again, the implication is that the question of whether it is possible to create institutions that will give life to a conception of rights—no less institutions that can effectively decide on the content of rights—can be left until later.

Much of the work in this vein—indeed, in much of moral philosophy generally and of the political philosophy that is akin to it—draws its inspiration from what is often termed "analytic" philosophy. Here, rigorous inspection of value terms to determine whether they can or should include other value concepts captured by other terms is the order of the day.[4] It is asked, for example, whether the idea of rights must include the idea of equality, and what kind of equality is consistent with the idea of people having rights? It is an exercise in conceptual analysis. But if our concern is with practice, with serving political-moral values in the world, we would do better to give an account of the institutions that are to give life to the values: can they co-exist together and under what conditions? This tells more about the consistency of our values than does an analysis of how we should use words.

Some moral and political philosophers working in the analytic tradition do give some consideration to institutions. Consider, again, van Parijs, who says that "the intellectual endeavor in which I am engaged, along with many other political philosophers in the Anglo-American tradition . . . consists in trying to rigorously clarify political ideals by proposing some explicit general principles and critically scrutinizing the concrete institutional implications."[5] Much plainly depends on what is meant by "critically scrutinizing." For van Parijs and others of similar inclinations, it seems mostly to mean asking whether we can think up institutions that would do the job.

This is important, but it is just a modest first step. For, to really "scrutinize," we would need to know whether the citizens of the political order that concerns us are inclined to support the institution under consideration; whether they can be induced to do so if they are not so inclined; whether those who are to operate the institutions will have the relevant skills and dispositions; and how the given institution will work in the context of other institutions. All this is to say that we must look at actual citizens with their history, virtues and vices, institutional inheritance, and so forth. If we are concerned with good political practice—which, after all, is the subject of constitutional thinking—we cannot deduce institutional means from valued ends. This is because how institutions are *supposed* to work is one thing, but how they in fact can or will work another. Institutions cannot be understood simply as a collection of rules that those who operate them follow. They are, instead, ongoing forms of relation among those who operate and are affected by them—and, as such, they are complex political entities, with all that entails by way of conflict, consensus, strategic behavior, responses to uncertainty, and the like.

The underlying problem with the kind of moral and political philosophy being considered is the premise that it is possible and useful to treat as two separate matters what we value and the institutional means of realizing it. If we are concerned with practice, however, we cannot know how much weight to give to our purposes unless we know what it takes to realize them. Evaluation in the context of practice cannot be an abstract exercise pursued, as it were, outside the features of the world in which the values are to be realized. In short, our evaluative weighings must combine the normative and the empirical. As Lon Fuller says in discussing equality: "[U]ntil we find some means by which equal treatment can be defined and administered, we do not know the meaning of equality itself."[6] In the context of practice, there aren't two separate judgments—one about values, the other about practices that will serve them. There is only one: how much we value something given what it takes to realize it.[7]

Our evaluations should therefore be a mix of what we value tutored by what it takes to realize it in the world. This is to say that, whereas we could start with abstract value statements, our interest in practice obliges us to consider modifying them once we see what it takes to realize such value.[8] For many readers all this will be obvious, as indeed I think it is. But a perusal of the contemporary literature in moral and political philosophy suggests otherwise. There is far too little acknowledgment that political-moral evaluation without institutional detail is seriously deficient. Justice— for some the first virtue of political institutions—is after all a practical virtue concerned with how our collective life should be carried on. It is thus a strong—even decisive—objection to a strongly egalitarian conception of distributive justice that it cannot be implemented in a principled way, that it will invite corruption among public officials, and that it will tempt them to abridge liberty.[9]

A similar disregard of the connection between values and institutions can be found in contemporary critiques of liberalism. Consider the talk about the contradictions within liberalism, in particular the argument that, while liberal theory and practice need some measure of community, they cannot accommodate it.[10]

Let us suppose that the meaning given to "community" is one that liberals must accept, although this is far from clear in many of the critiques. One possibility is that liberals would need some particular conception of community in order to get the liberty they value, and they are somehow precluded from articulating this view of community or putting it into practice. Notice, however, that it is highly probable that the political theories we are talking about here are going to be rather loose constructions. They are not geometric theorems.[11] Thus, it will not be nearly so obvious as many of the critics of liberalism suggest whether within it there is indeed a contradiction. More importantly, however, if our concern is with practice, we really don't know if there is a contradiction in our values just because they contradict one another "theoretically." Coherence in practice does not require coherence in theory. After all, it is not only possible but common for logically contradictory values to cohabit in practice: we routinely come across versions of liberty- and equality-enhancing institutions that pull in opposite directions but manage to co-exist.[12] Is there a contradiction?[13] Maybe. But it would be more accurate to say that discussions about conflicts among values typically smuggle in assumptions about how particular institutions do or will work. Thus, arguments about contradictions in values are, at least in part, arguments about contradiction in practices—and thus the attempted separation between values and institutions cannot be maintained from the beginning. To which we may add that coherence in theory does not mean coherence in practice. To assume otherwise is to give more weight to words than they can bear.[14] Thus, it has been argued, for example, that the demonstration that equal liberty, material equality, and equalization of capacities are all aspects of the value of equal respect tells us that they all can be simultaneously achieved, that pursuing one does not substantially impede pursuing the other.[15] This is, to say the least, unproven. And that indeed is the point: the proof is in an examination of the compatibility of institutions.

Behind these failures of what might be called "means-ends" moral and political philosophy lies a deeper failing, one that is of central importance for constitutional thinking. Implicit in such arguments is the dubious proposition that there exists a decisionmaker to whom advice is being tendered concerning the appropriate ends of political action. Or, what amounts to the same thing, a single mind (the reader's) is being addressed, with the implicit assumption that the fundamental political question is the person's stance on certain normative matters—as opposed to how a multitude of people with a variety of outlooks, values, and interests should organize themselves to carry on their collective life. Other styles of moral and political philosophy can and do proceed on the basis of these faulty propositions, but they are particularly characteristic of the kind given over to "means-ends" thinking. Those pursuing this style of moral and political philosophy are drawn to this decisionmaker or single-mind view, or find it easy to assume it, because it allows them to focus on the ends of political action while leaving the problem of means—just who is to choose them and how—to someone else. This kind of analysis is less likely to be attractive to someone who thinks that values and institutions, ends and means, are intertwined.

We cannot, however, assume that there is a single decisionmaker, whether Great Legislator in fact or, in the case of the reader, in fiction. This is to misconstrue the fundamental problem of political action, at least for the pluralistic political systems that have the allegiance of most of us. Political judgment ought instead to start with the design of the institutions that will interpret, elaborate, and extend the values that the political order is committed to serving. Fundamental to deciding what those values are— what we can hope to achieve—is whether those who are to do the job of judging what to do are likely to act in ways that are consistent with and give life to the values at issue. Similarly, if political authorities are not inclined to act in appropriate ways, are incentives available at reasonable cost that will so incline them? Providing incentives for the appropriate behavior is relevant not only for authorities but for citizens as well. At least in a democracy, citizens reward or punish these authorities depending on what judgments they make. Or at least they ought to. In saying all this, it becomes obvious that what we have here is a *constitutional* question: how to constitute the institutions that will do the job of judging. We have, that is, a problem of many minds, and we must consider what the terms of cooperation and conflict should be if the people involved are to carry on their collective life in a stable and attractive fashion.[16] And once again, the question of values merges into the question of institutional possibilities. But we are now concerned with multiple decisionmakers and the crucial questions become how they are to be related to one another, what will induce them to behave in the appropriate ways, what will ensure that they have the necessary abilities, and so forth. The evaluation of political practice is thus, at bottom, the evaluation of the constitution of a political order. In the most general way, the concepts we need are ones concerning the forms of relation between the multiplicity of people who compose these political orders.

Now, some will object that we cannot escape the language of means and ends. What are values such as liberty, justice, and equality if not ends, they will ask, and institutions the means to serve them? However, not all purposes are ends. If I say I wish to develop certain of my capabilities, I am talking about the ability not to achieve a particular end but a series of ends, many of which I cannot conceive. Instead, in effect I am saying that the best way to proceed is to prepare myself for a whole host of situations, many of which I cannot predict, where I will want to serve a variety of ends, and my purpose is to be able to respond intelligently to these situations. So it is with political orders. The substantive ends we wish to pursue are difficult to define: there is too much we do not and cannot know. We cannot, therefore, design our institutions as the means to serve a set of precisely designed ends. What then is the relation between political capabilities and such values as liberty and equality? The answer I am suggesting is that in creating political institutions we are thereby creating values. The institutions that define, interpret, and enforce free speech, for example, are not a *means* to liberty; they *are* liberty, which is to say, they are liberty at work.[17] Similarly, we create justice when we establish institutions that act in predictable ways and whose laws bind lawmakers and citizens alike. Justice cannot be fully understood as a concept that exists apart from such institutions. It is instead their workings, and it is thus embodied in them. We create capabilities, then, when we create relations among and between lawmakers and citizens, which relations are themselves value-creating. Thus, for example, we say that for a people to be equal means, in part, that it deals with its societal problems through institutions that define citizens as equals.

Institutional and, more broadly, constitutional design is thus a question of creating capabilities—and political values such as liberty are a means of describing those capabilities. To talk in this fashion is to leave behind the language of means and ends. Little is gained, and much is lost, by insisting that this language still applies. Yes, we might concede, many problems of political practice can be described in means-ends language. But we would then simply need to develop a vocabulary for different kinds of means-ends problems. We would be better off positing from the start that the problem of good political practice differs in substantial ways from other problems of choice, and develop our concepts and theories accordingly.

EMPTY FORMALITIES: HAYEK, EPSTEIN, AND POLITICAL INSTITUTIONS

The same difficulties that bedevil the style of moral-political theory I have been considering also appear in a common form of legal theory that is rooted in a certain kind of classical liberalism. Theorists guided by this legal theory, which aims to make law and legal institutions the center of a political regime designed to secure individual liberty, set out political values, typically centered on a definition of liberty as noncoercion,[18] deduce a few broad guiding principles from that definition, and then define the institutions that, it is claimed, will serve these principles. But little consideration is given to what will be required to make those institutions work in the necessary ways if liberty is to be served. If the theorists were to pursue such questions, considering, for example, whether citizens would or could act in the ways called for, it is likely that they would be forced to revise their value commitments. That is, they might well end up giving liberty a more modest place in their scale of values while according greater weight to political participation, political and economic equality, and a substantial role for government.

Consider Friedrich Hayek in this regard. More than fifty years ago he argued that popular government must be constrained by the rule of law. In this early formulation, he defended a kind of legal formalism. Law must have a certain form if it is to be law, and government ought to conform to what he termed (and capitalized) the "Rule of Law." Legislatures, Hayek argued, must obey the rule of law if government is to serve liberty. Here, Hayek meant more than the obvious point that good government requires that state action must be authorized by a formalized procedure of lawmaking. For Hayek, law properly understood is not whatever issues from institutions designated to make it.[19]

Hayek's argument that law, properly understood, is the centerpiece of a republican political order grows out of his criticism of the politics of contemporary democracies, which largely consist, he states, of efforts to satisfy the claims of particular interests:

> The idea that the aim of government is the satisfaction of all particular wishes held by a sufficiently large number, without any limitation on the means which the representative body may use for this purpose, must lead to a condition of society in which all particular actions are commanded in accordance with a detailed plan agreed upon through bargaining within a majority and then imposed on all as the "common aim" to be realized.[20]

In the last version of his theory, Hayek subsumes the rule of law within a distinction between two forms of social organization: *taxis* and *cosmos*. The latter is a self-organizing, spontaneous order that does not have an overriding purpose and that typically does not arise from anyone's intentions. It is instead a result of efforts to adapt to a wide range of facts and aims that are not known in their totality by anyone. A *taxis*, by contrast, is the result of an organizing intention. It is designed to serve a purpose.[21] A crucial example of a *cosmos* is the system of common law and the private property-based market system built on it. Legislative lawmaking, argues Hayek, should not aim to displace this and similar forms of social organization, but rather seek to perfect their workings. In particular, legislation should only occur when a decentralized, spontaneous order fails to facilitate the behavior of individuals engaged in serving their particular purposes and where there is no prospect of this order repairing itself. Thus, Hayek says that law should be understood as consisting "of abstract rules which make possible the formation of a spontaneous order by the free action of individuals through the limiting of the range of their action, but [it] is [not] to be the instrument of arrangement or organization by which the individual is made to serve concrete purposes."[22]

Law so understood provides rules of just conduct for a largely unknowable future rather than directions to achieve substantive purposes. As such, it does not consist of directives to known individuals, but aims at unknown persons with unknown purposes whose free choices will bring them into spheres of activity where the rules of conduct apply. The law will thus create domains of action where individuals can treat significant features of the world as relatively fixed. This will enable them to make plans with the reasonable hope that they can be realized.[23]

Hayek's theory of how liberty is to be secured depends on citizens understanding the centrality of a particular view of law in a regime of liberty. In the final version of his theory, this means that citizens must understand why decentralized rulemaking—which works through matching particulars to reigning general normative principles—is a superior form of lawmaking. In his earlier theoretical statements, citizens would have needed to appreciate the value of the rule of law. In both cases, the degree of understanding and self-restraint on the part of the people is crucial. But what will induce a citizenry to hold its lawmakers to such a conception of law? Will they even understand its attractions?[24] Citizens—who inevitably will be deeply concerned about their own interests, the interests of those of their intimate circle, and of those with whom they have something in common—may on occasion view lawmakers in this fashion, but will they do so regularly? It is unlikely, unless specific and powerful incentives are at work, which will, to say the least, be difficult to provide. In short, the problem will not take care of itself. While these sorts of questions are absolutely central to Hayek's theory, he gives very little consideration to them. In *The Constitution of Liberty*, he says that "if the ideal of the rule of law is a firm element of public opinion, legislation and jurisdiction will tend to approach it more and more closely."[25] Just so; but merely pointing to it is insufficient for a theory of how to secure liberty.[26]

Hayek, in short, needs to provide an account of what would foster a citizenry that will curb its predilection to serve its particular interests and how this might be done in a way that does not undercut liberty—which is, after all, his primary concern. Hayek, that is, needs a theory of classical liberal citizenship and the political sociology that will support it. A compelling theory of this kind will be difficult to construct because, in a Hayekian regime, the citizenry will have little experience with the consequences of not restraining their demands. There will, after all, be little in the way of direct citizen involvement in lawmaking insofar as that would lead to the interest group politics that Hayek argues is the bane of the rule of law. Hayekian citizens may thus be more inclined to action that undercuts this rule than they would be if they had continuous and direct involvement in political rule. They will have not gone to political school, and the absence of instruction shows as it usually does—in unruliness. In short, Hayek's design is incoherent: to learn the value of restraint the people must be politically involved, which is exactly what he wishes to prevent.[27]

An arresting insight into why Hayek gives little attention to the qualities required of the citizens of a common law or rule-of-law regime—and why, more broadly, he devotes little time to the design of the institutions of such a regime—is found in his remarks to a Chilean newspaper during the Pinochet dictatorship. He said that "it is possible for a dictator to govern in a liberal way. And it is also possible that a democracy governs with a total lack of liberalism. My personal preference is for a liberal dictator and not for a democratic government lacking in liberalism."[28] Hayek makes clear here that he does not think that the source of law is crucial for the limiting of government. As he has said, "it is not the source of power but the limitation of power that prevents it from being arbitrary."[29] Hayek is so fixed on what he takes to be the corruption of law by democratic politics that he tries to situate lawmaking entirely outside the ambit of the citizenry and its governors, who he believes use it to pursue their own interests. In doing so, he misses the essential problem: how to restrain such people. *Telling* them to be restrained, which is what legal formalism amounts to, won't do the trick. At his worst, Hayek sounds like a believer in the "parchment barriers" that Madison argued are of little use. That is, he seems to say that if we can just get clear on what the right rules are for governing, then we can get good government. Indeed, we could write them down in a constitution— which is to say that we can defend a set of values and leave to another time the question of whether the institutions necessary to give them life can be created and maintained.

If these criticisms of Hayek are persuasive, it matters relatively little whether, in some abstract sense, the common law and its extensions through legislative enactments are the "best" way to govern. More important is that the people and their lawmakers can be induced to see the value of doing so. The hardest part of the problem of republican political constitution is not one of finding foundational justifications for political values. There are many modes of justification for the values that are common among those attempting to practice popular and limited government. The real problems lie in whether workable institutions can be formed to give concrete meaning to these values and whether such institutions can be created to give them effect in the world. If this cannot be done in a manner consistent with Hayekian law-centered liberalism, or if it would be far too costly to try, then Hayek's version of republican institutions becomes significantly less attractive as an outline of the political constitution of a republican regime. Hayek, like many legal and moral theorists, wishes to keep lawmaking uncontaminated by politics—and this impulse seems to extend to theorizing about government: it will be corrupted by thinking about politics.

Richard Epstein's work is also an instructive example of the problems I have been considering.[30] His account of free government focuses on two closely related problems: the limits on the scope of government and the principles that should guide lawmakers and judges in deciding matters within the government's reach. The burden of Epstein's argument is that if we can establish precise principles for defining the proper relation between society and state and for guiding state action, we will have solved the essential question of free government. But is this so?

Consider that in a regime in which the people are to rule, that is, in democracies—which we can assume are encompassed by Epstein's notion of a free society—defining the scope of government is unlikely to be very effective in securing limited government. This is so even if the principles on which the definition of the proper scope are said to rest are simply and powerfully stated. The difficulty is the same one noted in the critique of Hayek and stated long ago by Walter Lippmann. In *Principles of the Good Society*, which was his attempt to breathe life into classical liberalism, Lippmann noted that it is inevitable that the people, in the form of the various interests that compose a free society, will work to use the powers of government to improve their lot, and that, in a democracy, this is entirely legitimate. Much the same point was made earlier by Madison with regard to factions, a particularly dangerous form of interest group. They cannot be eliminated and to try to do so is a cure worse than the disease. More so even than Hayek, Epstein looks to the definition of rules for decisionmaking when the essential problem of free government is the design of institutions that we have good reason to suppose will work in the necessary manner. In short, we must construct the political institutions that make for a free, self-governing people. The problem, we may say, is to construct a constitutional design that will allow groups of citizens to attempt to improve their lot through the exercise of governmental authority, but will prevent them from destroying republican government through factional rule.

Perhaps it is Epstein's training as a lawyer that makes him want to substitute hard rules for squishy politics. In any case, the result is a constitutional theory in which the account of political values is uninformed by a serious understanding of what it would take institutionally to realize them. Following Madison's lead instead, it is apparent that the central problem of free or republican government is the absence of precise rules or goals on which to rely either for keeping in check those who illegitimately wish to expand state power, or for guiding decisions on how that power is to be used. To say that lawmakers lack precise goals does not mean they have no goals at all. It is reasonable to suppose that under a free popular government that is working tolerably well there are some broadly agreed on purposes that government is to serve.[31] An essential task in constituting a free government is thus to put into place a set of institutionally generated incentives that dispose lawmakers to take these broad purposes seriously and incline them to give the purposes concrete meaning in particular acts of lawmaking. Similarly, the institutional design must provide lawmakers not only with the incentives but the capacity to give these purposes concrete meaning in particular acts of lawmaking—which, among other things, means structuring a political environment in which it is possible to think about the proper interpretation of public purposes. Otherwise said, in a well-designed republican constitution, the citizenry, through the political life of the regime, will be engaged in limiting itself, which is a matter to which I regularly return in this book.

An important source of Epstein's errors—which he shares with other neo-laissez-faire theorists such as Milton Friedman and James Buchanan[32]—is the belief that government is a necessary evil and that if we give discretion to public officials we invite arbitrariness and worse. These theorists deeply mistrust rule by the people and by those who speak for them.[33] But if one thinks the people are the problem, it is difficult to face the possibility that they are also (part of) the solution. This last is the implication of Madison's argument. In the language of an earlier era, Epstein and his fellow theorists, among whom for these purposes we can count Hayek, doubt that the people have enough "virtue" to govern themselves, and are seemingly unwilling to think about how such virtue might be fostered. Instead, they try, unsuccessfully, to finesse the whole problem, and in the process end up giving the citizenry lectures in political theory, explaining why they must restrain themselves and what rules to follow in order to do so. This must be counted as a dubious strategy.[34]

If we believe, with Epstein and like-minded theorists, that getting the rules right is the essence of creating republican government, we have a simple means-ends problem: the ends we already have, for they are the rules, in light of which the means are apparent—namely, to make the rules

clear and, presumably, to teach them to the citizenry. However, this theoretical strategy is flawed: what we value should be deeply shaped by the
institutional forms available to us. Moreover, and to extend a point made
earlier, if Epstein and his colleagues thought through the problems of institutional design, especially the requirements of republican citizenship, they
might well discover that it is impossible to secure republican government
and protect liberty by adhering to the rules they have set out. Or it might
be possible but at a cost few would willingly bear. To adhere to the kinds
of rules Epstein favors would almost certainly require governmentally imposed limits on the freedom of citizens to serve their particular interests.
This is unlikely to be an attractive strategy to those—like Epstein—whose
underlying view is that liberty consists of the absence of restraint and that
the exercise of political authority is a prime source of that restraint. Jonathan
Glover puts the point as follows:

> It is possible to assume too readily that a set of moral principles simply needs
> to be "applied." The result can be the mechanical application of . . . precepts
> about justice . . . and so on. When this happens, the direction of thought is all
> one way. The principles are taken for granted, or "derived" . . . and practical
> conclusions are deduced from them. What is missing is the sense of two-way
> interaction. The principles themselves may need modifying if their practical
> conclusions are too Procrustean, if they require us to ignore or deny things
> we find we care about when faced with the practical dilemmas.[35]

The kind of theoretical incoherence to be found in much classical liberal
theory suggests that its revival does not rest on the power of its arguments.
To put it differently, all liberal theories directly concerned with political
practice will probably end up looking much the same. They all must contend with the inevitable existence of active interest groups and the possibility
of faction—something they cannot successfully do, at least if their concern
is with practice in our world, by simply announcing rules to curb individual
liberty and collective action. All liberalisms must also consider how an institutional design that will help curb hyperactivity by interest groups and curb
faction is to be maintained. This suggests that any republican government
must be active government. Maintaining republican institutions requires
it. And making such institutions work over time is the key to keeping the
liberal republic that Benjamin Franklin proclaimed to be ours. It might be
said that the essential focus for a theory of good political practice is the
right roles, not the right rules.

AGGREGATORS

There are echoes of the faults I have been considering in another influential
body of work on the design of good political institutions—namely, that done

by economists on the problem of collective choice and by those who have followed their lead. Economists who study political practice tend to see constitutional design as a matter of properly organizing social choice, understood by many of them[36] as the process of aggregating citizen preferences. We may call such theorists "aggregators."[37] The fundamental premise of an aggregative view of political institutions is that the satisfaction of the preferences of individuals is the test of good political practice.[38] Institutions are evaluated in terms of their ability to ascertain and combine preferences concerning the possible outcomes at stake so that the extent of total preference satisfaction among those concerned is increased and, ideally, maximized. For aggregators, political institutions are essentially calculation machines: the best institution is the one that most accurately sums up the preferences of those affected by the decision being made. With some license, we can say that political conflict is transformed into a problem of arithmetic.

There is a connection between the conception of politics as the summing up of preferences and the idea of free-standing values independent of the institutional means of realizing them. An economizing mentality, where the aim is to homogenize everything into preferences, co-exists easily with a philosophical outlook that wishes to homogenize the problem of political choice into a matter regarding the choice of values. The tip-off that such an alliance exists lies in there being so much current talk about value preferences. Little would be lost if the talk focused on one or the other. For our purposes, however, the most important point concerning aggregators is that they miss the crucial connection between what it takes to make institutions work and their political and moral value.[39] Thus, if we assume that even regimes with perfect aggregation procedures will require more than one institution to do the job of governing, a central question for aggregative—and for all constitutional—theorists is how and whether the various institutions needed can be made to co-exist, reinforcing rather than undercutting one another.[40] Lawmaking must be concerned with securing the foundations of the institutions that give a regime its character—including, in the present case, those that do the aggregating—otherwise the regime will fail. But there is no reason to believe that what is necessary to secure these foundations coincides with the preferences of citizens as these are expressed in ordinary aggregation procedures. Citizens formed by aggregative institutions, with their emphasis on relatively narrow interests, may not—probably will not—have much interest in securing them.

In general, those who hold aggregative views seem remarkably uninterested in the problem of just how the institutions required by a good constitutional order are to be maintained. They seem to have in mind a machine that runs by itself. They thus avoid thinking about whether that "machine" can actually be made to work, and if it can, what is necessary for its maintenance. Like the moral philosophers and legal theorists just considered, aggregators typically do not take seriously enough that what they value politically must be informed by a consideration of the problem of getting political and economic institutions to work in a manner that will give those values life.

REGIMES

We have seen that values and institutions cannot be separated into means and ends. Of equal importance, I have suggested, is that we cannot usefully talk about institutions taken one at a time, as if they exist independently of one another. Thus, it is deeply misleading to isolate a problem—say, the distribution of income—analyze the institution at work, and, given a likely definition of equality, argue that there is an institutional failure. Instead, institutions come in packages, very likely in big packages, in what might be called "political regimes."[41] That, at any rate, is how I have discussed political practice in the foregoing critique of Madison and later theorists. The focus has been on how political institutions can be fitted together to make an attractive political whole. It is now time to address directly what it means to talk about political regimes and, by extension, to build a case that the principal concern of constitutional theory should be to realize these political wholes.

To begin, it is highly likely that there are limits on the kinds of institutions that can co-exist with one another. The human world is unlikely to be made up of random aggregations of social bits.[42] For this reason, when we consider how the various institutions that compose a political system are to be put together, we cannot pick and choose among the various possibilities in a kind of rationalism of the machine shop.[43] This might be called the "organ" theory of constitutional design (we ain't got no body, only individual organs). Political institutions, however, are not mechanisms but patterns of behavior, and some patterns will undercut others. Moreover, institutions are interconnected: what we can and ought to do about any one of them has strong implications for what happens or ought to happen elsewhere in the political-economic order.[44] Thus, Hayek comments that "we are not fully free to pick and choose whatever combination of features we wish our society to possess, or to fit them together in a viable whole. . . . We cannot build a desirable social order like a mosaic selecting whatever particular parts we like best."[45]

A similar conclusion emerges if we carefully consider the language of trade-offs among types of institutions, trade-offs that for many are a central aspect of political choice. Some institutions are good at one thing, it is said, other institutions at other things—and we should weigh up what each is capable of, trading off one outcome against another in a search for the right combination. The implicit assumption of those who talk in this fashion is that there is, again, a decisionmaker who has a set of values and will use them to make the institutional choices.[46] By contrast, to think about how an institution fits into a larger whole requires the recognition of a wide variety of actors seeking to operate an array of institutions that will enable them to live on some more or less acceptable terms with one another. The problem is one of the right terms of association, rather than a problem of calculation, which is where the language of trade-offs comes from.[47]

If institutions do indeed come in packages, what accounts for this? What makes a set of institutions and their underlying politics a political whole? The answer given in classical political theory is that these wholes—or political regimes, as I have been calling them, adopting classical terminology—are an institutional expression of a limited number of types of political rule and of the conception of justice that legitimates and helps to define the manner of that rule.[48] In classical political theory, the regime not only encompasses what we today understand by the "polity," but also what we now term the "economy" and "society." The latter two are forms of rule without the sword (or at least without continuous swordplay), and to a significant degree they extend the rule of the polity through other means. Economy and society each have their own rules, but the most important of them draw their legitimacy, at least in part, from the same conception of justice that helps to legitimate the polity. Widespread commitment to a certain conception of rule and to its accompanying conception of justice makes it difficult for certain kinds of institutions to flourish. For example, institutional forms lacking a measure of democratic accountability are difficult to sustain in strongly popular regimes, as are those whose express purpose is to foster inequality.[49] There is an ethos or a set of norms at work that, through the weight of opinion and the power that is a result of that weight, constrain the type of institutions that can exist and co-exist. Moreover, the form of rule and the accompanying conception of justice generates a set of lesser norms and normative practices that find expression throughout the society. Those who seek or already wield political power regularly refer to these norms and practices to justify their actions. Thus, institutional possibilities are constrained.

The manner of rule imparts, then, a logic to institutions, helping to create a political whole by giving the political institutions of the regime a broad form. Within that logic there are a variety of possibilities: not all regimes of a certain type contain the same institutions. Lawmakers, constitutional designers, and citizens have choices to make regarding the design of institutions and how best to combine them. Still, who is to rule and to what purpose are the defining elements of political life; they give a regime its distinctive character. The task of constitutional theory is thus to spell out the logic of rule for each regime type, and to specify institutions and their combination that will bring to life that rule and its attendant conception of justice.

Continuing in this classical vein, there is a well-worn typology of political regimes—the rule of the one, of the few, and of the many. There have been more or less convincing efforts to elaborate and modify this typology so that we can, for example, talk about totalitarian tyrannies and people's democracies.[50] In the present context, our concern is with a form of the rule of the many, which is directed at variously defined conceptions of justice built on the equality of all citizens.

As an institutional expression of a type of political rule, a regime also has a ruling stratum, those who are most devoted to this manner of governing and to the justice at which it aims. This stratum is the principal source of those who claim the right to rule and who, in fact, do so. The political influence of the ruling stratum reinforces the logic of rule in making what otherwise would be a disparate set of people, rules, and institutions into a political whole. This is as true of a popular regime, where the many are to rule, as of regimes where a single person is to rule. In a popular regime, the ruling stratum will be large in number, perhaps as much as a majority of the citizenry. As for the rule of one, even kings, not to mention totalitarian leaders, cannot govern by themselves. Their rule inevitably rests on the shoulders of a group of significant size that, together with the ruler, compose the ruling stratum.

The ruling stratum need not be politically dominant in the sense of controlling the full substance of law and policy. Indeed, in a modern, organizationally complex, and broadly democratic society, such complete control is unlikely, even impossible. The ruling stratum rules, at a minimum, in the sense that its conception of political rule and justice is the one given expression in the institutional design of the regime and is reached for when political justification is sought.

In the case of a fully realized commercial republic—the regime to which, I have argued, we Americans aspire—the ruling stratum is the middle class.[51] The conception of justice attendant on its conception of political rule dominates, and its views of just rule shape political talk and political action. Thus, in such a republican regime, no significant group of citizens may be systematically excluded from taking part in political rule; political discussion must be reasonable and polite; and distributive justice be so defined that enormous inequalities and strict egalitarianism are both excluded, and moderate inequality accepted. This middle-class conception of justice looks to the equality of citizens—and more specifically to the realization of a free and equal people engaged in governing themselves where there are limits on what that government may do. None of this means that, even in a fully realized commercial republic, the middle class will always succeed in making these norms (and their institutional expression) dominate. For one thing, the politically privileged role of business often gets in the way.[52] But as soon as any major departure from the ethos is widely recognized, the offending institution or practice is likely to be criticized and often modified.

In good regimes,[53] the conceptions of rule and justice are not just expressions of the self-interest of the ruling stratum. This stratum will benefit in significant ways from these conceptions: this, after all, forms part of the reason for their attachment to the conceptions in the first place. But as Michael Walzer emphasizes, the conceptions of rule and justice are standards by which the ruling stratum itself is judged.[54] They express what plausibly is a good way to rule and what plausibly really is a form of justice.[55] It also follows from the definition of a regime that each type has a characteristic form of corruption and failure. Thus, a commercial republic typically suffers from the sort of corruption in which money and economic power are used to weaken popular rule, in which case its characteristic form of failure is a transformation into oligarchic rule masked by a facade of democracy.[56]

The workings of a regime are not confined to the laws it makes and their direct effects on the citizenry. In republican regimes, the impact of public decisions on most people's lives in the sense of direct intervention—an injunction to do this or stop that—is, while significant, not the dominant mode of rule. It isn't the cop at the door or the check in the mail through which such a regime mostly works. The principal effects of the rule come through a complex background of rules, assumptions, and definitions of what is acceptable, all of which form the context within which individuals make their own decisions. In this sense, political life in all regimes where political power is limited does not consist only of political institutions making decisions. Political life to a large degree is instead a culture or way of life.

A regime, I have said, is not composed of only one possible set of institutions. Functional substitutes are possible. Thus, while there are limits imposed by the manner of rule on what combination of institutions is possible, within these limits there are various possibilities.[57] This must be the case if the idea of reforming a regime is to make any sense. If only certain institutions, working in certain ways, are possible in a given regime, then when changes in any given institution occur—whether intentionally or otherwise—another regime would come into being. But this affronts common sense: we regularly make statements about the need to reform American politics or the American political system, by which we mean that it has a continuing identity. In the same way, we think that we ourselves have a continuing identity, even though at age sixty-five, say, our bodies are much different from what they were when we were ten, as are our thoughts. There must be *families* of institutions that compose a given type of regime, if there are to be regimes at all. It is likely, then, that there is significant leeway in how institutions can be arranged. As well, the various things that must be done if a regime is to be more or less fully realized can be accomplished in different ways by different institutions. Thus, it is possible that the job that political parties typically have done in popular regimes can be done in other ways by other institutions.

To talk about good forms of rule does not mean that there are no conflicts in actual regimes over the terms of rule or even over whether ruling is being justly done. Political power can be exercised for a wide array of purposes, from self-aggrandizement to the salvation of souls, and in the process used to dominate those who dissent. The conflicts that issue from such behavior, and the tyrannical behavior that lies at the root of most of them, need to be distinguished from the conflict endemic to more or less fully realized good regimes. In the case of good popular regimes, such conflict is a healthy expression of the differences of opinion and interest that is one of the purposes of popular government to protect. But good political regimes must go further. They must be designed with these conflicts and temptations in mind, otherwise their instability will undercut efforts to realize the fruits of that rule, and will call into question the value of the form of rule itself. Thus, aggregative theorists—who think of political institutions as adding machines—are drawn to the idea that it is possible and desirable to have societies without power and conflict. They are not likely to be successful designers of the governing institutions for a regime of popular control— nor, for that matter, for any political regime.

It is worth emphasizing here that all of my discussion of regimes—not just the point about conflict—rests on the proposition that political institutions are patterns of political behavior. Institutions are not just bundles of formal rules. Thus, while we talk for the sake of convenience about institutions, our concern is for how they actually work—which is to say their politics; and this includes not just the politics internal to the institution but those that help shape it from the outside.

GOOD AND BAD REGIMES

If institutions come in packages, how are the packages to be evaluated? If there are several kinds of good regimes, what makes them good in the first place?[58] Why, as in the classical formulation, are kingship, aristocracy, and a mixed form of popular rule superior to tyranny, oligarchy, and direct rule by the mass? Which among the modern forms of rule are good regimes? That is, among constitutional or liberal democracy, people's democracy, strong democracy, mild authoritarianism, and totalitarianism, which are to be preferred?

I have suggested a promising start for answering these questions. What makes regimes good is simply that they aim at a defensible conception of justice, and in doing so they are lawful.[59] Power is to be constrained by standards inherent in the conception of justice. All good regimes have effective limits on how power can be used.[60] While they concentrate power sufficiently to serve public purposes, they constrain its use for other ends. Bad regimes either do not claim to serve justice[61] or their conceptions are indefensible. A signal trait of such regimes is that power is unbounded, unmarked by standards that transcend the desire of the rulers. Evil is frightening because it knows no bounds, its force is unlimited. It is antinomian.

Thus, large aggregations of people devoted to mass plunder are not regimes, good or bad, especially if they are held together by force. Nor are aggregations that aim at racial or ethnic subordination, whether on their own or with terrified populations in tow. This is again especially clear if force is the primary or only means that can hold the aggregate together. At their best, the cohesion of both sorts of aggregations depends on bribery mixed with fear, but they advance no conception of justice. It is at least possible, however, that the least ferocious of such aggregations may be regimes—albeit bad ones—if they advance a conception of political rule and of the justice at which that rule aims. They thus have a way to talk about limits on the use of political power. But these claims to good rule are unlikely to withstand scrutiny even though they may be widely accepted by those who live under them. Typically, in such regimes, there is an elite to whom the rules that are to guide the mass of its inhabitants do not apply, and no convincing case can be made about why this should be so. The claim to serve justice is thus greatly weakened and probably vitiated.[62]

The evaluation of regimes is not as abstract an exercise as the preceding discussion might imply, nor can the results of that evaluation be applied universally. We must look to the circumstances of the people who are attempting to realize a certain sort of regime, or to the circumstances of the people to whom a type of regime is being commended. That is, regimes—forms of rule—are not just good or bad; they are good or bad for particular peoples with their history, virtues, and vices.[63] Here again, as in considering the relation between values and institutions, any evaluation must be heavily empirical. An essential part of the normative inquiry is an investigation of whether the requirements for making these institutions work in the necessary ways are consistent with the habits and outlook of the people who are to operate them. The recent, sad outcome of attempts in many African countries to realize stable and attractive forms of popular rule indicates how important such empirical understanding is. The one obvious thing about political life is that it happens in particular places among particular peoples with their own histories. This does not mean that no universal definition of the right and the good is possible. But it does mean that if we are interested in political practice, we must tailor our judgments about how to proceed to the actual situation of the particular people with whom we are concerned.

A commercial republic is a good regime, then, because it aims at a defensible conception of justice. Americans are thus right to aspire to the full realization of this political order because it is an attempt to limit political power by reference to the regime's deepest purpose—namely, to create a free and equal people engaged in a form of self-government that is limited in what it may do.[64] That the commercial republic is the subject of our aspirations also contributes to its goodness. Both its general goodness and our aspirations are important for American constitutional theory because there are several types of good regimes other than the commercial republic, and none of them may be suited to us as Americans. It matters, that is, that a particular "we" wishes to see this regime flourish because, if not a guarantee, it increases the odds that a regime appropriate to our condition as a people will be constructed.

GOOD REGIMES AND GOOD PRACTICE

Much of the preceding discussion can be brought together in a single formulation: a regime is (1) a conception of rule aimed at a conception of justice; (2) the politics comprising the institutions that more or less realize the particular form of rule; and (3) the political sociology that helps give political energy to that rule.[65]

A theory of the political constitution of a good regime specifies the institutions that compose the regime—those that provide its characteristic manner of working—and how they are to be related to one another. Constitutional theory is built on the proposition that the most important step in the evaluation of political practice is the regime question. The institutional politics that compose the regime define how the people who are to carry on their life within it are related to one another. The institutions help establish how these people cope with the difficult-to-predict possibilities and problems that arise, and with the conflicts attendant on their common fate. Institutions create what may be termed an "environment of choice": they do not force a particular result but rather encourage those within their ambit to take account of particular kinds of considerations when they act. A republican political constitution is composed of the modes of association a people use to confront collective problems, cope with the conflicts that will attend such efforts, and deal with the continuing temptation to use political institutions for arbitrary purposes, including political domination—all in the service of constituting a free and equal people engaged in governing themselves where there are limits on that government.

By helping to define the terms under which people have access to one another, the political constitution of the regime helps shape the habits of mind and mores of a people. It also reflects in its institutions these mores and, more broadly, the dominant conception of justice. The political constitution shapes the people's overall way of life, and indeed makes them a people.[66] The constitution is to an important degree adverbial, fostering as it does ways to behave rather than specifying particular purposes to serve.[67] "Constitution" in the sense employed here, refers to the "shape," "composition," or "establishment" of a people in their political associations.[68] The constitution of a regime, then, sets out not only offices and powers, that is, the frame of government. It is more generally an "ordering" by which the organization (order) of something provides its constitution, thus enabling it to act. The political institutions of good regimes provide incentives for those who live within them to behave for a significant portion of the time in a manner that is at cross purposes with a narrow conception of their interests. The institutions are also formalities and are intended to give the power of authority a public and acceptable face. It is a face meant to give the commonweal dignity, and the design of the institutions is meant to encourage those who occupy their offices to act accordingly.

The central concerns of constitutional theory, we may thus say, are the realization of good regimes, their maintenance once established, the prevention of bad regimes, and the effort to transform bad regimes into good ones. By this focus on regimes, I am not only pointing to where our evaluative and practical energies should be directed. I am also emphasizing, once again, that empirical questions are deeply implicated in the evaluation of political practice. We must be able to recognize the kinds of packages of political practices present in the world, and just how and why these packages fit together as they do. Whether our political values are coherent is at bottom a question of whether the institutional politics that embody them can be made to co-exist in the world. Thus we cannot commend a form of rule and its attendant conception of justice without bothering to consider how and whether the institutional politics that will give it life can be made to work together. It is a mistake to separate the questions concerning which regimes are desirable and which possible—at least if our concern is with practice. In thinking about good regimes, we cannot decide first what to do, and *then* look for who is to do it and how. The question of what to do is deeply shaped by who is capable of doing it and who should be so authorized.

The kind of constitutional theory I have been commending might be called "realist theory"—if that is understood not in its usual sense of paying little attention to values, arguing that they only get in the way of effective political action. Realist constitutional theory is, instead, "realistic" about the kind of political value at which it is plausible to aim, given the sort of beings we are and the various forms of interaction of which we are capable. Realist constitutional theory, like ideal theory, concerns what is not present but might be if conditions were changed. Its normative claims, however, are more securely rooted in an assessment of the capabilities and limitations of human action. A constitutional theory that supposes that "men are angels"[69] is not only wrong in its fundamentals, it is dangerous. It diverts our attention away from the valuable actions we can take, and pushes us toward making people do things they can only do with tremendous cost, if they can do them at all.

Indeed, it might be argued that the very reason for having political theory and political science is to try to work out the features of good political regimes in the face of the facts of political behavior, many of which are far from pretty. If so, then the kind of constitutional thinking I am arguing for here should be the heart of political theory and political science. It is a resolutely empirical enterprise, but one oriented to a horizon of political value. It is an exercise animated by a tension between what is good or right and what is possible and likely. The frustrations that its practitioners will inevitably feel are not those of someone trying to solve a difficult puzzle, but of people who wish to behave well but who find it difficult to do so.

I want to conclude this discussion of values, institutions, and regimes by making explicit something only implied. In saying that, in the context of practice, we cannot usefully think about value separated from the institutional realities of giving it life, I mean two closely related things. We should think about the institutions that are to serve the values we have, but also about the institutions that are to interpret them. Indeed, the latter is the principal concern here, given that the discussion is about constitutional theory. A regime is not just a set of practices to give life to values, but a set of institutions through which we reflect on these matters. Together these institutions compose a political regime and in so doing help to form a people.

POLITICAL RATIONALITY

Political regimes are composed of parts that need somehow to be constituted into a workable and attractive political whole. In seeking the sort of reasoning necessary for that task, it is useful to start with a widely shared view of what is entailed, just as we did in considering the relation between institutions and political value: to reason about the political constitution of good regimes, especially republican regimes, is to exercise legal reasoning.

Before discussing legal reasoning, however, I want to quickly dispose of several other possibilities that, in effect, have been considered earlier. First, constitutional thinking does not borrow from the rationalism of the machine shop. Nor—given that it is substantially an empirical question whether the parts of a regime can hold together—is it akin to solving a problem in logic, fitting the pieces into a logically coherent whole. Neither is it like the reasoning employed in designing an elaborate calculating machine, as aggregators contend. Even though calculating machines, and indeed machines of all types, may have several purposes, these can and must be very precisely defined if the machine is to work efficiently. The purposes of regimes cannot be defined so precisely—not precisely enough, that is, to make the design problem one of simply deducing the shape of the institutional parts from the outcomes desired.

LEGAL REASONING

A number of legal theorists have argued that the design of republican regimes should be guided by legal reasoning. These theorists, who might be called "legalists,"[70] are bound together by the belief that, in being guided by legal reasoning, they are giving expression to the basic idea of republican government: that it be a government of laws and not of men (and women).[71] All such theorists are committed to the proposition that the law is the standard to which government must be held. At least with regard to the definition of the legitimate reach of governmental power, we should, in their view, have government by courts.[72]

For legalists, legal reasoning is distinct from the practice of politics and political judgment. Perhaps the most prominent expression of this view is by Herbert Wechsler:

> [C]ourts in constitutional determinations face issues that are inescapably "political" ... in that they involve a choice among competing values or desires, a choice reflected in the legislative or executive action in question, which the court must either condemn or condone.... But what is crucial, I submit, is not the nature of the question but the nature of the answer that may validly be given by the courts. No legislature or executive is obligated by the nature of its function to support its choice of values by the type of reasoned explanation that I have suggested is intrinsic to judicial action.... Is there not, in short, a vital difference between legislative freedom to appraise the gains and losses in projected measures and the kind of principled appraisal, in respect of values that can reasonably be asserted to have constitutional dimension, that alone is in the province of the courts? Does not the difference yield a middle ground between a judicial House of Lords and the abandonment of any limitation on the other branches—a middle ground consisting of judicial action that embodies what are surely the main qualities of law, its generality and its neutrality?[73]

A contemporary expression of the legalist position is given by arguably the most important legal theorist of the day, Ronald Dworkin, who states that

> individual citizens can in fact exercise the moral responsibilities of citizenship when final decisions involving constitutional values are removed from ordinary politics and assigned to courts, where decisions are meant to turn on principle, not on the weight of numbers or the balance of political influence.[74]

The underlying point in all claims for the distinctiveness and power of legal reasoning is that law is different from politics and that, in deciding on the essential characteristics of good regimes, we should rely on the kind of legal reasoning that Wechsler describes. There are available to us neutral principles, it is said, that are untainted by partisan advantage and that can guide our decisions about how the society is to organize itself. By implication, no other principles should direct us, certainly none arising from reflection on politics, since all politics is tainted by self and group interest. Law then is not only separate from politics, but legal reasoning should guide the decision as to what kinds of questions should be handled through the political system—and, in its most ambitious versions, how the political order ought to be organized to decide such matters.[75] Moreover, if we are starting *de novo*, the constitutional or institutional design of the regime should be the product of legal reasoning. If, however, there is a satisfactory or potentially satisfactory institutional design already at work, then the courts, especially the Supreme Court as the custodian of that design, should use legal reasoning to protect and, where necessary, to amend it.[76] Legal reasoning, in the legalist view, is the source of standards external to the politics of the regime, and so can be used to define the competences of political authorities. The day-to-day politics of the regime is to be enclosed in the legal standards that derive from what might be termed "higher law," as that is interpreted by the courts. The popular branches of government, according to the legalists, lack the ability—that is, the legal reasoning—needed to define these competencies and standards.

Legalists might content themselves with the argument that courts should operate in a certain way, relying on legal reasoning, and leave the overall design of the political order undiscussed. But, as suggested, most are tempted to go further. Legalism in America finds its principal expression in a kind of logical progression intended to guide the ordering of our republican constitution: the courts, and especially the Supreme Court, are the custodians of legal reasoning and the law; the Constitution is a form of law, that is, the higher law; the courts in their exercise of legal reasoning are the custodians of interpretations of the Constitution; the Constitution defines the basic structure of the American regime; and thus the courts, again especially the Supreme Court, are the interpreter, and, given the relative open-endedness of much of the Constitution, the definer of that basic structure. Some legalists might shy away from the brutal clarity of this progression, but it is fair to say that it captures the implications of their position. Others might be inclined to argue that, in defining this law- and court-centered political design, they are not really relying on legal reasoning. Perhaps, to take an obvious possibility, they might say that they are simply looking to a certain kind of political theory. This is no doubt true of some legalists. But consider the ease with which many legalists move from the juxtaposition of principled courts and unprincipled politics to an overall institutional design in which the courts define the boundaries of political choice. This tendency strongly suggests that most legalists think that, as custodians of legal reasoning, they have a particularly clear-sighted, even unique, understanding of the proper design for republican government.

The idea of legal reasoning as a guide to constitutional thinking is attractive for at least two reasons. First, in pointing to the rule of law, legalists reinforce the idea that even the rule of the people must be limited in a principled way. Second, by saying that any attractive regime must have a very large role for principled legal argument, legalists emphasize that a politics dominated by self-interest and political calculation is something we should resist. But legalist arguments are also badly flawed in two ways. First, it is difficult for legal reasoning to sustain a definition of the limits of the people's rule. This is true whether that reasoning is understood to be rooted in a conception of a public and private sphere or in neutral, nonpolitical principles of law, a matter I return to in the following chapter. Second, as a guide to the design of a republican regime more generally, legal reasoning is weak. It is this weakness that concerns us here.

The idea of law and legal reasoning as the basis for constitutional design derives from the early efforts in American jurisprudential thought to separate law from politics.[77] The effort was set in motion by the Marshall Court and given a more complete form by nineteenth-century writers on the law.[78] As Jennifer Nedelsky explains, the distinction between law and politics resulted in the argument that the "basics of politics would be called law" and the judiciary would be the custodian of these basics.[79] The unique competence of courts is to define and set out legal doctrine, understood to be "the law." As Robin West notes, the rule of law for "the vast majority of contemporary legal scholars" is an ideal "which insists on a strict separation between the methods, operations, and values of *law*...and those of politics."[80]

But talking about "the law" here conceals as much as it reveals. The Constitution is not a law just like any other, only more important. It is, instead, the outline of a political regime to which we as Americans are committed. It designates the purposes and constitutive features of that regime. It is "political law," not "ordinary law," and as such it must be interpreted by the various political organs that it calls into being, not just the courts. We might say that the Constitution, to the degree it is instrumental in calling into being a republican regime, is what makes the rule of law possible. In this sense, it is not itself law. Indeed, according to Sharon Snowiss, fundamental law was understood until the nineteenth century as an "attempt to bind sovereign power whereas ordinary law [binds] individual action."

It was understood, she says, that "it is impossible to enforce restraints on sovereign power in the routine way ordinary law is enforced."[81]

In this context it is worth noting Madison's understanding of the Bill of Rights, which has been at the center of our jurisprudence for a significant part of the life of this Republic. In his view, the Bill of Rights was an acceptable device to guarantee a sphere free from government intervention, although it was also unnecessary.[82] But Madison's deepest point was that promulgating a bill of rights, while it would reinforce the idea of limited, republican government, would not itself be the principal means by which those limits were defined and enforced.[83] In short, how best to secure fundamental rights—surely one of the broad purposes of republican government and thus essential to understanding how to design it—is not a task for legal reason.

Thus, while it is relatively easy to agree with the proposition that courts, and therefore legal reasoning, have a special competence with regard to settling disputes between private individuals, it is difficult to sustain such claims when it comes to the basic organizing rules of the political regime. Consider what is at stake when the courts undertake to rule on the content of property rights and the appropriate reach of government in economic matters.[84] Even if it is conceded that there is a natural and constitutional right to private property, the appropriate definition of property rights is still deeply bound up with questions of economic efficiency, justice, and the character of good political regimes. It is thus difficult to see just how a case could be sustained that legal reasoning should have a privileged status here. Even those who think that the organization of productive life is largely a question of property rights, and thus to be interpreted and enforced by courts, will likely concede that there remain many questions that can only be dealt with by legislation and political reasoning. These would plausibly include aspects of the conditions of work, what kinds of cooperative or collusive arrangements businesses may enter into, what kinds of quality assurances they must give to their customers, and what use they may make of the natural environment in which they operate. It is difficult to see in such cases how legal and political matters can be separated from one another. The interconnections are pervasive and deep and any attempt to sever them will be more like butchery than surgery. Successfully operating on the body politic requires knowing that its parts are deeply interconnected.

Consider here that the definition of the political prerogatives of business corporations can be settled only by what is usually thought of as legal argument so long as it largely avoids the question of the political power of business. The easiest way for supposedly legal reasoning to proceed—judging by how the U.S. Supreme Court has gone about its business—is to assimilate the question of limits on business power to the question of what sorts of political activities individual persons may rightfully pursue under the Constitution. A corporation is a kind of person, the courts have said—a "fictive" person. What is a right for the "natural" person is, broadly, a right for the fictional one. Thus, the question of limits on business power is turned into a question of the limits on public authority to regulate individual political activity. But this conclusion is far from obvious; indeed, it is usually part of a broad political outlook—one that is not very convincing. A corporation is, of course, not a person; from one point of view its very *raison d'être* is that it is not. Otherwise, corporate status would not provide limits on the degree to which its employees and owners can be held individually responsible for the corporation's actions and its debts. But even if convincing arguments can be made that a corporation is best understood on analogy with a person, surely there is something unsettling about assimilating whales to minnows. Yes, they are both living creatures. But they are alike in all but the ways that matter if one is trying to control their behavior. A "person" with the budget and assets of a medium-sized country is a different "person" than one with a poverty wage—and any thinking about the limits on private power that fails to notice this would seem to have a slippery grip on reality. More to the point, such thinking is likely to be rooted in a political theory that only has room for "individuals," to the exclusion of any sustained consideration of a central feature of the modern world: that many of its political actors are corporate, organized entities.

Perhaps the most important point of all regarding the inadequacy of legal reasoning for the kinds of issues we have been discussing is that most of the conclusions supposed to have been arrived at by such reasoning can be more convincingly reached through well worked-out arguments in political theory. The content of the basic organizing rules for a republican form of government is a staple of discussion by liberal political theorists.[85] Indeed, if the conclusions of legal reasoning in these matters are compelling, this is likely because they simply restate the arguments of liberal political theory. Thus, the importance of civil liberties, such as trial by jury and due process of law, can be straightforwardly derived from the requirements of popular self-government. They are, among other things, necessary for the security of property and person against governmental officials who would like to silence political dissent. Without the possibility of political dissent, there can be no popular government. Similarly, setting limits on private power and defining the appropriate means to restrain it are essential and usual exercises in liberal political theory. They arise from the idea that public lawmaking should not be beholden to private interest—it must in some sense speak for the public interest and have integrity—if it is to be worthy of the consent of the citizenry.

Consider also that the case for rights—in particular those that might be called "primary political rights" such as freedom of speech and assembly—is best understood as one of the conclusions of liberal thought concerning what is required if popular government is to work effectively.[86] There is little specifically legal in the argument. Similarly, freedom of religion almost certainly grew out of the political reflections—of those who came to be called liberals—on the need to keep religion from becoming the subject of political conflict.[87] Indeed, rights generally might be understood as abridgments of successful political practice—and reflections on those practices became the essence of liberal political thought.

Some will think that the claims of legalism can be strengthened, perhaps saved, by joining moral philosophy to legal reasoning, in the manner of Ronald Dworkin. Courts, they might say, are better equipped to decide constitutive matters if they add moral philosophy to their analytic arsenal than if they look only to legal reasoning. Thus Dworkin comments that

> judges should decide hard cases by interpreting the political structure in the following, perhaps special way: by trying to find the best justification they can find, in principles of political morality, for the structure as a whole, from the most profound constitutional rules and arrangements to the details of, for example, the private law of tort or contract.[88]

For Dworkin, courts are the very center of republican government. He does not much care for legislatures, or politics more generally, and his response to the problems that a majoritarian politics raises for republican government is to look to the judiciary, especially to the Supreme Court. A republican regime, he says, cannot be allowed to wallow in "mere majoritarianism"[89] and self-interested deals. The solution is to rely on the courts, which are to carry the burden of settling the constitutive questions of constitutional design, appropriate political purpose, and political means.

Here again we have entered the intellectual world of a certain kind of moral philosophy where empirical analysis of what is required if institutions are to work in the necessary ways is put to one side, to be considered after we get our values straight.[90] Whether the institutions can do the job at a cost any prudent person would accept is a matter perhaps to be studied by lesser lights concerned with the details of political organization. It is also worth noting in the work of legal theorists such as Dworkin the characteristic moral philosopher's assumption that the underlying problem of republican political practice is to give the right advice to a decisionmaker. It is a happy (but not wholly) coincidental fact for Dworkin that there just happens to be one available: the Supreme Court.

As a practical matter, it is almost certain that if we were to follow the lead of legalists, Dworkin included, the burden on the courts would be very great indeed. Since nothing useful is expected from "politics," the number and complexity of the decisions they would face would be overwhelming. What is puzzling is that legalists seem to believe that if the courts really become the central political organ of the regime, laying out all of the pathways within which the political organs should ply their trade, they would be able to behave much as they do now—and ideally, in an even more principled fashion. That is, the courts would still to be able to offer reasoned decisions and be largely immune from the exercise of political power by interested groups. This is unlikely. Once it became widely understood that the courts are, in effect, legislatures, those pushing various kinds of political agendas would soon find their way to bench and bar in great numbers, where they would apply the tried and true methods of political influence. Their efforts no doubt would include offering jurists fancy jobs after they retire and giving them advance information about lucrative financial transactions—and would finish by making it clear that judges are political actors, the proof of which is that they should be encouraged to stand for election. All this brings us back to where we are now, with the decided disadvantage of not having an independent judiciary. One wonders whether this is quite what legalists intend.

Perhaps the biggest failure of legalism is that it has little of a compelling nature to say about the institutional foundations for courts independent enough to engage in legal reasoning, no less the expansive kind of courts legalists contemplate. There can only be such courts because the institutional design of the whole regime makes it possible—and insofar as legalism addresses the question, the working assumption is of a kind of simple division of labor between principle and politics. Legalists' understanding of the problem of designing republican government is thus inferior to Madison's. Because he understood that preventing factional rule, serving the permanent interests of the community, and generally limiting the power of government were deep and difficult problems requiring the channeling of powerful political forces and impulses, Madison looked to a complex design for the whole regime to do the job. Quite apart from the tenability of the distinction between principles and politics, Madison implied that an attempt to simply divide the two would fail, and with it republican government. Or, at least the division would make it difficult to pursue the kind of active government needed to secure the permanent interests of the community. Because of their suspicion that politics is the realm of unprincipled majoritarianism, the arguments of legalists stop just where they need to begin: with the burden of Madison's thought—namely, that we should aim to ensure that day-to-day republican politics is not bereft of efforts to secure rights, serve the permanent interests of the community, and properly aggregate interests.

In this context, it is useful to consider the contrasting work of Alexander Bickel and John Hart Ely, two of the most thoughtful American constitutional theorists. Ely's work nicely illustrates whether the courts, as legalism calls for, are likely to be well equipped to handle the kind of large-scale constitutive questions we have been considering—whether the legal reasoning at which they are supposed to be adept is up to the job. Bickel, understanding the complex problems of "political questions," which overlap with what I have dubbed "constitutive" matters, argues that the courts ought to be very circumspect in venturing into such matters.[91] Ely, seized by jurisprudential enthusiasm, is inclined by contrast to jump right in.[92] The Supreme Court's role, he argues, should be to keep the gates of a pluralist democracy open, seeing that no group be kept in so "insular" a position that its voice cannot be heard. Maybe so. But opening the doors to political participation for them does not guarantee a grand entrance or, indeed, any entrance at all. If the courts are to concern themselves with such matters, they must concern themselves as well with what accounts for the group's insularity and outline what should be done about it. Maybe the group's political marginality is the result of the high level of poverty of its members. This, in turn, may be the result of the wage structure of certain industries and the privileged political access of business corporations. Are the courts, then, to analyze and rule on these matters? Again, maybe. But surely we ought to consider whether the legal reasoning courts employ gives them any special competence in this regard. Again, there is reason to doubt it.[93] Why suppose that lawyers are likely to be better judges of constitutive questions than members of Congress, who at least have spent some portion of their career in democratic politics. The most reflective among them are surely at least a match for the ordinary Supreme Court justice when it comes to thinking through large-scale constitutive matters. It might be another matter if law schools taught a lot more Madison. But then if they did, they wouldn't be law schools.

Legalists are undoubtedly correct that republican government must have substantial room for principled decisions—that the compromises of ordinary politics are unlikely to produce a political order that would remain republican or that otherwise would be attractive. But why suppose that the full burden of principled discussion can or should be carried by courts? They may indeed rely more than ordinary politics on reasoned analysis, but that is a far different matter from the claim that their writ should run across the full range of constitutive matters. In the design of a republican regime, we must look beyond courts for the kind of reasoned choices legalists rightly commend to us. In doing so, it would surely be an advantage if those who are to reason had regular, close contact with and knowledge of the day-to-day lives of the citizens who will be affected by their decisions. We might temper our enthusiasm for the most cloistered of republican lawmakers—judges—and consider the possibility that more principle can be introduced into ordinary politics where leaders regularly brush up against followers. To be sure, this will require a complex constitutional design that gives legislators the ability and the incentive to act in ways that they would not otherwise be inclined to do—especially given that they will be elected by a citizenry broken into a variety of narrow and parochial interests. But that is on balance a more attractive option than giving courts a privileged role in deciding constitutive matters.

Another step can be taken in understanding the appropriate role for courts. When it comes to constitutive questions, we may say, courts, especially high courts that are expected to concern themselves with these matters, are best understood as political bodies with a characteristic way of viewing constitutive questions.[94] Consider the situation where there is a written constitution that has been consented to by the people as constituent sovereign, as is the case for Americans. This constitutive law is a statement of the principles the people as constituent sovereign believe should guide the workings of the regime. It is, as noted, political law, and thus any court engaged in interpreting it is engaged in a political act. It shares with other agents of the people, notably the legislature, the task of giving concrete meaning to the rights and the permanent and aggregate interests of the community—that is, to the public interest of the regime.[95] Courts are likely to be more sensitive than legislatures to at least certain aspects of the public interest, perhaps in the area of due process, and in those areas in which questions arise concerning how to facilitate interactions among individuals such that the expectations they have of one another are stable and fair.[96] On other issues they are likely to be less thoughtful, their competence more limited. Such matters include crucial features of republican government, such as the degree of economic and political equality it requires—and, as such, they will almost certainly be a part of any plausible account of the republican public interest. It is worth adding that it is natural to speak of the "public interest" here and that this is political language. As such, it points away from the courts and toward the elected branches of government. As for their capabilities as practical reasoners, judges, like other lawmakers, must employ whatever skills of practical political reasoning they can command.

In general, courts in the Anglo-American legal tradition are likely to have the strengths and weaknesses of a body of lawyers trained in the common law, where reasoning that revolves around careful attention to the particulars of a case and its relation to similar cases is highly prized.[97] At their best, courts may thus pay substantial attention to their past efforts to interpret the public interest, and their actions may thus be informed by the rational virtue of consistency. Not being elected, they can also feel more free to insist on their views than those who must face the electorate at regular intervals. A reflective citizenry may well prefer to insulate some parts of the effort to give concrete meaning to the public interest from any hasty attempts on their own part to revise the results—and to this extent, they look to the courts as their agent. These are all no small advantages, not least since it makes it easier, as legal theorists have long reminded us, for us to plan our lives. But that is what they are—advantages—and not a case for a unique competence.

The foregoing argument does not reduce law to politics. It is to say that we wish for reflective political decisions when constitutive matters are decided on and that courts can provide some of this. If this is all that is meant by legal reasoning, there can be no quarrel with its proponents. Legal reason might then be understood as part of disciplined reflection that builds on and extends a particular body of historical thinking on how to secure republican government. Jurisprudence as applied to republican constitutive matters would then be a part of political theory understood as a theoretically informed abridgment of political prudence.[98] For the sovereign people to rely in part on courts to deal with constitutive matters is to employ one kind of political decisionmaking that is better suited for certain matters than for others. But this is only to say that there are a variety of ways to settle political questions politically.

Much of what I have said about the shortcomings of legalists and legalism can be captured by simply noting that the rule of law is not synonymous with the rule of courts. Republican government indeed promises the rule of law, but that has little to do with the supposed essential properties of something called "law." The promise of the rule of law is rather that we can have a popular government where the people cannot rule as they please. An essential problem of constitutional thinking, then, is how to combine the rule of the people with the idea that the people cannot rule as they please. As an ideal, this might be called the rule of law, but less is gained by calling it so than is often supposed—and something may be lost if, as a result, our attention is turned to looking for the essence of legal reasoning.

We can learn much by considering Madison's view of this whole problem, especially as, unlike most of us, he had considerable experience in dealing with the problem of constitutional design. He said that in being "called upon to give a decision... that may affect the fundamental principles of the government... and liberty itself," all that can be done "is to weigh well every thing advanced on both sides, with the purest desire to find out the true meaning of the constitution, and to be guided by that, and an attachment to the true spirit of liberty."[99] This does not sound like a job for a judge trained in the law, and since Madison had actually done the thinking he described, we can take him as a reliable witness.[100]

CONSTITUTIONAL THINKING, PRACTICAL REASON, AND SHIPBUILDING

If there is no special legal reasoning on which to rely when we think about the best design for a republican political order, what kind of reasoning should inform constitutional thinking? I have suggested that the answer is practical political reason, which we need to discuss more fully in order to clarify how we should think constitutionally; the discussion also adds to our understanding of the substance of the theory of republican constitution. Thus, we have good reason to believe from the discussion of political regimes that good ones, at least, have a public interest. The discussion of practical political reason will help clarify the character of this public interest: if, as Madison teaches, the public interest must be broad in character, lawmaking must be, in significant part, deliberative if the public interest is to be given concrete meaning. That is, lawmaking itself should involve the exercise of practical political reason. The discussion of practical political reason as constitutional thinking also clarifies just why the public interest must be broad in character. Altogether, we may say that constitutional thinking for a republican regime is an exercise in practical political reason, the purpose of which is to secure an institutional design for the exercise of that reason, a design in which such reasoning gives concrete meaning to a broadly defined public interest. Consider the following analogy between constructing a political constitution and building a ship on the open sea.

Those who wish to constitute a republican regime[101] are like shipbuilding sailors[102] on a partly uncharted sea who know the direction in which they wish to sail, since the kinds of ports they prefer lie that way. This much they can agree on. To attempt to agree on anything more specific will defeat them, their opinions on the matter differing significantly. They also know too little for substantive agreement to be possible. They do, however, know something about the conditions they will face as they sail in the direction they prefer. They are not entirely at sea, that is; otherwise they could not hope to build a seaworthy vessel. But they must build with an eye to a wide range of conditions because they are not sure precisely what kind they will face. As they sail and build, they learn what works well under what conditions and how common various conditions are likely to be.

Described in this way, it is clear that the relations among the shipbuilders are fundamental. Because they must build, rebuild, repair, and modify the vessel as they sail and learn—and because they must alter their course, taking different routes to the sort of ports they prefer depending on what they ascertain about how their vessel will do under various conditions—it matters whether the shipbuilders' modes of association are such as to facilitate this learning and the decisions they must make.[103]

These modes of associations are then at least as important as the ports toward which the shipbuilders sail, and are in some ways even more important. The ports are distant, and reports of them faint, even contradictory. Few people have been to them and thus accounts of local conditions are scant. As a result, to navigate is not a simple problem of instrumental rationality, where they know precisely where they want to go and have a detailed understanding of all the factors that bear on getting there. Moreover, as I have suggested, the shipbuilding sailors can only agree on the general direction in which to sail and must leave to later, more specific choices any precise determination of direction and destination, if that is even possible.

It is also unlikely that the sailors will ever reach port. As they learn what it takes to reach a given destination, it may become clearer that the particular route they have chosen is now too costly and they must change it, or even sail toward similar but less costly ports. This process of reassessment is ongoing because the shipbuilders' resources are limited. In addition, if the shipbuilders get close enough to glimpse a desired port, it may well look less attractive. Certainly—if the analogy is dropped for the moment—it makes sense for constitution makers to provide for the possibility that lawmakers may achieve enough equality, in a way that it does not make sense for the shipbuilders to say that they have had enough Madagascar (at least if they haven't actually arrived and spent three months shore leave there). In any event, the shipbuilding crew is always in a state of flux, as some die and others are born; and the routes that seemed attractive to one generation of shipbuilders may not seem so to the next. Still, they cannot sail in just any direction or organize themselves in any pattern: to do so invites shipwreck. Thus, again, the modes of association among the shipbuilders are at least as important as their purposes.

So it is with those who think constitutionally about a republican regime. Like shipbuilding sailors, their essential problem is one of creating a design that provides the capabilities that are needed to keep the regime oriented in the right direction. Similarly, they will need to foster dispositions among citizens and lawmakers that are necessary to keep the ship on course. This direction must, at least in significant part, be the one given by the liberal justice that a republican government aims to serve.

On rare occasions, constitutional thinkers will be present at the creation of a republic and thus be joined with other citizens in bringing to life a new regime. But even here the slate is never wiped clean: the founders of the American Republic inherited a legacy of popular self-government. Most often, republican constitutional thinkers will be plying their trade in the context of an ongoing republican political order, trying to convince their fellow citizens that some part of the institutional design needs repair or that some proposal to do so is misguided. They are mostly spared, therefore, the overwhelming task of trying to think through the whole constitutional design. They may take much as given, as can even those thinkers who wish to start afresh. In this, constitutional thinkers are very much like the shipbuilders who are born at sea and must keep in repair the ship on which they sail, or build a new one mostly out of the materials of the old.

The core of constitutional thinking, as in shipbuilding and sailing on the open sea, is to keep in balance the tension between politics as instrumental activity—things must be accomplished, policies defined, and so on—and politics as creating and maintaining durable modes of association among a people that enables them to cope with a world that reveals little beforehand of the dilemmas, possibilities, and conflicts it will pose. It is all too easy to think that politics is *only* instrumental—the pursuit of desired outcomes by the intelligent deployment of the means of reaching them. It is equally tempting to construe politics as nothing but a durable set of engagements, and political purpose as consisting only of maintaining those engagements within which individuals can pursue their own ends.[104] Each captures a truth about political life: it matters for a republic whether massive economic inequality is reduced. But, political life has few, if any, of the kinds of purposes that characterize, say, business corporations. Moreover, there is too much about political life that simply concerns creating and maintaining modes of association, whether in political parties, neighborhood groups, or legislatures.

Republican constitutional thinkers thus must have some conception of the direction in which they wish the political order to go. We may call this the public interest, which, I have suggested, is derived in significant part from liberal justice. They must design with it in mind: shipbuilders have ports, constitution makers have the public interest. If we take the shipbuilding analogy seriously, the purposes that compose the public interest may be defined as the creation and maintenance of the relations among those making the journey that enable them to head in the right direction. The public interest is to this extent institutional in content—and, at their best, those who operate these institutions learn how to secure and improve them by discovering what is essential to their working well. It is in this idea of an institutionally defined public interest that we can join politics as a purposive activity aimed at serving the public interest with politics as the effort to maintain a set of institutional capabilities for an uncertain and conflicted world. We can, that is, understand the public interest as concerned with maintaining the set of institutions that are needed to constitute a republican regime. For example, the equality that is part of the liberal justice at which a republican regime aims may be understood not as a place to arrive at, but as a particular kind of relation among citizens. Thus understood, achieving equality is a substantive purpose, but the substance is the maintenance of an ongoing kind of relation, not simply a distribution of valued things. To return to the shipbuilding analogy, this focus on institutions means that the sailors are *always* sailing, never quite making port. Their entire enterprise consists of maintaining the forms of relation among themselves—and the direction in which they choose to sail is that which facilitates keeping these relations in repair. But enough has been said for the moment about the nature of the republican public interest.

We may say then that republican constitutional thinkers, like the ship-builders, take as an essential component of their institutional design that the citizenry and its lawmakers will need constantly to learn, and, in doing so, regularly modify the design they have inherited. Moreover, citizens and lawmakers also never quite arrive. Republican constitutional thinking must, therefore, provide incentives for lawmakers to discuss the content of the institutional particulars of the institutionally defined public interest that helps to shape the relations among and between citizens and lawmakers. That is, the lawmakers must be given incentives to exercise practical political reason. Lawmakers and constitutional thinkers, at their best, are engaged in a similar enterprise: to constitute a people in such a way that allows them to continue sailing in the broad direction called for by republican government and liberal justice. A crucial part of these incentives for lawmakers will undoubtedly be a citizenry who through elections can reward lawmakers who take up this task. Republican constitutional thinking then must also make provision for citizens learning enough of the meaning of the public interest to enable them to hold lawmakers to account.

More generally, a constitutional design for a republican regime should foster the ability to adapt to changing circumstances. As I have said, at its best, the political constitution of a republican regime defines how the people of a regime should associate in the face of the difficult-to-predict possibilities and problems that arise and the conflicts attendant on their common fate. Far and away, the most important characteristic of republican constitution-making is that it is an attempt to cope with the irremediable uncertainty of political life. Purposes are not easy to define in advance with enough precision to substantially constrain lawmaking. Constitutional design is not an exercise to be judged by intellectual virtues such as economy and simplicity. The expertise appropriate to it is not that of a social engineer.[105] Here is an echo of the earlier criticism of those definitions of good political practice that look to precise delineations of the ends that political institutions are to serve. We cannot know these with any precision, and the problem of political design is what to do about this fact. If the situation were otherwise, it would not be easy to explain why lawmaking is always a political process. The reluctance to accept this fact appears to lie behind the regular attempt to turn lawmaking, and thus politics, into something more tractable. But the stubbornness of politics in the face of such hygienic efforts suggests that politics arises and continues for a reason: even with the best will in the world (which itself is often lacking and is another source of politics), it is not easy to spell out with precision the ends of public choice. Political life is much less of a goal-oriented activity than many suppose.

In the view of constitutional thinking and the public interest that I have been sketching, political institutions are not interchangeable tools. They help to constitute a people, to bring into being a mode of association, and, as such, each has a specific job to do. Political institutions, moreover, are not essentially a means to get some place. We are there already once they come into being because their operation creates something new—a new mode of association. Institutions are then simultaneously ends and means; they are formative, or in the language I have been using, they are constitutive. This being so, political institutions, and other institutions that form a people, help to create a regime, which is a complex of modes of association that defines a political way of life. The value of institutions and the politics that defines their operation thus lies in their being a part of a certain kind of regime that is itself of value. They help to constitute it.

Lon Fuller long ago said much of what needs saying on how to think about political institutions, regimes, and political values:

> We should not conceive of an institution as a kind of conduit directing human energies toward some single destination. Nor can the figure be rescued by imagining a multipurpose pipeline discharging its diverse contents through different outlets. Instead we have to see an institution as an active thing, projecting itself into a field of interacting forces, reshaping those forces in diverse ways and in varying degrees. A social institution makes of human life itself something that it would not otherwise have been.[106]

CONCLUSION

Constitutional thinking mixes empirical and normative analysis in a way that is characteristic of all practical undertakings.[107] There is one feature of it that I wish to emphasize in concluding this chapter—namely, the manner in which the republican public interest joins together what might be called the "purposive" and "procedural" aspects of politics.

The vocabulary of liberty, equality, and self-government—to focus on the components of liberal justice—evolved to help practically minded people to better shape new and evolving modes of association among their countrymen (and later, countrywomen). The terms of the vocabulary were not "values" in the sense of abstract markers imported by an enterprise from outside it by a special group of people—whether legal theorists or moral philosophers—and designed to be definitions of successful outcomes. They were, instead, ways to define desired relations among citizens, including lawmakers, that arose out of a critique of existing practice. The value of these relations was thought to lie in the enduring ways they organized the collective life of the citizenry so that it might deal with a wide range of questions of uncertain character and dimension that would inevitably arise in its collective life.

Liberty, equality, and self-government thus are best understood as features of a constitution, the array of relationships that constitute a people.[108] The promise of a properly constituted republic is not that the institutions will secure something separate from themselves: that is, liberty, equality, and self-government as ends, the serving of which is the task of institutional means. Rather, the institutions, to focus on the United States, will constitute us as a free, equal people engaged in self-government. The relationships thus established among us—our political way of life—will define the manner in which we consider our collective problems. We will attempt to cope with them standing in relation to one another as, among other ways, rights bearers and political equals. Our capacity to deal with an uncertain and inevitably conflictual present and future are given by these forms of relation.

Here, then, is why the metaphor of building a ship on an open sea without clear ports is illuminating. This picture helps us see that we will better understand the essential problem of republican constitutional design if we relax our grip on the vocabulary of means and ends, of freestanding values against which to measure each institution: not all purposes can usefully be understood as ends, and, at least much of the time, institutions and their associated values come in packages. Republican regimes indeed have purposes, but they are best understood as the maintenance of a package of long-term engagements to associate with one another in specific ways, namely, as free and equal citizens engaged in self-government. There is reason to suppose, moreover, that the public interest of a republican regime might usefully be understood in just this fashion: as the securing of the constitutive institutions that make a collectivity a republic and that enable it to maintain itself in that form. The next step in the discussion of the American republican political constitution is, then, an account of its public interest.

Also worth considering, before we take that step, is that the most comprehensive and sure road to realizing many of the goods moral philosophers commend is, very likely, the realization of good political regimes. If this is indeed the case, it would seem that the fundamental moral-political problem is how to foster and maintain such regimes. It is also possible that we need not choose among moral theories in the way many moral philosophers suppose. Thus, in a more or less fully realized republican regime, lives informed by utilitarianism, virtue ethics, and deontology, not to mention religious lives, can flourish—perhaps not as much as would be the case if there were a regime whose basic purpose is specifically to serve, for example, a virtue-ethic way of life. But how big a worry should this be? Since it seems unlikely that the superiority of one or another moral theory will ever be decisively demonstrated, we cannot be sure that a world made up only of people who acted, for example, as virtue-ethicists commend would be superior to the mixed moral world that would flourish under a well-ordered republican regime.

Now THAT some substance has been given to the idea of a political regime and to the kind of reasoning that should inform efforts to create good ones, it will help to set out the main features of the arguments that are elaborated in the remaining chapters.

A central purpose of a commercial republican constitutional design is to induce lawmakers to give concrete meaning to the public interest, since the public interest is crucial to creating the more or less fully realized commercial republic that we aspire to be. Moreover, much else that we care about also depends on this regime's flourishing, including serving our own interests in regular and peaceful fashion. A republican constitutional theory must then concern itself with how to foster a pattern of politics that results in lawmakers giving concrete meaning to the public interest. The theory, that is, outlines the politics of a self-limiting popular sovereign because to serve the public interest means to use political authority to serve specific, limited purposes.

At various junctures, lawmaking in the public interest may need to facilitate the creation of new institutions. But in a political society that to some degree has in place the constitutive institutions it needs, the central task will largely consist of maintaining these when they are well ordered, strengthening them when their operation is on the right track, and reforming them when things have gone awry. This is the case for the contemporary United States.

In order for republican lawmaking to serve the public interest, it must in part be deliberative: the public interest is unlikely to be secured without discussion of how this is to be done. But the public interest can also be served as a by-product of other kinds of lawmaking, notably the kind in which the self-interest of major social groupings dominates. If Madison is correct, it is unlikely that the public interest can be fully served unless there is an overlap between class interests and the public interest. A direct concern with the public interest is necessary but not sufficient for a well-ordered republican political constitution. A politics of the public interest includes, then, not only a politics of deliberation but also a politics of class interest.

In addition to providing an account of the public interest, republican constitutional theory, therefore, includes a theory of constitutional politics. Included in the latter are how existing political institutions are to work; specifications for new ones if they are necessary; and an account of the incentives that encourage lawmakers and citizens to operate these institutions in the appropriate ways. Without an account of what makes for a lawmaking process that gives concrete meaning to the public interest, efforts to define its elements lose much of their importance. We need to know whether there is any real prospect that the public interest can be served, given commercial republican politics as it is and can plausibly become. Conversely, if we have a clear account of the elements of the public interest and of the politics that serve it, we need not worry too greatly—contrary to much contemporary constitutional theory—about giving detailed advice to lawmakers concerning how best to serve the public interest. If there is the right sort of politics, they will be attending to the matter anyway. Moreover, they will have their own ideas on the subject—and, being elected, their proposals will have more legitimacy than those of constitutional theorists. Overall, thinking of politics in a broad sense, we can say that constitutional theory is a theory of constitutional politics. An account of the public interest and the actions needed to serve it is simply a statement about the purpose of a particular kind of politics.

With regard specifically to the theory of American political constitution, much attention in later chapters is given over to how to make existing lawmaking institutions operate so that the public interest is served. There is no prospect of substantially changing the institutions' formal characteristics, nor is this needed. In short, with some notable exceptions, the focus is on changing the pattern of incentives that helps to shape the actions of lawmakers and citizens.

It is worth emphasizing that theorizing about the American political constitution must be heavily empirically based because it is concerned with how a certain kind of politics works. If an account of this politics is to be convincing, it must be rooted in how the politics of broadly democratic regimes is in fact carried on. Most of the constitutional theory set forth in the following chapters concerns how things *can* work and why that is possible. But I am not engaged in making predictions about the future. Rather, the aim is to shape it: here is how things will work if such and such is true. Here are the conditions that must obtain if we are to have the politics we wish for. Not everything can be shaped in the way we desire; some features of our political universe are fixed, or at least unalterable given our political will, resources, and knowledge, and other features we cannot predict. The ones that can be altered are the subject of constitutional analysis, as is the question of how to act in view of the features that cannot be.[109]

Constitutional theory thus occupies the space between the strictly normative and the strictly empirical. It is not reducible to political philosophy, as that is widely understood, with its attempt to define and defend a conception of the right or the good. Nor is it reducible to ordinary empirical analysis, with its concern to describe what is presently the case and explain why things work that way. A concise definition of constitutional theory is offered by Friedrich Hayek, who says that "fruitful social science must be very largely a study of what is *not*, a construction of hypothetical models of possible worlds which might exist if some of the alterable conditions were made different."[110] We might say, then, that the animating concern of constitutional thinking is how things *could* work.

Constitutional thinking is rooted in what human beings are like and may plausibly become. But how are we to make credible claims about how humankind can act and thus how its political institutions can work? There is no simple way to provide empirical backing for such claims since we are talking about what may be the case if certain other things are true. What is to stop us from making extravagant, even utopian, claims about how human beings can act? In these matters, what you see can't be what you get, otherwise what is the point of constitutional theorizing? But what you hope to get must still be somehow rooted in what you see unless we wish to give ourselves over to the intoxication of imagining what political life could be if only we could fire the present human race. In short, knowledge of political behavior as it is, is central to making credible claims about how it might be. Often this will be a matter of pointing to some piece of existing behavior that holds promise if it can be expanded. Thus, to take an example drawn from the discussion in chapter 7, if we wish to foster a greater degree of public-spiritedness among the citizenry, we can point to some instances of it now at work, even if its extent is less than is desirable. We can then analyze the conditions that must obtain if more of it is to occur.

To some degree, therefore, the empirical backing for claims about what could be can take the form of pointing to widely shared observations about political behavior, or to easily derived inferences from it. It is worth noting in this context that if the behaviors of interest to a constitutional theory aimed at bringing something new into being were widespread, there would be little need for constitutional theory. For then the behaviors we wish for presumably could be found around every corner. Sometimes, however, my analysis in the chapters that follow departs from what might plausibly be counted as common observation and asks for greater faith on the part of readers that something is possible. The only kind of evidence possible in such circumstances is that which may be inferred from present behavior but not directly derivable from it. There is, therefore, little or nothing to point to by way of studies because empirically minded analysts rightly wish to stick to their trade. My aim here, therefore, must be modest: insofar as my arguments rest on claims about how the world will work if certain conditions are present, to so frame them as to invite cautious assent.

II

The Political Constitution of a Commercial Republic

5

The Public Interest

ANY ACCOUNT of the political constitution of an American commercial republican regime should start with the defining characteristic of
republican rule: that it is not only popular but also limited. The discussion
so far has indicated that these limits must be broadly defined and that an
account of them can be built around the form institutional relationships
must take if we are to be constituted as a commercial republican people.
That is, there is reason to believe that the commercial republican public
interest is concerned with the maintenance of the political institutions that
give a republic its form.

A first step in developing this view is to briefly consider other accounts
of the limits on republican rule. We have already considered some, but they
turned out to be substantially flawed. Madison's attempt fell short because
he did not manage to give much content to the permanent interests of the
community.[1] Hayek and other classical liberal theorists have looked to the
idea of law itself to provide the boundaries. In addition to the difficulties
already canvassed, however, there is a further one, particularly pertinent
in the present context. To paraphrase Amartya Sen, a law can be general
and perfectly disgusting.[2] Still, and probably of greatest importance given
the present manner in which we conduct our political business, there is the
Constitution as higher law as interpreted by judicial reasoners.

The Constitution too, however, is flawed as a statement of the limits on
popular rule. Leaving aside the question of how and why we the living are
bound by the hand of the dead—and worries about why political majorities
that need limiting must be bound by nine unelected judges—there is simply
the point that the Constitution lays out a theory of the constitution of
the American Republic that is insufficient for the task. Consider whether
a republican regime needs a public-spirited citizenry. Madison said that

it does.[3] But the Constitution says nothing on the matter. Consider also that the document says nothing about the business corporation and its appropriate role in the regime. These matters all raise the question of how to define limits on political authority. How much can the state do to encourage public-spiritedness? Should the business corporation be given a privileged political role, yet also be limited?

The Constitution does tell us much that is useful in our effort to constitute a well-ordered commercial republic, and thus what the limits of popular rule are, but it is not a complete statement of the problem and its solution. Nor, for that matter, was it intended to be, if Madison's writings are any indication: there is more that is relevant in *The Federalist* papers than there is in the document. Moreover, because we must add to what the Constitution says about how we should constitute ourselves, and thus inject additional considerations concerning the problem of limits, there is good reason to worry about whether courts and lawyers have the necessary understanding to take these next and necessary steps. In chapter 4, I argued that it is unlikely that there is a special kind of legal reason. It thus is also unlikely that looking to judges and lawyers to fill in what is missing from the Constitution is a satisfactory way to complete an account of the limits on the people's rule.

THE PUBLIC–PRIVATE DISTINCTION

There is yet another effort to anchor limits on popular rule outside of politics: the attempt to distinguish between a public and a private sphere. It overlaps to some degree the view that the limits on the people's rule are set out in the Constitution, and it may well have the greatest hold on American political thinking. It too, however, is flawed.

In the efforts to distinguish between the public and private spheres, it is commonly said that the state's domain is limited to the public sphere; that private property, the market, and the family are matters properly relegated to the private sphere; and that the law is the politically neutral vehicle for defining these distinctions. In this, as in other matters, law is said to be neutral in the sense of being nonpartisan: its conclusions do not systematically favor one set of interests over others.[4] Those who have looked to the public–private distinction have not necessarily argued for a strict separation between the two. But these theorists, no less than the ones who argue for a strict separation, have assumed that the boundaries of a naturally private sphere are more or less clear and can be used as the basis for legal decisions made by courts. The boundaries of public decision are anchored outside of politics. Political choice is to be bounded by that which transcends it.[5]

Beginning in the nineteenth century, a growing number of lawyers and jurists asserted the importance of keeping separate the public and private spheres.[6] Business corporations were stripped of their public powers and turned into private entities. Conversely, municipal corporations were stripped of their proprietary functions and turned into public entities regulated by state government. Similar changes also occurred in private law doctrine, in the wake of which arose the view that the public sphere was, or at least should be, the realm of power and the private sphere of voluntary cooperation. The distinguishing feature of the private sphere, it was asserted, is that its contours are not a result of the exercise of political power but of the behavior of actors who need to seek the cooperation of others if they are to serve their purposes. Public involvement was to be confined to enforcing the rules that made private cooperation possible.

This legally oriented effort to distinguish between the public and private spheres builds on some commonplaces of life in societies like ours. It seems entirely natural to contemporary Americans to conceive of family life as private, a sphere where the state writ ought not to run. Its goods are so different from those the public world offers, not the least of which is intimacy, that it is easy to think of it as a distinct sphere. Similarly, what one does with one's property, so long as others are not injured, seems obviously a private matter.

Such views as they have been developed by legal thinkers have, however, been subject to searching criticism: most pointedly, there are no coherent transpolitical standards to guide courts (and other authorities) in tracing the outlines separating the public and private spheres. Legal realists were perhaps the first in the twentieth century to criticize the putative public–private distinction, arguing that the content of law cannot be derived from something outside of politics. Rather, it is what judges say it is, and to an important degree this reflects their politics and the politics of the day. Any attempt to show that the law is an unfolding of specifically legal principles must fail, the realists argued, and the claims for any nonpolitical legal principles that may exist are no stronger. Law is, in complex ways, another arena for politics.

For legal realists, therefore, law, far from being neutral, at least as judges elaborate it, favors some groups over others. In practice, the realists argued, the groups favored are the already powerful. As Morton Horwitz comments, legal realists believed that "all law was coercive and had distributive consequences." Law was therefore to "be understood as a delegation of coercive power."[7] Moreover, as Cass Sunstein in an extension of realist arguments shows, much of the claim for the nonpartisanship or political neutrality of legal principles rests on taking as given existing distributions of economic and other resources. Perhaps not surprisingly, he is able to show that the existing distributions are hardly politically neutral.[8] To which it may be added that the distributions represent the result of past political struggles—and the winners and losers of these show a consistency that only an overwhelming desire to separate law from politics can obscure.

Once the door of nonneutrality was opened by legal realists and their successors, the various means of demarcating a "natural" private sphere—by looking to definitions of private property, markets, and the family—also became open to question. Legal realists and their successors have pointed out that private property, whatever it once was, is now a product of choices made by the state. As such, it can hardly serve to delimit the state's sphere of activity.[9] Moreover, unless the courts have some coherent way of saying when the state's redrawing of property rights is acceptable, then not only is the "giveness" of property no longer a barrier to state action, there are no coherent standards to replace it.[10]

This last is, in fact, what has happened. The courts have, with perhaps some recent exceptions, simply abandoned any serious attempt to define such standards.[11] Indeed, the Supreme Court has more or less conceded that, in the crucial matter of a state taking of property, property rights are what the political authorities say they are—as long as they claim that the property is being put to public use. Even more important, what counts as public use has been more or less left to the political authorities involved.[12] As Frank Michelman comments, since 1922 the Court has moved toward a "highly non-formal, open-ended multi-factor balancing method." "Never once" between 1922 and 1987, he says, did the Court apply this open-ended test and come out in favor of a taking having occurred and against a regulating government.[13] Jennifer Nedelsky simply comments that "since 1937 the Supreme Court has virtually abandoned the means it had established for preventing legislative interference with property rights."[14]

Just how far the courts themselves might go in reducing the extent to which property can be understood as a barrier to the exercise of political authority is suggested by the presiding judge's comment in a case brought against U.S. Steel. The case resulted from a suit filed by the local steelworkers union when the company announced it was leaving the Youngstown, Ohio, area. The judge suggested that the law might recognize "the property right [of the community] to the extent that U.S. Steel cannot leave [the community] area in a state of waste, that it cannot completely abandon its obligation to that community, because certain vested rights have arisen out of this long relationship and institution."[15] If communities have property rights by virtue of a long-standing relationship with a company, then presumably the community can exercise those rights through its government. They would have a claim to some portion of the firm's assets for community betterment and be in position to act on it. Jennifer Nedelsky, after extensive discussion of how the courts have treated private property, concludes, with similar judicial opinions and declarations in mind, that "[i]t is now widely accepted that property is not a limit to legitimate governmental action, but a primary subject of it."[16]

The confusion over the appropriate reach of state power can also be seen in the judicial response to the welfare state and its redistributive policies, as well as to the political activities of the business corporation. The courts have sanctioned the taking of the revenue of the property of some to increase the income of others. On the other hand, the courts treat corporations as "fictive persons," thereby giving them certain speech rights that seem to preclude at least some kinds of regulation of political activities. Which specifically legal principle could accommodate both is not easy to see.

The confusions of the courts and of legal discussion generally over the justification and prerogatives of private property have contributed to and partly reflect a powerful line of analysis: whatever rights there are—whether fully natural or simply beyond political choice—a strong right to private property, especially to an unlimited accumulation of what might be termed "productive property," is not one of them. Thus Dahl, in a widely discussed analysis, criticizes the most common argument for private property as a right. This argument, derived from Locke, says that a right to property comes as the result of mixing one's labor with what nature has provided. For Dahl, the idea of the fruits of one's labor being the source of the right to property can only justify acquisition by producers. It cannot justify either the ownership of stock or the collection of rent. It is important to note here that Locke also ruled out spoilage—one cannot take more than one can use—and that we must leave "enough and as good" as we mix our labor and create a right to property. This in itself would seem to set a significant limit on how much wealth can rightfully be acquired. Locke's argument is subtle, and he works to soften the impact of the statement about "enough and as good." Yet it still looms as a barrier to unlimited acquisition, and possibly even to significant accumulations of wealth.[17]

There are similar difficulties in justifying the present distribution of wealth and income in the United States. It is unlikely that it can be justified on the ground that those who have large incomes and holdings deserve them as a matter of right because they have, through their own efforts, significantly added to social wealth. All technological innovation—indeed, all wealth creation—rests on an extensive social inheritance. None of us could even begin to do our jobs as they now exist without an enormous legacy that has created the very consumers of our products, no less the tools of our trade. Our contribution to wealth creation must then be very small and the social contribution very large. If the successful mixing of our labor rests to a substantial degree on the results of the labor of others, it is hard to see how we are entitled to very much of the fruits of our own exertions. Such considerations suggest that arguments for a strong right to private property are difficult to sustain.[18]

If arguments like the ones just canvassed are correct, it is difficult to see how the idea of private property can in any straightforward fashion be used to demarcate the public and private spheres. It is not a sufficient reply to argue that courts can weigh the multiple considerations at issue and claim that the results are the product of reasoned argument.[19] For a start, we may doubt whether the weighing process can avoid considering which classes of people are to be favored. If equal protection of the laws does not encompass ensuring that all students in a state whose constitution guarantees a certain standard of education have more or less equal amounts of education dollars spent on them,[20] we might conclude that the U.S. Supreme Court favors the propertied against the propertyless. But more accurately, and at least as telling, we can say that in balancing various considerations, the Court has given little weight to the interests of the propertyless and those similarly situated who compose the population of poor school districts. The idea of the Court as non-nonpartisan—that is, neutral—between interests (as opposed to principles that end up favoring some interests as against others) begins to look rather shaky.

But there is a deeper point here, one to which legal realists have pointed. Once it becomes clear that there are no relatively clear and simple principles to guide the courts, and that courts then must get involved in a complex weighing process, is it the case that lawyers and judges have some particular facility to do so unavailable to others? This is a version of the legal reasoning question that I have already considered.[21] Enough has been said on this matter to raise serious doubts about whether judges have such a competence. Here we can add that, given the close ties between property and political power, we should be very skeptical indeed that there can exist any neutral competence that can save private property as the boundary between public and private.

If there were a strong right to private property, it is possible that legal practitioners might be able to defend a claim to a special competence in interpreting it.[22] But once the mix of relevant considerations for defining the scope of a right to property includes that the state may take property for a wide range of public purposes, that equal protection of the laws may call for an equalizing of educational expenditures, and that the funds generated by a natural resource endowment of oil can be distributed to all equally,[23] we surely have left the realm where legal practitioners have any obvious special competence to weigh up such matters. Perhaps it is enough to say here that the capacity for principled argument does not only lie in the hands of judges and lawyers, with the rest of political life consigned to the grubby business of cutting deals. We can hope for more from the legislature—a matter to which I return[24] and which is an underlying theme of much of the remaining discussion.

The public–private distinction is vulnerable in another way, this time because of arguments made by radical economists. They too have contended that it is not possible to maintain a distinction between a private domain of economics and a public domain of politics. They have argued that this version of the public–private distinction rests on the proposition of labor asset neutrality, that is, that there is nothing intrinsic to labor that prevents it from being bought and sold like any other commodity or resource. Thus, a good deal of standard economics argues that the use of labor should strongly reflect efficiency considerations as determined by the market. However, as radical economists have pointed out, labor is not a commodity like refrigerators or cars, because it cannot be separated from the person providing it. It thus requires the shaping of human behavior, in this case of workers, in a way that real commodities do not. This in itself suggests that defining labor as a commodity is a consequence of politics, because it is unlikely that the disciplining would be successful without the exercise of political power and political authority.

But more important is the assertion by radical economists that the reason capital hires labor, rather than the other way around, is not a matter of efficiency, as standard economic theory has it.[25] In the standard view, the fact that labor rarely hires capital means either that this is not efficient—a "technical" not a political fact—and/or that workers on balance simply prefer the usual employment arrangements in which they are subject to employer discipline. The question, however, is whether this *is* a technical matter, a question of how economic markets must work. This question becomes particularly pressing once we realize, as radical economists say we must, that what might be called "democratically organized labor" is often more efficient than disciplined labor: worker-owned firms can rely on group solidarity and a sense of a stake in the company to prompt workers to work up to their abilities. If such firms then are more efficient, why indeed do workers not hire capital: the return to owners of capital would presumably be greater.

The answer lies, say radical economists, in the difficulty of designing a contract under present economic arrangements such that those who lend capital to workers have sufficient security for their investment. There are, however, ways of alleviating this problem. That this is not done suggests that capital markets are probably biased as a result of political choice and action. The further result is, almost certainly, that some nontrivial numbers of workers are consigned to working arrangements that they would not choose if they faced politically unconstrained choices.[26] Moreover, an alternative is forgone that, because of its greater efficiency, would benefit the society as a whole. What is presumed to be "private" is, in fact, "political" in the sense that life chances and general well-being are significantly shaped by arrangements that are not necessarily, not even likely, the most economically efficient possible for the society. For essentially political reasons, capital is given an advantage in the competition for who should hire whom.

Recent feminist political and legal theory also makes clear that there is no easy distinction to be made between the public and private spheres. Political choice in the view of these theorists has always significantly shaped the private sphere, especially with regard to the roles of women, gender relations, and family life. Feminist theorists have shown that the demarcations between public and private that the law enforces are neither neutral nor justifiable because they do not mark off a naturally private sphere and do not follow a consistent set of principles. Taking note of a gendered division of labor within the household as well as in the work force, Susan Moller Okin argues:

> Public life is far less distinct from personal and domestic life for women than for men. Their experience in each radically affects their possibilities in the other. The claim that the two spheres are separate is premised upon, but does not recognize, both a material and a psychological division of labor between the sexes.[27]

To this we should add, as Okin herself recognizes, that the division of labor in the family is to a significant degree itself a political creation. A look at the history of family law strongly suggests that public authority has effectively constituted—and reconstituted—the family in the sense of who owes what to whom. Until the nineteenth century, fathers were generally awarded children in custody cases. Subsequently, it increasingly became mothers. Similarly, what was owed to children by parents has been continually revised.[28] What principles of law and specifically legal reasoning could explain and defend such redefinitions? Any satisfactory answer must be rooted in what liberal justice calls for by way of the organization of family life, the goods and dispositions families can foster, and the kinds of families that facilitate republican government. It is hard to see how referring to the "privateness" of families or to legal reasoning can help much in such an investigation.

The preceding are all compelling criticisms of the public–private distinction, and they indicate that the vision of political choice reined in by a supposedly natural private sphere beyond politics cannot be sustained. It is not possible for judges—nor anyone else—to rely presumptively on a naturally given private sphere uncontaminated by politics as they go about defining the appropriate range of political choice. The supposed private sphere is contaminated, indeed partly created, by politics.[29] This does not mean that it is impossible to create a sphere within which the intimate life of citizens can be carried on, civic life conducted, neighbors create cooperative schemes, and a wide range of politically unconstrained economic transactions occur. Indeed, we must be able to do all of these if we are to have liberal regimes at all. The point rather is that we cannot decide on the contours of the sphere in which all of this is to occur by referring to natural boundaries anchored outside of politics and to the conclusions of a special legal competence. How the private sphere is to look must emerge from struggle and debate over such matters as how much economic equality does republican government require and what role must government play in helping to structure economic transactions in order for such equality to be secured; what kind of efforts are necessary to rein in the factional propensities of powerful private actors; and what are the reasons to restrain government activity when it touches on civil association. These and similar questions cannot be avoided in a republican regime. Phrased as they are, moreover, it seems clear that arguments about them are and must be deeply political. If this is so, while republican regimes must have a private sphere, its contours will emerge from political argument. Indeed, the need to prevent faction, secure economic equality, and facilitate a vital civic sector are elements of the commercial republican public interest, to which we can now turn.

THE SUBSTANCE OF THE PUBLIC INTEREST

If the distinction between public and private, the Constitution-as-complete-guide, and legal formalism[30] do not settle the question of the limits on popular rule, where else should we look? By and large, the efforts just described try to avoid directly confronting the question of whether the limits on popular rule should be rooted in substantive value commitments. That these efforts are flawed does not mean that any such approaches must fail. But it does suggest that it may not be possible to answer the question of the proper limits on popular rule if substantive value commitments are laid aside. We have, moreover, already come on a possible alternative—namely, a substantive public interest that is rooted in such commitments.

But before discussing which such commitments might provide our bearings, there is another matter to consider: why conceive of the problem of limits on popular rule as a matter of defining the content of the public interest. To be sure, insofar as Madison is counted as a powerful theorist of republican government, it is of some importance that this is how he viewed the problem. As discussed in chapter 2, Madison argued that if they are properly chosen and lawmaking itself properly designed, lawmakers would be in a position to "discern the true interest of their country and [would] be least likely to sacrifice it to temporary or partial considerations."[31] Lawmaking would then aim at a progressive refinement in understanding the comprehensive interests of the country.[32] Lawmakers would give what Madison (and Hamilton) referred to as "the deliberate sense of the community,"[33] to discern, that is, "the permanent and aggregate interests of the community."[34] Moreover, as the earlier discussion of Madison also suggested, when considering the limits on popular lawmaking, we should not seek anything so specific that it reduces lawmaking to administration. But in a republic, of course, there must be *some* limits. That is what the idea of the public interest offers: a conception that provides substance to the limits on lawmaking but is not so specific as to obviate discussion on the appropriate content of the law.

That Madison thought that the idea of the public interest points in a useful direction, however, hardly settles the question of whether there *is* a public interest. This is an especially pressing matter given that social science and political theory are shot through with arguments that there is no such thing. Thus, there are the mid-twentieth-century behavioral political scientists and the late-century postmodern social theorists, and many in between, whose views run from one extreme (that the public interest is merely a rhetorical cover for the exercise of power) to the other (that individuals can have no other palpable interests beyond what will accrue to them personally). In the riveting assessment by Margaret Thatcher, there is no such thing as "society."[35]

Any conception of the public interest must walk a precarious line between this view that no such thing exists—there are only the aggregated interests of those who compose the society—and that there is such a thing and it contains detailed specifications for the laws' contents. The weaknesses of each are apparent. If there are only aggregated interests, what shall we say about the rules that make aggregation possible? Are we indifferent to how it occurs, whether it is fair? If we do care about such matters, what would promote and make the rules secure? A citizenry with a certain character situated in a certain economic condition? This begins to look very much like a discussion of the public interest. Moreover, if we think that the rules of aggregation must be fair, the justification of such rules very likely cannot itself rest on an aggregation of preferences. And so, again, we are more than halfway to a conception of the public interest, this time understood as the rules that ought to structure our decisionmaking on how politics is to be carried on.

Aggregators are proceduralists who attempt to finesse the problem of the public interest by looking to good procedures. There are other similarly inclined proceduralists who look, for example, to democratic deliberation to guarantee the goodness or rightness of the laws that emerge. Whatever comes out of a properly designed deliberative process, in this view, should be the law. But this way of proceeding is also flawed. Notice first that deliberation is exceedingly difficult if those involved are understood as living nowhere in particular. What will they talk about? Where will they start? Is any starting point sufficient? If not, why not? If yes, what if anything distinguishes this from the public interest? Again, many procedural theories smuggle in substantive conceptions of the public interest in their specification of the circumstances in which reasoning is to occur. Thus, it is sometimes said that the reasoners must be equal. Possibly so, but that amounts to saying that one of the things the reasoners or some other authoritative agent must do in their deliberations is to try to secure equality.[36]

Similarly, there are proceduralists—we might call them "strong democrats"—who argue that the only real test for the goodness or rightness of a political order is that the people shall rule. But what, in fact, is being claimed in this argument? That whenever a large aggregation of people come together, whatever they decide must be right or legitimate? Any aggregation? How about a howling mob? If not, there must be criteria to distinguish a band of thieves from other groups of people—and, if there are, then surely it is the task of good lawmaking to act on them. The difference between this lawmaking task and serving the public interest is not easily discernible.

To hold, as some do, that there is available to us a detailed conception of the public interest is both unwise and in any event impossible. No one can see far enough into the future to provide detailed guidance for lawmakers. Moreover, why should we attempt to bind lawmakers in this hard and fast manner if we want them to be lawmakers, not clerks? Why, indeed, do we want lawmakers at all, if the substance of the public interest is so readily discernible in all its detail? If we are to have lawmakers and lawmaking, lawmakers must have discretion—and a significant part of the burden of giving content to the public interest is theirs.

Tracing the intellectual journey of Robert Dahl, one of the leading democratic theorists of the past and present, is helpful for our thinking through whether there is a public interest and what its content might be. In the flush of the midcentury victory of the new science of politics over its supposedly unscientific and hortatory predecessor, Dahl, along with many others, was skeptical that the notion of public interest had any meaning.[37] In his later work, however, he has hesitantly suggested that there is indeed a public interest and has taken a few steps toward filling in its content. Thus, when Dahl says that an intelligent democratic citizenry should develop the right conditions to support democracy,[38] this is another way of talking about the public interest, as he clearly recognizes.[39]

Just as Dahl is led inexorably to giving meaning to the public interest, so those less insistent in thinking through the implications of their formulations can be led to take a similar path. Thus, one might gently ask whether democratic regimes need rules, and if they do whether any sort of rules would suffice. And when the answer is forthcoming that, of course, they do and not just any sort would do the job, then the prompt may be offered: ought lawmaking aim to secure the appropriate rules? Plausibly the answer would be "yes" and then one might ask whether securing the rules on which democracy rests is not in fact a perfectly comprehensible and compelling conception (of at least part) of the public interest. And if the interlocutor insists that the public interest is coterminus with the interests of the citizenry, it is easy to reply that securing the rules of democracy is precisely in the interest[40] of those who receive its benefits.

So, we are driven to talk about the public interest, even those of us who are skeptical of its existence. The earlier discussion in chapter 4 of the relation between political value and political institutions, moreover, suggests how we should proceed once the existence of the public interest is acknowledged: to know what we value in the context of political practice requires knowing what it takes to realize it. We thus need to consider the kinds of institutions needed to realize such values. In short, the substance of the public interest is institutional.

An institutional conception of the public interest has impressive advantages. For a start, it is broad enough to be applicable to changing circumstances. Whatever else the public interest is, it must provide direction across largely unknown circumstances, possibilities for action, and political conflicts. By contrast, a conception of the public interest made up of policy goals quickly outlives its usefulness; it provides little guidance once the particular world for which it was designed passes away, as it must. A focus on institutions, on modes of association designed to enable members of a community to cope intelligently with political unknowns, is more promising. To repeat an earlier point, in constitutional thinking it is crucial to think about capabilities as opposed to specific ends.

An even more important advantage of an institutional conception of the public interest is that it enables us to make sense of the common intuition that politics is concerned less about arriving at some particular destination than about how we stand in relation to others wherever we are going. We have already encountered this point in the discussion of shipbuilding as an analogy to constitutional design. Many political observers sense that defining destinations for a whole society is difficult to do; the world is too uncertain and the members of almost all societies differ too much to agree on anything very detailed. What seems more important is that we are related to one another in durable and attractive ways. Such a view also draws on a deep sense on the part of many in liberal societies that too great an insistence on seeking to secure substantive social purposes undercuts liberty: individuals are the principal holders of purposes. An institutional focus also draws on the sense that societywide planning has proven to be very unattractive and unmanageable. If there really is a public interest composed of a comprehensive set of substantive ends, should we not organize our politics around plans to serve them? But it is precisely this that we cannot do and should not attempt.[41]

In similar fashion, an institutional conception of the public interest does not carry the divisive freight of a morally insistent conception of the ends of politics and their relation to the good life. As many have argued, we are unlikely to agree to any great extent about such matters given our ethnic, religious, and racial diversity. The substance of the public interest as I have started to describe it is, in fact, largely procedural,[42] focused on securing institutional forms through which a variety of purposes may be sought. Being procedural in this sense, it is more likely to be widely accepted.[43]

Finally, an institutional view of the public interest makes sense of the idea that if we desire a certain political way of life we must create and maintain the institutions at its core. Something as complex as a political way of life is unlikely to come into being by itself, and it is not very likely that it could maintain itself through its ordinary institutional workings. If we value a regime, we must value the efforts of lawmakers to secure its crucial institutions, which is to say we must have a conception of the public interest.

A similar institutional conception of the public interest has been offered by Samuel Huntington, Bernard Crick, and John Finnis. Huntington comments that "the capacity to create political institutions is the capacity to create public interests."[44] Crick says that the public interest is simply a way of "describing the common interest in preserving the means of making public decisions politically."[45] Finnis, more cumbersomely, defines the public interest (which he terms "the common good") as a set of conditions "which enables the members of a community to attain for themselves reasonable objectives, or to realize reasonably for themselves the value(s), for the sake of which they have reason to collaborate with each other . . . in a community."[46]

In addition to its institutional content, there is a second thread to follow in giving substance to the public interest. I have argued that political institutions come in packages, in regimes. I have also argued that, as one of several kinds of good regimes, a commercial republic is a conception of rule aimed at a conception of justice. It is a liberal regime, and, as such, it aims at a conception of justice that centers on the creation of a free and equal people engaged in self-government that has limits on what it may do. There may be some disagreement about whether I have properly characterized liberal justice. But for the purposes of constitutional theory and, in particular, for an account of the commercial republican public interest, this matters much less than is often supposed. *Any* conception of liberal justice as such is too broad to offer much direct guidance to lawmaking. Moreover, it is unlikely that differences in the conception of liberal justice would point lawmaking down substantially different paths.

Our aspirations also provide normative guidance for giving content to the public interest. They are the flip side of liberal justice, and concern the kind of liberal regime that is to realize this justice. But our aspirations are also too broad by themselves to define the public interest. It could hardly be otherwise, since normative commitments of the kind found in aspirations are likely to be very general: they are meant to orient us in a wide range of situations, many of which cannot be predicted beforehand.

The next step in an account of the public interest is to see what can be derived from liberal justice and our aspirations when we think about them in institutional terms.[47] That is, lawmaking in the public interest is broadly concerned with securing the institutions that compose a commercial republican regime. There are at least seven components of the public interest that can be derived in this way, each of which has also been the subject of considerable scrutiny. It will be best to consider them first in general terms and then give them the institutional specificity that enables them to serve as the public interest.

These elements of the public interest of a commercial republic include:

1. *Developing a means to prevent the capture of lawmaking by those whose aim is to use the power of the state to serve unlimited purposes, whether for self-aggrandizement or for aims said to be of the greatest worth.* This is what Madison called the problem of "faction."[48] The concern here is to ensure that lawmakers are not precluded from attempting to give concrete meaning to the public interest. This element of the public interest derives from our commitment to republican government, which is impossible if faction is not controlled. It is also included in the idea of a free people engaged in self-government: there cannot be self-government and liberty if there is factional government. Madison's constitutional theory is an elaborate defense for including the prevention of faction as an element of the public interest.

2. *Developing deliberative forms of lawmaking.* This element derives from our commitment to be a self-governing people. Self-government is valued because it allows a people to serve whatever collective purposes they have. If they are actually to serve those purposes, they must be able to talk about their specific content and how to realize them. In short, they, and more importantly their lawmakers, must deliberate. There is reason to think that deliberative lawmaking must rest on a citizenry with some experience of deliberating about the public interest. Otherwise, citizens are unlikely to be regularly able to choose deliberatively minded lawmakers. They must

have a measure of public-spiritedness. Madison's constitutional theory also points to the importance of securing deliberative lawmaking and the citizen foundation on which it rests as part of the public interest.

3. *Securing those rights that characterize a commercial republican people— namely, those that make them a free and equal people engaged in self-government.* At the least, these consist of what Dahl calls "primary political rights,"[49] as well as rights that ensure due process of law and a significant measure of private ownership of productive assets. The commonly used language of "respecting" rights suggests that these and other rights are in some sense simply there, and that a principal task of government is not to trample them—whether by arbitrary behavior or by actions that invade the sphere of liberty that rights define. By contrast, to talk of "securing" rights points to the need for state action in their service. This is especially clear when due weight is given to the idea that if human beings have rights, each of them should have the same or *equal* rights. Moreover, insofar as rights are more than promises, to have one means to be able to exercise it.[50] Since the life situations of citizens vary markedly, some adjustment in the lot of some of them is called for insofar as their condition impedes enjoying these rights. One source of the capacity to exercise political rights is steady work. Without it, a person is unlikely to have the resources necessary for political engagement. Franklin Roosevelt pointed to the importance of work for republican citizenship when he included in his "Economic Bill of Rights" a "right to a useful and remunerative job."[51]

4. *Securing a degree of political equality sufficient to ensure that the politics of interest aggregation—a feature of any modern free society—is not so heavily biased that significant portions of the citizenry regularly find themselves on the short end of law and regulation.* Whatever else being an equal people may mean, it surely means that all nonfactional interests have at least some prospect of getting the attention of lawmakers. Lawmaking in a commercial republic will have both deliberative and aggregative elements, not least because the freedom that republican government promises includes the freedom to pursue private interest. Moreover, a free society cannot attempt to suppress interest group politics if it wishes to remain free. Faction can only be prevented, small homogeneous societies aside, by preventing the citizenry from talking to one another in order to better pursue their interests. As Madison said, this would be a cure worse than the disease. Moreover, commerce itself generates a multiplicity of political interests who will demand an aggregative politics—one that allows them to pursue their interests and, if necessary, bargain with others until agreement can be reached on law and regulation. An aggregative politics is the home of the political pluralism that is both inevitable and a constitutive feature of a modern commercial republic. An aggregative politics is also necessary if so complex a society is

to hold together by peaceful means: its major interests need to be satisfied. The fact that we are talking about a liberal regime means that there are substantial limits to how much it can be held together by common purpose.

5. *Securing a degree of economic equality sufficient to provide the foundation for an equal people capable of self-government.* Republican government requires a measure of economic equality as the basis of an acceptable form of its aggregative politics. Gross inequality of economic resources reproduces itself as political inequality. Republican government also requires a measure of economic equality because, if there is to be deliberative lawmaking, the citizenry cannot be characterized by great economic inequalities. Significant portions of the citizenry must themselves be engaged in a deliberative effort to give concrete meaning to the public interest if they are to be public-spirited, a quality necessary for effectively judging the deliberative inclinations of lawmakers. Citizens who are highly unequal economically will find it difficult to give one another the mutual respect that makes deliberation possible. The result is to undercut the public-spiritedness on which deliberative lawmaking must rest.[52] Moreover, economic insecurity compromises the independence of political judgment that a self-governing people require. Economic want and its corollary, economic dependence, are poor foundations on which to build self-government. To worry about whether you can pay your bills wonderfully concentrates your mind—but not on political life.

Since we aspire to be a commercial regime, the principal source of economic equality must come from a system in which there is a significant measure of private ownership of productive property. Again, Madison is helpful. He argued that republican lawmaking should aim to "reduce extreme wealth" and "raise indigence," and to do so "without violating the rights of property."[53] In a fully realized commercial republic, the fruits of prosperity should not be available only to a few; neither should economic production be in the service of creating an oligarchy with the status and material comforts of an aristocracy. There are several ways to accomplish these things, including significant inheritance taxes with the proceeds directed to the less well-off, and substantial redistribution of income and wealth. A politically more acceptable way to "raise indigence" is to make widely available work that pays enough to keep a family out of poverty. This is especially true when economic independence for most people can no longer rest on ownership of productive assets. The great majority of us are wage earners, and what economic independence we can achieve depends on steady and reasonably well-paid work. Thus, a significant part of the economic equality a commercial republic needs will come through a wide availability of at least moderately remunerative work.[54] This is one area in which lawmaking in the service of the public interest should focus.[55]

6. *Developing ways to give those who control productive assets a significant degree of discretion in their use—so that they can use their detailed knowledge in efficiently deploying these resources—and providing these asset controllers with inducements sufficient to encourage them to take the risks that are an inevitable feature of large-scale wealth creation.*[56] This is what a commercial regime requires (and very likely any regime in which high levels of economic growth are desired). It is perhaps a measure of our lack of political-economic sophistication that this basic point about controllers of productive assets is not widely appreciated. When asset controllers proclaim that some program of government regulation is too heavy a burden to bear, they are not only trying to fatten their bottom line while keeping prying eyes from their affairs, but are also pointing out, however tendentiously, that if we want economic growth we must give those who control productive assets room to try various strategies. They are also reminding those willing to listen that they need various kinds of inducements—not least of which is that they can accumulate sizable sums of money—since the failure rate for large-scale investment is not trivial.

7. *Developing a vibrant civil society in which private cooperative undertakings are common.* The organizations and modes of association that compose civil society are public but not part of the state. They are not private, if by this is meant that they are concerned with the intimate spheres of our lives. They are instead nonstate forms of public cooperation, which are public in at least three senses: they are open to everyone, or at least to a wide array of citizens; their activities are of the kind that could be undertaken by a liberal state; and their activities are broadcast to the larger society, partly to gain support, partly because of the extent of their impact on others. A neighborhood organization is an example. It is open to all in the area; it undertakes neighborhood projects that might be carried out by local government; and its actions are known to a wider public.

A free people cannot allow all of its important business to be carried out by the state. If it did, the state in time would eventually issue detailed directions governing the behavior of its citizenry and quashing all criticism of its actions. For much the same reasons, the people would find it impossible to engage in self-government. The associations that compose civil society teach the skills of self-government, most notably the art of political association, without which a citizenry would be helpless before its governors. More generally, liberty and self-government can only flourish in a regime where there are multiple centers of power.

A vibrant civil society is also needed if the moral pluralism that characterizes a free society is to be achieved. In order for different understandings of what it means to live a good or just life to be meaningful to more than a few people, association with like-minded others must be possible. In any more or less fully realized American republic, a substantial portion of such moral associations are likely to be religious at their base and will include not only associations built around common worship, but also various kinds of organizations devoted to self-help and community service. As Tocqueville observed long ago, religion is the first of our political institutions.[57]

It is possible that a vibrant civil society can be built more easily on a system of common law courts and judge-made law. A civil society is composed of groups of people who come together for common purposes and whose activities are facilitated by a system of law that is not itself a product of the central government.[58] These civic associations must not depend on nor be authorized by government lest they become agents of governmental authority.[59] The animating ideas of the common law and civil society thus are similar: that there be a substantial civic realm, not of the state, whose actions are significantly concerned with increasing public well-being; that the organizations and associations of that realm be able to engage in social problemsolving without central direction; and that these organizations and associations to some degree be self-regulating.

EACH OF these elements of the public interest can be restated in an institutional form, which provides sufficient precision to guide the efforts of lawmakers involved in giving the public interest concrete meaning. To serve the public interest means to secure political institutions that control faction, that are deliberative in form, that secure rights, and that aggregate interests in a politically equal fashion. It further means to secure private-property-based market institutions that create widely available and at least moderately remunerative work, and whose political counterparts give significant discretion and inducements to controllers of productive assets. Serving the public interest also means securing institutions that facilitate creating and maintaining a vibrant civil society in which nongovernmental forms of cooperation flourish.

The emphasis in this conception of the public interest is on creating, if necessary, and otherwise securing the crucial institutions—constitutive institutions—that give the regime its characteristic manner of working.[60] Serving the public interest helps bring into being a political way of life that has at its center a free and equal people engaged in a form of self-government that is limited in what it can do. More generally, to serve the public interest of a political order whose citizens wish for a good regime is to create and secure the institutions that help constitute the regime. In the case of Americans, it means to work for the realization of a commercial republic and its attendant conception of liberal justice. The realization of the regime is the realization of our wish to be a certain sort of people.[61]

In addition to its normative character, the public interest of any good regime—in this case, of a commercial republic—has a strongly empirical cast. Its content is given by identifying the constitutive institutions of the regime and what is needed to create and secure them. Its empirical character helps to discipline discussion of its content by lawmakers (as well as by public-spirited citizens, constitutional theorists, and statesmen). Not everything supported by a large group of citizens, nor for that matter any otherwise desirable state of affairs, is in the public interest. Although certainly complex in character and requiring substantial effort to give it concrete meaning, the public interest has a relatively small number of elements. For this reason it can direct the attention and energy of those who care about its realization. Otherwise, this institutional conception of the public interest would go the way of most other candidates for the honor, becoming one more piece of empty rhetoric trotted out in civic celebrations and in the race for political advantage.

My definition of the public interest helps us define faction. This should increase our confidence in the meaning given to the public interest because it provides a way of dealing with the fundamental question of how to distinguish acceptable assertions of group interest from group behavior that is a danger to republican government. That the aims of such groups are "adverse to the rights of citizens" presents few problems of definition so long as there is agreement on at least a basic bundle of rights that we all have, as there in fact appears to be. But what about actions that are "adverse... to the permanent and aggregate interests of the community?"[62] We now have an answer. Those groups who aim at undercutting the elements of the public interest are factions. Thus, if their intentions are to weaken or eliminate the devices needed to prevent faction; to make deliberative lawmaking significantly harder; to increase inequality beyond what a moderate amount allows for; to undercut the political equality necessary for an attractive aggregative politics; to prevent asset controllers from having significant discretion in controlling their assets or from receiving any inducements to invest; or to make it harder for civil associations to form—then they are factions. They are transformed from the interest groups that a commercial republican form of government is designed to protect into groups that the design of republican government must control.[63]

Understanding much of the public interest of a commercial republic requires no heroic discernment on the part of the lawmaker (or citizen, theorist, or statesman).[64] Its elements are deeply rooted in the ordinary experience of the collective life of a people who have already realized to some degree a commercial republic. The desirability of market institutions that provide steady work for at least moderately remunerative wages is rooted in the experience of a society where those without work are marginalized, relegated to the sidelines not only of the economy but of the polity and community as well. Also, experience of the business world suggests that those who run businesses need discretion if resources are to be used intelligently. Similarly, in a society that accords some measure of individual liberty, few need to be instructed in the need for political institutions to protect rights, and that the strong should not be allowed to use government to devour the weak. Nor do many need much reminding of the importance of political equality in a republic; or of the need for lawmakers to attach at least some value to serving the public interest if lawmaking is to be composed of anything other than insider deals; or of the necessity for a free people to manage a significant part of its affairs without direction from government.

Knowing these things, however, is a far cry from acting on them. The public interest cannot be served without the right sort of politics, a matter we need to consider at length.[65] Regardless, those who share the aspiration to see a fully realized commercial republic must wish that this republic be the best it can be. This means keeping in good repair the institutions that would provide its distinctive character. Therefore, lawmaking in the public interest must, for example, concern itself with fostering a public-spirited citizenry and a moderate level of economic equality. Doing so helps to secure the institutions necessary to a commercial republic. In the broadest terms, it is serving the public interest that makes a commercial republic possible—that secures a regime whose institutions help to realize liberal justice.

We may say, then, that the public interest is both "subjective" and "objective": it derives from the citizenry's aspiration to realize a certain kind of regime whose lawmaking must take a particular form if it is to remain that sort of regime. The content of the public interest does not depend for its fundamental features on agreement among the citizenry or on aggregating their preferences.[66] While it does depend on our having political aspirations, it may be that a significant number of Americans will disagree with the account of the public interest offered here. Although that is not likely, their disagreement in and of itself has no bearing on whether this account is correct.[67] This will be especially clear if these dissenters share the aspiration to realize fully a commercial republic. On the account given here, they simply will have misunderstood what is required.

Nothing said here precludes extensive disagreement about the concrete meaning of the public interest: to know its elements is not to know how best to interpret them in particular cases. Theoretical arguments that focus on the kind of justice a regime pursues and the character of its constitutive institutions, on the one hand, and empirical investigations that ascertain what is necessary to create and secure these institutions, on the other, cannot be so powerful as to end all disagreement. They provide, instead, a principled way to carry on the discussion. Moreover, disagreement over the specific interpretation of the public interest need not be worrying; it is likely to indicate a healthy concern for its concrete meaning.

The substance of the public interest is thus defined not by abstract considerations of justice or other moral-political values, but by a political theory that looks to the character of political regimes. A people wishing to secure a flourishing commercial republic and the liberal justice it promises must be committed to serving some version of the public interest as it has been sketched here. Wishing the one, they must, if they are instrumentally rational, wish the other.[68] The public interest is how we talk about normative matters given the world as it is and plausibly might be, and the means that we have to act within it. It is in giving concrete meaning to the public interest—attending to the complex business of seeing what will work to serve it, and revising the weight given to its normative components in light of such investigation—that the real work of lawmaking as a normative undertaking gets done.

The spirit of the conception of the public interest offered here is nicely captured by a remark of Neil MacCormick's who ties this sort of view of the public interest to a "long spun-out thread in Western thought" that "politically-oriented societies . . . each have a 'common good' not in principle divisible into individual goods, but a condition of them."[69] A more or less fully realized good political regime is the foundation for the realization of the particular goods of the individuals that comprise that regime.

It would be odd indeed if something very much like what I have described were not the public interest of a good political regime, and of a commercial republic in particular. If the regime is good, so must the institutions be that help define its character. Again, to wish for one is to wish for the other. It would be equally odd if regimes did not have any public interest: what it takes to realize a good regime is surely its public interest, and thus all good regimes must have one.

RIGHTS AND THE PUBLIC INTEREST

In the preceding discussion, the task of securing rights has been absorbed into the effort to serve the public interest. More broadly, the value of rights does not stem from something valued over and above a republican regime.[70] Rights do not provide a standard external to the regime, a means by which to judge it. Rather, their value ultimately stems from the value of the regime itself.[71] This, in turn, is what allows us to say that rights are part of the regime's public interest, not values set out to limit what can be done in its service.[72]

The institutional conception of the public interest also tells us why rights should be treated in this fashion. To serve the public interest means to create and secure political institutions whose workings give life to rights. Conceived in this fashion, rights are relations,[73] not absolute claims against those who may wish to control our behavior. Rights, that is to say, are properties of a political regime, not of individuals, and indicate in part how that regime should function.[74] They are best understood, therefore, as one among several good features of a political order, and the problem for good lawmaking is to determine the best balance among them. Moreover, once we understand rights as institutionalized relationships—one of several important ones that, in the present case, constitute a commercial republic— it is implausible that one kind of relation can be said to outweigh all others, a matter to which I will return just below.

The merit of treating rights as part of the public interest is also suggested by the point made earlier—that to secure rights means to secure equal rights—and that this, in turn, requires the exercise of political authority. If rights are essentially negative, bulwarks of some sort against the power of the state, then it is natural to think of them as independent of state action. But if we see that rights need to be secured, and that this requires governmental action, then it is more natural to balance efforts to secure rights with other necessary exercises of state authority.

Opposing the view that rights should be assimilated to the public interest, it has been argued that rights are transconventional: they do not derive from a commitment to a specific sort of regime and its public interest. Indeed, they are in some sense natural or universal and thus do not derive from politics at all, which must be local and whose values can only be conventional. In the strongest form, rights are said to be not only transconventional but "trumps." They outweigh any considerations of the public interest, whether understood as the common good or as an aggregation of interests.[75]

Not all those who believe that rights are transconventional also think that they are trumps. Rights do not derive from politics, they might put it, but they do not outweigh all other political considerations. Those who take this stance[76] need have no quarrel with my argument that rights are best understood as part of the public interest of a liberal republic. In effect, they do the same when, as they must, they consider how to weigh rights against whatever conception of the public interest or other values they hold. More importantly, such advocates of universal rights need not worry that assimilating rights to the public interest makes them merely conventional. The foundation for the value of rights in the public interest view lies with the value of a republican regime, and I have argued that the distinction between good and bad regimes is not itself conventional.

Moreover, it is worth noting in this context that nothing that has been said here implies that there are no transconventionally grounded rights. It is probable that there are such rights, which are tied to preventing cruelty, preserving bodily integrity, and securing a substantial degree of autonomous choice in our lives. Each of these is a necessary feature of personhood, which is an attractive starting point for almost any discussion of political value. Together, they point to preventing the kinds of humiliations that deny the value of our lives, and thus our efforts to give meaning to them, and they promote the dignity of persons conferred by the ability to reason. Michael Ignatieff puts it well:

> Why do we need an idea of God in order to believe that human beings should not be beaten, tortured, coerced, indoctrinated, or in any way sacrificed against their will? These intuitions derive from our experience of pain and our capacity to imagine the pain of others.... That we are capable of this thought experiment—i.e., that we possess the faculty of imagining the pain and degradation done to other human beings as if it were our own—is simply a fact about us as a species.[77]

Talking about rights brings specificity to transconventional values, and may be understood as pointing to features of our existence that give us claims on others. Rights consist of the minimum set of transconventional values that we are obliged to honor. Each of us is to forbear from actions that will dishonor these values—and thus we are all equals in respect of both being protected by the values and being obligated to respect them.[78]

The principal objections to understanding rights as an element of the public interest will likely come from those who think that rights are both transconventional and trumps. Few such theorists would go so far as to say that rights essentially have infinite weight. But some are certainly drawn to the idea that rights are very weighty indeed.[79] Again, the question here should be whether there is a way to avoid talking about the value of rights as against other desirable features of a political regime. A convincing case that rights really are trumps, meaning that they outrank all other considerations, or, what amounts to the same thing, that they are lexically prior to other values, is difficult to make.[80] Thus, if it is argued that rights must be served first and made fully secure before anything else can be done, this leaves us with the problem of how we know when rights are completely secured. This cannot be measured easily, if at all. Moreover, must there be a state of perfect liberty before we aim at anything else? An affirmative answer is absurd, not least because such a state looks to be beyond us as human beings. For rights really to be trumps, we must be willing to incur any amount of negative consequences for other values to which we are committed. This is political theory for those with strong stomachs.[81]

The crucial point is that, while each of us has certain irreducible and inalienable claims on others, we have other concerns besides such rights, and, while we cannot abrogate rights in the service of some other purpose, how we interpret and weigh them depends on what else we care about. Consider a right to equal respect. The inclination of most of us is probably to say that this is an important right indeed, and if the right is being violated by an effort to degrade a group of people—say, by forcing them to clean sidewalks with a toothbrush—then enforcing that right comes first before any other sorts of gains that might be made by ignoring the humiliation.[82] But it is much less clear how much weight should be given to the right to equal respect if it is understood as requiring that each of us must be addressed in a respectful way.

The upshot of this and related considerations is that it is plausible to claim that rights, especially insofar as they reflect transconventional values, should be given special attention. They ought to be considered early in the deliberations of lawmakers and weigh heavily in their decisions. But beyond that, the problem is largely one to be solved by the exercise of practical political reason by political authorities. This is especially obvious if, as I have argued, the effort to serve rights is best understood as an effort to secure rights-creating institutions. The practice of rights creation strongly suggests that taking rights seriously is a lot more complicated than arguing that respecting them is extremely important.

The public interest, then, is a complex mix of the transconventional and the empirical. It is not about what the people and those who speak for them happen at the moment to agree on. But given the broadness of the values on which the public interest rests, and especially that the meaning and weight given to the elements of the public interest changes with the times, its interpretation must include conventional elements.

LAWMAKING AND CONSTITUTIONAL THEORY

Because the public interest focuses on the constitutive institutions that help give the regime its character, the task of lawmaking in the public interest[83] and the task of constitutional theory mirror one another. Both are concerned with the appropriate working of these constitutive institutions; and both concern themselves with the manner of association that makes for the kind of people Americans wish to be. Constitutional theory and lawmaking have as their ultimate purpose constituting a free and equal people engaged in self-government where political authority is limited and where a property-based market system operates.

Still, lawmaking is the principal means by which the constitutive institutions set out in constitutional theory are given life. The constitutional theory of a republican regime thus focuses on a reflexive process: lawmakers aim at securing the constitutive institutions defined by the public interest; and, in doing so, they shape the political patterns that affect how they themselves make law. The politics should be nonfactional, have both deliberative and aggregative elements, take place in the context of a vibrant civil society, and so forth. The elements of the public interest, understood as centered on the constitutive institutions of the regime, define, in effect, how republican lawmaking itself should be organized. In addition to defining the public interest, therefore, constitutional theory's central concern is an analysis of the politics that prompts lawmakers to act in this reflexive fashion—namely, to legislate in the public interest.[84] I turn to an account of this constitutional politics in the succeeding chapters; before doing so, however, additional features of republican lawmaking in a fully realized republican regime are worth noting.

Republican lawmaking in the public interest, I have said, is reflexive. It consists of looking in an expansive, regime-encompassing way at itself. Lawmakers trying to serve the public interest will often find themselves trying to bring off that quintessential political act—lifting themselves up by their own bootstraps. Political reform by definition requires lawmakers to move beyond where they presently are and rise above the pressures and incentives at work to ensure their conformity with present practices. Republican lawmakers, therefore, are likely regularly to try to reform institutions to reduce faction at the same time as strong factional pressures are brought to bear on them. And they must regularly seek to increase the extent of deliberative lawmaking in a legislature where particular interests flourish.

At the center of lawmaking in the public interest will be the "tensions" or "contradictions" that reflect the features of the regime. It is due to these fault lines of the public interest that the efforts to secure one constitutive institution makes it more difficult to secure others. Securing the institutions of civil society, for example, may pull in the opposite direction from strengthening institutions that are designed to secure rights: the autonomy that a vibrant associational life requires may free these associations to undercut civil rights. Similarly, strengthening the separation of powers in the service of preventing factional government may make it harder to maintain political institutions that give life to political equality: to secure such equality likely requires concentrated legal authority.[85]

Perhaps the most difficult of such contradictions arises from the need to keep up a steady flow of the kinds of inducements to asset controllers. This is necessary if there are to be effective market institutions and is part of business's privileged position, as is lawmakers giving the most careful attention to the views of asset controllers on how to operate an enterprise-based market system. This last is itself one of the inducements to significant investment, and it ensures that the other inducements offered are ones that asset controllers find attractive. As a result of these features of the business–state relationship, lawmakers, hoping to keep in good repair the economic institutions of the regime, will regularly be tempted to act in an overenthusiastic manner. Thus, the content of our present laws has been largely indifferent to and sometimes actively hostile to fostering the public-spirited citizenry that is necessary if lawmaking is to have a deliberative quality. Since much in the politics of a commercial republic will cut against deliberative lawmaking—attending to particular interests will remain high on lawmakers' agenda—there must be strong countervailing forces at work. Large-scale asset-controllers, sensing that fostering a public-spirited citizenry is likely to require greater economic equality than is presently the case, have at least been unenthusiastic about doing so. So, yes, as Bernard Crick says, the bourgeois state contains inner contradictions, and that is its point.

THE PUBLIC INTEREST AND LIMITS ON THE PEOPLE'S RULE

Lawmaking in the public interest ties the exercise of governmental power to a conception of governmental purposes. By delineating these purposes, the public interest defines the appropriate exercise of political authority. And it does so for an active, limited government, which is the inevitable result of a regime of popular control where the citizenry is heterogeneous and has freedom of association. Active, limited government is also a consequence of a popular regime whose citizens and lawmakers believe that there is a public interest and that, as such, it must be served. Indeed, it is difficult to see how else, except through a conception of the public interest, that the ideas of active and limited government can be combined. In a well-ordered republican regime, lawmaking gives concrete meaning to the limits on governmental authority by giving definition to the public interest; and it is active in the effort to serve that interest. Limited government need not be small or passive government. So long as government has clear purposes to guide lawmaking, and lawmakers attempt to give specific meaning to them, government is limited—and probably in the only fashion possible in a regime that has genuinely popular government as its heart. The public interest as it has been defined here treads a line between, on the one hand, active government that is a result of responding to whatever claims significant numbers of citizens and powerful interest groups make, and, on the other hand, passive government that is indifferent to the common purposes of the society.

The "objective" qualities of the public interest, then, provide the limits on the people's rule. If they aspire to be a commercial republican regime, they cannot rule as they please. If the constitutional design is successful, and there is a sustained effort to give the public interest concrete meaning, the people will be engaged in self-limitation—their rule principled, and hence according to law.[86] The principles, however, are not specific destinations but institutional capabilities, the specific forms of relation among citizens that constitutive institutions help to create.

The commercial republican public interest is capacious. A narrowly conceived one could hardly serve in any complex and heterogeneous society. But capacious does not mean empty. The public interest is broad enough to invite discussion and clear enough to indicate what kind of arguments are appropriate in defining its concrete meaning.[87] Thus, it is plain that arguments for the passage of laws that simply assert that they serve the interests of major constituencies are not arguments in the public interest. Nor are arguments that all those affected by laws should derive something like equal benefits from them. Thus, while there is no single right answer to the concrete meaning of the public interest, there are wrong ones. The public interest points to the kind of reasons that are to count in lawmaking. It is not an empty phrase—invoked whenever we wish to argue for the use of public authority for reasons that are not in themselves likely to be very convincing.

The various elements of the public interest have such a status because they derive from the liberal justice at which a republican regime aims or because they are constitutive elements of such a regime. The elements are valuable, therefore, quite apart from whether their value is widely recognized by the citizenry. They are in the interests of citizens just to the degree they wish for a republican regime—even though they may be unable to say what that entails. These interests are then public interests because they follow from the citizenry's aspiration to be a commercial republic. A fully realized republican regime is government by the people, but it is not simple majoritarian government, nor is it a government that takes its bearings from what the people say they want at any given moment. If the public interest is regularly served, however, it gives the great mass of citizens the chance to fashion a life of their own choosing. While a liberal regime is not neutral between ways of life,[88] it can accommodate and even foster a range wide enough to suit most citizens. The public interest, in *this* sense at least, will be the subject of wide agreement.

A commercial republic is one of several kinds of good political regimes. Even if we believe that one or another of these good regimes suits us better as Americans than a commercial republic, we still are obligated to defend our aspirations and the republic that issues from it. More precisely, we are obligated to defend the commercial republic in argument and deed so long as doing so does not prevent any of us from advocating the merits of other good regimes and the steps needed to realize them. If this is so, the public interest ought to have at least some hold on those who wish for something other than a commercial republic. It is the public interest for them as well, at least until another good regime is capable of being born.

6

A Public Interest Politics I

OUR ASPIRATIONS to be a fully realized commercial republic point to features of our constitutional politics that need modifying. We rely too heavily on the Supreme Court to carry the deliberative burden of the regime and, concomitantly, have allowed Congress to become the permanent home of particular and narrow interests. The result is that the public interest has, at best, been given only intermittent attention and truncated definition. This, in turn, has meant that the constitutive institutions of commercial republican government are in poor repair. For example, sustained consideration has not been given to limiting the political privilege of large-scale business. Thus, efforts to foster a market economy that provides a significant measure of at least moderately remunerative work have faltered. Nor have the qualities republican citizens need for deliberative lawmaking been given much attention. The same can be said about the other elements of the public interest, including the need for a strong deliberative politics at the center of the regime.

If our constitutional practice is flawed,[1] we must *in medias res* do for ourselves much the same thing that Madison and the founding generation did for themselves and their successors. We must set out a theory of political constitution to guide us in constituting ourselves in a manner that better serves the aspirations that have defined us as a people. We need a more compelling constitutional theory than even Madison provides if we are to strengthen the major political institutions that are weak but appropriately constituted; maintain those that are in good repair; and alter those that are significantly flawed.

The great question in this undertaking is whether we the people, acting through the organs of self-reflection that we ourselves have created (or at least assented to) can secure and strengthen the foundations of a commercial republican regime. This must be a self-levitating set of actions. A well-designed constitutional politics means that the public interest is regularly served. And since the public interest consists of creating and securing constitutive republican institutions, serving the public interest, in turn, means that such a constitutional politics would itself be strengthened: these constitutive political institutions are at the center of a constitutional politics, and to strengthen one is to strengthen the other. Thus, the heart of a theory of republican political constitution is an account of the politics that serves the public interest. In serving the public interest, we work to constitute ourselves as the people we wish to be. To the degree that the commercial republican institutions composing the public interest are realized, a free and equal people engaged in self-government is constituted.

I have already given an account of the public interest. The next step is to consider the central features of a constitutional politics to serve it.[2] Given that only a broad conception of the public interest can be set out, the aim of a design for a constitutional politics is to increase the odds that lawmaking regularly focuses on giving concrete meaning to the public interest. This is only likely to occur if lawmakers have substantial incentives to do so. Just occupying the office of lawmaker is not sufficient.

In developing our account of a well-ordered constitutional politics and of the constitutional theory that is to guide it, we can take our bearings from some remarks of Walter Lippmann. Commenting on the kind of vision we need to have in large-scale political reform, Lippmann said that we should look to the "latent promise in the actual world. . . . In the unfolding present man can be creative if his vision is gathered from the promise of actual things."[3] The task of providing a theory of political constitution, then, is made more manageable not only because we can build on the thought of Madison—we may say that it is a neo-Madisonian theory we are constructing—but because our existing practices are not in such a state of disrepair and corruption that they cannot serve as starting points. As a popular regime with a long history and established institutions that have not simply failed, however imperfectly they have operated, we need not look to a Great Legislator to provide us with a new start.

A PUBLIC INTEREST POLITICS

A precondition for a public interest politics is the control of faction. Unless lawmakers are largely free from its grip—they cannot be completely so since faction cannot be eliminated—they will be unable to concern themselves with the public interest. Madison remains the preeminent teacher here. Although there are significant flaws in his analysis, as we have seen, his is a compelling view of how best to approach the problem of faction.

Beyond some remedies for these flaws, which will emerge as the account of constitutional politics unfolds over the remaining chapters, we need here only add a few comments to Madison's account.

In particular, a fully developed politics of the public interest both strengthens the backbone and informs the efforts of those who aim to resist faction—in contrast to those who simply engage in defending the prerogatives of their institutions. Moreover, these same actors, who resist factional government from an understanding of what it portends, are likely to be more acute students of the public interest. They will better appreciate the importance of various elements of the public interest as they consider what will follow if factions are politically successful.

It is also worth emphasizing that because a theory of republican political constitution cannot do without a conception of the public interest, republican politics cannot only be designed to prevent one of the worst of political outcomes, that is, factional rule. The politics of a republican regime must also include governing—that is, acting. As Hamilton commented, "we forget how much good may be prevented, and how much ill produced, by the power of hindering the doing of what may be necessary, of keeping affairs in the same unfavorable posture in which they may happen to stand at particular periods."[4] What is valuable enough to be guarded is worth actively serving. Said differently, republican lawmaking must be concerned not only with disciplining the exercise of public power. A great deal of damage is done to people's lives by private power: the strong really do attempt to gobble up the weak. Thus, republican lawmaking must discipline private power as well. Nor should this be surprising, for the essence of liberalism is subjecting power to principle and this includes private power.

Turning to the politics of the public interest itself, unless a significant portion of republican political life is devoted to giving concrete meaning to the public interest, the regime must rely for serving it on the by-products of a largely self-interested politics. This reliance at first glance looks attractive. As Madison teaches, self-interest is a sturdy motive, and further, much of modern economic theory is built on it. However, while economists can provide themselves with an attractive life by pointing out the beneficial consequences of self-interest, theorists of a republican political constitution are not so lucky, at least if they think there is a substantive public interest. A careful assessment of efforts to harness a process driven by self-interest to serve that public interest would likely reveal that the creation and maintenance of the process itself—which is part of the public interest as outlined here—often escape the net.[5] It is apparently assumed by many partisans of self-interest that the social processes driven by it come into being through a kind of immaculate conception, which is followed by something equally wondrous—automatic institutional maintenance. Thus, the magic hand is added to the invisible one. Giving concrete meaning to the public interest, however, is too important a matter to leave solely in the hands of the wonderful. Whatever its limits, conscious attention is needed.

How then should republican political institutions be arranged to promote direct consideration of the public interest? If a central task of republican lawmaking is to give concrete meaning to the elements of the public interest, lawmakers must be capable of reasoning about how these elements can be brought to bear in particular choices. They must deliberate.[6] We can say, therefore, that a central feature of the theory of political constitution embodied in the American Republic is a design for a deliberative core made up of institutions capable of deliberative ways of lawmaking. A deliberative politics, however, is not an intrinsically valuable part of republican government. It is instead necessary for republican government because it is the best way to give concrete meaning to the public interest. The design of this deliberative core encompasses how the separation of powers should work, since we will need to improve on the institutional design we have inherited, strengthening, reforming, and maintaining its components where appropriate.

In a fully realized American republican regime, as Akhil Amar says, "all three branches of government...are agencies of the People. No branch...can uniquely claim to speak for [the] People themselves; no branch is uniquely representative."[7] This was Alexander Hamilton's view at the founding of the Republic when he said that the Constitution does "not suppose a superiority of the judicial to the legislative power."[8] With specific reference to the Supreme Court, Justice Ruth Bader Ginsburg pointedly comments that judges "play an *interdependent* part in our democracy. They participate in the dialogue with other organs of government and with the people as well."[9]

The separation of powers is thus not only a political device geared to prevent factional rule. Properly designed, it can, through the different political bases and grants of power to each branch, also facilitate broad-scale reasoning about the concrete meaning of the public interest. The separation of powers, then, is best understood as a way of distributing authority in order to facilitate appropriate governmental action[10]—that is, lawmaking in the public interest. Because the task of giving concrete meaning to the public interest is complex, having multiple voices to reflect different perspectives is an advantage. We might reach the same conclusion by asking whether a convincing case can be made that the people acting as constituent sovereign should, instead of the separation of powers, prefer that law be made either by a simple majority of citizens and those who speak for them, or by an appointed group of officials who are to be the custodians of a tradition of inquiry into the appropriate limits on state power. As constituent sovereign, the people would surely want both—lawmaking that reflects current majority opinion about what the state should do, and lawmaking that is informed by experience with how proposed state action might be wrong. A thoughtful citizenry would also want to hear in lawmaking the voice of an agent who sees the need for immediate action. The people might reasonably conclude that the public interest is sufficiently complex that it cannot be entrusted to only one agent, to only one voice. A better system would amalgamate the partial views of the people's agents into a more comprehensive view. Properly organized, this is what the separation of powers can do.

A central feature of the institutional design for a fully realized American republic should then be one of separate institutions sharing powers. Guizot makes the essential point:

> [L]aw needs to be sought; it is a difficult task to discover and practice it. But, any isolated will, any independent force is reluctant to do this work; it must be constrained to do so and constantly led to it by necessity. Let then that de facto sovereignty which must command be the result of an effort, of the confrontation of independent and equal powers capable of reciprocally imposing on each other the obligation of seeking the truth in common in order to come together in its bosom.[11]

The separation of powers, again, is a *grant* of authority to do something—secure the public interest—and, being a grant, it is not unlimited. But it *is* a grant—designed to ensure that the authority is used under specific terms.[12] In the process of giving meaning to the public interest in a fully realized republican regime, there must be extensive cooperation between the branches: it is the whole deliberative core that is to do the work. Given that each branch of government is an agent of the people, no branch is able to coerce the others. Each needs to rely on its ability to argue persuasively what the concrete meaning of the public interest is.

In a fully realized republic, disputes among the branches about the meaning of the public interest are unlikely to come to a rapid conclusion. This is how it should be, for the presence of an impasse would not be immediately apparent. Furthermore, the public struggle and debate among the branches will be educative: the citizenry will become gradually apprised of the contours of their disagreement. Moreover, an impasse means that the people must decide: they are, after all, the constituent sovereign.[13] But there will be no formal way for the people to so act, unless by constitutional amendment, which, if past experience is any guide, is a difficult, clumsy process that should not be often invoked.

And yet there is an alternative that would allow the people to speak as constituent sovereign albeit in an informal way. As the argument among the branches proceeds and the citizenry is drawn in, groups of citizens and opinion leaders can make their views known in the usual manner—giving support where they believe it is merited, ridiculing positions with which they disagree, pronouncing themselves to be bored by the whole matter, and so forth. As the balance of opinion becomes clearer, this in itself could induce one of the branches to modify its views and bring the matter to a close. But it is more likely to take one or more elections for the president and the Congress to make clear what the balance of opinion is. If, after several elections, the division of citizen opinion were to remain constant, this is as good an indication as is likely to be possible of how the citizenry as constituent sovereign views the matter. After such elections, it is probable that the branches of government will find a way out of the impasse: electoral advantage will lie in doing so for many elected officials.[14] In all this, the formal constitutional separation of powers is an advantage. All broadly democratic regimes have at least some informal division of powers but only a formal one is designed to force public discussion of disagreement among the branches.[15]

For the separation of powers to work in this deliberative fashion, statesmanship may not be required. In any case, as Madison argued, it is too often absent. But a kind of prudent ambition *is* required, one in which the leading members of each branch work to ensure that their views on the public interest are heard: "the interest of the man must be connected with the constitutional rights of the place."[16] Also crucial is that leading members of the branches have that degree of prudence necessary to recognize the dangers of prolonged public dispute; similarly, they must see the importance of not taking all disagreement among the branches to a bitter conclusion. They would also need to weigh these considerations against the merits of their own branch's case. The machine "can go of itself,"[17] but if it is to do more than limp along and not crash into all kinds of barriers, it needs the right sort of people to operate it. Institutional design has its limits. It can provide incentives for struggle and debate, but the quality of the leaders is also important, a point that will regularly assert itself as our discussion of republican institutions proceeds.

Because we cannot expect the regular presence of a sufficient number of political office holders whose understanding of the public interest of the republic is profound, whose allegiance to it is great, whose ability to act on it is large, and whose inclination to serve it is deep, in designing a republican constitution we must make good use of the capabilities that are likely to be available. We also cannot look to any one institution to speak for the people. The chance that most or all of those who serve in a particular branch of government would have these sterling and startling characteristics is virtually nil. It may not be the case that the greater the number of voices the better. But it almost surely is the case that all the voices coming from a single institution—with the same limited set of concerns, history, and tradition—is not a good bet for lawmaking that will serve the public interest.

Let us now fill in this sketch of how a fully realized republican separation of powers would work. In particular, we need an account of the roles of the particular branches of government: what in their character makes each branch fit for its role, and what may push them into actions that weaken the deliberative core of the regime.

THE HIGH COURT

In considering which agents are to speak for the people, there can be little doubt that, among those who are capable of practical reasoning, we should start with the Supreme Court. Whatever else might be said about it, the Court is the most visibly deliberative institution in the American Republic as it is now constituted[18] and it has a long history of attempts to define the limits of public power. In general, the Court has on occasion shown itself to be capable of serious reflection on the foundations of republican government, even if its arguments have generally failed to take account of the several elements of the public interest.

One possibility for the design of a separation of powers system capable of deliberation is to anchor it in a simple division of labor between the high court and the legislature, with the judicial body bearing most of the burden. Reasons have already been given in chapter 4 as to why such an arrangement is unattractive. Perhaps the most important reason is that many of the essential elements of the intellectual tradition from which the Supreme Court takes it bearings can be arrived at without thinking about the "law." They can be deduced from the essential features of liberal political theory and, indeed, have been. High courts that are expected to concern themselves with large-scale constitutive matters are, therefore, best understood as political bodies with a particular kind of view of such questions.[19] There may be real advantages in having a significant set of constitutive decisions made by courts. But this is only to say that there are a variety of ways to settle political questions politically.[20]

To these arguments we can add that, because serving the public interest includes securing the foundations of deliberative lawmaking,[21] doing so requires focusing on the character of the citizenry. Deliberative lawmaking, as we have seen, is unlikely to occur without a public-spirited citizenry.[22] A high court may have much to say about, for example, the prerogatives and responsibilities of citizenship. But it is unlikely either to be interested in or compelling in its remarks about, say, whether republican citizenship requires a certain distribution of wealth or employment. On the broad relation between citizenship and the organization of economic life, a high court can have no privileged view, while, at least in principle, a legislature will have much of value to say. As regards another element of the public interest—promoting widespread economic prosperity through an enterprise-based market system—the point is much the same. A high court would have important things to say because the question of property rights is sure to arise. But there should be little disagreement that a legislature must also have a significant role. In decisions about how to secure the foundations of the constitutive institutions of the regime, both legislature and court must play a role.

In the same vein, even in a well-ordered republican regime, the high court will be "conservative."[23] This also suggests that there should be limits on how much it can be relied on in any design for the deliberative core. One of the central concerns of any high court is likely to be consistency of doctrine, if only to make good on its natural claim that it decides cases on the basis of reasoned deliberation. It will generally be reluctant to make great departures from established doctrine and practice. This conservative character of the high court offers advantages. Compared to the legislature, a high court is likely to be less hasty. This is beneficial not least because, if the rules under which we plan our lives change constantly, rational people are likely to use their resources in ways other than for investing in the future. Still, there will be occasions when significant changes must be mounted if the public interest is to be served.

A high court is apt to be conservative in another sense. The kinds of arguments it hears and the social backgrounds from which its judges are likely to be drawn, when added to its concern for precedent, suggest that the courts' judicial deliberations are unlikely to canvass anything like a full range of views pertinent to any judicial decision. Thus, for example, arguments about the effects of the distribution of wealth and the organization of economic production on the quality of republican political life would probably not be given a substantial hearing. It is particularly likely that any American high court—concerned mostly, as it should be, with disputes between individuals and conflicts between individuals and the state—will find it difficult to assimilate such arguments to what will be its more usual concern with the rights and legitimate expectations of individuals in social interactions. And yet the proper organization of production and the distribution of wealth are elements of the public interest.

At the broadest level, the strengths and weakness of a fully developed republican high court are likely to be those of a body composed of lawyers trained in the common law tradition and having life-time tenure. Their training and experience as judges are likely to lead them to think of the society's central problems as concerning the relations between individuals or between those, like corporations, who can be so construed. And because they are unlikely to be elected to the bench, they will find it relatively easy to value continuity in their decisions. In a fully realized republican regime, such a high court can be described as a "common law legislature."[24] This perhaps sounds like an oxymoron, for we ordinarily do not associate the making of common law with a legislature; moreover, common law and statute law are often juxtaposed. But the term is useful for conveying that, even in a well-ordered republican regime, the high court will be a political body making collective decisions about the content of the public interest.[25] It cannot avoid doing so, given the understanding of the public interest I have been proposing. Hence we should think of it as a legislature of sorts, which would arrive at its decisions differently from the more familiar legislative body. At its best it would draw on a large body of reflection by judges and other juridically minded thinkers that is rooted in a long line of cases about the appropriate uses of political power and the limits on private power. Hence the term "common law." We might say that the common law of this "legislature" is constitutional law.[26] Talking about a common law legislature conjures up a body whose decisions, being deeply rooted in reflection and practice, are not to be regularly judged according to whether they are approved of by overtly political bodies. They are simply good practice, tested by experience and fitted to the problem at hand.

The attractions of a fully realized high court will arise from its being an inheritor of a long and sophisticated tradition concerning the proper exercise of public and private power, and from its ability to emphasize the value of continuity in public decision. Its claim, in the American case, to speak on large public matters has been settled in its favor. Hence it is important to be clear just how that settled role should be understood. The Supreme Court has successfully established its claim to review whether legislation conforms to the Constitution. But it is not a settled matter that the Court is supreme in this regard, having the final say about constitutionality.[27] The reservations about such a role reflect in part the sense that the Court should not be supreme in interpreting the public interest, and the impossibility of disentangling constitutional matters from efforts to give concrete meaning to that interest.

Thus, while a republican high court may be a republican schoolmaster,[28] it is ill equipped to be the only one. Its contact with the citizenry is infrequent at best and its discussion of the public interest uses language that ordinary citizens are unlikely to comprehend.[29] The appropriate role for the high court follows from an account of the whole regime, particularly from the shape of its constitutional politics. Depending on how that is understood, the role of the court will vary: what we ask of it cannot be settled by simply talking about "the law," whether constitutional or otherwise.

On balance, in a fully realized American Republic, the present Supreme Court's concern with individual liberties and the smoothing of transactions between individuals should be strengthened, while its intermittent claims to be the sole arbiter of constitutive matters should be restrained. Just how to do this is not clear. What *is* clear is that any such combination of strengthening and restraining cannot be achieved by altering the institutional design of the high court itself (there isn't much to alter). However, some restructuring of the whole federal court system might help, particularly of the processes by which cases arrive at the high court. Even more potent would be reform of the law schools so that prospective judges are educated in liberal republican political theory and through it learn that a vital public interest politics cannot be centered on a high court. Indeed, an overbearing court will subvert it. That we must look to the cast of mind of lawyers and judges should not be surprising. As one of the greatest republican theorists indicated, we must think about the spirit of the laws. Why not then think about the spirit of the lawyers?

This view of the role of the high court in the separation of powers will likely be resisted by those I have termed "legalists." Enough has been said in chapter 4 to indicate why their general position on the design of republican government is badly flawed. But my position on the separation of powers will also likely be resisted by many contemporary American liberal believers in the activist state who have placed their faith in the Supreme Court as the principal vehicle through which the American regime should realize their own political-moral vision. Their position, however, has been undercut by recent developments, and it is now clear that the high court as a liberal engine can be thrown into reverse. Consequently, liberals are tempted to call for reining in the Court, and many have succumbed, even if it does not square with their previously expressed preference for an activist Court. In short, there is reason to doubt whether the views of many liberals rest on a carefully considered account of the role of the Court in a fully realized republican separation of powers. They may now even be inclined to reject any principled view of the high court's competence, preferring instead to look to whatever branch promises at the moment to advance most the liberal cause.

Other contemporary liberals, having argued that liberalism rests on a marriage of law and moral theory, now are also likely to be discomforted by recent events. They must face the problem that moral philosophy comes in several flavors, some of which they gag on, and that a group of nine people cannot be trusted to always read the right philosophy books. Consider in this context Ronald Dworkin's argument that history has decided that the Supreme Court is the final arbiter of the Constitution. He claims that, if the view were accepted that other branches of government have something to say about the Constitution, then "the Supreme Court could not have decided, as it did in its *Brown* decision in 1954, that the equal protection clause outlaws racial segregation in public schools."[30] To which the obvious reply is "Why not?" If the Supreme Court does not have the final word, would the justices stop thinking about complex and difficult matters? One might just as easily argue the reverse and with a good deal more plausibility: not having the final word might make the Court take on even more demanding questions.

In the same vein, Dworkin attempts to scare those who adopt the position presented here by arguing that "religious independence and personal freedoms" are "almost universally thought not only sound but shining examples of our constitutional structure working at its best."[31] Is the argument that, absent the Court as final arbiter, we would not have these freedoms? This seems doubtful in the extreme, not least because these freedoms do not consist of nor rest on the words of Supreme Court decisions. Those decisions must be put into effect and, more or less by definition, this requires at least the acquiescence of a wide range of political authorities. So even if the acceptance of constitutional decisions by other branches of government is not formalized, in fact this is what is required—and we thus have the freedoms we do not merely because the Court says we do. Moreover, we could have those freedoms *without* a high court like ours. Other Western democracies do.

In general, the Supreme Court seems to exert a peculiar fascination for otherwise highly intelligent, learned students of republican government. They seem drawn into ever more complex and unconvincing arguments about why liberty and other good things require exactly the constitutional setup we have. As often as not, they continue by saying that the Court in interpreting the Constitution exercises a special kind of reasoning denied to lesser mortals; that such reasoning is learned in law schools; and that the heart of the law is moral theory—as if those who developed liberal democratic institutions never noticed that they were persons of a practical bent trying to secure a variety of liberties that political experience, their own and that of others, told them they should have. The most acute among them—Madison being a notable example—thought that their liberties rested on a politics rooted in a complex institutional design that, while dispersing power, also provided incentives for it to be assembled and employed in the service of liberty and other permanent interests of the community. We could do a lot worse than follow them.

Thus, no matter how unsettling it is to some, a substantial portion of the burden of republican self-limitation must be borne by the legislature, a matter to which I turn below. The people have reasonably deputized a high court to act as their agent in giving content to the public interest. Similarly, they have authorized it to announce when their agents, chosen through elections, are exercising political power in ways that undercut that interest. But unless we suppose that the only limits on government that we should care about are ones that courts are likely to feel comfortable talking about, placing the principal burden on a high court to define the limits of our rule means that we are imposing needless and ill-considered limits on ourselves. If we rely only on courts to bind us, we are likely to find it very difficult, for example, to act on the proposition that the public interest includes that our economic institutions should generate a modest level of economic equality. Yet a strong case can be made that this is so. A similar point could be made about other elements of the public interest.

Those who are now ready to cheer a convert to the conservative cause of judicial restraint might wish to pause here and consider my account of the public interest. I have already suggested that the public interest includes fostering a citizenry with a certain kind of character, one able to operate a republican regime. To serve such a public interest requires energetic government: a high court that believes its job is to parse the sentences of the Constitution in light of how people in the last quarter of the eighteenth century used words is unlikely to find such bracing governmental action very attractive. Judicial restraint is not coterminous with governmental restraint. Equally, if republican government cannot rest on an all-purpose high court, neither, as I will argue, can it rest on a legislature unwilling or unable—in part because it is the very inviting home of private economic interests—to concern itself with serving the public interest. In this respect far too many conservative thinkers cut off the argument about the substance of republican political constitution just as it gets interesting. After they argue that a high court must show restraint, their arguments mysteriously stop—as if everything else can be left as it is, including that the legislature shows little aptitude to legislate in the public interest. Friends of republican government ought instead to wonder just how the whole task of republican lawmaking should best be organized.

THE EXECUTIVE

In light of the need for a deliberative core in a fully realized American republic, what should we say about the presidency?[32] The primary thing to note is that the institutional presidency presently lacks a complex differentiation of views. This would almost certainly be the case even in a reconstituted republican regime because much the same forces would be at work. Those who directly work for the president do not typically bring with them large-scale policy positions and views of the public interest that differ substantially from his. They are largely chosen because of their compatibility with the president's views—and disagreement among them, while sometimes thought to be valuable by White House denizens and others, is often repressed so that the president and his administration can speak with a single voice. There is, to be sure, plenty of infighting within the institutionalized presidency and among the president's staff, but this is, as much as anything, about who is to get the president's ear. And while there is certain to be policy disagreements and even differences about larger matters, there is unlikely to be the wide range of views necessary for a vigorous discussion of the concrete meaning of the public interest. The result is that it is uncommon for the president and his administration to develop a view of the public interest that is tested through a process of regular and public argument in which there is a premium on making clear the reasoning behind their positions. They need not engage in such argument and, indeed, public discussion, not to mention disagreement, is likely to be politically costly. In short, the presidency is not a legislature. Montesquieu, one of the greatest theorists of the separation of powers, said that "an executive power belongs to the legislature only through its faculty of vetoing, it cannot enter into discussion of public matters."[33]

The presidency, then, is presently not structured to function as a deliberative institution, and even with the best will in the world it probably cannot and should not become one. Its virtues lie in its unity, as the founders of this Republic realized when they considered the question of whether the executive office might be composed of several members. The structure of the institution is such that the premium for those working in the administration is on getting their views to the president and convincing him to adopt them, rather than arguing them out with others. The president's policy advisors may be equals, but they are equals much in the way that courtiers are in the court of a king. It is only his ear that counts.

Of equal relevance to the presidency's contribution to the deliberative core of a well-ordered republic, the president—for two reasons—is likely to be impatient with limits on the use of governmental power: (1) As the only official elected by the whole of the citizenry, a president can easily think of himself as a kind of tribune, speaking for the people as a whole. Having ascertained the will of the people, he might conclude that action is all that is required, not careful consideration of whether the specific purposes to be served and the means of doing so actually serve the public interest. (2) As a single official, the president will find it relatively easy to act, a disposition that is reinforced by the task-oriented nature of the executive job. The president, more so than the other branches, will be inclined to fall (or jump) into the belief that if he wants something done—especially if he thinks that the mass of citizens approve it—then it ought to be done. This is not a good foundation on which to build a deliberative separation of powers that will give careful consideration to whether governmental action serves the public interest.[34]

None of this means that the presidency in a fully developed republican regime would not have much to contribute to the struggle and debate with the other branches over the meaning of the public interest. Indeed, it has and will continue to have advantages that largely stem from a view of the public interest that is, at bottom, the product of a single mind: the loss of comprehensiveness in giving concrete meaning to the public interest is likely to be compensated for by the consistency of vision that is the natural corollary of that single mind. In any case, the president, of course, is likely to be a vigorous participant in lawmaking, able to talk and act with clearer purpose than the other branches since he will have, if not quite only himself to please, at least no one else in the executive branch with whom he shares authority. Moreover, his impatience with limits will almost certainly have the corresponding virtue of promoting a view that to serve the public interest requires action. This can work to counterbalance the high court's likely focus on significant limits on the exercise of public power. In general, institutional reform of the presidency ought not be high on the list of things that friends of republican government should worry about. Rather, its present strengths need to be maintained. The real changes, institutional and political, that need making are in the legislature.

THE LEGISLATURE

Even though the branches of government are equals, the legislature is the key to republican government. Only the legislature can be deliberative in its workings and have the breadth of vision to consider the whole of the public interest. A high court can be deliberative but its purview will be limited. The president can have breadth of vision, but he is less likely to have it than a well-ordered legislature. The legislature is thus the engine of the separation of powers if there is to be deliberation on the concrete meaning of the public interest.

If, however, the legislature lacks the inclination and energy to be the engine, the separation of powers will continue to make factional rule more difficult. But it cannot serve as a device to secure wide-ranging deliberative lawmaking. At best, the other branches could merely insist on their own truncated view of the public interest—whereas, if the legislature acts deliberatively, the other branches will have to counter the broad view of the public interest that a well-organized legislature can offer, reconsidering in the process their own versions of it. The legislature as a public-spirited interlocutor may not be the only way to galvanize the other branches' contemplation of the whole public interest. But it is likely the only way to make them do so consistently and with real attention. At the least, pride and ambition are likely to prompt office holders in the other branches to attempt to respond to the arguments that the legislature makes. If they are seen by attentive citizens to be uninterested or slovenly they will lose prestige and, possibly, public office. Deliberation within the legislature promotes deliberation among the branches. And this is one of the keys to the constitutional politics that is at the center of a developed republican political constitution.

In a sense, there is nothing new in this view of the legislature as the key to the separation of powers. Theorists of a republican political order have long known that it is fundamentally legislative government—rule by representatives meeting in open congress. As already noted, Justice Jackson said, "With all its defects, delays and inconveniences, men have discovered no technique for long preserving free government except that the Executive be under the law, and that the law be made by parliamentary deliberations."[35] The lawmaking of the legislature is public, the arguments made in it are (mostly) open to inspection, and they are recorded so that their value can be reflected on at leisure. It is the excellence of the legislature to make law publicly starting from the diverse viewpoints that its members bring. Only it is equipped to foster public exchange of argument about the appropriate content of the law in language accessible to ordinary citizens.[36] My argument here simply takes this staple of republican thought to its conclusion: if there is to be deliberative lawmaking in a separation of powers system, the legislature must take the lead.

Still, it is not a particularly happy matter for friends of republican government to have to place so much weight on the capabilities of the legislature. A high court even in a well-developed republican regime will have some significant advantages over a legislature. It would be small, for one thing, and have a body of doctrine to guide its discussions. Together these would help the court to deliberate in productive ways. In addition, such a court would likely inherit a set of expectations that it should reach its decisions in reasoned ways and be seen to do so. By comparison the legislature will be large and, at least initially, without a body of doctrine on which to rely; and there will probably be fewer people who believe it should deliberate in the first place. Moreover, the present behavior of the Congress with regard to deliberative lawmaking suggests that it will not be easy to foster in it even a modest and sustained effort to give content to the public interest.

It should thus be apparent to all but the relentlessly optimistic that even a reformed version of the present Congress will not be a superb device for reasoning about the concrete meaning of the public interest. At present, noted legislative careers do not require any great talent for hammering out how the elements of the public interest should be brought to bear in policy decisions. The need for so important a role for the legislature seems to be lost on those who think of themselves as policy entrepreneurs or paladins of the interests of their home districts.[37] Many contemporary members of

Congress seem especially drawn to the idea of a political career graced by the regular appearance of their face on television, enjoyment of the perks of office, and the pleasures to be supplied by those who finance election campaigns. More wholesomely, but of not much greater help, legislators presently can also pursue happy careers attending to the concerns of private and public interest groups focused on a single policy issue.

We must look to the legislature largely because we have no other place to go. And as Locke says, the "Legislature is the Soul that gives Form, Life and Unity to the Commonwealth."[38] It is a clumsy contrivance—large, filled with members unlikely to be more intellectually acute than the ordinary citizen, and open to all kinds of narrow pressures often felt as riveting by members seeking reelection. But with all its weaknesses, the legislative is the only kind of body that can claim to represent the citizenry in the sense of reflecting something of its diversity of opinion and interest. An elected executive can be found in several kinds of regimes that few would count as desirable. But a freely elected legislature able to make law is a clear sign that, at least so far as those devoted to republican government are concerned, the regime is on the right track. Thus, what a legislature loses in a kind of institutional clumsiness it potentially can make up in the broadness of its concerns.[39]

A legislature in a well-ordered republic cannot be the domain of private interest, of the parceling out to particular interests of the largesse generated by government that is one of the regular features of contemporary lawmaking. Republican lawmaking must limit the extent to which legislation is the art of the political deal. It is all too easy to be blinded by the taste of contemporary political science for the informalities of political life. There is too little sense in its literature, and in our politics, that Congress as a formal institution is crucial to republican government. Instead, the Congress is too often understood as just one more arena in which interests fight it out, and reform proposals as often as not concentrate on changing the balance of power among the interests that ply their trade within its precincts. William Leggett, a passionate commentator on American politics in the Jacksonian period, warned of the results if bargaining between private interests were to dominate the legislature. In doing so, he points to the distance we must travel from contemporary legislative life at its worst if we are to have republican lawmaking:

> Nothing could be more self-evident than the demoralizing influences of special legislation. It degrades politics into a mere scramble for rewards obtained by violation of the equal rights of the people; it perverts the holy sentiment of patriotism; it induces a feverish avidity for sudden wealth; it fosters a spirit of wild and dishonest speculation.[40]

THE ORGANIZATION OF THE LEGISLATURE
THE CHARACTER OF DELIBERATION

A central concern, therefore, in the design of the commercial republic is to ensure that the legislature engages in deliberate ways of lawmaking—not to the exclusion of other modes, but on the occasions when the public interest is at issue. It is relatively clear what deliberation would entail in a high court operating in a more or less fully realized republican regime. What does it mean for the legislature to engage in deliberative ways of lawmaking?

Madison suggested that what is crucial is a disposition to think about public matters in terms of how they might affect one's country as a whole, instead of solely in terms of one's own interest or the interest of some particular group in the society. As Arthur Maass says, legislators must have "breadth of view"[41] as they seek to answer the implicit question posed by a piece of legislation—Is it in the public interest?—by *discussing* it. That is, they have to argue, adduce evidence, point to comparable cases, and so on.[42] They must not just speak but also listen to one another's arguments, and respond, if necessary, by pointing out mistakes in analysis, adducing evidence that points to a different conclusion, presenting stories that illustrate that the world works differently than is being proposed, telling anecdotes to invite others to see the world as they do—and, perhaps most important of all, arguing for principles drawn from the public interest that encompass both the respondent's position and those of his or her interlocutor. Deliberative lawmaking aims, then, at transforming statements of wants into reasoned argument, will into judgment. As William Galston says, lawmakers must possess "deliberative excellence."[43]

Agreement, of course, may not result from efforts at deliberation. Bargains often must be struck and trades arranged. This can be an extension of the deliberative process so long as what is compromised are versions of the public interest. And that is the crucial point. It is not desirable or even possible for lawmakers to attempt unaided heroic feats of discernment of the true public interest, as if lawmaking in the public interest were an exercise in logically deducing conclusions from first principles.

By contrast, in deliberative ways of lawmaking, the question—What is in the public interest?—is not an abstract one. Instead, lawmakers start from what they believe are the policy views, interests, and conceptions of the public interest of their constituents, modified by their own views on these matters. They will, after all, have run for election, and in the process will undoubtedly have articulated some policy preferences and at least an implicit view of the public interest to which substantial numbers of voters will have given their assent. The crucial point is how they go about arguing for and making sense of their initial positions. Deliberatively minded lawmakers understand that these are indeed their initial positions. These are partial viewpoints that are subject to expansion and revision,[44] especially as lawmakers, alone and in common, try to reconcile these positions with the broad principles of the public interest. Their policy positions are not then to be counters in a trading game, but partial, tentative answers to the question of what is in the public interest. The intellectual traffic runs in multiple ways. Constituents' views and initial policy positions are argued for as plausible interpretations of the public interest; they then become modified in light of other partial views; and all views eventually are modified as the effort is made to reconcile them with the components of the public interest. And as the meaning of the public interest is made more concrete through such efforts, it in turn is used to judge further proposals in an attempt to make the new and the old consistent. As Hayek says in his account of such practical reasoning, those exercising it move "within an existing system of thought" engaging in "immanent criticism" to make the various pieces or arguments advanced "more consistent both internally as well as with the facts."[45]

Lawmakers who stand in relation to one another as deliberators thus have a disposition to reach beyond that to which they are already committed, revising their positions in light of argument and evidence. For them, lawmaking is a search for the concrete meaning of the public interest—a search, however, that cannot stop with a simple juxtaposition of private and public interests, as if the two were wholly distinct. Their commitment to the public interest is not a pledge to remain unacquainted with private interest but to engage in a deliberative process that transforms such interests.

While deliberative lawmakers offer reasons for their positions, lawmaking in a well-developed commercial republic is no counterpart to a debating society where great speeches are delivered by a queue of modern-day Pericles. Because wide-spread agreement on important legislative measures is not likely to emerge quickly or easily, but must be built up from diverse starting points, for deliberative lawmakers the premium is less on oratory and more on drawing out, making concrete, and reconciling various policy positions. Similarly, there would also be a premium on constituting a set of people who work together over time to give patient attention to public problems, and who then would be able to implement the "train of measures"[46] necessary to give concrete meaning to the public interest. Deliberative lawmaking does not involve debate so much as a search for a good resolution of a problem. Just as with a high court, deliberative lawmakers do not start each attempt at lawmaking from scratch. Lawmaking of this sort can be neither synoptic (Lindblom)[47] nor constructivist (Hayek).[48] But because it builds on past attempts at lawmaking, it may in this sense be called "public interest law" and be comparable to what is now constitutional law.

What is wanted, then, for lawmaking in the public interest is a kind of "principled inclusivity" on the part of lawmakers, a disposition to attend to diverse views and to make an effort to reconcile them. In short, they must act as people ordinarily do when they reason together. A deliberative way of lawmaking involves nothing more taxing than (1) that lawmakers have breadth of vision, most notably some sense of the public interest; (2) that they offer reasons for their views; (3) that they be receptive to the reasoning of others; and (4) that they thus see their own views and the views of others as starting points open to revision. Edwin Haefele offers a concise description of what is called for in deliberative lawmaking: it is a "creative resolution" of a public problem that "leaves more friends than enemies" and "redefine[s] the issue in broader terms rooted in deeper and more generally shared principles." It is an "entrepreneurial task" that seeks to find the "highest level of agreement." Deliberative ways of lawmaking do not rest on a simple compromise that leaves "the underlying issue[s] unresolved."[49] Nor do they leave the preferences of the participating parties unaltered. In deliberative lawmaking, the aim is to change preferences, to redefine the views of the parties involved about what is at stake for themselves and for the larger community in the choice at hand.

Finally, deliberative lawmaking in the public interest need not and should not be innocent of the degree of societal support behind a piece of legislation. Since it is legislation being considered, not some abstract pronouncement, the question of whether the proposed legislation can actually be made to work is central to making good law. Lawmaking in the public interest is rightly, in part, rhetorical in purpose—it announces what the public interest is—but if it is to serve that interest it must actually make something happen. Thus, which major societal actors support the proposal, which can be induced to support it, which are likely to at least acquiesce in it, and which will probably work to prevent its implementation are hardly irrelevant. So, lawmakers engaged in deliberation are not only engaged in testing each other's argument but also in judging how much political support lies behind each proposal. In a well-functioning deliberative process, the arts of practical reasoning meet those of political calculation.

ORGANIZING THE LEGISLATURE

What will make the legislature work in a deliberative way? If there are few lawmakers whose ambitions include being a powerful advocate of the public interest and a lawmaker of note, then the separation of powers cannot work as the foundation of efforts to give concrete meaning to the public interest. Legislators who see little connection between their ambitions and the role of the legislature as crucial to public interest lawmaking have little incentive to resist the ambitions of presidents and high court justices to be chief lawmakers.

Being more or less free to engage in legislative deliberation—a well-ordered republican regime controls faction—does not mean lawmakers will do so. If the legislature is to play its proper role in a republic, we must understand what, in the first place, will make lawmakers take seriously the need to limit the power of the state by concrete definition of its purposes—even when many of their constituents do not wish it and when it will thus be politically costly. Legislators, unlike high court judges, are unlikely, as a matter of course, to understand their job to be centrally concerned with defining the limits on the exercise of state power. In a popular regime where the citizenry is reasonably well organized and has some information about and is attentive to public matters—both of which will be the case in a more or less fully realized commercial republic—the situation is, if anything, likely to be the reverse. Legislators will be under constant pressure to use public power to relieve private misery and advance private interest. What can counterbalance such pressures?

Four features of our present working constitution prompt a concern for limiting governmental power. In a more or less fully realized commercial republic, these features will be strongly at work, and, in this respect at least, the road from where we are to where we aspire to be is not terribly long. Modest reform will probably be enough. The first feature is simply the separation of powers, which makes expansion of state activity more difficult than if power were concentrated in one governmental body. The other three require greater discussion.

In a society where commerce is highly developed, there will always be those who worry about any large-scale exercise of state power—even one that, putatively, would benefit them in direct ways. This is the second force promoting limited government. Most notably perhaps, the existence of private property results in political pressure on lawmakers to be chary of marked state expansion. Those whose property holdings are large can regularly be expected to sing the praises of limited government in the service of preserving a private sphere. They may also be expected to use their considerable resources to see that their concerns are given careful attention. Many among those who control substantial property are likely to think that, regardless of what they may gain immediately, they will pay for it in the long run as state authority becomes a regular presence in their day-to-day affairs. Property, moreover, is a potent symbol of limited government as it is concrete and tangible in a way that other limiting principles—such as the right to free speech—are not.[50]

Similarly, those who engage in nonstate civic problemsolving are likely to be attentive to the need to limit governmental power. Experience in civic life helps develop a sense of just why government should be limited and where the limits should be drawn. For it is through the experience of actually participating in such civic problemsolving that one appreciates just how clumsy government can be, not least because it must deal in general rules if it is not to be corrupt. Correlatively, those who run civic organizations are likely to develop a sense of the kinds of things civic organization can handle well and what matters are best left to the state. If there is any doubt here, consider that citizens whose entire experience of public life—voting aside—consists of being on the receiving end of rules and benefactions are unlikely to think carefully about the appropriate limits of public power. They may approve of the exercise of such power because it provides for their group. Or they may resent it and seek to overthrow it out of a concern for the immense impact it has and its tendency to feed corruption and arbitrariness. Neither of these responses is likely to be the foundation for any careful thinking about the appropriate limits on public power.[51]

More generally, so long as there are organizations and interests, including those rooted in ownership and control of property, that are strong enough to engage state officials and force them to listen—especially through credible threats of appealing to the citizenry and of not cooperating with governmental schemes—there will be voices for limitation on the exercise of state power that cannot be ignored. This is the real meaning of pluralism: the existence of sources of power independent of the state.[52]

A third force promoting limits on state power is simply the logic of a great expansion of state power. Even in a situation where no one major interest can be assured of controlling the levers of state power, it will still be dangerous for any major societal interest to acquiesce in the destruction of boundaries on its use because there would then be few barriers to remaking the society in the image of whoever happens at the moment to control the state. In short, each major societal group has an interest in seeing that there are some limits on governmental power. And, even though there are collective action problems, the small number of societal actors likely to be involved will allow conventions, written and otherwise, to grow up that will work to prevent such a remaking. These conventions are necessary if constitutional government is to survive, and it is no great leap to argue that they will be valued by large numbers of public officials and leaders of major social interests long after they are first put in place.[53]

The fourth force at work in limiting governmental power is competition between political parties. If the above factors are at work and the citizenry has any inclination to limit state power, the question of limits on government will be an issue in the competition between political parties. One of the parties will find it politically advantageous to present itself as speaking for limited government. In recent years, this has certainly been true of the Republican party: the Reagan "revolution" and its aftermath can be understood as one long reminder to the nation's electorate and political elites of the reasons for limits on governmental power.

In addition to the above generalized pressures that work to limit governmental authority, a well-ordered republic will also give lawmakers incentives to use political authority to serve specific elements of the public interest. In a republic, limiting public power means using it for the broad purposes delineated in the public interest and by means consistent with its requirements. Again, we can point to forces at work that, with modest reform, will increase the likelihood that the public interest will be served.

To illustrate, consider those elements of the public interest concerned with securing a vibrant civil society and a variety of rights. Here the essential point, already suggested, is that once there is a network of civic organizations that rests on the exercise of these rights, their existence provides a basis for exerting continuous pressure on government to respect the rights. In addition, we may note with Robert Dahl[54] that the existence of popular government itself increases pressures to institute and secure primary political rights. Rather than popular self-government simply being a danger to rights (a worry for both Madison and Tocqueville), the evidence suggests that the more reflective members of the demos can see that, for the people to rule, there must be a system of rights that secures their ability to meet and discuss public affairs, to vote for their governors, and to not be subject to the arbitrary exercise of political power. To subvert rights is to subvert popular rule. More reflective citizens will for much the same reasons see the general need to control faction.

Similarly, a system of property rights will provide the foundation in self-interest for its own defense and thus of an enterprise-based market system.[55] Moreover, taken together, a system of relatively fair and free popular elections, and an economic system in which the citizenry's income comes largely from salary and wages, more or less guarantee that promoting economic prosperity will be a central item on the political agenda. And since there is a system of private ownership of productive assets, any attempt to promote widespread prosperity will have to focus on the workings of the business enterprise system, particularly the inducements necessary for high performance. As for political equality, given the inclination of a republican citizenry to resist a state with unlimited powers, its citizens will find it natural to use the language of rights: "You can't do that to me, I have rights too." It is the "too" part that is crucial because it implies a kind of political equality, or at least a source for it.[56]

More generally, a well-organized commercial republic needs political parties that perform two tasks. First, they must speak to different aspects of the public interest, and in doing so check each other's propensity to emphasize some elements of it at the expense of others. Second, at their best, political parties must be *constitutional* in their concerns, arguing for maintaining, strengthening, and reforming those elements of the public interest whose embodiment in political institutions give the regime its essential character. A plausible and attractive party system will have one party that welcomes those who find the expansion of the national government a threat to some of their most important interests; the same party will likely defend the virtues of local political life and of civic life generally. The other party will be drawn to advancing different elements of the public interest and thus work to attract those who wish to mitigate the economic and political inequalities produced by an enterprise-based market system, and who look to the expansion of national political power to mitigate such inequalities. The roles of the parties can be expected to alter over time because their attraction to voters will result as much from disaffection with the course of government as from choices made by party leaders.[57]

The pressures I have described are, however, unlikely by themselves to produce deliberative ways of lawmaking. Not least of the problems is that there are few reasons why lawmakers should, in fact, deliberate. They may recognize the need to concern themselves with elements of the public interest, but what will induce them to think through and argue about the interconnections between these elements? In addition, the pressures I have pointed to, while real, are probably not strong enough on their own to do the necessary work even if they are strengthened. Moreover, while most lawmakers will show that modicum of attachment to the public interest characteristic of all decent people in not completely wretched regimes, such attachment to the public interest is itself insufficient to generate a consistent and ample disposition to engage in deliberative ways of lawmaking. We thus must extend the argument. In doing so, it is worth emphasizing that republican lawmaking does not require civic virtue in its legislators—not if that is understood as involving a disinterested attachment to the public good, exclusive and independent of all private and public attachments.[58] This cannot be common among lawmakers in a commercial republic nor, given that in a commercial republic public and private interest are not so disconnected as this phrasing implies, is it desirable.

Even then, if lawmakers feel pressures to attend to the various elements of the public interest, why will they *reason* about the concrete meaning of these elements in arriving at a decision on particular pieces of legislation? Engaging in bargaining and vote-trading would, at least, make lawmaking less intellectually taxing. Lawmakers, even in a well-ordered republic, are

not, after all, likely to be Solons but ordinary people who in the end act in deliberative ways, if at all, for the same reasons that most people do—because
it is personally rewarding to do so. They will be, in part, self-interested.
But, for many, their self-interest is unlikely to be narrowly understood, and
thus will probably include a desire to be held in esteem by their colleagues
for showing great knowledge of public matters and a concern for the public
interest. In addition, lawmakers are likely to be motivated by the fear of
being revealed by their legislative adversaries as ignorant and in the pocket
of special interests. They will also undoubtedly find satisfaction in political advancement that a reputation for being devoted to the public interest
and knowledgeable about public affairs can bring.[59] Moreover, some lawmakers harbor a deep and abiding desire to be famous, to go down in the
history books of their country as a lawmaker of great distinction, devoted
to the well-being of its citizenry.[60] As one contemporary lawmaker puts
it: "[Y]ou've got being part of history, looking back 5 or 10 or 30 years
from now and saying, 'we did it.' "[61] Or as Gouverneur Morris more suc-
cinctly put it: "The love of fame is the great spring to noble and illustrious
actions."[62]

It is in the motives just canvassed that part of the hope for deliberative
ways of lawmaking lies. For these motives can be built on and extended in
ways that bring lawmakers to a regular concern for giving concrete meaning
to the public interest. The legislature, if properly organized as an institution,
can teach; it can help to form the outlook of lawmakers and thus be a school
for learning the arts of deliberative lawmaking.[63]

To be sure, as I argue in chapter 7, if the legislature as school is to succeed, the pupils must come to it with something more than the above by way
of dispositions towards deliberative ways of lawmaking. If the legislature
does not have the right pupils it cannot succeed as a school. But equally
important, it cannot be the appropriate sort of school without the right
teachers. These teachers must be legislative leaders who are willing to organize a legislature that encourages a deliberative concern with the public
interest—notably those who hold its formal positions of leadership, such as
majority leader and committee chairs—but also the informal leaders who
have reputations for knowing how the business of legislation works and
should work. A legislature largely composed of abject mediocrities cannot
by some hidden hand miraculously turn itself into a lawmaking body of
great distinction. John Stuart Mill tartly said in this regard that

> a school of political capacity . . . is worthless, and a school for evil, instead of
> good, if through want . . . of the presence within itself of a higher order of char-
> acters, the action of the body is allowed, as it so often is, to degenerate into an
> equally unscrupulous and stupid pursuit of the self-interest of its members.[64]

What will attract persons of great ambition and competence to pursue life purposes through politics? What will dispose them to see politics as a place for accomplishments that will make their name? Why will they become legislative *leaders*, people who give up the relatively quiet life of large offices and staffs, modest prestige, and modest power that grace the careers of most lawmakers? Indeed, legislators of great ambition need not look to a career as a leading lawmaker. They might look instead outside the legislature and seek the accolades of the media and of those who shape reputations among corporate heads, university professors, and Hollywood stars. They might even become instead the president's helpmate.

No great legislative leader will be mistaken for a shrinking violet. Still, it is hard work, and for the most part it must be done inside the legislature, without the constant monitoring of the political breezes fanned by daily headlines. It is hard to see how lawmaking in the public interest can be fostered if legislative leaders are constantly changing their own minds and trying to get their colleagues to do the same because the leader's stock with the media or major interest groups has dropped a few points. There is nothing at all obscure about all this: those who think good law can be made in an open stadium buffeted by the winds of opinion may know something about football, but not about republican government. Legislative leaders in a republican regime must see the connection between their own ambitions and a great and powerful role for the legislature in carrying on the business of republican government. Lackeys of presidents are comparatively easy to come by.

What then might prompt the ambitious and the competent to undertake such burdens? The answer—again leaving aside any inclination of the citizenry to elect public-spirited lawmakers—is a heightened form of what motivates ordinary lawmakers to at least consider moving beyond the narrow interests of their constituents and their own self-regarding desires: they wish for the fame that accompanies a reputation for being a great lawmaker. Therefore, it must at least be possible for those of large ambition to realize their desire for great public esteem through a career as a legislative leader. If the organization of the legislature and the manner of choosing its members is such that even those with the greatest concern for the public interest cannot expect to shape the legislature into a great engine of the public interest, then those with the requisite appetite for fame will look elsewhere—and the legislature will be run and populated by non-entities and by those with appetites for fame that require no more than holding public office. This means that the committee structure, the process of appointing committee chairs, and other features of the internal organization of the legislature must not defeat the efforts of aspiring leaders to shape the legislature as a deliberative lawmaking body. If this is exceedingly difficult to do,[65] the ambitious and the talented, being no different from their more ordinary counterparts and thus possessing some measure of rationality, are unlikely to waste their energies in fruitless pursuits.[66]

In order to realize their ambitions, those who wish to be great legislative leaders need the help of a substantial proportion of their colleagues—and they must thus devote considerable effort to seeking reliable ways to achieve such cooperation. Here is where the legislature as school is crucial. And here again care must be taken to distinguish a deliberative-minded legislature from a debating society, which is one of the least likely forms of organization to accomplish much of anything except to hone the skills of debaters and provide either delight or boredom for the audience.[67] How then should the legislature be organized?

Of fundamental importance, leaders must devise ways for those with the inclination to enlarge their purview and that of their constituents to do so, and to do it without being punished at the polls. Leaders must also find ways to reward such lawmakers both inside and outside the legislature. The rewards inside might include good opportunities for ordinary lawmakers to be involved in the legislative process in ways that garner public attention and please the folks back home; positions of influence in the legislature; and attention to the projects that are closest to the hearts of lawmakers' constituents. Outside of the legislature, leaders must look for ways to emphasize that ordinary lawmakers are persons of such integrity and acumen that they deserve seats at the tables of the momentarily mighty.

Lawmakers must also be *seen* to deliberate, which to some degree is in tension with actual deliberation insofar as it cannot usefully be carried out through the whole chamber meeting in floor debate. Thus, the real task of leaders is to see that deliberation occurs in committees, where it is both easier to prompt and more fruitful in result, and to make the course and outcome of those deliberations widely available to anyone willing to pay modest attention. The organization of a republican legislature must be such as to allow publicity so that voters may judge the deliberative qualities of their lawmakers, and thus reward those who make the effort. But the legislature must not be organized in a manner that makes it impossible for lawmakers to move beyond the appeals they have made when seeking election, especially if these reflect relatively narrow and particular interests among their constituents.

How might all this be accomplished? Among other things, leaders must be adept at sounding out the views of members of the legislative body. This means listening carefully in an effort to discern what most concerns each lawmaker, particularly if their views are based on a strong grasp of the matter at hand. In the absence of strong feelings or well-informed views, or when the legislator's views are at variance with the leadership's, leaders might present arguments and evidence. Or more likely, leaders will put lawmakers in touch with those who may convince them of the error of their ways ("See Jones. She's a genius at this stuff and she will set you straight.") Leaders might also give members a reading of support for their position, as an exercise in backbone strengthening or in the wisdom of being flexible. Probably most important of all, leaders can convene those who seem to be the most articulate and persuasive advocates of positions that show some affinity to one another, and that broadly conform to leadership thinking, and charge them with deliberating until a position is reached on which they agree.[68] Leaders could then direct these advocates to talk to a wide variety of other legislators to whom they will teach the merits of the proposed legislation.

Legislative leaders, now with the help of friends of the bill, will also spend a good deal of time, especially when an important piece of legislation is on the agenda, in arguing to the faint of heart that they need to show courage, that they will be widely admired for taking a stand, that they will go down in history—and that, if necessary, their pet projects will be given loving attention. The crucial thing in all this is that the leadership and its helpers so run the legislature that there are incentives for doing the hard work of making good law, listening to arguments, offering concrete proposals, suggesting amendments, and so forth. In short, the legislature must be organized as an elaborate system for rewarding those who work at lawmaking—in contrast to those who work at getting on television, those who work at doing the bidding of powerful constituents and sources of campaign finance, and those who work at sitting in their offices admiring the look of the pictures on the walls.

Leaders who can manage all this over time—and who have built up a stable of those willing and able to take the lead on specific pieces of legislation—develop an aura about them. It will be said that they can be trusted; that they should not be double-crossed; that they should be fought with only when something of great moment is at stake and the fight cannot be avoided; and that they should be applauded in public as great lawmakers on whose shoulders all should be willing to stand.

Can we expect such leaders and those who help them on particular pieces of legislation to be in evidence? If what is required is a deep and sophisticated grasp of the public interest—call those who have such a grasp "statesmen"—then Madison gave the answer long ago: we probably cannot do without them, but neither should we build a regime around their regular and continuing presence.[69] Lesser mortals may be enough because all that leaders may really need is some sense that there *is* a public interest and some grasp of its contours. These they can have, if what they learn in their schooling, imbibe from the common culture, and read in the newspaper does not regularly convince them that they are foolish to believe such things. It would of course be better if all leaders were statesmen, but fortune is unlikely to be so bountiful.

For leaders to do the job of lawmaking in the public interest, they probably must themselves be party leaders. Parties are essential if leaders are to discipline followers who stray too far from the party line. Leaders also need ways to protect legislators who are out ahead of their constituents and to provide benefactions to those who cooperate with their legislative plans. Moreover, legislative leaders cannot succeed in running the legislature as a school of the public interest if they must put together new coalitions for each piece of major legislation, and, what is even more difficult, if they are to legislate with due regard to the connections between issues. They must have a solid foundation of support on which to build: a set of lawmakers inclined to see issues in similar ways and who, once convinced to modify or expand their views, can be relied on to argue and vote in the appropriate manner. Deliberative lawmaking cannot rest on a legislature composed of highly independent lawmakers. All this party organization can help provide.[70]

In addition to having a significant measure of internal coherence, parties in a well-ordered republican regime must not be sectarian, geared toward representing a particular ethnic, racial, or religious grouping. Thus, proportional representation systems that encourage multiple parties and the representation of narrow interests are best avoided—especially if they contain a low threshold for the number of votes needed to secure seats in the legislature. They make the maintenance of encompassing political parties and the expression of broad interests, both of which are necessary if the public interest is to be served, more difficult to achieve.[71] It is thus doubtful that republican government of the kind outlined here can flourish with proportional representation or indeed with any electoral system that creates incentives for representatives and parties to represent interests rather than people who have interests. Representatives need to be able to respond to the full range of their constituents' concerns and to shift among them as debate in the legislature unfolds. The only electoral device that seems capable of allowing for this—although, of course, it does not guarantee it (consider Britain)—is the single member district in which representation is territorially based.

Regional parties present similar difficulties for lawmaking concerned with the public interest of the whole political community. A republican constitution needs a mechanism to substantially reduce the incentive for regional parties to form. The electoral college is one such mechanism insofar as it reduces the incentives for parties to pile up "wasted" votes in one area of the country since votes over and above those needed to carry the state are of less value in winning an election than carefully spreading votes across all regions. Regional parties are just that—advocates of regional interests—and thus undercut deliberative lawmaking in the service of the public interest of the whole regime.[72]

Similarly, political parties in a well-ordered republican regime must not be ideological, if by "ideology" we mean being rooted in *alternative* accounts of the public interest. It is hard to see how members of parties that differ on the most fundamental questions of governmental purpose can deliberate. Thus, (1) if one party believes that government is simply a result of a contract, that its task is to guarantee the rights of the contractors, that there is no such thing as society, only contracting individuals, and that we thus do not owe one another anything; and (2) the other party believes that we are all members of a political community in which our actions shape one another's lives in profound ways, and that we thus owe one another a good deal including making life chances more equal and attending to the poor and weak among us—then it is hard to see that party members would have much to talk about with their opposite numbers. Legislating in such circumstances would look much like a trial of strength. By contrast, it is an advantage for republican government if parties offer competing views of the *same* public interest giving, say, differing weights to its elements. If they do so in a coherent fashion they educate the citizenry. And because such parties compete around a shared public interest, it is probable that this in itself will stimulate a measure of legislative deliberation. Deliberative lawmaking requires just enough party discipline in the legislature to narrow down what needs to be discussed, and not so much as to preclude deliberation among the body of lawmakers.

In a more or less fully realized republic, parties will be broadly based and concerned with the full range of public issues. Republican political parties cannot then be essentially aggregations of local interests in the fashion of the American party system at some points in our history. That all politics is local is not a good slogan for those who wish to promote a republican political regime.

In addition to broad-based parties, ambitious legislative leaders oriented to broad public interests will be helped by a similar kind of interest group system. The present situation in the United States is one in which, to the old producer groups and to organized labor, have been added new groups concerned with policy domains that have come about as a result of the expansion of government. As government has grown, its activities have generated a wide array of interest groups anxious to shape these new policy arenas. A majority of such groups have relatively narrow interests and are thus unlikely to be swayed in their criticism of government by its successes in domains other than those that concern them. Many of the leaders of these groups, moreover, seek to increase organizational membership by repeatedly pointing out how much more must be done and how those in authority are impeding the effort.

Interest group activity in general has mushroomed for reasons over and above governmental expansion: (1) congressional reform has led to the proliferation of subcommittees, which in turn has created more points of access for groups and thus reduced the costs of forming new groups; (2) the weakening of political parties along several dimensions and the related rise of independent campaign consultants have made members of Congress more vulnerable electorally and thereby increasingly reliant on interest group money;[73] and (3) the growth of new communications technologies has made it easier for interest groups to raise money and promote grassroots activity, and has reduced the costs of forming groups in the first place because all that is really necessary is a headquarters staff and an electronic mailing list.

The United States now has an extraordinarily large number of interest groups that do not represent much of anybody as measured by an involved membership but who claim to represent tens of thousands of people. Moreover, producer groups are more fragmented than hitherto—the number of trade associations engaged in lobbying has multiplied—and organized labor as a political force has been weakened considerably. We have, in short, an interest group system that is prone to great narrowness and fragmentation of views. The growth of so-called public interest groups has, in spite of the name, done little to help matters and, very likely, has made things worse. The dominating concern of these groups is not with the public interest, which requires that environmental, product safety, and similar groups involve themselves with the full range of republican lawmaking as it intersects with their fundamental concerns. On the evidence, this is precisely what they have trouble doing. Many such groups seem to think that the public interest consists of doing as much as possible about the particular policy concern they happen to have.

What would be preferable, by contrast to an interest group system largely supportive of narrow and fragmented views, is a larger array of groups with broader purviews—that is, ones that focus not on a single issue but, like peak labor or business organizations, are interested in the full range of public matters. Such organizations are also likely to recruit a membership with a wide array of interests, which should reinforce the groups' broad stances. Together, these features of groups are likely to make them sensitive to two matters: (1) that the public interest is not the serving of one goal, or even a few goals, and "justice" is not to be found simply in affirmative action or securing rights for women: there will need to be a weighing-up of a variety of considerations; and (2) that deliberation in lawmaking that attempts to consider matters in broad perspective is thus a good idea, not a "sell-out" to special interests: if something is given up in order to gain something even more valuable—if we have slightly less clean air but educate more children—this may well be an attempt to serve the public interest.[74] To see the extent of the problem, it is worth reflecting on the fact that over eleven hundred groups were involved in trying to shape the Clinton administration's legislation for the reform of the health care system.[75]

As I have said, the various forces I have been canvassing plausibly can be strengthened: they are within our grasp or are already at work. Friends of republican government should support legislative reforms that facilitate the emergence of legislative leaders whose ambitions are tied to serving the public interest. Similarly, they should seek institutional changes that increase the odds that the legislature as a school of public interest lawmaking can flourish.[76] If both are done it is much more likely that we will have a constitutional politics that seeks to give concrete meaning to the public interest. Friends of the commercial republic also need not give in to that spurious kind of realism that says the only political reality is the deal, the tactics of bargaining and the political pay-off. While such a view is not without some truth, it is deeply unrealistic if its adepts think this is all that is needed for a republican regime to survive and flourish.

Alas, however, even if the forces discussed here are considerably strengthened, we would still not have a more or less fully realized republican regime. If this account contains all that would be at work in the public interest politics of a republican regime, then there is unlikely to be much in the way of deliberative lawmaking. The motives and forces canvassed, while important, are unlikely to be strong and reliable enough. Unless the citizenry itself asserts regular and significant pressure on lawmakers to give the public interest significant weight, lawmakers are likely to tread the more usual paths of satisfying vocal and resource-rich constituents and interests. Some students of republican government have argued that legislative lawmakers "should not reflect those who choose them,"[77] implying that the lawmakers will somehow be a cut above those who elect them. But this leaves unanswered how citizens might rise above their inadequacies in judging those who are to represent them. The citizens of a commercial republic must be in their way as capable as its lawmakers. They must have those qualities of judgment that allow them to say which prospective lawmakers understand lawmaking to be, in significant part, a deliberative process and who have either the skills necessary to make to make it so work or the inclination to learn them. It is in the combination of the legislature as school and the capacities for judgment by the citizenry that the hope for lawmaking in the public interest for a commercial republic lies. How then will the citizens learn to make the necessary judgments? The political constitution of the commercial republic must make provision for their education as well. The citizens of a republican regime must have the experience of deliberating and struggling over the content of the public interest if they are to judge the inclinations and capacities of their lawmakers.

7

A Public Interest Politics II

A PUBLIC-SPIRITED CITIZENRY

What provisions can be made in a republican design so that deliberative-minded lawmakers concerned with the public interest are likely to be elected? Americans already have some measure of public-spiritedness as a result of living in a free society. But there is good reason to believe that the citizens of a commercial republic will not, as a matter of course, have the measure of public-spiritedness necessary to regularly elect such lawmakers: the pull of self-interest in a commercial society, whose workings reinforce it, will likely be too great.[1] In this they reflect the natural human propensity to prefer one's own and to discount the future—to which may be added that a market society rewards those who are adept at serving their own interests.[2]

How, then, can public-spiritedness and the ability to judge whether lawmakers are disposed to consider the public interest be strengthened? A citizenry without such a character is not likely to elect legislative leaders who are interested in creating a legislative school of the public interest. And if the leaders of the legislature are to succeed in this undertaking, they will need a significant number of lawmakers similarly inclined, who must also be elected by the same citizenry. If the legislature as school, and the other forces already discussed, cannot overcome the problems presented by a large contingent of legislators without talent and concern for broad public interests—as very likely they cannot—then the political constitution must make provision for fostering a citizenry with the ability and inclination to judge which legislators will engage in republican lawmaking. No amount of institutional contrivance can overcome a citizenry that regularly chooses for office time-serving self-interested mediocrities, those who lack

"due acquaintance with the object and principles of legislation."[3] A legislature composed of those who see their office as essentially a pleasant,
prestigious way to make a living, and their role as being a high-class gopher
fetching benefactions for their constituents or as a dealer in interest group
rewards, can do little to further the central concerns of a well-ordered republican government. Jefferson, while exaggerating what would be possible
in a commercial republican regime, put the point as well as anyone:

> May we not even say, that that form of government is the best, which provides
> the most effectively for a pure selection of these natural *aristoi* into the offices
> of government.... I think the best remedy is exactly that provided by all our
> constitutions, to leave to the citizens the free election and separation of the
> *aristoi* from the *pseudoaristoi*.[4]

Not surprisingly, the commercial republic, being a republic, stands or falls
on the qualities of its citizens. They must have a significant measure of
public-spiritedness.

Public-spiritedness is a disposition to give significant weight to the public interest. It consists of the not very demanding belief that there is a
public interest and that political life should devote significant effort to giving it concrete meaning. For present purposes, the principal expression of
public-spiritedness is the disposition to judge lawmakers by whether they
show a concern for the public interest and its necessary corollary, deliberative ways of lawmaking. If citizens cannot make such judgments, lawmakers
will likely understand that voters lack the ability to tell the huckster from
the great lawmaker, and act accordingly. The task of constitutional design,
however, is not only to devise ways to educate citizens to the fact that
there is a public interest; it must also aim at fostering the development of
the skills necessary to judge whether lawmakers have a disposition to engage in deliberative lawmaking. Citizens must also have some conception
of the substantive elements of the public interest. Public-spirited citizens
thus have two characteristics: they have some knowledge of the broad elements of the public interest and a concern that lawmaking aim to give
it concrete meaning; and they believe that lawmaking must, therefore, be
deliberative.

Where shall we look if our aim is to foster public-spiritedness? John
Stuart Mill said that "free and popular local and municipal institutions" are
part of "the peculiar training of a citizen, the practical part of the political
education of a free people." Mill added that without the habits of mind
learned through participation in local political life—specifically, the inclination to act from "public or semi-public motives"—"a free constitution
can neither be worked or preserved."[5]

Tocqueville said:

> It is ... in the township that the force of free peoples resides. The institutions of a township are to freedom what primary schools are to science; they put it within reach of the people; they make them taste its peaceful employ and habituate them to making use of it. Without the institutions of a township a nation can give itself a free government, but it does not have the spirit of freedom.[6]

Tocqueville also said that local political life allows a citizen to practice the art of government in the "restricted sphere that is within his reach...; he habituates himself to the forms without which freedom proceeds only through revolutions, permeates himself with their spirit, gets a taste for order, understands the harmony of powers, and finally assembles clear and practical ideas on the nature of his duties as well as the extent of his rights."[7]

Mill's and Tocqueville's formulations suggest that local politics is the only forum in which citizens can consider an array of public decisions wide enough to draw them into the full range of matters encompassed by any plausible conception of the public interest. Moreover, local government is the only context in which matters of direct and compelling interest to the mass of citizens can be decided in a manner that makes vivid the interconnections between them. Local political institutions are the only governmental arena in which a significant number of citizens can put into practice any disposition they may have to be public-spirited—and, in doing so, reinforce and refine it.[8]

Local political life is also especially important in a republic because fostering public-spiritedness can only be done in this kind of regime through indirect, "mild" means—that is, through experience rather than through tutelary or even harsher methods.[9] To rely on direct and even coercive means is to undercut one of the fundamental purposes of the regime: securing the rights of its citizens. In addition, local government offers the only possibility for large numbers of citizens to become involved in exercising public authority—that is, to take responsibility for the use of powers that affect others, many of whom will not share their views. Civic associations cannot do the job: the element of authority is missing. To be responsible in such a fashion is likely to prompt a healthy skepticism concerning whether one's own views are quite so obviously right as they seem. Judiciousness of this sort is necessary if a politics of the public interest is not to degenerate into a deep conflict that might pull the regime apart.[10]

If properly structured, local government also makes plain that there is no easy escape from our fellow citizens. They are in close enough proximity that their travails and successes become ours to some degree. And if the most powerful and wealthy among us are prevented from building legal walls around ourselves, that message—that we are all in this together, that there is something more than the interests of me and mine, that there is a common or public interest—becomes, not an abstraction, but a fact of everyday life. A nation, or even a state or region within it, is too big to make this point in any concrete way. Moreover, if the point *is* made in these larger contexts, the sheer size and complexity of the larger political system will impede the ability to respond to it.[11]

Tocqueville summed up the crucial point about the relation between local political life and republican government: "It is in fact difficult to conceive how men who have entirely renounced the habit of directing themselves could succeed at choosing well those who will lead them."[12] His point can be extended: for citizens to have any concern for the public interest of the regime, they must have the experience of grappling with its elements. And for any significant number of citizens this can only happen through local political life.[13] Thus, the kind of constitutional politics a commercial republic needs must be anchored in local political life.

There is much to be said about how the public interest can be made manifest in local political life, what motives can be harnessed to draw citizens into a local politics that considers it and gives it concrete meaning, and what the structure of local political institutions must be. But before considering these matters, we need to consider the qualities citizens must bring to local political life if it is to have the features just noted. The formal structure of institutions does not ensure that they will work in the manner just described. This is as true for local government institutions as it is for any others. To be sure, institutions help form the outlook and dispositions of those who work within them, but they cannot do so for just any kind of individuals. What is worse, institutions that are designed to be participative and deliberative— as I will argue local governments must be—can easily turn into teachers of cynicism and frustration if those who operate them are ill equipped and disinclined to have them work in the appropriate ways. Moreover, even if those who participate are receptive to what the institutions might teach them, they need other qualities if they are to act on these lessons in public-spiritedness.

THE QUALITIES CITIZENS MUST BRING TO LOCAL POLITICAL LIFE

There are at least six qualities that citizens must bring to local political life if its institutions are to foster public-spiritedness:[14]

1. the beginnings of the idea that there are public interests as well as private interests;

2. a significant measure of proud independence;
3. a degree of trust in other citizens;
4. the capacity to make moderately complex judgments about public matters;
5. a degree of respect for other citizens (and thus a substantial degree of mutual respect among the citizenry); and
6. a concern for the esteem in which others hold them, central to the granting of which must be a reputation for reasoned analysis of public matters.

THE BEGINNINGS OF PUBLIC-SPIRITEDNESS

To even get started on the project of fostering public-spiritedness, we must assume that a significant number of citizens have some inclination to judge political life in terms of interests and concerns larger than their own and those of their immediate circle. They may only be weakly inclined, but the disposition to do so cannot be absent. They may also have only a weak idea of how to go about such judging and what its content should be, but there must be something to build on. Political life can only reinforce or diminish what is already present, not create dispositions from scratch. Those who cannot imagine just why they ought not to litter or why they ought to help the frail across a busy intersection are people for whom political life can do little—except possibly to secure their possessions and act as a source of largess that will make their lives and the lives of their intimate circle more comfortable.[15]

What are the sources of such minimal concerns with the good of something larger than oneself? Presumably the usual places. Among the first lessons we learn if we are emotionally healthy is that there are other people in the world and that the well-being of some of them at least is important to us. Call this a "functioning family." Sometime after that we learn that we are part of some larger group—of neighbors, of members of a religious congregation,[16] of families connected by a common place of work—and we come to see that our well-being is tied to the fate of these others. Call this "community."[17] While not everyone will grow up this way, a great number must if there is to be a public-spirited citizenry.[18]

A concern for the public interest starts, then, with a basic connection being made in the outlook of a child between his or her own interests and those of others. On this foundation, an interest in civic life can grow: the child moves into adulthood and becomes a part of the various groups and organizations that compose civil society. Such experience reinforces the idea that my well-being includes attending to the well-being of others. All of this may, of course, go no further than fostering a realization that I share my private interests with others and that we can act together through an interest group to serve them. But interest groups can also be civic organizations insofar as they engage in informal social problemsolving, the effects of which reach beyond serving the specific set of interests for which the organization was founded. In this way, a concern for the good of the political community can be built: engaging in such problemsolving both reinforces and stretches further the connection between one's own good and the good of a larger whole.[19]

There is more: because any conception of the public interest can only be a partial one—no one person is capable of thinking through its complete concrete meaning—if we are to be public-spirited we must also have the self-confidence to face up to the fact that our view is only one among several. This may not be the only source of the tolerance necessary for the clash of interpretations of the public interest, but it is certainly an important one. And as before, we must look to the family, to our neighborhoods and our places of worship—that is, to the contexts in which our identities are first formed. In general, if we do not see ourselves as belonging to some group larger than ourselves, we are unlikely to make much sense of a good as complex as the public interest: if our feet are not anchored somewhere we will not be able to lift our eyes to the horizon.

PROUD INDEPENDENCE

However public-spirited citizens may be, it matters little to their behavior if they do not have confidence in their own opinions and think that they are worthy of being heard, that their views ought to affect public action, and that their efforts will meet with some success.[20] Only those who have faith in their own abilities—who are *proud* of their independent powers of judgment—can act in a public-spirited fashion.[21] They will think it their right to judge their lawmakers and not be overawed by them or by the size of the task facing them. As men and women who respect their own abilities and accomplishments, they will, however, also understand that being a lawmaker is a demanding job, difficult to do, and that a cavalier dismissal of the job and those who do it is beneath them.

The roots of proud independence are to be found, in part, in the world of work[22]—among other things in the experience of nonroutine, complex, loosely supervised work that, in allowing workers to exercise considerable discretion, fosters the independence of judgment and self-respect that are at the core of proud independence. As both of these traits are also necessary for mutual respect and the ability to make complex judgments—virtues discussed below—the structuring of jobs and the broader world of work is of great importance for the political life of republican government.[23]

Markets also engender a degree of proud independence by offering the regular possibility of exercising independent judgment. They also help foster the sense that there is some connection between one's exertions and a desired result, what Robert Lane calls "self-attribution." We learn that we can affect our environment, and in so doing develop a sense of efficacy crucial to proud independence.[24]

Similar are the effects of job security. The traditional argument was that independence came from owning property—that is, the ownership of a portion of the productive assets of the community with which to earn a living. This source of independence is now effectively gone: few of us own productive property of the kind that we can deploy on our own to make a living. For economic security, most of us must rely on wages and salaries. Thus, the economic insecurity that results from not having steady and reasonably well-paying work makes it difficult to develop the feeling of proud independence that underlies our conviction that we can make political judgments.[25] For republican government it matters, therefore, how wealth and income are generated. The same distribution—in one case characterized by gross economic insecurity among a substantial part of the citizenry, in another by relative economic security—can produce quite different socio-political environments. And the insecure environment is much less hospitable to republican government.

An additional source of proud independence is to be found in deliberative lawmaking itself, where citizens are assumed to have the ability to understand and profit by the reasoning that goes into the making of law. That this is a plausible outcome can be seen by contrasting to a politics centered on deliberative lawmaking a politics that treats citizens as objects to be manipulated by spin doctors—as if they are too stupid to understand what is being done to them and lacking in self-respect to such an extent as not to resent it.[26] If the only consistent message received by citizens is that lawmakers think they are fools,[27] then it is unlikely that citizens will take seriously the notion of a public interest. How citizens are addressed is especially crucial in a continental-sized republic like ours, where national political life is remote for most people, and the rhetoric of public leaders is often the only political message that reaches them.

Finally, participation in a vital civic life brings individuals into concrete, day-to-day contact with public matters transcending their private interests. If this experience *is* concrete and regular, it will plausibly promote a sense of confidence that one has something to say about public life.

TRUST

Trust is one of the principal ways we orient ourselves to the social world. It concerns whether, with due regard to circumstances, we can expect others to act with some concern for our interests and not to take every opportunity to serve their own interests at the expense of ours. More generally, it concerns whether we suppose that those doing the work of the world can be relied on to give something like their best most of the time and to attend to larger interests rather than their own and those of their immediate circle.

If citizens have little trust it is doubtful that they will have any inclination to join with others in deliberation about public matters. Nor are they likely to trust national lawmakers, about whom they inevitably have little detailed knowledge and with whom they have even less contact. Citizens without trust in their lawmakers may be humbled by the power these officials project through carefully managed mass media, and this may quiet distrust for the moment. However, as soon as things go a bit wrong, distrust quickly dissolves the trappings of office and turns them into the perquisites of unearned privilege, in the process engendering a kind of all-purpose cynicism that is an infertile ground for a politics of the public interest.[28]

As with public-spiritedness, the deepest roots of trust are in family and neighborhood. It is difficult to imagine a child growing into a trusting adult who has learned early in life that one cannot trust even those to whom one looks for love and bodily comfort. In much the same way, a child growing up in a neighborhood filled with predators is unlikely to feel drawn into cooperative dealings later in life.

It would be surprising if popular culture and the mass media also did not have some effect on children's and adults' sense of trust. For example, if the reporting of violent crime strongly implies that each of us is in imminent danger,[29] this can only reinforce feelings of mistrust of our fellow citizens. If the ordinary fare of television and the movies shows that elected officials take bribes and cut deals to further the interests of wealthy constituents, and that businessmen regularly and illegally dump toxic waste at the first opportunity, many of us will suppose that this is the way things are. After all, television and movies are vivid in the way that our timid little surmises about how the world really works never can be.

Those lucky enough to grow up in an environment where feelings of trust emerge as a matter of course are to some degree inoculated against the cynical maneuvering, naked display of self-interest, and policy failures that are the inevitable and frustrating features of even the best political orders. They are less likely to mistake these parts for the whole, and more likely to believe that mendacity and foolishness will inevitably garner more public attention than the earnest, little-noticed, plodding competence that characterizes most of the work of the political world in which they live.

COMPLEX JUDGMENTS

Without some measure of cognitive complexity[30] it is unlikely that citizens can make the kind of judgments about lawmakers that I have said is necessary. They would not only be unable to judge what elements of the public interest are at stake in any particular effort at lawmaking, but they would also find it difficult to judge whether lawmakers have any real concern with the public interest.

A principal source of the ability to make complex judgments—of cognitive complexity—is likely, again, to be in the domain of work. While it may be too much to claim that having complex, nonroutine, and loosely supervised work promotes such a capacity, it is at least plausible that the lack of it dulls what powers people have. Since work consumes the single largest portion of most adults' waking hours, if experience there does not reinforce a capacity for cognitive complexity, most people are unlikely to develop it to any high level. Here again, Adam Smith is suggestive. He commented that the "understandings of the greater part of men are necessarily formed by their ordinary employments" and that the person engaged in repetitive industrial work "becomes as stupid and ignorant as it is possible for a human creature to become."[31]

MUTUAL RESPECT

A deliberative mode of association must rest on a foundation of mutual respect among citizens. Unless citizens regard one another as equals, they are unlikely to deliberate, whatever the formal rules of the institutions require.[32] Mutual respect is the minimum form that equality in a republic must take, and it can be roughly understood as respect for persons as against abilities or attainments. Mutual respect is especially important if the natural inequality of reasoning ability—and reasoning is the center of deliberation—is not to subvert the education of judgment that is to flow from political participation. The fundamental feeling at the heart of mutual respect is that I am as good as you, no better perhaps, but certainly no worse. The enemy of mutual respect is a sense of power so great among some that they consider themselves to be in a position to inflict cruelties on others, and a corresponding sense of servility and fear among the victims.[33]

A measure of material equality is likely to be a minimum condition of mutual respect. But how much material equality is required? Perhaps a modest amount would suffice—more than, say, presently characterizes the United States but less than any strong egalitarian standard would call for.[34] The prospects for a deliberative local politics very much turn on how stringent a standard must be met; any very substantial degree of material equality would probably be difficult or even impossible to achieve within the minimum requirement of a commercial republic, that is, with some form of the private ownership of productive assets.

The dimensions of the problem that economic inequality poses for mutual respect are the following. It seems likely that persons in families with incomes around the year 2000 median family income of just under $51,000[35] are not likely to be overawed by someone who comes from a family with an income of $175,000. They inhabit something like the same world economically, and different incomes can plausibly be attributed to differences in talent and luck. The better-off person, in turn, is unlikely to think of the less well-off person as someone who lacks a character and talents worth respecting.

The problem for mutual respect lies with those at the top and bottom of the income distribution. When those in the bottom 25 percent of the distribution of American household incomes (with a mean income of just over $10,000) come into contact with those in the top 5 percent (with a mean income of just over $260,000), they are meeting people who inhabit another world.[36] They are all too likely to be deferential to those they think have won the economic race. As the political economy is now organized, moreover, the top 10 percent holds—and will continue to hold under virtually any set of reforms now possible—the major organizationally powerful positions in the society. Additionally, the top 10 percent are more or less completely insulated from contact with the poor and near-poor, and being so, some number of them are fearful of the motives of those at the bottom. Mutual respect is unlikely to be a feature of relations between the two groups.

The real difficulty for republican government, therefore, is not so much the size of the top income stratum (the highest 2–3 percent)[37] but their fear of a bottom that is too large for comfort and to whom they mostly respond without generosity. The extent of their wealth is not the problem. It is rather their response to those at the bottom and the substantial political influence they wield, which is not often mobilized to bring the poor into the system of mutual respect. Even more problematic for republican government is simply the number of the poor and near-poor. Something like a quarter of the population—those living in households with yearly incomes of just under $18,000—is outside the system of mutual respect. In short, a political economy like the present United States—characterized by an income distribution that has a significant part of its citizenry (the lowest quintile) living in poverty and near-poverty, and a top decile composed of people whose incomes run from six times to several hundred times as great as those in these lowest deciles—is not likely to be a place where mutual respect can flourish.[38]

The difficulty in achieving some measure of material equality is eased by the reasonable assumption that the core of mutual respect is self-respect. While one's material circumstances in a commercial society plainly have some bearing on self-respect, it is unlikely to be determinative. Think of the effects on a person's self-respect of possessing a skill or a body of specialized knowledge. The relatively low-income specialist in ancient Greek philosophy is less likely to feel overawed by the rich merchant banker than would the moderately well-paid middle manager of a corporation.

Similarly, the modestly paid violin maker is unlikely to think that he or she is a lesser person than the rich corporate raider. To have a skill means to have the ability to create something—and where such a skill is of a complex sort, those who have it are given or naturally have a sense of their own worth and are likely to be accorded respect by others. This, in turn, will not only be communicated to those of greater material means, but the latter will probably to some degree share their evaluation of skills and knowledge. A basis for mutual respect is in place.[39]

Here, then, is one recipe for mutual respect: each person is to have income sufficient for that measure of self-respect that will result in mutual respect. This formulation does not point to anything like strong economic equality. But it does suggest that our present distribution of income and wealth is too unequal if there is to be a republican citizenry. It is entirely possible, however, that the measure of equality required is within our economic means.[40]

But two points must be emphasized. First, self-respect is unlikely to be very strong among persons with little or no income regardless of their skills—at least not in a commercial society. In much the same way, their self-respect is likely to be eroded if they have so low a level of economic security that it will take little to tumble them into poverty. Second, many, and perhaps most people in a commercial society, will not have a level of skill sufficient in itself to promote self-respect or possess the kind of knowledge that is in short supply. The basis for their self-respect is thus likely to be closely tied to their material circumstances, including income and the prestige of the job they do. There is still some room here to get quit of the tyranny of money: there is a good deal of evidence[41] that, once people are above a certain modest level of income, it is the amount of discretion they have on the job rather than money that is more important in determining their sense of well-being. People who can exercise initiative, or are not treated as replaceable parts in a giant human-mechanical machine, are likely to feel more fully human and thus have a greater degree of self-respect. Nonroutine, complex, and loosely supervised work is important for self-respect. Those whose work is closely monitored, whose job is so routine as to require little of them must look for self-respect elsewhere.

The central questions concerning mutual and self-respect are captured in the remarks of Franklin Roosevelt:

> Our aim is to recognize what Lincoln pointed out: The fact that there are some respects in which men are clearly not equal; but also to insist that there should be an equality of self-respect and mutual respect—at least an approximate equality in the conditions under which each man obtains the chance to show the stuff that is in him compared to his fellows.[42]

How much mutual respect is needed for the kind of local politics that would engender the capacity for judgment that republican citizens need? If a commercial republic needs very substantial displays of mutual respect, it probably cannot succeed. If, on the other hand, mutual respect can be of the kind to be found among decent people who are encouraged to act in mutually respectful ways—by, for example, a modest measure of material equality—then the prospects are brighter.

THE ESTEEM OF OTHERS

Citizens can be drawn to reason-giving and deliberation because it allows them to enjoy the esteem of others, which, as Tocqueville pointed out, is a powerful motive in all popular regimes.[43] A significant number of citizens must come to local political life believing that those among them who show an awareness of interests larger than their own, who try to give content to such interests, who attempt to demonstrate why such larger interests should be attended to, and who listen attentively to the views of others on these matters should be held in high esteem. Conversely, a significant number of citizens must also believe that those who never rise above their own interests and unrelentingly pursue them are citizens from whom decency requires that one avert one's eyes.

Concern for the esteem of others is a motive that can be harnessed in the context of local political life. Indeed, this is probably the only context where such a private-regarding motive can be systematically employed in ways that will lead republican citizens to engage in a deliberative politics.[44]

LOCAL political life, and political life generally, cannot perform miracles of transformation. Deeply self-interested, unreflective citizens unable to think very hard about political life will defeat virtually any effort to induce them through constitutional design to think more carefully about public matters. In a commercial republic, the world of family and work is where the foundations for a public-spirited citizenry are laid. It would be very odd indeed if it were otherwise. Political life is much like any other undertaking: what we learn as children has a powerful impact there. And work takes up much more of our time than politics, and more powerfully affects our day-to-day lives. If it helps to form our character in ways that are deeply adverse to the requirements of republican citizenship, we should not be optimistic about realizing the regime that rests on it.[45]

LOCAL POLITICAL LIFE IN A REPUBLICAN REGIME

How must local political life be organized if it is to foster public-spiritedness? Even if citizens come to local political life with the qualities just discussed, it is unlikely that without a local political life that can build on and reinforce these qualities the measure of public-spiritedness needed for republican government can be achieved. Local government institutions in a commercial republic must create a mode of association among citizens that, by giving expression to public-spirited sentiments, reinforces them. The institutions need to stretch the regard of citizens for a good larger than their own and that of their circle so that it encompasses the public interest. In giving these sentiments expression, the citizenry's powers of judgment will also be refined and its confidence in them increased. Such institutions will need to provide a range of opportunities for citizens to act on these sentiments, thereby strengthening their capacity for judging whether their lawmakers are disposed to concern themselves with the public interest.

Republican citizens, then, must have some experience of deliberative ways of lawmaking in which they attempt to answer the question: what is the public interest? Since the concrete meaning of the public interest is a difficult matter to address, and the incentive on the part of present and aspiring lawmakers to sham is great, without experience the citizenry can be easily misled. As V. S. Naipaul says, "When men cannot observe, they don't have ideas; they have obsessions."[46] If we substitute "participate in deliberative processes" for "observe," the possibility for mischief and worse is apparent. Walter Lippmann simply said that "the kind of self-education which a self-governing people must obtain can only be had through its daily experience."[47] Something of how properly structured political experience can pull people toward a concern for larger interests is suggested by Hanna Pitkin:

> Drawn into public life by personal need, fear, ambition or interest, we are there forced to acknowledge the power of others and appeal to their standards, even as we try to get them to acknowledge our power and standards. We are forced to find or create a common language of purposes and aspirations, not merely to clothe our private outlook in public disguise, but to become aware ourselves of its public meaning. We are forced, as Joseph Tussman has put it, to transform "I want" into "I am entitled to," a claim that becomes negotiable by public standards. In the process, we learn to think about the standards themselves, about our stake in the existence of standards, of justice, of our community, even of our opponents and enemies in the community; so that afterwards we are changed. Economic man becomes a citizen.[48]

There is nothing very difficult to understand in all this. We enter the politics of a free government and, simply by having to answer questions that invite, indeed require, that we at least talk in terms of broader interests than our own, we end up thinking about what these interests might be. From perhaps knowing little and caring less about these broad interests, we now find ourselves at least trying to find the words of the public interest to cloak our narrow interests. We now know more than we did and, as in learning anything, we come imperceptibly to see the point of at least some of the elements that compose the public interest. We are on our way to becoming more fully public-spirited.[49]

In much the same way, and more mundanely, we become better at spotting bad arguments and learn something of how to craft good ones. We come, that is, to understand that if we are to be involved effectively in the broad range of matters that comes under the heading of the public interest, we must rely on the judgments of those who have thought long and hard about a given question. We thus learn how to spot just who is genuinely knowledgeable and has an eye to larger, public interests; and we learn that if there is open and vigorous debate, shoddy arguments based on rank prejudice are soon exposed. In short, we learn to be better deliberators ourselves and better at identifying those who have the requisite talent and inclination.

The assumption underlying this account of the relation between citizens and lawmakers is Madison's, who argued that we cannot rely on statesmen being our lawmakers. Republican lawmakers for the most part will be ordinary mortals who require incentives to deliberate and, most importantly, to deliberate about the concrete meaning of the public interest. A crucial set of such incentives must come from a citizenry able to reward by election those they believe have the disposition to engage in deliberative lawmaking in the public interest. First and foremost then, local political institutions must place citizens in relation to one another as deliberators, as those who think that a crucial feature in decisions about public choices is the giving of reasons. Where possible, the making of public choices should elicit arguments about what is beneficial to the members of the community and not just reflect the summation of wants and interests. It follows that local political institutions must be relatively open in their operations as well as participative because each citizen must be a prospective deliberator. In a word, the design of local political institutions should not be executive-centered, as if the principal tasks of local government were administrative in nature.[50] The latter is, in fact, the dominant contemporary vision of local political life. Instead, local political life in a fully realized republican regime must center around legislating, that is, around lawmaking in open congress for the whole community. Citizens will be directly involved in exercising the legislative power of the local polity. Just how this all is to be done is no small matter to work out. Suffice it to say that neighborhood governments and other institutional innovations are necessary.[51]

MOTIVES AND DELIBERATION

It is one thing to say that institutions must emphasize deliberation and reason-giving; it is, however, another to ensure they actually work that way. They are, after all, not bits of machinery but forms of human interaction.

We need, therefore, to consider what kinds of motives must be at work in the citizenry if local government institutions are to function in the desired ways. If their upbringing and adult experiences are like the ones I have sketched, some citizens can be expected to enter local political life believing that politics ought to concern itself with the public interest. But such motives are unlikely to be strong enough to draw a significant number of them into any kind of local political life, no less one built around deliberation and the public interest. We must seek to harness powerful private motives in addition to an abstract concern for the public good.

For most citizens, political argument about the public interest is of little interest unless it concerns such issues as neighborhood matters, schools, the land-use patterns of their localities, and public safety—all of which deeply affect their day-to-day lives. Most citizens are unlikely to accept that something is in the public interest unless it is connected to their private interest. For most people living under free popular government, there is no other starting point in public matters than the interest in their own safety and well-being and that of those dearest to them. It is from such natural concerns that a concern to serve the public interest must grow, and it is from such motives that most citizens most of the time will participate in local politics. As J. A. Gunn has put it, "[T]he raw materials for discovering the public interests are the concerns of private men as understood by these men themselves."[52] A society that has commerce at its center will reinforce such an understanding because its engine is self-interest.

The literature on collective choice, however, teaches that even such a direct connection to self-interest is unlikely to be a sufficient motive for participating in a public interest politics.[53] Consequently, additional motives—such as, for example, the esteem of others—must be at work if republican citizens are to be involved in such a politics. These too must be private-regarding. As already noted, Tocqueville pointed out that a concern for the esteem of others is a powerful motive in all popular regimes:

> [W]hen ... the public is supreme, there is no man who does not feel the value of public good-will, or who does not endeavor to court it by drawing to himself the esteem and affection of those amongst whom he is to live. Many of the passions which congeal and keep asunder human hearts, are then obliged to retire, and hide below the surface. Pride must be dissembled; disdain does not break out; selfishness is afraid of itself. Under a free government, as most public offices are elective, the men whose elevated minds or aspiring hopes are too closely circumscribed in private life, constantly feel that they cannot do without the population which surrounds them.[54]

Those whose involvement in public affairs is motivated by an informed and serious regard for the public interest are likely, then, to be held in high esteem. More broadly, Tocqueville teaches that, in democratic societies, it is the opinion of others that dominates our motives[55]—in contrast to those societies in which honor, salvation, or virtue are the dominant forces. In one sense, societies *are* democratic because opinion is so dominant. So, if political institutions are to act as I have been describing—if they are to be more than formalisms—they must transform the desire for the esteem of others into a disposition to act politically by the giving of reasons.

The design of republican local government institutions must, however, do more than promote deliberation and foster citizen participation. Public-spirited citizens wish to see that the specific, substantive elements of the public interest are served. They must thus be able to judge whether law-makers are both disposed and have the ability to deliberate about the interpretation of the elements of the public interest.

How are citizens to learn about the elements of the public interest and become adept at judging whether their lawmakers are concerned with giving it content? The broad answer is that local political life must promote deliberation about the concrete meaning of the public interest. For local political life to act as a school of public-spirited citizenship, citizens must have the experience of grappling with the meaning of the specific elements of the public interest as these are manifested in local politics. The elements of the public interest must be alive to them, attached to questions they care about and to matters they feel must be resolved.

THE STRUCTURE OF A REPUBLICAN LOCAL POLITICS

How might local political life be structured so that citizens are drawn into attempts to give concrete meaning to the elements of the public interest? In arriving at an answer, it is useful first to list again what those elements are. Thus, to serve the public interest means to secure political institutions that control faction, that are significantly deliberative in form, that secure rights, and that aggregate interests in a politically equal fashion. It also means to create and sustain private property-based market institutions that create widely available and at least moderately remunerative work, and whose political counterparts give significant discretion and inducement to controllers of productive assets. And further, it means to create institutions that facilitate a vibrant civil society. Of these elements, local political life can do the least for fostering a concern for controlling faction and securing political and civil rights. Indeed, small polities invite factional efforts by majorities to squeeze the rights of minorities. As for civil and political rights, again small polities are more likely than their larger counterparts to invite majoritarian efforts to undercut minority rights. Still, there are some modest things local political life can do in these areas, which I consider below.

We have already considered how local political institutions can foster a concern for deliberative ways of lawmaking, and found that if such institutions were deliberative in form, a significant number of citizens would have the experience of reason-giving and see something of its value. They would then be likely to seek lawmakers who also appreciate its value. This leaves us the other elements. How might local politics be structured to foster a concern for these?[56]

It will help to start by noting some features of contemporary American local, especially city, political life. This will tell us what is already being done with regard to the public interest as well as point to what must be remedied. At the heart of most local political systems of any size is an alliance between what may be termed "land interests"—large land owners, developers, downtown interests, and the like—and city political officials. The former are concerned to maintain the value of their holdings and increase their value if possible, and, for them, redevelopment and the rearrangement of land use are central concerns. Public officials, on the other hand, see redevelopment as a way to improve the city's tax base, to show their constituents they are energetic leaders, and to provide a flow of material benefactions such as jobs and contracts that can be used to secure the loyalty of their political supporters.[57]

There are two important, closely related consequences for the present discussion of a local political system dominated by land-use politics. The first is that, as things now stand, the major political actors, and many citizens, participate in a politics where the belief that government needs to provide inducements to private controllers of productive assets is central. They are unlikely to be in much doubt about its importance, as local governments go about the business of offering tax rebates, using the powers of eminent domain to create attractive land packages, and constructing municipal buildings in places that increase the value of developers' land holdings. In much the same way, citizens understand that secure property rights are central to a prosperous society. Municipal political leaders are always telling them this, if for no other reason than that the leaders' political careers depend on good relations with major property holders. In short, many, probably most, citizens get a good education in the value of these elements of the public interest.

The problem, however, is that the education is lopsided. For at bottom, the lesson being taught is that local polities must accommodate themselves to market forces. They have few powers with which to deflect these forces and so must, through inducements and other forms of accommodation, try to shape them as best they can—which is not much—and live with the results. What is missing is the opportunity, and what it may teach, to consider whether the inducements are too large, the accommodations too great—an opportunity that would come with greater governmental powers and a more open and deliberative politics. Local political life induces citizens to overvalue as elements of the public interest the strengthening of market institutions and the securing of property rights. Moreover, the structure of local politics makes it difficult to gain a hearing for the proposition that there are other elements of the public interest. There is, therefore, little room to engage in the kind of deliberative weighing of the elements of the public interest that a public-spirited citizenry must have if it is to judge whether its lawmakers have any inclination to do the same. Indeed, since the present pattern of local politics affords few opportunities for deliberation, citizens have little sense of its value, especially as compared to decisions reached by bargaining. If bargaining is the only game in town—it is at the center of the relationship between land interests and local officials—few will have any experience of a deliberative alternative.

The point is much the same for the value of institutions that secure economic and political equality and that facilitate civil society. To repeat, the path to local prosperity is presently seen as lying essentially in the support of market institutions—and through political institutions that offer substantial inducements to those who control productive assets and that give a generous interpretation to property rights. Alternative paths that rely on differently structured political and economic institutions are given little consideration. In particular, little weight is given to versions of local economic and political institutions that might ease present levels of economic inequality with a view toward making local politics an affair of, if not political equals, at least one where more players get seats at the bargaining table. In much the same way, little thought is given to institutional forms that would allow more modest inducements to asset controllers than at present, including giving them less in the way of political privilege. Similarly, little consideration is given to a version of local institutions that would work to strengthen neighborhoods, and with them the civic associations that are crucial to their health.

In short, the present workings of much of American local politics direct the attention of citizens away from an expansive conception of the public interest. A more or less fully realized republican regime rests on a moderate citizenship, one disinclined to give extravagant weight to particular elements of the public interest. A republican regime is no less threatened by an undue regard for the political and economic institutions that reward asset controllers and give them the room they need to operate than it is by an unqualified embrace of economic and political equality. To the degree that local political life fosters such narrowness in the outlook of citizens, it is a deeply flawed school of the public interest.

I have implied that a, if not the, central barrier to local politics fostering a broad conception of the public interest is a combination of the limited legal powers local governments presently have and the accompanying pattern of politics. The two are connected: if local officials had a larger array of legal powers with which to promote local prosperity, they would not need to rely so much on rearranging land-use patterns. Land interests would then be less attractive political allies and, in general, local politics would be open to a wide variety of alternative policies and institutional innovations. It follows that if friends of republican government want a constitutional politics with a broad view of the public interest at its center, they must consider alterations in local government powers and politics.

Because any serious deliberative politics concerned with the public interest depends on weakening the alliance between public officials and land interests, how might this be done? To sever that alliance requires that localities be able to pursue other strategies for securing local prosperity than pursuing mobile capital.[58] Localities would then be in a better bargaining position vis-à-vis mobile capital and less worried about the ability of their localities to attract fickle investors. Less anxious local officials would not be as vulnerable to the blandishments of land interests. It is also necessary that local officials be able to turn away from relying on the streams of material incentives generated by large land-use projects to cement their political alliances.

If localities are to pursue other strategies they must have the legal powers to do so. Municipal corporations are presently restricted in how directly involved they may be in economic matters, and thus with a large portion of the public interest.[59] This, in turn, restricts the extent to which citizens and officials can struggle over the public interest. The need is to expand municipal authority, which probably involves altering Dillon's rule and the rulings that parallel it, all of which limit the city's powers.[60] Much of what is required by way of new powers and a different politics can be grasped by simply focusing on what would be required to alter the present overwhelming focus in local political life on securing business investment. Again, how might this be done? Two possibilities may be quickly eliminated. One is to allow city financial deficits to be made good by the federal government, so that cities need not worry about their revenue bases. A second is simply to eliminate private ownership of productive assets, allowing city governments to control the local investment process. The first is unpromising because central finance would bring with it more central control than is consistent with the kind of vital deliberative-minded local politics that is required for republican government. As for the second, eliminating or even substantially reducing private control of investment is not a proposal for reforming a commercial republican regime, whatever else it may be.

This leaves less drastic proposals. Probably the most promising is to build on the proposition that property is not a thing but a "bundle of rights,"[61] the elements of which may be separately adjusted. This adjustment of rights is, of course, currently being done as restrictions are placed, for example, on how factories may dispose of their waste products. This suggests that there is nothing in the concept of private property itself that prevents local governments under certain conditions from exacting repayment for public investments made to attract investment. Thus, if public authorities utilize common resources for public benefit, and if the realization of those benefits is jeopardized, it would be appropriate to attempt to recover the investment.[62] Such a proposal has much in common with those whose basis is that the costs of a firm leaving a locality should not be borne only by local citizens. Both proposals aim to alter the calculus of controllers of productive assets when they make decisions concerning the location of their businesses, but to do so without stripping them of the right to make such decisions.

There would be at least two immediate effects of such a repayment scheme. Businesses attracted to a new locality by new road facilities or property-tax abatements would be more reluctant to relocate than they are at present. And if repayment were made, city coffers would not need to be drawn down in order to attract new investment because a revolving fund of sorts would be established. For both reasons, officials and citizens would be less drawn into alliance with land interests.

Increased powers to consider land-use questions and the freeing of those who exercise city authority from the need to seek an alliance with land interests will not, however, free city residents from the need to be concerned with the economic vitality of the city. What they will gain is the ability not to be strongly drawn toward businessmen's definitions of the commercial dimension of the public interest, a matter to which I will return. It suffices to say here that citizens and those who speak for them will be freer than they now are to consider alternative formulations for promoting local prosperity. They will also be able to focus on the connections between doing so and other aspects of city life. Thus, altering the structural features that shape local politics will give the deliberative politics set in motion by new deliberatively oriented city political institutions a chance to flourish. Expanding city powers will allow citizens and officials to be less attentive to mobile capital, and increased city powers will likely bring in their wake political organizations that rely less than they presently do on the flow of political benefits from capital investment projects.[63] Structural change at the local level, then, is fundamental to a politics whose core concern is the public interest.

The broad effects of such a change can now be considered, particularly how a major part of the local citizenry will be drawn into a general discussion of the concrete meaning of the public interest. We can start by expanding the preceding discussion of how, in a reformed local politics, market-securing policies will fit into an overall discussion of the public interest. In a fully realized system of republican local government, attracting and keeping mobile capital will continue to be an important source of local prosperity. But with expanded powers to affect that mobility and alternative ways to promote local prosperity, local citizens, and those who speak for them, will be able to consider more fully than at present the terms under which such capital is worth pursuing. Moreover, citizens and officials will also be in a position to ask whether there are good reasons why, under a variety of circumstances, it should be made more difficult for businesses to move. Since local governments will have the powers to affect the extent of business mobility, citizens and officials will be forced to consider whether the locality ought to enter into contractual agreements that require departing firms to repay some portion of the benefits that initially attracted them to the municipality. Similarly, if localities can exercise powers of eminent domain to buy businesses threatening to depart, citizens and officials will face the question of whether exercising this power will make it more difficult to attract new businesses. In the ensuing policy debates, it will become apparent that the prosperity of the locality depends not only on what local government can do but also on whether businessmen have substantial discretion in how they invest their capital. There is no way to compel them to make investments given a private enterprise system, and if their discretion is sharply curtailed by local government, they will likely be disinclined to make them.[64]

In short, citizens and officials will be forced to consider whether efforts at public regulation of private investment may reduce the level of prosperity that is itself a part of the public interest.[65] Similarly, they will be drawn into considering whether such regulation may also reduce the degree to which this prosperity is widely distributed among the citizenry in the form of moderately remunerative work, that is, whether such regulation may affect yet another element of the public interest. It should not be surprising that such discussions will occur. Even with limited local powers, thoughtful citizens and officials undoubtedly believe that inducing private investment, relying on market institutions for prosperity, and being careful to maintain substantial discretion for those who control productive assets are elements of the public interest.

More broadly, in a republican local politics, politically engaged citizens and local officials will face the following situation: having significant power to promote local prosperity and to reduce the dependency of local governments on mobile private investment, and participating in a politics that can support such initiatives, they will be induced to consider the value of relying on and strengthening market institutions as against the claims of other elements of the public interest. Thus, attentive citizens and officials will be drawn into considering whether it is appropriate to use local taxing powers to attract businesses, especially as the principal benefits are likely to flow to one part of the citizenry while the costs fall on another. If, as past experience suggests, the costs tend to fall most heavily on the poor and weak, citizens and those who speak for them will likely find themselves weighing the value of promoting the modest level of economic equality required by the public interest against another of its elements, the strengthening of market institutions that inducement of investment produces. Similarly, once local governments have such powers, and once local politics is freed from the alliance between land interests and elected officials, local citizens and their representatives will be able to address the question of whether the politically privileged position of land interests in local politics needs to be as great as it presently is. In turn, by considering the degree of political privilege that is appropriate, citizens and officials might well see the danger of factional rule. It is all too easy, they may say, for local governmental power to be used to ride roughshod over the due process rights that should be at the core of a public taking of land, as well as over the political rights that make possible public scrutiny of large-scale rearrangements of land use.

In much the same way, in the efforts to promote local prosperity and keep city revenues high, it will be possible for citizens and officials to appreciate that localities with large poor populations are less attractive to employers considering moving their business there; they prefer an educated and energetic workforce. Also, large numbers of poor people are a drain on local budgets, which means that money that could go into growth-supporting initiatives does not. The breaking down of the alliance around land use and the creation of participative local institutions will make it easier for such considerations to be raised. To the degree that this is so, local political life will, again, provide the experience for many citizens of weighing the claims of economic equality against other elements of the public interest. In much the same fashion, as those who realize that something must be done about local poverty look for political allies, they will no doubt realize that the poor themselves are politically weak. This might prompt a concern for political equality and inject this element of the public interest into local political life.

In all these ways, the citizens of a republican local politics will develop a concrete sense of the ways in which the politics of business inducement is in tension with other elements of the public interest. Thus, to illustrate further and return to an earlier comment, the citizens and officials of republican local governments will be drawn into policy discussions that reveal the tension between the politics of business inducement needed to keep market institutions functioning at a high level and deliberative ways of lawmaking. In much the same way, such a citizenry and its representatives will have experience of weighing the claims of business inducement that would lead to large-scale redevelopment of neighborhoods and the value of civic associations anchored in these neighborhoods. Each of these—business inducement, deliberative ways of lawmaking, and a vibrant civil society—are needed. A public-spirited citizenry will be wrestling with questions whose answers give concrete meaning to the public interest as that is manifest locally. In the broadest sense, many citizens will be part of an attempt to define limits on the power of government. They will come to realize that too great a scope for government endangers the necessary discretion of asset controllers and the rights of citizens, and will invite factional strife; against this they will develop a sense that excessive limits on government make the availability of modestly remunerative work, economic and political equality, and appropriate limits on the political privilege of business harder to achieve. Equally important, many citizens will likely come to appreciate that deliberative ways of lawmaking are necessary if reasoned discussion of such matters is to occur.

There is nothing in such efforts by citizens and those who speak for them that requires deep acquaintance with major policy questions. Neither do they rest on sophisticated analyses of the roots of local prosperity nor a theory of the public interest. Most citizens are unlikely, in any case, to have such comprehensive and detailed ideas. In this, they are not likely to be much different from their lawmakers. For the fostering of a public-spirited citizenry, all that is necessary is that citizens see the need for their officials—and they themselves if they are engaged in significant ways in local political life—to give consideration to the claims of business discretion, the necessity of public deliberation, the value of a measure of economic equality, and the like. Citizens can see the need to do so if local politics is so structured that such natural considerations for local lawmaking are not screened out, and, indeed, attention to them is facilitated by the design of political institutions and the politics they support. In turn, if these considerations do find a purchase in local political life, many citizens will be a party to political struggles that will help them develop a sense of what—even if they don't refer to it as such—the elements of the public interest call for. Different citizens are likely to have different competencies in this respect, and moderate acquaintance with any policy area will provide them with a good test for reaching a judgment about their lawmakers. If prospective or sitting lawmakers say they know something about a policy area and hold considered opinions regarding its connection to the public interest, but they plainly do not, citizens will not need to think very hard in deciding whether such persons should be given the power to speak for them. Properly structured, local political life can reduce political fantasy and slovenliness about public matters and generally discipline the thinking of citizens.[66]

Not all citizens can or need to hold local political office or otherwise be directly and intensively involved in local politics if public-spiritedness is to be fostered. Many will indeed so participate, and if local politics is structured as I have said it ought to be, they might be called "fully" public-spirited. They would have both of its elements: a concern that political life revolve around a reasoned effort to give concrete meaning to the public interest; and a sense of the concrete elements of the public interest. They would be public-spirited not because they have thought through a theory of the regime and its public interest. Such people are not political theorists disguised as ordinary citizens.[67] It is experience, properly structured, that will have taught them what they need to know. If such learning cannot be the source of a full public-spiritedness, it is difficult to see how there can be lawmaking in the public interest.

All citizens need not think of themselves as, or in fact be, fully public-spirited. They need only call to mind some standard—for example, that the discretion of businessmen in how they deploy productive assets should not be too greatly limited—in light of which lawmakers are to be judged. In doing so, they effectively will be promoting lawmaking in the public interest—so long as other citizens are drawn to judging lawmakers by reference to other elements of the public interest. Such people we might call "minimally" public-spirited, and the form that minimum takes will vary, with different people being concerned with different parts of the public interest. There will inevitably be those for whom local political life holds no charm or interest or who otherwise find it difficult to gain entry to its precincts. Such citizens are likely to lack public-spiritedness altogether. But so long as they constitute substantially less than a majority of the citizenry, national lawmakers will find themselves facing a citizenry that pushes them toward lawmaking in the public interest.

Is it really likely that a majority of citizens, a body large enough to substantially affect the process by which national lawmakers are selected, can display at least a modest level of public-spiritedness? Can a significant proportion of them make judgments about human types who are not significantly different from themselves? It would be one thing if the problem for republican citizens were to choose philosopher-kings, for then they would be asked to choose a kind of being whose existence was inconceivable to all but of few of them. But the problem for republican government is different and easier: all that is needed is for citizens to be able to recognize among themselves those who have a strong and abiding concern for the public interest. They need only recognize a modest kind of excellence, of the sort that is regularly encountered in day-to-day life—the sort of person who is sensitive to the concerns of associates but tries to get them to think more broadly, to see that they are a part of a larger world whose well-being is as much their concern as their own immediate needs.[68]

Public-spiritedness is not perhaps an easy virtue to learn—certainly not in a regime like the commercial republic we aspire to be and to some degree are. In such a regime, and probably in all those that afford some measure of individual liberty to its citizens, the natural disposition is to favor our own interests and those of our immediate circle. Familial and other relationships that can provide the foundations for public-spiritedness must do a great deal of work if the outlook of republican citizens is to approximate what is needed for there to be deliberative ways of lawmaking. It is important, however, not to make the task greater than it is. Republican citizens need not be indifferent to their self-interest, and self-interest is thus not displaced. To be sure it must be enlarged and the connection to the public interest made vivid. But republican citizens will still have a lively sense of and be inclined to pursue self-interest in its more straightforward meaning. In the end, perhaps the hardest thing about republican citizenship is to learn when a concern for public or private interest is appropriate.[69]

SOME ADDITIONAL FEATURES OF A REPUBLICAN LOCAL POLITICS

It is worth adding here that if republican local governments are to do the job of fostering public-spiritedness they must be sufficiently diverse so that, in their efforts to give concrete meaning to the public interest, citizens and officials will have to accommodate a wide variety of views.[70] Otherwise, they will be in danger of supposing that the conclusions they reach as a homogeneous municipality are in fact the only compelling ones. And they will be inclined to suppose that, when national lawmakers come to different views, it is probably because of their dark purposes rather than a result of their efforts to take account of the interests of a heterogeneous citizenry. Moreover, the citizens of homogeneous localities will be less likely to recognize the possibility that, even though a lawmaker has policy views different from their own, the legislator could still have a good grasp of the public interest. The citizens of a commercial republic need the regular experience of seeing that the concrete meaning of the public interest is the subject of considerable conflict. Perhaps they will not need much experience to convince them. But, and more difficult to grasp, they also need to learn that such conflict is no bad thing (indeed it is inevitable) so long as disagreements are settled peacefully and with due regard to the merits of various arguments. We may say that a political order composed of a mosaic of homogeneous localities is a poor base on which to build a commercial republic.

Another feature local political life must have if it is to be a school of public-spiritedness is a significant degree of residential stability. Those who regularly move their households are unlikely to be very interested in or informed about local affairs. Learning requires memory—of what has been tried before and with what results.

The key to the design of a republican local politics is thus a set of institutional arrangements that can harness the concern for securing their own interests that most citizens feel when issues such as the state of their neighborhood and schools emerge.[71] What they will learn about the public interest in such a politics is, in part, a side benefit of a concern for their own interests.[72] Citizens will be drawn into a process in which they must do more than argue that some proposal is beneficial to them and people like them. They will have to give reasons and be able to connect them to the questions that a properly structured local political life will raise, namely, those prompted by the form the public interest takes in local political life. In a commercial republic, virtue must either begin in private interest, or at least be compatible with it. Private interest is to be accommodated, made use of, and stretched.

If the structure of local government is such as to attract widespread citizen involvement in local political life, a significant number of citizens will have the kind of experience necessary to judge their national lawmakers. They will likely respond to legislative proposals that on their face make little sense not by assuming that such matters are beyond them, but instead by realizing, in light of their own experience in related matters, that many proposals are in fact foolish or unworkable. Such citizens, while certainly more public-spirited than the vast majority of present-day Americans, are not so different as to be unrecognizable versions of ourselves. Given present proclivities and even a modest experience of a republican local politics, it is not hard to imagine large numbers of citizens being brought to the point of saying: "I don't agree with all or even many of a candidate's stands on issues, but I believe him to be a straight shooter, someone who has thought about the positions taken, and whom I respect." To state as much is to say: "Here is a candidate I can trust to use his powers of reasoning to arrive at decisions that, if I had more time to think about the matter, I might well arrive at myself. And if his votes in the Congress are different than ones I think I might have arrived at if I were there, this too is acceptable. After all," our imagined citizen might go on, "the lawmaker's vote on legislation plausibly derives from listening to other lawmakers and weighing evidence, which is something I would try to do myself." In short, such citizens might conclude that the lawmaker is disposed to deliberative ways of lawmaking in the service of the public interest.

More broadly, it is likely that a significant number of citizens will be able to evaluate how prospective lawmakers talk about public matters. Do they try to make it appear that there are no costs other than monetary ones to major policy proposals, that there is, in short, no conflict among the values that citizens know to be encompassed by the public interest? Probably many will conclude that candidates who speak about public questions without attending to these conflicts are either fools or demagogues, or both.

Here is a sense of community appropriate to a commercial republic and liberal regimes generally. It is rooted not in identity or ties of culture. Nor is it at bottom an affective community, although local citizens can, of course, have an affectionate regard for their localities and principal institutions. Local communities in a more or less fully realized commercial republic will be rooted in practical affairs, in the need to make a life among those whom fate has caused to occupy a locality. The communities of a commercial republic are rooted in the fact that we must live with others and must take account of them. But something more can be made of this than just the grudging acceptance of propinquity: self-interest can be stretched and an inclination to be concerned with larger interests reinforced.

In the end, the most important thing to say about a republican local politics is that two streams of activity and affect meet there, both of which point beyond self-interest. One is a kind of moral learning that has its roots in the intimate sphere, another in political life. Both are needed to foster public-spiritedness. A politics structured to promote public-spiritedness will instead promote cynicism if it lacks a foundation in the moral teaching of the intimate sphere. Similarly, a politics to which citizens bring a nascent public-spiritedness, but that lacks institutions promoting deliberation, will degenerate into a scramble to benefit me and mine as public-regarding impulses are stifled.

In its choice of deliberatively minded lawmakers with a concern for the public interest, a public-spirited citizenry illustrates the first law of social science: it takes one to know one. If local political life is characterized by the kinds of political institutions I have sketched, if local communities have the kind of socio-economic structure that I have described, and if the citizenry that can give life to these institutions brings to local political life the virtues I have set out, then a local political life characterized by a more or less reasoned attempt to give concrete meaning to the public interest is likely.[73] And those citizens who have themselves participated in deliberative ways of lawmaking will expect of their lawmakers what they expect of themselves. They will also be in a position to judge whether deliberation is occurring. Moreover, even those who have not participated in a local politics concerned with the public interest will likely be impressed with the fact that local lawmakers can be induced to concern themselves with it, and be inclined to judge their national legislators accordingly. To be sure, they will be less adept at judging national lawmakers than those who have participated in local political life, but they will be more skilled than if they had never witnessed a local politics concerned with the public interest. Citizens will learn as a byproduct of local politics a significant portion of what they need when judging their national lawmakers. Learning that occurs in this fashion will go a long way to reducing the otherwise high costs of acquiring the skills they would need for such judging.

CIVIC MAJORITIES AND THE MIDDLE CLASS

There is more to the story about the character of a public interest politics. I have said that a political regime has a ruling stratum, and that in a fully realized commercial republic this is the middle class. If this is so, the middle class should be receptive to a politics that aims to foster a public-spirited citizenship. It is, after all, *its* conception of justice and the good regime—and thus of the public interest—that is being fostered by a republican local political life. Nor should this be surprising: it is a standard argument that liberalism was created for and strengthened by a social stratum that was neither aristocratic and concerned with honor, nor deeply concerned about distributive justice. Liberalism's political and moral center was to be a class with a secure basis in material well-being and in the exercise of individual initiative—in short, the mass of ordinary people who, as Montesquieu said, wished to have a feeling of tranquility arising from the opinion each has of their own security.[74]

If such a public-spirited middle class exists, a republican regime can safely be majoritarian. Its existence would allow us to solve a problem that we have inherited from Madison. Madison was a majoritarian but not a simple one. His worry was not about majorities *per se*, but factional majorities. He was clear that majority rule was the "republican principle" of governing, a view powerfully expressed by Lincoln.

> A majority, held in restraint by constitutional checks, and limitations, and always changing easily, with deliberative changes of popular opinions and sentiments, is the only true sovereign of a free people. Whoever rejects it, does, of necessity fly to anarchy or to despotism. Unanimity is impossible; the rule of a minority, as a permanent arrangement, is wholly inadmissible; so that, rejecting the majority principle, anarchy or despotism in some form is all there is left.[75]

Not any sort of majority should rule, Madison believed; but neither should rule be by anything other than majorities. Madison thus hoped for rule by "civic majorities,"[76] by those committed to serving the public interest, and he designed a set of institutions to impede factional majorities and encourage those committed to rights and the permanent interests of the community. However, Madison's reliance on the propertied meant that he needed to make the formation of *any* majorities relatively difficult, and he hoped that the refining and enlarging of opinion that would occur in republican lawmaking would produce the needed civic majorities. But he failed to provide a compelling account of why the kinds of lawmakers needed to make this refining process work would, in fact, be elected. He did not have an adequate theory of republican citizenship.

The heart of Madison's problem, we might say, is that he did not think there was a reliable majority on which to rest a republican regime. In the end, he seems to have placed his faith in the process of lawmaking itself, and thus in lawmakers who might be supposed to rise above and compensate for the failures of the citizenry. Much in his thinking, however, makes this a bad bet. What Madison did not foresee was that an attractive possibility for a steady majority would emerge with the rise of a mass middle class. The emergence of a numerous and politically active middle class was not easy to see at the very beginnings of capitalism.[77] Madison, in fact, still inhabited an economic world in which scarcity was a real problem and the coming of widespread abundance necessary for such a middle class to form far from obvious. We, however, have seen such a class come into being and know that the societal wealth necessary for economic well-being to filter down to the mass of people is possible. Regardless, with the rise of the middle class comes the possibility that republican politics can be majoritarian and, even more important, that it can revolve around the actions of civic majorities. Moreover, such a middle class also makes possible a different, more self-interested kind of majoritarian politics, a matter to which I turn in chapter 8.

Who is to mobilize these civic majorities? There is no reason to suppose that public-spirited majorities will somehow mobilize themselves. The plausible candidate, again, is party leaders. But friends of the commercial republic should not be overly optimistic here. In a republican legislature, it is probable that party leaders can organize the agenda and provide the cues for lawmaking in the public interest. The outlook of party leaders in this context will likely have elements of both an abiding concern for the success of the party they lead and a measure of concern for the public interest. Importantly, in this sort of legislature, it will not be easy for party leaders to turn their backs on the question of the public interest. Legislation will inevitably be introduced that has a direct bearing on the public interest and some visible response on the part of the leadership will be necessary. Leaders might be inclined to walk away, but this will only be to the dismay of their public-interest-minded colleagues and at some cost to their own view of how lawmaking should be carried on. Or this will be the case if the fostering of a public-spirited citizenry has succeeded.

In the electoral arena, however, and in the world of mobilizing citizen opinion, matters are likely to be different. Here it will be easier for party leaders to look the other way. There will be no formal agenda requiring them to deal with the policy proposals that surface and complicate their partisan lives. Moreover, there will probably be little in the way of costs for not pleasing public-spirited citizens. Not being much mobilized in the first place, they can hardly exert themselves very effectively to punish party leaders. In short, party leaders can keep their attention on, as it were, their official job.

The question, then, is whether there are any possible incentives that might make these leaders more attentive to matters of the public interest. One possibility is to rely on so-called public interest groups, the members of which have no significant material stake in the outcome of the policy struggles in which they are involved.[78] But the present array of such groups is, for the most part, not the kind that would be needed. As we have seen, their focus is too narrow; they are not greatly concerned with ensuring that all or indeed any elements of the public interest be given life. It is possible, however, that with a public-spirited citizenry, those with political ambitions may take it on themselves to organize groups genuinely committed to at least some aspects of the public interest. If this occurs, party leaders who wish to remain among the most visible and powerful leaders in the regime will regularly face other political leaders who make it clear to them that they cannot maintain their leadership positions if they do not regularly turn from political mobilization, directed at strengthening party positions, to building support for the public interest. Such movement by party leaders—between party matters and matters of the public interest—will be more likely insofar as some of these same leaders will be doing the same thing in the legislative arena. Almost as useful would be parties well-enough organized that there is regular contact between leaders who take the lead in the two arenas. Those plying their trade in the legislative arena would press their electoral colleagues to take questions of the public interest seriously.

To summarize, if the legislature is organized in the manner described,[79] and if there is a public-spirited citizenry at work, then it is likely that the separation of powers will work to enhance deliberative lawmaking. The legislature, as an interlocutor with the other branches of government, will provide incentives for those branches to broaden and strengthen their own views of the public interest. Not least of the reasons that the other branches will likely enter into struggle and debate with the legislature over public interest matters is the existence of a public-spirited citizenry, one unlikely to look kindly on branches of government that do not make some attempt to respond to efforts to give tangible meaning to the public interest.

SELF-LIMITATION, STATESMANSHIP, AND THE ORDINARY POLITICS OF THE PUBLIC INTEREST

To the degree a public interest politics is firmly established, the danger of factional government is reduced. It may thus be possible to have milder "auxiliary precautions" than Madison supposed to control faction. These would also allow majorities substantial scope in organizing and giving direction to government. Less need for stringent means to control faction would be especially apparent if the majorities that regularly form are civic majorities. If such majorities were a regular feature of our political life, a self-limiting popular sovereign would be created, that is, a constitutional politics in which the people limit themselves. Since it is the agents authorized by the people who give concrete meaning to the public interest, subject to the people's consent, it is the people who limit themselves. They do so in the act of giving the public interest substance. In a fully realized republic this cannot be regularly done in any other way. There is no other agent than the people that can, within the confines of republican government, legitimately limit the people's rule. In limiting themselves, the people also prevent the destruction of popular government likely to follow on a citizenry unable to moderate and direct its demands on the state—a destruction that (most of) the citizenry will not wish for. Crucial to this effort of self-limitation is the prevention of factional government, which by its nature is hostile to the idea of limited government. And central to this whole effort of creating a deliberative, self-limiting politics is a citizenry with the capacity and energy to induce its leaders to limit government by preventing faction and serving the rest of the public interest.

In giving the public interest sufficient substance to direct governmental action, good arguments are what must count—in particular, arguments aimed at showing what the public interest calls for in the case at hand. Neither the fact of having an argument nor, more broadly, having an interest in the matter at hand is sufficient warrant for one's views to carry any weight. In contrast to questions where aggregating interests is appropriate,[80] the response to an unacceptably powerful voice for large-scale controllers of productive assets, for example, cannot be to aim for political equality among relevant interests. This would amount to saying that there cannot be deliberation. It would also—if not deny that there can be a public interest politics—turn efforts to serve the public interest into a process that relies on something other than reasoning about it. This is to take a valuable point: that serving some valued purposes may require processes other than ones built around reasoning—for example, bargaining or other forms of exchange—and make them bear the whole weight of realizing republican government.

What has been described so far might be called the "ordinary politics" of the public interest. No statesmen are needed. Even the political leaders of the legislature need not be engaged in more than ordinary political acts, although their ambitions are such as to make them carry a large part of the burden of legislating in the public interest. But will all this be enough for the public interest to be well served? The ordinary politics of the public interest is just that—ordinary. This does not mean it is placid or unruffled by conflict. But it is not likely that a public interest politics can always have a work-a-day form. At some points, there are bound to be deep conflicts over the meaning of the public interest, and ordinary lawmakers and ordinary political leaders are apt to be uneasy with taking big risks to see that the conflicts are managed and, if possible, resolved.

While such intense conflicts can continue as the ordinary politics of the public interest moves along, at some juncture their continuation can become dangerous: ordinary politics threatens to be engulfed by intense conflict. And yet the risks of attempting to resolve such deep conflicts are great. Here, statesmen are needed—leaders who understand the political risks of acting but discount them because of their deep devotion to republican government and to serving the public interest.[81] They not only have the energy of legislative leaders and an equally intense desire for lasting fame as a great lawmaker; they are also willing to take chances when ordinary leaders hesitate.

Even with a well-designed republican political constitution, then, there are likely to be occasions when more is needed than the ordinary politics of the public interest. A commercial republic is no different from any good regime. Not every problem or threat that might arise can be planned for in advance through securing a constitutional politics. And if the crisis of the public interest is an especially deep one—if it cannot be contained within an ordinary politics of the public interest—and if no statesmen are present to take up the burden, then the regime itself is in danger. But constitutional theory has its limits. Madison is correct that we cannot rest our design for a constitutional politics on statesmen being present and men being angels. Nor did he think, and neither should we, that *statesmen* are angels. Their motives are likely to be mixed, with a belief in republican government existing alongside an appetite for fame and glory. Founding statesmen, as well as those involved in refounding regimes, are particularly likely to wish to leave their imprint on the world. As Madison himself understood—not least because he participated in a great act of statesmanship in the founding of the American Republic—we are probably unable to wholly dispense with their services. It would not have been prudent for him to spell out at any length that the new republic that he was commending would be vulnerable in ways for which no great provision could be made. Since he also believed that a commercial republic was the regime best suited to Americans, and since all good regimes must at various points rely on statesmanship, he likely thought reticence was called for. Whether statesmanship is necessary at the present juncture is another matter. We are not in the midst of founding a new regime, although we may be in the midst of refounding it.

The question of statesmanship as a limit on the design of a constitutional politics points to an additional limit. A commercial republic promises to provide for bodily security and the freedoms that flow from it, and for at least modest levels of material well-being. To accomplish this is no mean feat; indeed most peoples have never achieved it. While this may be enough to inspire affection for the regime on the part of the people, it may not be enough to gain the hearts of what Machiavelli called the "princes," those present in all regimes who are driven to perform great deeds and to acquire for all what is necessary if the goods of a civil life are to be secured and maintained.[82]

CONCLUSION

No constitutional design is free from difficulty and the one being set out here is no exception. Thus, if local polities must be heterogeneous if they are to be republican, and if achieving such a population mix requires judicial decisions as well as legislation by the states and the national government, as it undoubtedly will, how can such lawmaking co-exist with a vital local political life? Without the latter, it is difficult to see how a public-spirited citizenry can be fostered. However, it is equally difficult to see how the heterogeneity needed can be promoted without substantially constraining the local autonomy necessary for a local political life worthy of the interest of its citizens. Similar problems are present in any systematic attempt to reduce the number of communities so poverty stricken that grappling with the public interest can have little meaning for their citizens and even less interest. In the context of trying to secure a commercial republican regime, the economic condition of localities cannot and should not be equalized because, quite apart from whether this is justified or politically feasible, the only means for doing so is through the federal government. This in turn would make many localities financial wards of the national government and, consequently, diminish the possibility that they can be schools of republican citizenship.

These sorts of difficulties are compounded by the high rate of American residential mobility. Between March 1999 and March 2000, more than 43 million Americans moved their residences. Of these, 56 percent moved within the same county, the rest within the same state or state to state.[83] However, even those who moved within the same county are likely to have their interest shifted from one set of local government institutions to another. Population mobility and local political engagement pull in different directions.

It is not clear how best to navigate among these various requirements of a republican local politics. Whatever the difficulties, however, if local political life is to foster public-spiritedness, it must combine a stable population, a significant measure of heterogeneity, substantial economic resources, legal and fiscal autonomy, and broad political authority. A problem worth considering in this context is that there is a substantial tension between an economy that must be built around widespread mobility of labor and a vibrant politics of place. People with jobs that can easily be moved are unlikely to be deeply interested in local politics. Nor are they likely to invest very heavily in developing the relations of mutual respect that are fundamental to local politics as a school of public-spiritedness. The reforms of city powers and of local politics mentioned here will make capital less mobile and thus the issue less pressing. Still, the dimensions of the problem are more easily stated than the solution. The central question is this: is it possible to have reasonably high levels of national economic growth without undercutting the level of residential stability needed for a republican local politics?

Similarly, expanding the powers of local governments is not without risk to basic rights. The problem of faction returns with vengeance in small-scale political units such as towns and cities. Thus Hamilton, echoing Madison, commented that "the spirit of faction . . . ill humors, or temporary prejudices and propensities, which in smaller societies frequently contaminate" "beget injustice and oppression of part of the community, and engenders schemes which though they gratify a momentary inclination or desire, terminate in general distress, dissatisfaction and disgust."[84] It is plausible that guarantees of rights rooted in national political institutions can do much to reduce the danger, but there is no denying the problem.[85]

There is also the problem of a race to the bottom. What will prevent a process developing in which each local government attempts to outbid others by refraining from exercising the expanded powers they would have in a republican political constitution? Part of the answer is simply that, in itself, such a bidding process is self-limiting. The financial burden for any locality at some point will start to rise dramatically. Moreover, a participatory and deliberative local politics will likely bring to light the looming financial crunch and thus prevent the competition from proceeding to the bitter end.

Even as localities operate now, while there is certainly bidding, it is not a case of abject surrender to land interests. In much the same way, how far the competitive process can go will be shaped by how free localities are to shift the costs of this competition onto the backs of the weak and poor—for example, by giving away tax revenues that might otherwise go to services for them or by simply clearing them off land needed to attract mobile businesses. Both the fact of mutual respect and its economic underpinnings, and the relatively open nature of republican local government will likely set some limits on how far the process can go. But since pressures on republican local governments to compete will remain strong, it is unlikely that these features of local politics will be sufficient to prevent a certain amount of stumbling toward the bottom. National policies that lessen the need for localities to worry about local economic growth will thus be necessary. A full employment policy is one candidate for the job. If successful, localities will not be as worried as they presently are about attracting businesses. Whether this will be enough is another matter.

Again, there are those who argue that power is leaking out of local governments to such a degree that a local political life vital enough to foster public-spiritedness is no longer possible. Local governments are indeed losing autonomy in two ways. Power is moving "above," to transnational economic actors and to states and the national government thought by many to be better equipped to deal with a fast-changing national and international economy. Power is also leaking "below" (and sideways) to privately incorporated communities that wield many of the powers of local governments, and to various kinds of special districts. Even the supposed globalization of the economy, however, has not altered fundamentally the possibility of creating viable local political units, unless it is argued that it is no longer possible to modify, deflect, and harness for our own purposes economic forces. This seems too extreme a view and, if actions are any indication of what people believe, it is not shared by most government officials and citizens. They seem to think it is still worth trying to respond to and direct economic forces. In short, local political actors apparently believe that there are still reasons to have government—other than as devices through which the greedy can line their pockets. Nor has the carving up of the local, all-purpose municipalities gone so far as to make it impossible to sustain a vibrant local political life—one that allows and provides incentives for citizens and officials to think broadly and in common about how to make the locality prosper while attending to other elements of the public interest. Reports of the demise of local government are exaggerated.[86]

Finally, unless provision is made in the design of local governments for a kind of structured participation in which decisions of real importance get debated in serious ways—in which, that is, there are substantial penalties for frivolity, gross stupidity, interminable prolixity, and rank self-interest—local government as one of the foundations of a republican regime can be consigned to the same rubbish bin in which are kept all the other failed schemes to foster republican citizenship. It is the quality of local politics that is crucial, not the mere fact of substantial local government powers and citizen participation. Nothing is gained and a great deal lost if there is power without responsibility, mass entertainment (or boredom) without consequences. The danger for a republican local government is the one that Oscar Wilde identified as the trouble with socialism—too many meetings.

A republican system of local government will not be easy to design, much less put into place. However, it is not as if friends of the regime have much choice. There is no other place to look for a school of republican citizenship. As I have argued, no other political context offers the possibility of significant political participation in the making of important political decisions on the range of questions likely to be encompassed by any plausible conception of the public interest—and where, moreover, the idea that we need to be concerned with the well-being of our fellow citizens is not an empty abstraction. To put it differently, if they are to be public-spirited, citizens of a republic must find it a reasonable use of their time to engage in a politics that broadens their concerns. The context must be one that touches on some of their most important day-to-day concerns and that is not so large as to be, on its face, irrational for most people to involve themselves. This local political life can offer. Nor should this be surprising because it is in our localities that most of us carry on many of the activities central to our lives. Some of us may be able to live with little or no concern about what happens in our local community. Our children may go to private school someplace else; our work may take place in cyberspace; and our homes may be protected by private security measures including literally walling ourselves off from those with whom we share the locality. But most of us still live someplace and in the old-fashioned way. What rolls up to our door, what happens around the corner and in other parts of the community, has direct effects on us from which we cannot easily escape. Local life is still sufficiently important to most people that it can provide a foundation for republican citizenship.

Local political life is crucial for republican government for an additional reason. Unorganized citizens are no match for organized interests with a clear sense of their goals. If the public interest is to be served, there must be a significant counterweight to such groups, especially the ones with narrow interests, and a major part of that resistance must be the citizenry at large. Local government can *organize* the citizenry. It can provide an institutionalized context in which to form judgments about the public interest. Citizens need not raise money to make their views known or create organizations to carry their message. All this is ready to hand if there is a well-ordered republican local politics.

It should come as no surprise that some of the foundations of public-spiritedness, and thus of republican citizenship, depend on restraining various features of an enterprise-based market system. Local governments need powers to make capital mobility less easy, and citizens need to be freed from the need to regularly move their residences in the pursuit of work. Curbing important aspects of property rights and markets is especially difficult—and especially important—in a commercial society where private property and markets are valued. Still, like everything else in a capitalist system, "all that is sold melts into air"[87] under the pounding of the pursuit of pecuniary advantage. It would be odd if the settled and the nonpecuniary foundations of republican citizenship were not assaulted by the force of capital. However, a commercial republic is just that—not only commercial but republican. It is thus no weakness of will or lack of comprehension that makes reflective friends of the regime wish to protect substantial domains of our collective life from the measuring rod of money. In this they are better friends of the regime than those who, out of ignorance or the peculiarities of academic specialization, either proclaim that republican citizenship can take care of itself or simply fail to consider the forces that make them free citizens able to be ignorant or foolish.

Some will wonder at this juncture whether the design offered here for a local politics, just as with constitutional politics generally, asks too much of ordinary men and women. Will they find it difficult to hold simultaneously in their hearts and minds public- and private-regarding motives and a concern for their own and the public interest? Very likely. But it is worth remembering that most of us manage to get through life concerned with our own good and with a whole variety of concerns that pull us in other directions—for example, towards the good of others to whom we are bound by ties of loyalty and affection. A concern for the public interest is more demanding than this, but there is nothing here that requires the transformation of humankind of a sort that has made reckless the pursuit of other schemes of political improvement. It is also worth remembering in this context that a large number of Americans have learned to value private property, civil and political rights, and cooperation in civic tasks. We surely have not been born into an appreciation of these in a miracle of biological determinism; we have undoubtedly learned to value them, at least in part, through political experience. Republican local government can rest on the same foundation.

In any event, the fundamental fact about republican citizenship is that its virtues must be learned anew each generation. In one sense this is a banality. But once it is understood that the learning is not just or even importantly a matter of one generation teaching another the best of what it knows, but is instead largely a matter of ensuring that the necessary range of experiences for learning republican citizenship is widely available, then the importance of the generational point is clearer. As I have said, this is a matter of attending to the foundations of republican citizenship, and as such it is part of the public interest of the regime.

Moreover, each generation must inherit a political culture that points them in the right direction. Each generation bequeaths to the next such a culture, with all its diverse roots in family, church, workplace, school, and so forth. It is through this culture that they teach the young. In the end, the essential problem of forming citizens is not just one of the right institutions and the politics in which they are embedded, but of a culture that opens the door to the learning of public-spiritedness itself.

Class and Self-Interest in the
American Commercial Republic

THE TWO preceding chapters will leave some readers with an intoxicating vision of citizens strong in their regard for the public interest. Such citizens will see to it that lawmakers feel the lash of their disdain should they sink into the pleasures of office, give their attention largely to the rewards of serving their most prosperous constituents or indulge a taste for economic equality to such a degree that they attempt to drastically reduce the discretion that asset controllers need. But Madison points to the flaws in such a view. In constituting a republican government, he said, we cannot rely only on the better side of our natures, blind to human character as it is revealed in the collective life of the species. A political constitution cannot rest solely on "higher motives," and self-limitation must therefore depend on more than a politics focused on the public interest. Thus, a fundamental part of the design of republican government is creating a politics of self-interest that can, as one of its products, limit the power of government, thereby serving the public interest. The citizenry must not only have the requisite virtues: a significant portion of it must have the right interests. Republican government must be anchored in the self-interest of a significant number of citizens, that is, in a particular class or classes. However, we cannot simply substitute another ruling class for Madison's choice of the propertied. The problem is more complex and we must do better than Madison, who neglected to take the full measure of it.

It would be best if, instead of resting on class, the design of a republican constitutional politics could be anchored in social groupings defined by their attachments to different elements of the public interest. If each grouping were disposed to promote politically these elements, there would then be, in effect, a vigorous politics of the public interest rooted in something other than public-spiritedness.[1] However, Madison's views are compelling. A constitutional politics, he argued, must in part rest on reliable motives, and among the most reliable is economic self-interest.[2] We must look, he said, to class. This means that for outlooks that encompass substantial non-economic elements, as in the case of the public interest, we should rely on social groupings that are defined by economic position. Reliance on class is a crude device, however, not only because we must suppose that broad political outlooks are highly correlated with economic position, but also because we must believe that members of particular classes see a nontrivial connection between their economic interests and a broad political outlook. To serve one, they must think, is to serve the other. Classes, however, are almost certainly more heterogeneous than such correlations and connections imply. Still, the reliability of class motives for constitutional calculation compensates to some degree for their crudity.

Not only should constitutional theory look to class, there will in fact be classes, even in a fully realized commercial republic.[3] It is highly likely that all societies that are possible of realization, by humankind as it is and may plausibly become, will be divided by interests that stem from the position each of its members has in the organization of its productive life and how the product of that organization is distributed. This is as true of a regime built on private ownership as for any other, at least so far as we know. Even a fully formed democratic socialist regime will have a noticeable degree of economic inequality rooted in the organization of productive life, partly because that inequality cannot be eliminated if the foundations of democracy are to remain intact,[4] and partly because there will be a widespread desire to reward merit.

Regardless, and focusing on the commercial republic, those who own large-scale productive assets and those who exercise effective control of these assets—those who are more or less independent fiduciaries of asset owners—comprise one class. Another larger class will be composed of citizens who occupy economic positions that include owning small-scale productive assets and working in supervisory positions in large business firms. To their number will be added others who occupy various kinds of knowledge-based positions in industry and government. Yet another large grouping will be sellers of labor power. In a rough and ready way, the first (asset controllers and their broadly independent fiduciaries) are members of the business or asset-controlling class; the second comprise the middle class; and the lower reaches of the third comprise what I will call the "have-littles," in order to distinguish them from those who occupy middling positions as sellers of labor power who can be assimilated to the middle class.[5]

None of this means that there must be a large class of have-littles in a fully realized commercial republic (or in a social democracy for that matter).

Concomitantly, it seems entirely likely that there can be a very large middle class. Indeed, as I suggest below, if there is to be a flourishing commercial republic, an expansion of the current size of the middle class will be necessary. Thus, while a well-ordered commercial republic will have classes, a good deal of variation is possible in the size of each class. This makes it at least possible to produce that measure of economic equality that the public interest of a commercial republic calls for.

In much the same fashion, there is nothing in the class structure of a well-ordered commercial republic that would prevent class mobility. Those occupying the various economic rungs may move around, as may their children. Class mobility may then also contribute to the kind of economic equality that a commercial republic needs if economic circumstances over a lifetime and perhaps over that of two generations are central to the citizenry's outlook. If most citizens have at least modest economic resources at some significant points in their life, or come from families who have had such resources, this may not provide all the equality a commercial republic may need, but it very probably is a significant step toward it.

Thus, we can say that, if there are going to be classes even in a fully realized commercial republic—and if Madison was right that we must look to self-interest for the political energy needed to serve the public interest—we must seek to harness its class politics. We must look to divisions in the society, even if on other grounds we might find the existence of such divisions objectionable. Class is not desirable for its own sake, but it is very probably ineluctable—and, more importantly, it is useful. The place to start the discussion of class is with the propertied, who have been central to the discussion so far.

BROADENING THE INTERESTS OF THE PROPERTIED

The preceding chapters have argued that those who control large-scale productive assets cannot form the base of self-interest that gives a republican regime energy and direction. To rely heavily on them is to invite the great danger to republican government—faction—and even worse, minority faction. Yet, as Gouverneur Morris made clear in the founding debates, the propertied must be politically accommodated. Moreover, as Madison suggested, and as the analysis of advanced capitalism indicates, they should be given a politically privileged role. In short, if we wish for a commercial republic, we should not attempt to keep the propertied from playing a political role, or even to keep them from playing a substantial one. We must, instead, worry about the kinds of interests they pursue. That is, to ensure that the political privilege of the propertied does not lead to factional government, the interests of the propertied must be broadened. Such broadening also makes business privilege an advantage for republican government in that the political efforts of large-scale asset-controllers can serve the public interest, and—what amounts to the same thing—the politics of the regime can have the kind of political energy it needs. A fundamental constitutional question thus is how to broaden the interests of the propertied.

In thinking through this question of broadening interests, it helps to recall the essential features of large-scale business' political position. Changes in the character of private property, the rise of the privileged position of business, the growth of the administrative state, and the shaping of citizen volitions by the business class—when taken together with our constitutional impediments to a majoritarian politics and Madisonian advantages for the propertied—have all worked to weaken elections as a control on minority faction. These features of our constitutional life have increased what already were significant dangers to republican government generated by resting it on the self-interest of the propertied. Nevertheless, because those who control large-scale productive property manage the means by which economic prosperity is generated, their voice must, will, and ought to be politically privileged to some degree, particularly when economic aspects of the public interest are at issue.

A crucial concern in the institutional design of a commercial republican regime, therefore, is how to provide businessmen with a role attractive enough to make them staunch adherents of the regime, while so broadening their interests as to increase the overlap between them and the public interest, and by otherwise controlling their factional tendencies. That is, a privileged political voice for controllers of large-scale productive assets need not mean a failure of republican constitution. To be sure, the propertied at present may sometimes act factionally, and their voice may be too large and the interests they pursue too narrow. But these are not inevitable features of a commercial republican political constitution. The political privilege of asset controllers is an inevitable feature of a regime in which the citizenry expects high and increasing levels of economic well-being, where the responsibility for providing it is placed, in significant part, in the hands of the private parties we call businessmen, and where those businessmen will not on their own make the kinds of investments necessary for great and widely distributed prosperity.[6] But the propertied need not have narrow interests.

There are at least two ways to broaden the interests of the propertied. One is to alter the ownership and control of capital so that the interests pursued by those who control capital will be broader than is now the case. This is an effort to broaden the interests of the propertied directly by altering the group's composition. The other method is indirect, and relies on an effective version of the Madisonian effort to use the separation of powers. Before considering these methods, it is worth noting that, in addition to efforts to broaden the interests of the propertied, we might also look to a design that gives them fewer political advantages than they now possess. Previous discussion has suggested that the combination of Madisonian advantages and the political privilege that the rise of modern capitalism has brought in its wake is more than is needed for ensuring that the commercial aspects of the public interest are served. The combination also gives the propertied too much power, given the dangers of faction. We might, then, consider diluting the Madisonian advantages. If we can do so, the effect on the success of republican government of the narrow interests of the propertied would be diminished. Thus, if larger, more populous electoral districts advantage the propertied, as Madison contended, we might consider smaller ones. The complexities here are great: the design of electoral districts is a subject unto itself. Not least of the reasons is that smaller districts, which would probably be more homogeneous, would also probably make it harder for a robust public interest politics to take hold. And such districts would, of course, result in a larger legislature, which has its own problems. It is also worth noting that if this sort of reform were put into place, the probability of factional government would be lessened: majorities can control minority faction if they are not themselves factional. The likelihood of factional government would be similarly reduced if there were civic majorities at work, and this would be facilitated by loosening generally the impediments to majoritarian government.

There have been various proposals to enlarge the ownership of capital through a wider distribution of stock. The most notable is in the form of employee stock ownership plans (ESOPs),[7] and indeed, on account of this program, some have argued that there is now widespread ownership of capital. It has been argued[8] that if many ordinary citizens own significant amounts of stock, they may succeed in pushing business corporations to take a broadened view of business interests. Corporations would be more likely than at present to worry, for example, about the impact of their decisions on communities, and thus about the effects of their actions on the character of the citizenry. Such corporate behavior in these matters would come about, it is said, because ordinary citizens are vulnerable to what large corporations do in their communities, and so these citizens might wish to take this into account in exercising the authority stock ownership confers.

There are several problems here. First, the extent of ownership of stock by ordinary citizens would have to be significant if they were to have any noticeable impact on corporate policy, particularly in view of the way corporations presently are governed. This is not now the case: most ownership of stock involves small amounts.[9] Second, the argument assumes that ordinary citizens would not have as their primary concern the return on their investment. If they in fact do, they would presumably vote their stock in much the same way as present shareholders do. Moreover, if they were to own significant numbers of shares, they would of course cease to be ordinary citizens and their outlook might well change. Perhaps most important of all, it has long been clear that corporations are not run by their shareholders but by their chief executives.[10] It is their interpretation of their duties to shareholders, their self-interest, and the impact of competition that are at the base of the narrow interests of corporations. Broadening ownership without doing more would not change significantly any of these forces. Indeed, widely dispersed ownership might increase the power of corporate executives, because it is unlikely that a large number of shareholders would be able to concert their efforts: the problems of collective action would be great. It is when stock ownership is concentrated that there is some counterbalance to executives.

What about changing the character of capital ownership rather than its extent? There are several ways in which the ownership and control of capital can be organized other than through our present form or through state ownership, which is by definition not consistent with a commercial republic. These alternatives run from various kinds of publicly constituted investment funds in which all citizens own stock, to forms of worker ownership. In the first, most investment capital would be provided by such funds, and business firms would be run by much the same sort of people as they presently are. In the second, some or all of the business organizations that make up the economy would be owned by those who work within them, and professional managers would be hired to run the firms. At the risk of oversimplification, in both kinds of schemes ownership is cooperative. That is, each person owns property but can only dispose of it in ways consistent with cooperative ownership. Thus, shares in the funds and firms cannot be bought and sold at will. Worker-owners, for example, can only sell them either to incoming workers or to existing workers, that is, back to the firm.[11] Similarly, in some versions of investment funds, the shares cannot be converted to cash but can only be exchanged for shares in other funds. These restrictions are meant to ensure that the cooperative form of ownership continues, a form, it is argued, that has intrinsic value and is therefore worth preserving.[12]

It is not possible here to do more than make one essential point about these forms of ownership. In all of them capital is held "privately," that is, not by the state in any of its guises, whether national or local. To this degree, the proposals are consistent with a commercial republic. Moreover, such decentralized forms of ownership provide a counterweight to the state, as does, it is widely argued, the usual form of private ownership. These alternative forms also provide the independent sources of income that are probably necessary for liberty. Additionally, they all rely on the market system and, to the degree that the market is central to securing a high degree of economic well-being, they promise high levels of prosperity. In short, these cooperative forms would plausibly provide much the same benefits as the present form of ownership, being decentralized in character and relying on markets and individual choice. Moreover, these forms make use of the same large-scale business organization that is likely to be necessary for high levels of economic well-being.

Given their similarities to present forms of ownership, then, there is every reason to conclude that these intermediate cooperative forms are consistent with a commercial republican regime. The fundamental question, therefore, is whether such forms of widespread ownership would broaden the interests of those who control capital? Robert Dahl, for one, thinks so, at least with regard to worker ownership. He comments that employee-owners are a "more representative part of the public, as consumers, residents and citizens" than owners of large-scale capital. They are "closer to the average citizen" and thus, he says, "more likely than managers [and owners] to bear some of the adverse consequences of their decisions." The implication is that worker-owners would have a broader view of the interests of large-scale property since their own day-to-day concerns would affect their understanding of those interests.[13] The case, however, for investment funds is less clear, because those who run them would presumably act as fiduciaries for their citizen-owners, and be likely to interpret this as meaning that they must focus on increasing the value of the fund's holdings. In short, they are likely to act much like present providers of capital, and, again, given that there would be many citizen-owners for each fund, it would not be easy to compel fund executives to adopt any broader view should some number of citizens wish it.

It is worth remarking here that a wide distribution of capital would have one straightforward advantage in a commercial republic. It would directly serve the public interest as one of the few ways to achieve a modest measure of economic equality and the more robust measure of political equality it undergirds.[14] If promoting modest equality is our concern—as it should be if we are friends of the commercial republic—then it also is worth saying that, in addition to ways of more broadly distributing ownership of productive assets, we should consider ways of directly bolstering a more equal distribution of income. One possibility is a program of basic income grants, which in themselves can take several forms, running from a yearly payment to a one-time "life grant" at age eighteen.[15]

As for indirectly broadening the interests of property, as noted, Madison looked to the effects of the separation of powers.[16] As we have seen, he assumed that the various components that go into making up the propertied class would be spread among the branches of government, and in greater numbers than their presence in the population warranted. If this were the case, and with an attentive citizenry, property holders of various kinds would find themselves arguing in public about what they have in common—and they would look to a version of their common interests broad enough to attract significant support from such a citizenry. The rise of the administrative state requires an addendum to Madison's argument. This attentive citizenry must also prompt legislators to engage in sufficient oversight of the administrative branch to prevent components of the business class from exerting influence inside the federal bureaucracy to serve their particular interests. All this is to say that there must be effective electoral controls at work.

What will be the sources of such a citizenry and what will be its composition? My discussion of the politics of the public interest provides a partial answer. The fostering of public-spiritedness in a well-ordered commercial republic will counterbalance efforts by the propertied to shape the volitions of the citizenry. In particular, the middle class will likely have a normative vision that prompts a measure of skepticism about whether the contours of a commercial society are best decided by the propertied. It will thus have some inclination to prompt legislators to give more attention than they presently do to the efforts by particular industries to serve their interests within the administrative process. More generally, a public-spirited citizenry will provide just the sort of attentive audience that will encourage the various components of the business class to search for a broad and appealing account of their common interests.

But, as Madison teaches, we should not rely too heavily on such better motives for the energy behind a broadening process. It is safer to assume that the politics of the public interest will not have effects broad and deep enough to eliminate class interests. The importance of class for the political life of the regime will doubtless be less than it presently is. But it is prudent to assume that in a well-ordered republic we must still take the medicine of self-interest in a largely undiluted form and make use of less than noble motives. In particular, a self-interested middle class—that is, one without the dose of public-spiritedness supplied by a republican local politics—alone or in concert with others, might be able to form the basis for electoral majorities. The result would plausibly be a politics that would overcome the political advantages that stem from business privilege with its narrowing effects. Is any of this likely? This question is part of a larger one concerning the sources of political energy in the self-interest of the classes that compose a well-ordered commercial republic.

THE MIDDLE CLASS AND POLITICAL COALITIONS

How shall we characterize the ordinary interests of the middle class? That is, what are the contours of its behavior likely to be in a more or less fully realized commercial republic? To begin with, given a public interest politics, some significant portion of the political life of the regime will reinforce the middle class's conception of how politics should be organized and the purposes it should serve. Its members thus will feel a measure of security and confidence, a feeling that likely will be at work when it acts in the service of its self-interest. Thus our concern in a more or less fully realized commercial republic is with the self-interest of a secure and confident middle class, most of whose members will plausibly have the kind of confidence in their own judgments that leads them to act politically.[17]

With regard to the specific content of their interests, the principal source of income for the middle class stems not from controlling large-scale productive assets; nor does it come from selling muscle power in the manner of much of the traditional working class. Rather, most members of the middle class will be salaried, and the skills they exchange for a salary will be in greater demand than for relatively simple bodily exertion. This position— in between asset controllers and those who rely on exchanging unskilled labor for a wage—is likely to make the middle class skeptical of some but sympathetic to other classes' claims.

Because the salaries of members of the middle class are typically large enough for them to afford small investments in the form of stock ownership and to own consumption property in the form of houses and other large consumer durables, they can reasonably be expected to support relatively strong property rights and wish to live in a flourishing commercial society.[18] Most middle-class people living in such a society are likely to see a direct connection between the flourishing of a business enterprise economy and their own economic well-being—more so certainly than the have-littles. In this sense, the interests of the middle class will overlap with those of the controllers of large-scale property. We may go further. Because of its concern for the security of property rights, the middle class is also likely to share with controllers of large-scale productive assets the view that the latter should have considerable discretion in deploying those assets. Owning property themselves, they plausibly will have a concrete sense of the reasons for such discretion because they will wish to have it for themselves. Generally, they are likely to understand that national economic prosperity—on which their own prosperity largely depends— requires considerable discretion for these controllers of large productive assets.

However, a significant portion of such a middle class will likely find unjust a markedly unequal distribution of income in which controllers of productive assets routinely are paid twenty or even thirty times more than the middle class.[19] They plausibly will be at least moderately suspicious of those who do work that bears some relation to their own but that garners vastly greater rewards. The greatly privileged political voice of large asset-controllers is liable also to make them uneasy.

On the other hand, most members of the middle class are unlikely to wish to see substantial sums given to those who have been unable to earn their keep in the market place.[20] Most middle-class people will probably share the view of our greatest exponent of the dignity of work and free labor, Abraham Lincoln, that idleness is to be discouraged and high regard given to those who work for a living.[21] All able-bodied people should work for their keep, they will think, and they are likely to hold to the corollary that their own class status is the consequence of hard work. And, although it does not necessarily follow, many among the middle class will at least find plausible the idea that reasonably paid work should be widely available. The result of such a policy, many are likely to believe, will be a substantial reduction in the extent of poverty and thus in the number of people who lack the self-respect and proud independence to be republican citizens. With regard to secure work, the point is likely to be much the same: most middle-class people can understand the importance of economic security since it plays a substantial role in their own well-being. For similar reasons, they are likely to be skeptical of the value of federal agencies' granting favors to particular business interests. This smacks too much of not playing by the rules—that we all ought to work for a living and thus deserve what we get.

Enough has been said to indicate that the commercial republic's middle class, especially if it is moderately secure and self-confident, would likely support elements of the public interest that focus on the importance of markets and private property as keys to prosperity. But if the arguments are properly framed, it is also probable that many among the middle class would be made skeptical of the claims of asset controllers that full employment at reasonable wages for all is neither possible nor desirable,[22] and that very great economic inequality is necessary if we are to have real economic prosperity. When to this skepticism is added a worry about handouts to businesses, it is more than likely that controllers of productive assets will end up having to argue their case in public on a substantial number of matters. It will not be easy to convince a substantial number of citizens and those who speak for them that the country needs to give great benefits to industries through the administrative process and in other low-visibility ways. A middle class acting in this skeptical way will facilitate the broadening effects of the separation of powers on the interests of the propertied.

Still, our deepest concern here lies elsewhere than with this broadening process. It is this: the middle class in a fully realized commercial republic will be at the center of a politics of broad self-interest built around class coalitions.[23] Such a politics, through an overlap between class interests and the public interest, will increase the odds that the public interest will be served. The Madisonian anchoring of the regime in self-interest can be made to work better than Madison's own constitutional scheme promised or, in fact, ever delivered.

We should perhaps start this discussion of the broad politics of self-interest with the simple observation that, even though the middle class in a commercial republic will comprise a majority of the citizenry, it is unlikely that much or all of the class can be consistently mobilized across a wide range of policy matters. This is likely to be true regardless of whether a commercial republican regime is fully realized, whether the middle class has a significant measure of security and self-confidence, and whether it comprises a majority of the citizenry. The commercial republic's foundations in self-interest cannot rest alone on the middle class. It will typically need to join in coalition with other classes if it wishes to shape public policy. The constitutional design of a commercial republic would be a good deal easier if we could simply assume that the middle class will dominate day-to-day politics and provide the political leadership of the regime. But this assumption runs up against the fact that this is to be a *commercial* republic, and thus that the propertied will play a very significant role in its day-to-day politics. Much the same point emerges when we consider that, because of the political privilege of the propertied and the cost of getting elected, even though the middle class will almost certainly be a majority of the citizenry, it is unlikely to hold the lion's share of high offices.

A significant measure of the day-to-day politics of a well-ordered commercial republic will then be carried out by coalitions of sectors of the middle class in alliance with sectors of other classes. The politics of republics have always had at their center alliances between classes. A more or less fully realized commercial republic will be no different. What *will* be different is the substance of those alliances. For the reasons given, coalitions between significant sectors of the middle class and propertied class are likely to be particularly important as a source of political energy in the regime, especially if they constitute a majority on the issues at stake. These coalitions will be easier to form insofar as large-scale asset-controllers have a broad conception of their interests. To the extent that this is the case, the overlap with the interests of the middle class will be great. Coalitions with the have-littles will also be more likely to form so long as those who control productive assets do not devote considerable energy to defeating them. They are less likely to do so to the degree they have a broad conception of their interests.

Similarly, coalitions between the middle class and the have-littles will be more likely if the latter have that measure of political organization that makes them useful allies. An important potential alliance between the two classes is around economic inequality. A more equal distribution of income than exists at present is required if we are to have the kind of economic and political equality a commercial republic requires. A secure and confident middle class will likely find such a coalition appealing if greater income equality results from a wide-spread availability of reasonably remunerative work. Significant parts of the middle class will plausibly also find attractive an alliance with the have-littles built around strengthening the ability of local governments to affect capital mobility. Not the least of the reasons is that, like the have-littles, members of the middle class, especially those at its lower end, cannot insulate themselves against the economic consequences of jobs and taxes moving out of their towns and cities. They too will feel the effects in their pocketbooks and in declining public services. To be sure, because they own some property, middle-class citizens of a commercial republic will probably be more sensitive than the have-littles to the necessity of allowing controllers of productive assets substantial discretion (and that of course is the point insofar as it means that no likely political alliances centered on the middle class will undercut the public interest in this respect). Still, those middle-class persons who find it difficult to leave their communities undoubtedly will find schemes to bolster its economic base attractive.

As indicated, a confident and secure middle class will realize that businessmen ought to have discretion in deploying the assets they control. But it will more than likely also be suspicious of large inducements to businessmen to get them to invest at a scale necessary for widespread prosperity—especially if very large inequalities of income and wealth is the inducement. Similarly, such a middle class will tend to be skeptical of blandishments by asset controllers to join an effort to squeeze the wages of workers in order to increase profits and otherwise promote prosperity. Still, the middle class is also likely to resist pleas of the have-littles to attack in wholesale fashion the prerogatives of asset controllers. More generally, it can be expected to support a balanced view of business discretion—one that gives some weight to its necessity but also recognizes its dangers. It is even possible that a nontrivial number of the middle class would appreciate that the success of a commercial republic depends in large measure on how intelligently controllers of productive assets invest: if they are short-sighted and generally swinish, they themselves may survive in good fettle while the rest of the society will not.[24] In short, some number of middle-class persons may well see that, while asset controllers must have considerable discretion and, concomitantly, a privileged political voice, investment decisions cannot be left entirely in their hands.

In a well-ordered commercial republic, then, the middle class will act as a kind of pivot moving between coalitions with asset controllers and with the have-littles. In doing so, it will not necessarily modify the self-interest of these classes, but it will likely persuade a significant portion of their number of the tactical advantages of supporting policies whose effect will be to serve the public interest. Asset controllers will likely find themselves supporting or at least acquiescing in policies that lead to smaller gains in incomes than they presently receive in return for organizing large-scale investments. And the have-littles will likely find themselves in the same position with regard to policies that aim to improve their economic position by loosening restrictions on what asset controllers can do.

There are forces pulling in other directions from those promoting a system of alliances with the middle class at the center. Those in the middle are always vulnerable to an alliance between the top and the bottom— as those on the top emphasize their experience in running the country's economy and argue that only they are qualified to manage the real business of the society. Some number of have-littles will probably find it difficult to resist such claims of deference.

There are also areas in which the middle class is likely to find itself on its own, but not because of an alliance between the other two classes. Thus, a secure and confident middle class might well find itself alone in supporting the importance of deliberative lawmaking. With allowances for substantial oversimplification, the propertied, as befits those with a privileged voice in the affairs of state, will prefer quiet negotiations carried on in the corridors of power to public lawmaking. After all, it is in such quiet places that the full force of their accomplishments and standing can make itself felt. The have-littles, on the other hand, are likely to be mostly interested in substantive results that alleviate their plight, and just how these results are achieved is, therefore, of less concern. But a secure and confident middle class will be drawn to deliberative lawmaking, we might say, because of its deep concern with public rectitude—that things be done for the right reasons and be seen to be done in that fashion. Thus, lawmaking built around the giving of reasons confirms the broad moral outlook of the middle class.[25] Moreover, it may not be too much to say that many members of the middle class generally sense that it is only public government—government open to scrutiny, where reasoning carries the day—that can serve their interests. Private government can only serve the powerful—in the particular case, those who control large-scale productive assets.[26]

Alliances between the middle class and other classes that result in serving elements of the public interest are more likely to occur, I have said, not only if the middle class is secure and confident. It will also help if controllers of productive assets have broad interests and the have-littles have at least a modicum of political organization.

Thus, a middle-class/have-little alliance is only likely to work if significant numbers of middle-class people believe that the have-littles are not dangerous and disorganized. If the have-littles are seen to contain large numbers of the feckless, the angry, and the incompetent, little profit is likely to be seen by the politically minded among the middle class in an alliance. Indeed, if the have-littles are widely thought to be dominated by such people, this fact will be exploited by the asset-controlling class, with the likely result that a significant portion of the middle class will be frightened by the specter of the unruly poor. As a consequence, proposals from the business class that the country cannot afford social welfare for the poorest of the society, that they don't deserve it, that it will cut down on national competitiveness, and that it will subsidize a way of life that is costly to the rest of us will likely get an attentive hearing. On the evidence of the political discussions of the last twenty to thirty years, a great many people now believe such arguments. In general, the distribution of income must be such that the have-littles do not lead lives so different from the middle class that the latter cannot understand the former because there is little in the way of shared experience of married life, the raising of children, and the world of work.

In a similar vein, if the interests of asset controllers are narrow, and the lives of the have-littles are seen to be threatening by large numbers of more advantaged citizens, we can expect asset controllers to seek an alliance with the middle class built around improving the morals of the lower class. And because asset controllers have considerable resources, they might be able not only to paint a convincing picture of a dangerous lower class, but to indoctrinate the middle class into believing that only asset controllers know how to govern and should be given considerable power to do so. This in turn may call for efforts by elements of the middle class (notably intellectuals) to mobilize the have-littles for an assault on the economic and political privileges of the business class.

At their worst, we have seen, the aims of asset controllers are factional, and an alliance of the kind just described between the business class and substantial elements of the middle class will result not in minority factional government, but in factional rule by a majority. A factional alliance of this sort will almost certainly find it attractive to deny to a major portion of the have-littles effective use of their rights and the modest level of material well-being they need to join in the system of mutual respect that is one of the foundations of republican citizenship. Under these conditions, the have-littles will be right to believe that the commercial republic is a factional scheme of the haves, including the middle class, against the have-nots.

But the path to the subversion of republican government does not stop there. A majority faction may also emerge if the alliance between large elements of the middle class and the have-littles aims at denying to the holders of productive assets relatively free use of them. This was the factional scheme that animated Madison's constitutional theory. It is more likely, however, that a potential and, in some cases, an actually realized factional alliance between businessmen and the middle class has posed the greater danger to republican government in the United States.

The fundamental point in this discussion of class coalitions is that a secure and confident middle class—able alternately to attract asset controllers and the have-littles as allies, and with sufficient unity to make the separation of powers work—can prevent the factional behavior to which the propertied and those who lack it are inclined. By reducing this possibility, a confident middle class makes real the electoral controls that Madison argued was essential to the control of minority faction, and with that, the possibility of serving the public interest. What is required is a middle class (1) that is large and unified enough; (2) whose definition of its interests is not such as to lead the business class to think that it is in imminent danger of losing a significant portion of its economic, political, and social standing, as well as its property; and (3) whose definition of its interests is such as to convince the have-littles that a commercial republic is not an elaborate set of devices designed to keep them in their present condition. A secure and confident middle class will be all these things.

Even though a politics of self-interest can do much to serve the public interest in a fully realized commercial republic, it is too much to ask for a comprehensive overlap between the self-interest of its classes and the public interest. If such an overlap were likely, creating and maintaining republican regimes would be relatively easy. We would not need to be concerned about such difficult matters as public-spiritedness and deliberation; neither would we need to dream up institutional contrivances to induce political actors to behave in ways other than pursuing a narrow version of their self-interest.

As it is, not only must we look to the politics of the public interest, but friends of a republican government must rely as well on a good deal of indirection, attempting to accomplish things that cannot be dealt with directly.[27] They must, that is, look to the devices and conditions that will facilitate alliances between classes. These alliances will also reflect real tensions within the public interest. In a more or less fully realized commercial republic there will be, for example, conflict over how to balance asset-holder discretion and the need for a modest level of economic equality; similarly, tension is likely to develop between this discretion and the economic stability that local governments need if their politics is to foster public-spiritedness. The politics of a more or less fully realized republican government will contain real and enduring conflict. But if it is to flourish, these conflicts must not be fueled by exploitative versions of class interest. However, it is unlikely to be easy to constrain such an exploitative politics, no less eliminate it.

It is both fitting and perhaps unsurprising that the middle class should be the key to a well-functioning commercial republican regime. After all, as noted, liberalism was created for and strengthened a social strata that was neither aristocratic nor deeply concerned with distributive justice. A secure and confident middle class creates an opportunity for a commercial republic to have a secure social basis. It provides something Madison did not appear to believe he had—a class between the propertied and the propertyless. Around it and its alliances, majorities can be built whose concerns overlap with the public interest. In addition to providing political energy for the republic, alliances between the middle class and the have-littles will increase the odds that the separation of powers can do its work of broadening the interests of the propertied. More generally, the process of building alliances will itself broaden interests among all classes and thus increase the odds that the interest-driven politics of the regime will serve the public interest. The fundamental point here is that a secure and confident middle class can work through electoral controls to restrain a class with large political resources and a privileged political position. Indeed, without such controls it is unlikely that the powerful can be restrained. Elections are clumsy devices for political control, but they are the only reliable device for a secure and confident majority to ensure that its concerns are given serious attention. The need to get elected to public office can concentrate the minds even of officials who bask lazily in the arms of powerful interests.

THE FORMATION OF CLASS COALITIONS

Class coalitions do not form on their own. They need to be brokered and the partners mobilized. This is part of a larger point that undoubtedly has long since occurred to most readers: the conditions necessary for the class alliances we have been considering will themselves be a product of, and may indeed require, the efforts of the coalitions discussed. There is a potential virtuous circle here, but the self-reinforcing process is unlikely to occur without leadership. Who is likely to wish to and be able to play this role?

The leaders of political parties are one obvious answer.[28] As the middle class forges alliances with other classes, the central political role of the middle class will be facilitated by a party system that enables large sections of the class to move between the parties. For this to happen, a republican regime must have parties that find it possible to adjust their appeals to make such movement attractive. The competition between political parties can harness self-interest in the service of a commercial republic, this time building not just on class interests but on the interests of political parties. Assuming that there are two principal main parties,[29] it seems likely that one will draw significant support from the have-littles, the other from the controllers of large-scale productive assets. Thus, a central task of party leaders will be to draw large numbers of middle-class persons to their standard in order

to create electoral majorities. In doing so they will be organizing and ce-
menting class alliances. In response to any such successes, leaders of the
opposition will craft appeals meant to peel off middle-class voters from the
majority party.

But more than self-interest is at work in the efforts by political parties
to put together majority coalitions. Party leaders, at least, are likely to have
some concern for the public interest. Consider a party system in which
one party emphasizes liberty and the other equality (note that the public
interest of a commercial republic has elements of both). If the party system
is thus organized, there will be pressure for limiting public power that
flows from a concern for a vital civil society and from a desire to protect
rights, including property rights. The leaders of this party of liberty would
probably also sense that a principal inducement for business performance
is, in effect, a substantially unequal income distribution, and hence would
attempt to keep the question off the public agenda. We can also suppose that
they would argue that controllers of productive assets must have privileged
access to the corridors of power. The party of equality would likely attack
these inducements and this access, thus strengthening the foundations of
mutual respect and thus of republican citizenship. In doing so, they would
also be working to prevent factional government. The party would further
be receptive to curbing the discretion of asset controllers, which includes
increasing the ability of local governments to affect the movement of capital
in and out of their localities. At stake, once again, is one of the foundations of
republican citizenship—namely, public-spiritedness as it is fostered through
a deliberative local politics.

A party system like the one I have been describing is not farfetched. It
requires only that parties present broad-stroke arguments about the need
to secure liberty and equality. It is thus within the reach of those who wish
for a fully realized commercial republic. Indeed, at various points in its history, the American party system has looked something like this.[30] At any
rate, consider that the parties of liberty and equality would have different
homes—the former being most appealing to controllers of productive assets, the latter to the have-littles. As I have described the interests of the
middle class, aspects of both parties' principal concerns would appeal to it.
A party system structured in this fashion can thus facilitate efforts by the
middle class to find allies and cement such alliances.

It is worth emphasizing that while the parties of liberty and equality
may be based in a view of the broad purposes of republican government,
they cannot be deeply ideological—talking exclusively about either liberty
or equality. This would force members of the middle class to choose and
stick with one party, thus eliminating the class as the fulcrum of political
alliances. In general, ideologically defined parties can be expected to offer

two different conceptions of what the public interest is, rather than different versions of it. If the theory of republican political constitution offered here is correct, such a party system would make the maintenance of a republican regime extremely difficult.[31]

Political parties in a more or less fully realized republican regime must each have the sort of outlook and internal organization that the middle class can find a home in either. For it is in the movement between parties that the mix of public interest elements is secured. The parties must be such that they are hospitable to the two basic alliances: the party of equality to a have-little/middle-class coalition and the party of liberty to an asset-controller/middle-class coalition. Any dispute between those who think that parties must be "bland enveloping coalitions"[32] and those who think they must be disciplined[33] is then misplaced. A republican regime cannot rest on strongly disciplined parties if that discipline is rooted in ideology. To this degree, advocates of loosely organized and heterogeneous parties are correct. But advocates of disciplined parties are correct that the parties must stand for something and not be simply aggregations of those who aspire to public office. They need not have well-developed programs, but they must each embody an interpretation of the public interest or at least be attached to crucial aspects of it.

There is another potential source of political leaders able to put together class coalitions: those commonly called policy entrepreneurs, and particularly those with broad policy agendas. The two obvious current examples are leaders of the neoconservative and the New Deal/liberal democratic strands of American politics. Such entrepreneurs are likely to be close in style to the coalition builders among party leaders. Indeed, in our recent political history such entrepreneurs, in fact, *have been* party leaders.

However, many entrepreneurs will not be interested in putting together what I have been calling civic majorities. They will aim instead at narrowly focused majorities, even factional ones. Leaders on both the Right and Left have been thus occupied at various junctures in American political history. Indeed, a case can be made that contemporary American politics is being partly shaped by such sectarian entrepreneurs. They are ideologues in the sense of being intent on remaking the American citizenry according to a broad political vision—as against trying to build on the interests and opinions already present, and working to modify them as part of a sustained effort characterized by discussion, bargaining, and compromise. Of great importance here is that, unlike party leaders, these entrepreneurs do not have large, complex, and (most important of all) heterogeneous organizations to maintain. Because party leaders in a well-ordered republic will likely be in charge of such organizations, they will be pushed toward moderation in their political appeals and will be inclined to build coalitions out of existing materials. Such leaders will be mostly indifferent to the pleasures and rewards of manufacturing new political men and women.

By contrast, the efforts of ideological policy entrepreneurs are likely to be divisive insofar as they cut against the grain of a large section of the citizenry's conception of its best self. Thus, for example, in contemporary American politics the radical Right pushes hard to remake the citizenry according to its vision of a country built around Christianity and a muscular patriotism. This hits many liberals, so to speak, where they live because they see themselves as secular and in favor of a foreign policy built around peaceful negotiation. Similarly, multiculturalists and their identity-politics allies cut into the self-conception of many Americans in their claim that particular racial, ethnic, and sexual groups should be treated differently because their particular histories are characterized by discrimination and struggle. In this context, it is worth noting that if sectarian policy entrepreneurs capture political parties, the parties will be unable to facilitate the role of the middle class as the pivot of a broad class politics.

IF WE CAN rely on the self-interest of the middle class and on the coalitions in which it is the center, we have a tremendous advantage over Madison in any effort to realize republican government. We no longer need to rely, as he appeared to believe was necessary, on the self-interest of a *minority*, that is, on the propertied. We have seen the difficulties to which this leads, most notably the possibility of minority faction. If we can look to a class that is likely to comprise a majority of the citizens, we can make good on the promise of republican government as a majoritarian regime. This is a promise Madison understood and valued. But we can rely much more than Madison ever could on what he called the "republican principle," and in doing so, we can become a more fully realized republic than he could contemplate. Not least, we would no longer need to worry as much as Madison thought necessary about majorities. There is a strong case to be made that the middle class that has emerged in the United States is unlikely to be hostile to the deepest interests of the propertied. Moreover, if there were a well-mobilized middle class capable of acting with effective purpose, the republican principle would more than likely prevent factional government by the propertied. Such a middle class could broaden the interests of the propertied and alone, or in concert, provide political energy. Altogether, because we can plausibly look to the middle class, we can erase a central anomaly in the Madisonian design: giving a central political role to a minority in a regime of popular self-government. Moreover, we can look to a class whose self-interest not only overlaps with the public interest but does so to a greater extent than the propertied. This is especially obvious if we compare a secure and confident middle class to the class of asset controllers who have taken over from the men of landed property.

It is worth emphasizing in this context that, if republican government is animated by the politics of both the public interest and the broad interests centered on the middle class, we can—indeed we must if we wish to realize further republican government—dispense with some of the Madisonian auxiliary precautions that prevent the easy formation of majorities. Factional majorities, in our present politics, pose less of a danger than Madison supposed. Not least of the reasons is that majorities in the United States generally seem to be more transient than he imagined they would be. As well, a majoritarian politics has often been associated in our history with increased security for individual liberty.[34] Additionally, the wide dispersal of consumption property has probably reduced any desire on the part of a majority of the citizenry to expropriate or otherwise significantly devalue privately held productive assets. Nevertheless, factional majorities have appeared in our public life—more often than not with the aim of weakening or abrogating civil and political rights—and some provision must be made to prevent them from securing a substantial hold. Still, a commercial republic need not be as uneasy with majority rule as our constitutional tradition has been. Neither then should its theory of political constitution.

Given that we cannot expect a politics more or less completely concerned with the public interest, if a class politics of the kind I have been describing is not possible to sustain and if the only kind of politics of self-interest possible is a narrow group politics, then it is unlikely that a commercial republic can be realized to any significant degree. The existence of such a class coalitional politics, moreover, cannot be taken for granted. The decline of labor unions in the United States does not bode well in this regard, because that is where the have-littles have historically found a political home. It is through them that they have, in fact, found effective representation in the party system and in class coalitions. More generally, unless there is a secure and confident middle class, the kinds of coalitions described here are unlikely. In addition to its intrinsic value, the presence of such a class may also call forth a measure of class consciousness and organization on the part of the have-littles. This may help make up for the decline of a strong labor movement. We need not, of course, worry about the class organization of the controllers of productive assets. There is little possibility that it will disappear or become measurably weakened.

How large a role will the class politics I have been describing play in a well-ordered commercial republic? After all, there will be at least two other kinds of politics at work—a public interest politics and an aggregative politics.[35] If we follow Madison, we must suppose that class politics will play a large role. What cannot be done directly by lawmakers, prompted by the electoral connection, to give the public interest concrete meaning—and that will be a good deal—must be done by self-interest. Thus, if the form that a politics of the self-interest takes in a commercial republic is one dominated by ordinary, narrow-gauged interest groups, then friends of the commercial republic will need to urge their fellow citizens to resist the pleasures of pluralism. Finally, it is worth remarking here once again on the limits of political equality as a measure by which to judge a commercial republic. Not only is such equality not pertinent to judging whether a public interest politics is successfully at work (that is, we want good arguments, not everybody's arguments), but, in the class politics described here, we want good interests, not any interests.

THE RELATION AMONG A PUBLIC INTEREST POLITICS, THE POLITICS OF BROAD INTERESTS, AND AN AGGREGATIVE POLITICS

In addition to being the result of a public interest politics and of coalitions among broad class interests, commercial republican lawmaking must also aggregate the many relatively narrow interests that will be at work in a large-scale commercial republic. Madison thus spoke of the "aggregate interests of the community,"[36] suggesting that law in a republic should result, in part, from a summation of the interests of the various small groups that compose the society. It could hardly be otherwise in the complex, heterogeneous society that any commercial republic is likely to be. Moreover, lawmaking should be organized, at least partly, around bargaining in order to increase aggregate well-being, as representatives trade votes on issues about which their constituents care little for votes on matters about which they care deeply. Bargaining, in addition, allows those most knowledgeable, because most interested, to shape legislative outcomes. It may thus help to solve the problems of how to weigh the intensity of citizen preferences and how to encourage the application of expert judgment, both of which are likely to be greatly needed, given the complexity of modern legislation.[37]

There will be little need to promote an aggregative politics, for it will be a natural by-product of the workings of private-property-based markets and civil society. Indeed, if aggregative lawmaking were all that is needed in a fully realized commercial republic, there would be little difficulty in creating the necessary institutions. By its very nature, a commercial republic will engender citizens skilled in advancing their own interests. Similarly, such a republic will naturally produce legislators adept at paying attention to the particular interests of their constituents and well-versed in the arts of trading and bargaining. For a commercial people, it is natural to see politics as an extension of economics. Thus, there is likely to be little difficulty in getting the legislature to concern itself with the aggregative interests of the community—at least to the degree that it attempts to bargain and compromise over the various particular interests represented in it.

When is the aggregation of interests the appropriate form for republican lawmaking? The short answer is when the public interest is not at stake and when those engaged in coalition building among social classes have not latched onto the issue or problem. For example, the design of a national transportation system—and transportation policy generally—is an issue that is only tangentially related to the public interest and is unlikely to attract the leaders of class politics. There is probably little harm and much good if it is treated as a distributive issue where the central question is how much federal largesse particular localities should receive. In general, relatively pure distributive questions are good candidates for an aggregative politics. Similarly, whether to send astronauts to Mars, whether there should be crop subsidies, and even how stringent air pollution laws should be are not matters of the public interest. Nor are they likely to be taken up by a class politics.

To avoid misunderstanding, the point here is not that these questions are unimportant. They are important, but less so than the questions that touch directly on the public interest. These latter affect the purposes of the regime and its ability effectively to serve them, including whether an effective aggregative politics will be at work. A well-ordered aggregative politics makes its own contribution to republican government. The bargaining reflecting the intensities of preferences among competing groups will reinforce the belief that such aggregation is an appropriate part of republican government and its public interest. It will also reinforce the attachment to republican government that its citizens must have if they are to support a public interest politics that will sometimes undercut the serving of their own immediate and particular interests.

A commercial republican regime, then, cannot be held together solely out of a concern for the public interest. Indeed, one of its reasons for being— to ensure that citizens can pursue their own interests—precludes any such exclusive focus. Moreover, aggregative lawmaking is inevitable, not only for the reasons given above. Secure personal and political rights will produce the same result. Any effort to significantly curb efforts by societal interests to shape lawmaking would be, as Madison pointed out, a cure worse than the disease. If a commercial republic is to flourish, private interest ought and must be given its due: its lawmaking must be pluralistic and characterized by political equality. If it is otherwise organized, the public interest is violated. Thus, serving the public interest requires keeping open the channels of political influence for interests that are resource poor and "insular."[38]

Moral questions such as abortion will also arise in a republican regime. Some of these could be turned into aggregative questions. But given the principled nature of opposing views in such cases, this is not likely to happen frequently. Some of these questions could also be resolved in the struggle to give concrete meaning to the rights citizens have. Moreover, features of a republican institutional design aimed at curbing faction will undoubtedly curtail the political activities of some of the most passionate protagonists in moral disputes. Still, morally charged issues will not be easily assimilated to the political processes described here. How then shall they be treated? One possible approach is to say that, insofar as moral questions are not more or less naturally assimilated into the kinds of lawmaking we have been considering, they should not be the subject of lawmaking at all. This has the advantage of being consistent with the reluctance of liberal regimes to use the force of law to foster particular ways of life. It is also consistent with the deep purpose of liberalism to allow individuals to live their own life in their own way. And it is consistent with the argument that a theory of republican political constitution is not a moral theory: we must live by politics, and the only real question is what kind. Still, it may not be possible to prevent moral questions from becoming the subject of lawmaking. If so, there will be little to do except live with the conflict as best we can, ensuring that it does not become violent and hoping that the passage of time will modify opinion.

THE POLITICAL CLASS AND PARTY LEADERSHIP

The invasion by an aggregative politics of deliberative lawmaking is a danger to republican government. Like a factional politics, this too is a corruption of the public sphere by private interest. The public interest is undercut by an aggregative politics that overwhelms the deliberative ways of lawmaking necessary to serve the public interest. Deliberation depends on reasoning, aggregation on bargaining. Unlike in the case of faction, however, those involved in pressing their own interests on lawmakers may modify their behavior when it is pointed out that the public interest is being damaged. Undercutting the public interest is not necessarily their intention, and their ignorance may be curable.

Institutional devices are needed, therefore, to keep as separate as possible deliberative and aggregative forms of lawmaking. The two sorts of politics—three, if we add the politics of broad class interests[39]—will occur simultaneously. But given the attractions of an aggregative politics, keeping separated the two kinds of politics will not be easy to do. Similarly, it is not easy to say what will enable the legislature to move, when appropriate, between the several ways of lawmaking.

In assessing whether such switching between legislative modes is likely to occur, it helps to see that the problem has two dimensions. One is the switch between modes of lawmaking at a single point in time, the other is

the movement between them over time. The latter is almost certainly easier to secure because American lawmaking has, in fact, generally moved
in cycles, with some periods being more attentive to public interests and
others being more concerned with class and group interests.[40] However,
a republican regime is likely to be in some danger if it goes through long
periods during which lawmaking is mostly concerned with private interest,
especially if it is in a narrow form. A possible and almost ideal pattern would
be that public and private interest lawmaking are at work in all periods but
the mix between them shifts to take account of what kinds of problems press
the hardest on the citizenry. It seems unlikely, however, that such a pattern
of alternation would happen on its own. Citizens may indeed, at some point,
tire of a politics that does not regularly aim to serve the public interest. But
this is not to say very much because we do not know whether they would
do so often enough and in an appropriate manner. And even were we to
be satisfied that this has happened in the past, we cannot be certain that
it will continue into the future. A wide-eyed optimist might think that the
movement between the different types of politics will occur just when it
is required: when the public interest is visibly at stake we will have deliberative lawmaking, when we need a broad politics of interest we will have
that, and otherwise we will have an aggregative politics. The rest of us, for
good reason, are likely to be skeptical. We may have to content ourselves
with supporting a constitutional design that simply provides incentives for
all three kinds of lawmaking to occur.

It is worth emphasizing here that whether the types of lawmaking can co-
exist is not the real problem. There is nothing peculiar about the same citizens and their leaders moving back and forth at any given moment between
a concern for the public interest and group (and class) interest. Such move-
ments are mysterious only if it is supposed that we do not do much the same
thing in our private lives. But of course we do. Our relationships are composed of a mixture of other-regardingness and self-interest, empathy and a
wish to see our own desires served. The problem is not how to get movement back and forth between narrow and broad views of our interests, but
how a republican political order can balance them, keeping each in its place.

Part of the answer is the character of political leadership and, more
broadly, the political class. It is crucial that they be able to distinguish
between the different types of politics and when each is appropriate. We
need not, however, leave the discussion with the equivalent of a prayer that
the political class is up to the job. Some sense of how the political class
will work in this regard can be gleaned from the actions of party leaders.
I have already argued that they are crucial to the class and public interest
politics of a well-ordered commercial republican regime. And I have also
indicated that there can be incentives at work that make them attentive to

both class concerns and matters of the public interest. Party leaders are, of course, not the only lawmakers who have some disposition to give the public interest concrete meaning. But assuming that political parties are needed to organize the legislative process if it is to focus on the public interest, party leaders will be the most important public-spirited lawmakers: they will sit astride two of the crucial forms of the politics that will compose a well-ordered commercial republic. Whether moving between the two domains is done well or badly will depend heavily on their judgment.

What is likely to inform such judgments? It will clearly matter whether the issue at hand is one in which the public interest is obviously and powerfully at stake so that a political party that does not act with this in mind will be punished by a public-spirited citizenry. Beyond that, we can point to some impediments to party leaders attending to the public interest when it is at issue. Two are especially important.

First, a forceful aggregative politics will be at work. Not only will such a politics inevitably be robust in a commercial republic, it will find ready allies among the many lawmakers who find it easier to ply their trade by being attentive to the bigger and noisier interest groups. Attending to the public interest and building class coalitions are much harder jobs, and those who are interested in the quiet life will look for easier ways to stay in office. In any event, leaders of interest groups and their lawmaking allies will inevitably press to have even those issues with direct consequences for the public interest treated as a subject for group bargaining. Equally, they will resist forming class coalitions that push aside their group's interest. Party leaders must resist such pressures if the public interest is to be served.[41] At the same time, they must ensure that an aggregative politics has all the room it is supposed to have in a republican form of government. None of this is easy.

Second, those who speak for business interests inside government as well as the heads of major business organizations are likely to push to keep the focus on an aggregative or class politics. They will have considerable advantages in these domains, more so than in a public interest politics, where good arguments count for more than interests. Even in a more or less fully realized commercial republic, controllers of large-scale productive assets will have irreducible political advantages. Party leaders thus must be careful about pressing so hard against business interests as to raise what might be called the "Gouverneur Morris question": whether the propertied will maintain their attachment to the regime. Moreover, in the face of such attacks, businessmen will be prompted as a matter of defense to press narrow versions of their interests. Party leaders will undoubtedly find carefulness easier to come by than the resources needed to fend off narrow business interests. And that is precisely the problem. It will be all too easy for party leaders to be responsive to business interests at the cost of serving the public interest.

What kind of parties would have the right kind of leaders, that is, those who can fend off, when absolutely necessary, the kinds of pressures just considered? Even though a commercial republic cannot flourish without a particular kind of party system, the internal organization of parties and the character of the party system cannot, to any great extent, be the *direct* subject of lawmaking. The temptation to treat the party system in this way will be great, but it will open the door for factional-minded lawmakers to use the power of the state to control the political organizations of their adversaries. Yet, without the kinds of party leaders and political parties we have been talking about, a commercial republican regime may exist, but it cannot flourish. It is reasonable to suppose, however, that, if all of the constitutive features of a commercial republic are well developed, the odds will increase substantially that the appropriate party system and party leaders will emerge. Nevertheless, even though ordinary political leadership and statesmanship are inextricable parts of the various kinds of politics that compose a well-ordered commercial republic, they are the hardest of its attributes to shape. Not least of the reasons is that they depend so heavily on individual talents. The need to balance the various types of lawmaking is thus a source of considerable vulnerability for republican regimes. For the most part, it will be ordinary men and women who will exercise judgment about complicated matters. Not only are they likely to get things wrong at least some of the time, they probably will be seriously tempted to disregard the need to move between lawmaking modes. Once again we run up against a fundamental feature of republican regimes: a group of people able and willing to devote themselves in a more or less selfless manner to its solution—the best ruling—will unlikely be present.[42] We must instead rely for the most part on those with ordinary powers of practical reasoning who have ordinary inclinations toward a comfortable life and the serving of their own or narrow but useful political interests. A central problem for the political constitution of the American regime is how to get some of us—ordinary men and women—to do the necessary work. In the end, just as republican government must rest on the public-spiritedness and proud independence of its citizens, so must it rest on the judgment of its leaders. Institutional mechanisms can only take us so far. As Madison said, if we lack the necessary virtues we are lost.[43]

A MIXED REGIME?

It is no accident that the political sociology of a fully realized commercial republic is best anchored by the middle class, for its self-interest significantly overlaps with the public interest. It is conceivable, however, that a commercial republic could be anchored in the self-interest of a different stratum. Such a sociological foundation may work, and some republics at some junctures in their history may have no choice in the matter: those who advocate a conception of justice that legitimizes a republican regime may be too weak to serve as its foundation in self-interest. Still, there can be little doubt that this is a precarious state of affairs. At some point, it would be widely noticed that there is little relation between the justice that a commercial republic embodies at its best and the actual politics of the regime. It is obviously desirable that the weight of public opinion, which reflects that a particular ruling class is at work, parallel the actual pattern of self-interest found in the day-to-day politics of the regime.

A more or less fully realized commercial republican regime will, therefore, almost certainly have a large, secure, and confident middle class at the center of its politics. The middle class, with its greater receptivity to the kind of public-spiritedness needed by such a republic, will be a crucial source of support for the deliberative lawmaking that is distinctive of a republican regime. Its view of the public interest will be fostered through an appropriately designed local politics, and the day-to-day politics of the regime will include regular efforts to give its view concrete meaning. It will also be at the center of the broad-based coalitional politics that, in addition to a public interest politics, will be a principal source of political energy in such a regime. When to its centrality in the politics of the regime is added the foundation of the public interest in both a middle-class conception of justice and its view of what constitutes a good political regime, it is clear just why the ruling class of a fully realized commercial republic will almost certainly be the middle class.

Put differently, as a public interest politics flourishes, so also do both the political and economic position of the middle class and the values that give it a distinctive outlook. Such a politics not only reinforces the middle class's confidence that its views are right and ought to carry a good deal of weight in political life. It also, if past and present experience are any indication, benefits the middle class significantly by reducing economic inequality through the use of income transfers, social insurance, and the provision of subsidized social services.[44] Similarly, efforts to secure a vital civic life and to ensure, as part of a concern for political equality, that interest groups will flourish will also advantage the middle class. It has more time and greater organizational and political skills than the have-littles; and, quite possibly, it has a greater inclination to participate in civic life than large-scale asset-controllers, as well as a greater need to organize politically. If so, the results of a group politics will parallel that of the politics of class coalition. In a fully realized commercial republic, the two streams of politics will reinforce one another.

It only remains to add that bolstering the position of the middle class cannot be the declared aim of a public interest politics. Cynicism is one possible response to this assertion, especially given that favoring the class is likely what will often happen. A more moderate response is that, as a good regime, a commercial republic aims at justice and the public interest that rests on it. But like all political undertakings, the aim and the effort that accompanies it are characterized by partiality. As Harvey Mansfield writes, the classical idea of "the regime is the rule of the whole of any society by a part of that, which by its rule, gives that society its particular character."[45] This partly disguised form of class rule is a delicate and complex matter. Consider that a secure and confident middle class will help reduce the danger of factional rule by the propertied: class advantage directly serves the public interest. In general, there seems to be no way to serve the public interest without class advantage, not only because such advantage is inevitable but also because it is part of the means of serving that interest. Moderation is a political virtue because political life is filled with situations and conditions that are unattractive but inevitable.

Even as a ruling class, the middle class cannot, however, rule alone. Most importantly, it cannot rule without the cooperation of those who control large-scale productive assets. The latter group will have discretion on the deployment of those assets and as a result their political views must be accommodated. The character of the public interest also indicates that they should be regularly consulted. Nevertheless, the privileged political role of asset controllers can only be sustained in a well-ordered commercial republic with at least the acquiescence of the middle class. Thus, the politics of a commercial republic will to a significant degree revolve around the political claims of numbers and property—and around the effort to reconcile a liberal conception of justice with the political weight of the propertied. The "effectual truth"[46] of the commercial republic is that it is a mixed regime. We may once again suspect that lawmaking cannot, in the full light of day and in the full openness of public speech, aim expressly at serving the interests of those who control large-scale productive assets. Dusk and careful speech are probably needed.

There is a piece missing in this discussion of the class politics of a commercial republic. A new class may be emerging in the United States, one with roots in the recent and rapid growth of knowledge-based professionals. Those related to the productive apparatus in this fashion may be in the process of developing an outlook and political and economic interests that over time will differentiate it from the broad middle class. Here we need only note that, should such a class emerge and develop some measure of political organization, the character of the commercial republic as a mixed regime inevitably will be different from the one sketched here. There are at least two possibilities. If what we may call a "new" or "upper-middle class," with all its considerable resources and organization,[47] joins with the traditional middle class, the balance of power between the middle class, now in a broad form, and the controllers of productive assets will shift toward the former. In particular, the effort to broaden the interests of the propertied is likely to go further than it otherwise would, and the result will be a more nearly realized commercial republic. Alternatively, the new class may believe its interests are better served in an enduring alliance with the propertied. Whatever else it may do, such an alliance between, so to speak, the top and the top against everybody else is not a good recipe for the politics of a well-ordered commercial republic.

The preceding considerations prompt the thought: how can a regime that aims at a mixture of liberty and equality, of a combination of private property and significant participation by ordinary citizens in the act of governing, be other than a mixed regime?[48] Similarly, the idea of a commercial republic can be understood as pointing to a close connection between republican politics and economics. Politics is to be used to secure a certain kind of economic life because a free and equal people engaged in a form of self-government with limited powers requires a certain kind of economy. Therefore, in a reversal of much contemporary political talk and academic thinking, we should be guided in our economic thinking by political theory—that is to say, by constitutional theory. We should resist efforts to understand our political life through economic analysis. The idea of a mixed regime plays virtually no role in contemporary economic theory—with the usual dismaying outcome that ignorance invites.

CONCLUSION

Some additional general comments can be made about the political constitution of republican government. These broad considerations can serve as a conclusion to the discussion in this chapter and in the preceding two. They can also serve as a bridge to the final chapters.

A theory of republican political constitution is addressed to the people as constituent sovereign[49] who are the rightful authorizing agents of the political order by which they will be governed. At their best, the people authorize a government that will serve the public interest and be based in popular consent. The legitimacy of a republican regime rests not only on the people ruling but also on how they rule. The goodness of the regime has the same basis: who is to rule and how they are to do it. The aim of a theory of the political constitution of a commercial republic is to contrive a regime where substance (the "who") and procedure (the "how") reinforce one another.

A republican regime works not because clear and precise principles to guide lawmaking are laid out in advance, for who is to enforce them? We cannot presume a body of disinterested statesmen to do so. Nor can a republican people countenance a political force greater than themselves. A republican regime rests on a constitutional design that pays due regard to the various motives of political action—and that looks to the most reliable and powerful of such motives to induce the appropriate forms of lawmaking.

A free and equal citizenry engaged in a self-limiting exercise of self-government is the result of a properly designed politics. More narrowly, liberty is a product of government. Even the most strict libertarian must concede that liberty in a complex society requires a legal framework within which citizens can pursue their interests. As Hamilton said, "[T]he vigor of government is essential to the security of liberty."[50] Property and markets are also a product of government—unless by a sleight of hand courts are said not to be part of government even though judges are selected through governmental processes and their budgets are paid for out of governmental revenues. Those less given to strict orthodoxies should have little trouble in accepting that the real question with regard to liberty is not whether to have little or no government or a great deal of government, but what *kind* of government: how is it to be organized and operated? Since government is simultaneously the only agent able to give rights meaningful content and is a danger to them, the core of a theory of rights—and, by extension, a theory of liberty—must be a design for a self-limiting government and people.

In defining the limits on government, we are effectively defining the limits on how private power can be used. In saying for what purposes public power can be used, we are saying in what ways the actions of private agents can be regulated. This being so, the public interest, understood as that which will secure and maintain a well-ordered commercial republic, is also a definition of its public and private spheres.

The political constitution of a republican government not only limits government but enables it to act: it creates the kind of power appropriate to serving the purposes that define its limits. Constitutional design simultaneously limits governmental power and creates and enables it. A properly constituted republic is designed not just to prevent something—faction—but also to create effective government. A constitutional theory aimed only at preventing things from being done is dangerous. It makes no provisions for those matters to which a republican government must give attention if it is to survive and prosper. Worse, it must either assume that the important features of the world are simply fixed or that its changes can be easily predicted and provision for them readily made. Neither view is believable—and the result of a political constitution shaped by such views will likely be a diminution in the legitimacy of government itself, as pressures to cope with the consequences of inevitable and broad social changes are directed at public officials to deal with them in however an irregular fashion. As a consequence, government is likely to become corrupt, arbitrary, and inefficient, and citizens are likely to judge it so. It is a failing of much of libertarian thought not to see the likelihood of such a process unfolding. Thus, as noted, those libertarians who think of themselves as constitutionalists are badly mistaken if, as many of them do, they take Madison as the prototype of a libertarian constitutional thinker. It is central to Madison's thought that government can and must be active as well as limited.

Republican lawmaking—and with it the design of republican political institutions—must simultaneously prevent faction, serve the public interest, and properly aggregate private interests—all in the context of difficult-to-predict possibilities and conflicts. A crucial aspect of the problem is how to marry a deliberative, public-spirited and rights-respecting politics to a class politics—and to join these to a pluralist, interest-driven politics. To accomplish all this requires showing how a design for a constitutional politics can restrain overbearing private interests, combine moderate private interests, and secure the public interest.

If in the service of restraining faction, barriers are put in place that make it extremely difficult for *any* majorities to form, then republican government will be weakened. Whatever else it is, republican government is a species of majority rule. The alternative is rule by a minority.[51] But the substance and outlook of majorities matter: not just any majorities will do. A central feature of a successful republican design is that it retards factional majorities while giving full scope to majorities that are public-spirited and to those whose outlook and interests overlap with the public interest.

Moderate safeguards against faction—combined with a public-spirited citizenry, a social basis for the regime in which the private interests of the ruling class significantly overlap with the public interest, and a political class adept at encouraging movement between types of republican lawmaking—are the keys to republican constitutional design. Such a design provides reasonable security against faction while providing enough authority, political energy, and direction for the active government that serving the public interest requires. Republican government at its best is simultaneously strong, active, and limited. Strong because it has the necessary powers and energy to serve the public interest. Active because the public interest is broad in scope. But limited because its purposes are limited.[52]

Since circumstances may change dramatically, so may the specific concrete meaning given to the public interest. A republican regime can undergo significant changes in its politics—including substantial changes in the operative understanding of the public interest—and remain the same regime in the sense of being recognizably the one to which its citizens aspire. This is possible because at the core of political institutions and political forms more generally are generic modes of association that define how lawmakers are to stand in relation to one another, how they are to stand in relation to citizens, and how citizens shall stand in relation to one another. These relations can take different institutional forms.[53]

The political constitution of a fully realized commercial republic is built around the four modes of constituting political rule that the tradition of political theory has given us. It rests on class rule, to which classical political theory, most notably Aristotle, points; a mix of class outlooks, to which Tocqueville, Montesquieu, and, once again, Aristotle point; and enlightenment and institutional design, to which Tocqueville points and which is at the heart of Madison's political theory. It also needs republican political leadership whose greatest student is, perhaps, Machiavelli.

Republican constitutional theory is least developed with regard to political leadership. This is not surprising because a republic is supposed to rest on consent, self-government, and majority rule. The role of republican leaders is often disguised, and there is some reluctance to address it squarely among those who think about republican politics. We need say no more about the first of these four, except to note that more emphasis has been given here to class coalitions and to a ruling class that cannot rule on its own than classical political theory did. Tocqueville, moreover, on the evidence of his account of American democracy, would also probably be skeptical of the emphasis given here to class interest. In the present context, it is not possible to say more than that Madison is a better teacher than Tocqueville in this particular respect: we cannot do without the reliable motives that class interest provides. Moreover, this emphasis on class reflects the existence of a political economy more complex than the classical one and the one Tocqueville investigated. It is also rooted in the possibility, and hence in greater popular desire, for material well-being. Tocqueville was aware of the possibility of such a political economy but, while he thought an industrial aristocracy might emerge, he did not think it likely enough to consider in detail the way it would shape political life.[54] Nearly two hundred years later, we are in a better position to understand such matters as the political role of business. As for classical theorists, although they knew that a desire for unlimited accumulation of material goods existed, they gave little explicit consideration to what a regime would look like if this were one of its dominant motives.

On class outlooks, the opening comments in this chapter indicate that a well-ordered commercial republic needs not just the reliable, because self-interested, political energies of a class or classes. It also needs a mix of political outlooks that are concentrated in particular classes. The discussion offered here, which concentrates mostly on those outlooks that are more or less closely tied to economic class interests, provides only the beginnings of a full account of the mix of political and social orientations that a fully realized commercial republic requires. Tocqueville, for example, had much to say about the necessity in a commercial republic of elements of an aristocratic outlook.[55] If we believe, as I think we must, that a republican regime, like all good regimes, is an integral part of what Tocqueville calls a "social state," that is, a nexus of mores, civic and political institutions, habits of cooperation, and the like, then it will be clear that the mix of outlooks considered here is indeed only the start of what must be considered.

My account on enlightenment and institutional design as the key to constituting a commercial republic is more elaborate than that on class outlooks. Madison is one of the great teachers in this regard, especially on the matter of institutional design. I have had to go beyond him, however, on the matter of enlightenment—to consider in some detail the content of one of its essential components, public-spiritedness, and how it may be fostered. A full discussion of the content and role of enlightenment would have to take account of the thinking of Locke, Rousseau, and Montesquieu, among others—and it would need to consider, as the first two make especially clear, how children are to be educated in a republic.

The political constitution of a commercial republic is designed to harness in tandem two forces that pull in opposite direction: transconventional standards and popular sovereignty.[56] The problem is how to reconcile in practice what is difficult, perhaps impossible, to reconcile in theory. If we can get the institutional design and political sociology right, they may be practically reconciled. The essence of this reconciliation is likely to be that, each day, in giving concrete meaning to the public interest, the people and those who speak for them rebind themselves to purposes and standards whose claims on them transcend their particular wills.[57] The essential task in designing the political constitution of a commercial republic is how to get a self-governing people to secure transconventional rights and serve the permanent interests of the community, to rule but not just as they please. They must limit themselves so that enough room is left for lawmaking that takes account of a wide variety of interests and preferences that is an inevitable feature of the sort of complex society that a commercial republic will be. At issue here is whether we as a people can come to the sort of political understanding necessary to secure the essential features of a commercial republican political constitution. In political life there is always enormous pressure to focus on the here and now. The fruits of a well-functioning political constitution are diffuse and many of them are only apparent a fair way down the road. They are, therefore, easy to discount and difficult to explain to people who are rightly concerned with the problems that lie just before them.

But in the same way that the citizenry must often move beyond narrow self-interest in its choice of lawmakers, so it must also, at least some of the time, act constitutionally. This is where our real mettle as a people is shown. But our mettle is not determined by some genetic endowment or even by an inherited culture, if by that is meant a set of ideas dancing around in our heads. Whether we as a people have the ability to think and act constitutively depends on the political forms through which we can act. Our political institutions must act reflexively and, as such, they are institutions for learning as much as doing. Thus, whether we can more fully realize an American commercial republic depends very much on our political inheritance—what the founders of this republic bequeathed to us—as well as what succeeding generations have put in place. We may reform ourselves, but not just as we please: there is no "we" to so act apart from the existing institutions that form us as a people.

Thinking Constitutionally About the American Republic

MY ACCOUNT of the commercial republic is not about the best regime, nor is it even about the best regime for Americans. Rather, it is an account of the regime to which we Americans aspire—and of the best version of that regime—given who we are and might plausibly become. I have only argued briefly for the value of such a regime, and then only to defend the idea of taking our aspirations and the liberal justice associated with them as a guide for a theory of political constitution. My account is thus only incidentally a work in political philosophy, as that is now commonly understood. But this does not mean that it lacks a defense of the value of a commercial republic for Americans. I have tried to show how such a regime could work and how it would be broadly attractive. My defense, in short, has been a practical one, which is, after all, a good thing for an analysis that hopes to rise to a theory of political constitution. Moreover, it is a defense that asks the reader to look to the whole regime—not just to its particular parts or institutions. This too befits a theory of political constitution, which is a theory of a whole political regime. It is difficult to say whether this sort of defense will be convincing to those who think that the defense of political purpose must build outward from a justification of abstractly stated first principles. In chapter 4 I indicated some of my concerns with such an approach, and my remarks here are meant to echo these earlier ones.

A thread runs through the criticisms offered earlier of relying on moral, legal, and economic theories as guides for thinking about the constitution of popular self-government. These theories, at bottom, can be viewed as attempts to evade or—more dramatically—to escape from politics.[1] In their different ways, moralists, legalists, and economists think that politics rests on a mistake. What they fail to see is that constitutional theory is a theory of constitutional politics. Thus, many of them argue that political practitioners do not seem to understand that politics should be, respectively, an exercise in applying moral philosophy, legal reasoning, and the application of economic expertise.[2] The theories are efforts to find ground outside of the messiness of politics on which crucial collective decisions can rest, whether in foundational moral principles, the logic of the law, or economic efficiency. It is as if such theorists think that once the appropriate norms to constrain popular rule are defined—whether as moral, legal, or economic propositions—the hard part of the job is done. Some even argue as if, somehow, the norms themselves will do the work of securing limited, republican government. Otherwise, we may ask, why put so much effort into getting the norms precisely defined if not that their blinding clarity will itself significantly shape behavior? Some moralists, legalists, and economists go so far as simply to call for the replacement of politics and politicians by philosophy, law, and markets—or more precisely, by philosophers, lawyers, and economists. As Grant Gilmore warned, however, in hell there will only be law (and lawyers).[3] While perhaps a place where there is only philosophy or economics will not be equally dreadful, ordinary people there would likely have a devil of a time.

But once we realize that major political choices cannot be made by a single decisionmaker,[4] we know that broad general principles are all that can guide lawmaking. The rest, which is quite a bit, has to be filled in by politics. Moreover, the attractiveness of political principles depends heavily on whether they can be given institutional life, that is, whether ways can be found to make them politically effective in the world. And considering how political institutions can be made to work will almost certainly lead us to revise the content of our values.

There is thus no place to go to escape from politics—at least in the sense that, having arrived at such a place, we will find a comprehensive and detailed normative guide to political decision as it concerns constitutive questions and, more broadly, limits on the people's rule. Although efforts to escape politics may be characteristically American—moral philosophy, law, and economics play a large role in our intellectual culture—they are also very odd given the manner of thinking of those who founded this Republic. Rather than assimilating the idea of rights to an argument in moral philosophy, for example, they assimilated it to a political theory, in particular, a theory of how to constitute the new American regime.

The kind of matters we face when considering the fundamental questions regarding a republican constitution can, at the end of the day, only be settled by practical political reasoning that takes account of how the world works and can be made to work. We may need moral philosophy to help us decide which are good forms of rule or to point to the aspects of our lives that need the special protection of rights. Similarly, we may find helpful the history of high court decisions and legal commentary in our efforts to define the public interest and, perhaps, even to aid us in thinking through the design of political institutions. We may also need economic theory to appreciate fully the importance of aggregating interests for republican government. After taking account of these things, however, we must still rely on what we always rely on in deciding what to do when practical questions confront us. We first get the question straight: What are we trying to do and why? We then gather the available information about how the particular part of the world that concerns us works or might be made to work, and we think through the interconnections among our purposes and how they are, and may be, related to the workings of the world. "Thinking constitutionally" is the name we can give to such practical reasoning when we are in the business of creating, reforming, and maintaining political regimes.

RAWLS AND IDEAL THEORY

A prominent example of the impulse to escape from politics is found in the work of John Rawls. Since Rawls is widely considered to have been the most important Anglophone political philosopher during the last half of the twentieth century, an examination of his work is important for what it reveals about how political and constitutional theory, not to mention politics, are understood in the contemporary United States.

Rawls offers a theory of justice anchored in an account of the organizing principles for a whole society that rational people would choose if they made their choices behind what he calls the "veil of ignorance." Behind this veil, people do not know what their position would be in a society designed to serve these principles. The rest of the theory develops the implications of what Rawls calls the "principles of justice" for the organization of various important elements of a society. Rawls sees this effort as an exercise in ideal theory,[5] the concern of which is "the form a just society would take in a world in which, for theoretical purposes, everyone is presumed to act justly."[6] As Rawls puts it, ideal theory assumes

> that (nearly) everyone strictly complies with...the principles of justice. We ask in effect what a perfectly just...constitutional regime might look like, and whether it may come about and be made stable...under realistic, though reasonably favorable, conditions....Justice as fairness is realistically utopian:...that, is, [it concerns] how far in our world (given its laws and tendencies) a democratic regime can attain complete realization of its appropriate political values.[7]

These reasonably favorable conditions are what Rawls terms "the circumstances of justice." They are features of the social world that those choosing the principles of justice behind the veil of ignorance will know. These features include that this world makes cooperation possible and necessary, that individuals are roughly similar in physical and mental powers, that they have conflicting claims on the resources available, and that there is moderate scarcity.

Let us suppose that an important aim of political philosophy is to help create the best political regime of which we are capable. This seems to be a view that Rawls shares, as the quotation above indicates. Moreover, Rawls is clear[8] that he is concerned not only with a "strict compliance theory" of justice, where everyone is assumed to act justly, but also with a "partial compliance theory" that concerns "how we are to deal with injustice."[9] Indeed, he says that "the reason for beginning with ideal theory is that it provides the only basis for the systematic grasp" of the "more pressing problems" such as "weighing one form of institutional injustice against another"—and he goes on to say that "I shall assume that a deeper understanding can be gained in no other way."[10]

There are other reasons to pursue political philosophy besides a concern to promote good political practice. These include developing utopias that highlight the differences between where we presently are, what humankind is capable of, and what would simply be best. Utopian theory such as this may provide humankind with an impulse toward great change.[11] It can also tell us much about the human condition and the sort of enterprise politics is compared to other kinds of human endeavor.[12]

If I am correct that Rawls's enterprise is indeed, in part, an undertaking in practical theory, there is good reason to doubt its adequacy.[13] The fundamental question here is whether we are more likely to succeed in creating the best political regime of which we are capable if we start with an account of the "circumstances of justice"[14] or the "circumstances of politics." The first, as noted, is Rawls's term, but I want to use it differently in order to point specifically to the idea that people are presumed to act justly. In this second sense of the circumstances of justice, the presumption is that there is no problem of compliance once the content of justice is known. The central task, then, is to depict how a political order should look among people who are already committed to a particular common sense of justice.

The "circumstances of politics," on the other hand, may be defined as a state of affairs in which there is a large aggregation of people who (1) have conflicting purposes that engender more or less serious conflict; (2) are given to attempts to use political power to further their own purposes and those of people with whom they identify; (3) are inclined to use political power to subordinate others; and (4) are sometimes given to words and actions that suggest that they value limiting the use of political power by law and harnessing it to public purposes. These circumstances are not "the best of foreseeable conditions."[15] They are simply the conditions that obtain as we Americans, like others, go about our political business.

Again, where should we start? Contrary to Rawls, we should start from the circumstance of politics because they define the problem of how to secure any good, no less an ideal political order: we must *first* prevent the worst before we can achieve even the good enough, let alone the best.[16] Any plausible account of human motives will posit that human beings are capable of the grossest cruelty, of a desire to tyrannize over their fellows, and of a whole host of lesser evils. If we do not prevent these motives from being widely acted on, there is little reason to suppose that citizens and those who speak for them will have leeway to pursue even the good enough. This is not only Madison's point, but also the fundamental premise of all liberal theory, and it means that, contrary to Rawls's claim, we do not best grasp the nub of partial compliance theory by focusing on ideal theory. Rather, we can best understand partial compliance when we understand just why there can only *be* partial compliance, and what we need to do to achieve even this modest state of affairs. Thus, Madison teaches that we cannot have republican government if it is necessary that men act like angels.[17] The circumstances of politics are, to an important degree, irremediable, and our account of good political regimes should be tempered by this knowledge. We either build our institutions on reliable and plausible motives or they will fail—and with them our hopes for realizing an attractive political order.

More generally, we can say that the good regime is unlikely to be a stop along the way to the ideal regime.[18] This is, in fact, the point behind the theory of the second best,[19] and behind the phrase that "the best is the enemy of the good." Thus, the pursuit of the ideal, which is by definition beyond us, may bring out the worst in us: consider the consequences of some of humankind's efforts to find unity with God. Moreover, effort expended on the ideal is effort lost for seeking the good enough. Additionally, pursuit of the ideal *must* fail, and is thus dispiriting. Finally, if we shape institutions with an eye to moving toward the ideal, there is little reason to suppose that these institutions will be of much use in securing a good regime—which is, in fact, all we can hope to achieve. Following the road that is supposed to lead to the ideal is likely to engender major conflicts that, because we are unlikely to have made provision to handle them, will be devastating.[20]

More generally, the institutions called for by ideal theory will make it harder to achieve a good regime because they will not be well designed for the politics that will inevitably be practiced on the road we will travel.[21] And *post hoc* efforts to graft devices meant to prevent the worst onto institutions designed to achieve the ideal are unlikely to be successful. It would be much like the couch potato deciding he needs karate lessons when the barbarians are at the gates: it's a bit late. Against Rawls, therefore, we will be better off if we start our thinking about the constitution of a republic from the circumstances of politics—where "better off" refers to achieving a political order that garners widespread support as a result, at least, of civil peace, and that is widely thought to be good or decent. Indeed, it is entirely possible that more of Rawlsian justice can be achieved if the theory that guides our practical efforts takes full account of the circumstances of politics and uses it as the starting point. It *is* possible to gain a "deeper understanding" of the problems of partial compliance other than by starting with ideal theory.

The "ideal" for our theoretical reflections about political practice ought, therefore, to take account of the circumstance of politics, not abstracted and thus escaping from them: an "ideal" political regime is one that ideally copes with the circumstances of politics. Our efforts to create good political regimes would meet with greater success if we start from—to give the circumstances of politics a different name—the "political whole."[22] Rawls, by contrast, invites us to conceive of political and social institutions as either embodiments of moral-political ideals or simply the means to achieve them. We would do better, however, to focus on the fact that the political institutions of any good political regime must somehow enable people with conflicting interests and political views to live together in productive ways and to avoid the evil of civil disorder. More generally, the good we can bring about in political life must be achieved not by putting to one side unattractive, even evil motives, but by considering how they can be moderated and made use of. Political institutions are a principal means for doing this, as they form a citizenry by creating enduring relations within it. Good can and does rest on the unattractive and even on that which is worse. More broadly, the political institutions of an attractive political regime cannot be understood in the apolitical fashion to which Rawls's theory directs us. The good, the bad, and the ugly cannot be separated in the Rawlsian manner. Indeed, if we follow Machiavelli's teaching, good political orders must rest on vice, and even that may be too optimistic a view. The task of a political constitution is to take what cannot be changed—or changed only at prohibitive cost—and make the best of it. We need ideals to help us identify the various kinds of "good" regimes, but we also need to have our efforts at political constitution informed by a clear-eyed understanding of the circumstances in which they will be carried out. Getting the moral theory right does not solve the political problem.[23] In the end, what theorists like Rawls find difficult to accommodate is that the real subject of political philosophy is politics—the often self-interested play of ambition, power, and interest that is only intermittently principled.

THE DEVIL IS IN THE IMAGE

Attempts to escape from politics are usually prompted by a bedeviling fact: politics cannot be trusted. If my arguments in the preceding chapters are correct, however, the real problem faced by friends of republican government is how to get political choice to be self-limiting. We must rely on politics because it is the only way that we can govern ourselves; it is all we have. But that does not mean that we only have bargaining, strategic maneuver, and the exercise of power. Politics can be and is carried on in different ways, and the challenge is to make use of the full range of possibilities so that some kinds of politics can be used to restrain other kinds. Thus, when we are told to look to higher law, the implication is that such law is the source of the limitation on governmental power. But this cannot be right, for the obvious question is why those who are engaged in the ordinary politics of the regime give credence to such law. Is it simply because they believe in the higher law? Some may do so, but without incentives built into the politics of the regime to give its interpreters the means to defend their interpretation, it is unlikely that other public officials will be much inclined to constrain their behavior. Politics provides the institutional muscle for limitation.

The arguments concerning the limits on popular rule that I have criticized are surely correct, however, in one thing: a political system wholly characterized by the play of power, bargaining, and the pursuit of narrow advantage would be a deeply unattractive politics. Among other things, it would probably endanger the kind of primary political liberties that the citizens of Western countries have come to expect are theirs. Moreover, the ordinary politics of narrow advantage and strategic maneuver is too unprincipled. But again, there are different kinds of politics, and we Americans need not accept the form ours currently takes. Indeed we cannot if we are to have any prospect of further realizing our aspirations to be a well-ordered republican regime. To say that something is political does not mean that reasoning about it is futile.

There is thus no substitute for politics—if by politics we mean the various ways we arrive at collective, authoritative decisions in a world in which people legitimately hold different views about the purposes of government and the manner in which it should be carried on. To exclude politics is to require either that we all agree on purposes and the manner of carrying them out (or at least on an agent who will define and implement them for us); or that we not make any collective decisions; or that purposes and the manner of governing be imposed. There are no other choices—and since we do not in fact all agree, we are left with no government or force. Politics is better, even nobler, than these twins of anarchy and despair.

We must rely on politics, then, to bind politics. This is no paradox. It is simply a way of saying that only the people can bind themselves: in a republican government, the people must be a self-limiting popular sovereign. Republican citizens must devise ways to limit their own rule so that popular government is neither arbitrary nor tyrannical. Simultaneously, they must create the institutional powers that enable them to accomplish what their commitment to commercial republican government and its attendant conception of justice calls for. In constituting themselves, they create the ability to serve their purposes just as they devise the means to prevent their subversion. This is the heart of a republican politics. To bring this capacity into being is the key to reconciling the claims that the people are to rule and that there need to be limits on their rule.[24] To achieve such reconciliation is to design a self-limiting popular sovereign capable of practical reason.

To say that republican citizens must live by politics is also to say that the problem of how to reconcile popular and limited government has no theoretical solution. There are no principles precise enough to resolve most of the questions concerning the extent of the people's legitimate power. The people and those who speak for them must have considerable leeway in deciding what is the concrete meaning of the public interest—and the task for constitutional thinking is to ensure that they make the effort to do so.[25] This is the core of what it means *not* to escape from politics. A public interest politics and a politics of broad interests are used to limit a private-interest politics and to control the powerful. Indeed, those living in places without such a civilizing politics know only too well that before they can do very much about things as elevated as law, economic progress, and even individual morality, they must create a politics that, when properly organized, reduces the arbitrariness and precariousness of collective existence.[26]

In talking about self-limitation I might only be making the obvious point that standards external to politics must be implemented because they are not self-enforcing. This is, of course, true. The argument here, however, is that the concrete meaning of the limits must be worked out by the people themselves or by those authorized to speak for them. Even this can be interpreted as trivially true since few will doubt that limits on the people's rule, whatever their source, need to be interpreted—unless one believes that the finger of God has written down the limits of political authority in elaborate detail. The idea that rules must be interpreted is closer to what I am arguing—except that, in the view I am defending, this is a complex normative and empirical exercise in which the objective features of the public interest are given specific meaning in light of a wide variety of practical considerations. This is not only a rather more complex activity than is usually meant by the term "interpretation," it also puts the burden on the people and those who speak for them. In particular, it emphasizes how the people must be organized if they are to give concrete meaning to the public interest. If they and their agents do not do the job, no one else can. The difficulty of the job is suggested by the fact that self-limitation means not only that the people cannot rule any way they please, but also that they cannot define whatever sorts of limits they desire. There *is* a public interest, and if they are committed to realizing a commercial republic, they are bound by it.[27]

In order to understand what is at issue in limiting the people's rule, it helps if we are not mesmerized by a picture of popular self-government in which the people collectively vote on everything of importance, including proposed limits on their own rule. This is not the only form of popular rule nor, very likely, has it ever been tried. Nevertheless, this picture of how popular will is to be exercised has misled many thinkers concerned with limiting the people's rule. For if we think that the problem is to restrain the demos, treated as if it were a single actor, then we naturally turn to those bodies of thought relevant to deciding what individual actors should and should not do. We look, that is, to the study of moral rules, whether they are to be found in moral philosophy and legal philosophy or, in disguised form, in economic theory. Constitutionally minded theorists have long known, however, that the key to constructing republican government is not to treat the demos as a single agent. Instead, they say, we ought to think of the people as organized, as acting through a variety of institutions, indeed as being constituted by these institutions.

A theory of the political constitution of the American republic must give the central role to politics, especially the manner in which representatives are chosen and the way in which the legislature works in limiting popular rule. The legislature is where popular rule meets the problem of limits on that rule. It follows that the theory of liberty is a theory of political institutions and the politics in which they are embedded. It explains how the discretion necessarily given to lawmakers can be harnessed to serving the public interest, and thus be limited.

NATURAL LAW AND REPUBLICAN GOVERNMENT

I have argued that a set of transconventional values comprehensive and precise enough to guide republican lawmakers is not available.[28] However, natural lawyers and others drawn to the idea of a transconventional source of comprehensive guidance for political life need not be discomforted by this conclusion. Nor need they be worried by my arguments on behalf of the centrality of practical political reason to deliberative lawmaking, as it brings together the normative and empirical considerations that compose the public interest. Practical reason is in fact essential for natural lawyers as well—unless they believe that not only is comprehensive guidance available to us but that it is precise enough to bind lawmakers in detail.[29] Leo Strauss, one of the greatest modern commentators on natural law, put matters this way in discussing Plato and Aristotle: "There is a universally valid hierarchy of ends, but there are no universally valid rules of action. . . . One has to consider not only which of the various competing objectives is higher in rank but also which is most urgent in the circumstances."[30]

In a similar vein, Stephen Salkever, in a remarkable account of Aristotelian moral and political reasoning, argues that theory of the kind that posits natural ends or purposes "is useful to practice in clarifying the real issues involved and exposing false solutions . . . but not in providing answers." He goes on to say that "theoretical rankings of the virtues are possible, but action-governing rules—on the order of natural laws—are not."[31]

In short, natural lawyers and those who subscribe to the more modest role for transconventional values that is defended here, should be drawn to the same kind of institutional design for republican government. Each should find attractive a design that not only gives the central role to practical political reason in lawmaking, but also gives considerable attention to what can induce lawmakers to behave in the appropriate ways. We might say that the need for practical political reason is simply an aspect of our condition as human beings. Politics—understood as the organized effort to determine collectively what to do without access to standards that are comprehensive and precise enough to compel specific decisions—is simply one of the modes of human experience. This is a broadly Aristotlean view insofar as Aristotle simultaneously argued that judgment is not entirely conventional and that there are no transcendent truths applicable in all circumstances from which decisions on actions can be directly drawn. The circumstances of judgment are as important as the good at which the judgment aims.[32] The crucial point thus is not likely to be whether transconventional standards exist. Plausibly they do. Rather, the principal question is whether ways can be devised to induce lawmakers to attend to these standards—making them more concrete while also taking account of less abstract values and of empirical considerations about how the world works and can be made to work.

Happily, the design problem for republican government will also be much the same as I have sketched it for those who argue—in contrast to natural lawyers and the like—that there are no transconventional values to inform the setting of limits on the people's rule. So long as these skeptics concede that a working political regime must have rules, and that the institutions that give these rules life are not self-maintaining—that is, so long as they concede that conscious efforts must be made to enforce rules and maintain institutions—they have conceded that there are transpolitical values. And this means that they have accepted the existence of standards with a claim on us over and above what may be agreed on at the moment by "we the people" and our agents. Whether these values are also trans-conventional—binding on all polities—matters little in this context. Either way there are limits on popular rule. Republican lawmaking, therefore, cannot consist only of trades, compromises, and the aggregation of interests if republican government is to prosper. Lawmakers must attend to the problem of how to maintain republican institutions—that is, to the public interest—at least some of the time. It thus makes surprisingly little difference for republican constitutional design whether it is believed that there are transconventional or transpolitical standards. In designing republican political institutions, natural lawyers, moral conventionalists, and those of modest mien in these matters face essentially the same problem: how to limit the people when we can have only a broad conception of what those limits are to be.

To some, perhaps, this conclusion will seem to entail a loss of certainty in political judgment. But it is only a loss for those who suppose that certainty is both necessary and possible. We are where we have always been with "all of the sense and discernment we have ever had."[33] The point is nicely made by Martha Nussbaum:

> When we get rid of the hope of a transcendental metaphysical grounding for our evaluative judgments . . . we are not left with the abyss. We have everything we always had before all along: the exchange of reasons and arguments by human beings within history, in which, for reasons that are historical and human but not the worse for that, we hold some things to be good and others bad, some arguments to be sound and others not sound. . . . For it is only to one who pinned everything to that hope [of metaphysical grounding] that its collapse will seem to entail the collapse of all evaluation.[34]

CONSTITUTIONAL THEORY AND PRESENT POLITICAL PRACTICE

We can now consider how the constitutional theory I have outlined illuminates key features of our present-day politics, particularly its failures. The judgments offered in this regard must be tentative; anything more confident would need to rest on extensive empirical investigation, which would require a book in itself. However, it is possible to mount a full case for the value of the constitutional theory presented in the preceding pages. That is, if the theory helps us to determine whether we are moving along a path toward a fuller realization of our aspirations, then it is valuable.

To start, we now have a clear and simple way to raise the question of whether those who control the large-scale productive assets of the society are, in some sense, too powerful. The answer turns on whether they behave factionally, and there is reason to believe, I have said, that they have. To complete the case we would need to show in detail, for example, that asset controllers have worked to prevent serving the modest economic equality called for by the public interest. Or we could show that they have worked to prevent the political equality and public-spiritedness that is crucial to the full realization of a commercial republic. Regardless of which elements of the public interest we focus on, it is important to distinguish factional behavior from the distinctively large role that asset controllers play in shaping public decisionmaking. The latter is not in itself indicative of constitutional failure insofar as a commercial republic requires that asset controllers have such a role. Therefore, the question of whether asset controllers have *too much* power is largely a matter of whether the purposes served by their large political role overlap with the public interest. In other words, this is largely a question of the broadness of asset-controller interests.

This way of understanding the problem has the signal advantage of paying due regard to the fact that asset controllers cannot simply be the enemies of democracy—at least not if the citizens of democracies wish for high levels of material well-being. This approach also gives full recognition to the fact that large-scale businessmen have also at various points undoubtedly stood athwart the full realization of popular self-government. The theory of commercial republican political constitution thus invites the kind of discrimination between different aspects of the political role of businessmen that other kinds of theories have difficulty making—whether they argue that there is something approaching political domination by large-scale capital or have difficulty distinguishing between giant corporations and the corner grocery.

Again, the sketch of the constitutional theory offered here suggests just why our present distribution of wealth and income is a serious problem: it is at variance with the public interest.[35] More generally, when commercial republics fail it is often because they have been turned into thinly disguised oligarchies. There is enough in our present politics on this score that ought to make uneasy any defenders of the wealthy who also appreciate the value of republican government—especially if they believe that a flourishing commercial republic is likely to be the best long-term guarantee that large rewards will accrue to the propertied.

On a different dimension of republican constitution, most American citizens today do not participate in the political life of the society beyond voting and, when they do, it is largely with people very much like themselves. If the constitutional theory presented here is even approximately correct, this too undercuts the public interest.[36] Public-spiritedness is an essential ingredient of the deliberative politics that a commercial republic is built on and, in a heterogeneous society, interpretation of the public interest must take account of the multiple understandings of its concrete meaning.

In the same vein, the theory of political constitution I have been developing makes it possible to see why the present condition of our local politics may well be carrying us along the road to constitutional failure. Indeed, it is entirely possible that even if citizens were to come to local political life with all of the qualities I have discussed, unless it is structured very differently than at present, little public-spiritedness will be fostered. The present character of local political life promotes a narrowness of concern on the part of citizens and does little to stretch self-interest to a concern with broader, public interests.[37] Citizens quickly learn that local politics is about the advancement of private interests; naturally enough, they conclude that their interests too should be given serious attention. The present pattern of politics, moreover, offers few opportunities for deliberation. More importantly, it stands in the way of opening up more opportunities.

Equally serious, it is currently unlikely in a significant number of localities, particularly homogeneous, well-to-do suburbs and towns, that citizens can be drawn into a consideration of the concrete meaning of the public interest. The residents of these municipalities are the beneficiaries of a political economy that insulates them from the need to decide the question of how best to deal with the interconnections among the elements of the public interest. Although others might struggle with this question (and, struggling or not, are strongly affected by the tensions among elements of the public interest), for the citizens of more or less uniformly prosperous communities local political life is all of a piece: those who run business corporations can have very wide discretion in how they employ their assets, local prosperity can be high, and government can be limited. By contrast, those living in other kinds of communities will likely need to consider that if business corporations have wide discretion in how they employ their assets, they may decide to leave the locality, thereby reducing local prosperity. Rather than being drawn into a local politics that teaches the citizenry something of such tensions among elements of the public interest, those who live in homogeneous prosperous communities can move happily through life oblivious of these tensions. Indeed, they have the luxury of responding in a puzzled way when someone points out that serving the public interest is a very difficult matter. After all, for them the pieces of the public interest seem to fit together rather nicely.

While citizens of prosperous localities need not face the question of how to understand the elements of the public interest, those in other communities cannot do so:[38] their socio-economic condition allows them few, if any, choices. These communities, too, are homogeneous: a substantial majority of their citizens are poor or nearly poor. Thus, at present, East St. Louis and East Cleveland operate in a different world from Bronxville, New York and Winnetka, Illinois. East St. Louis and East Cleveland cannot pay their bills, no less devote resources to weighing up how best to manage their local economies. East St. Louis' property values have fallen to below 50 million dollars from 200 million dollars in the mid-1960s. Its per capita income is now approximately one-half that of the United States as a whole, and two-thirds of its residents at various points in time have received some form of public assistance.[39] East St. Louis may be the extreme, but other localities share many of the same problems, and for all intents and purposes, such localities are economically and politically bankrupt. Their politics are much more likely to teach futility than lessons in giving concrete meaning to the public interest.

To these difficulties concerning the present state of local political life may be added that local government is now balkanized because of the large number of special districts and separate governing boards for a number of public services. When local political life is fragmented in this way, it is exceedingly difficult for citizens and those who speak for them to consider the full range of matters relevant to the public interest.

Through the lens of the theory of political constitution set out here, we can also see why the present role of the Supreme Court ought to make friends of republican government uneasy. The increasing reliance on the Court to settle a wide variety of questions of political principle—such as the rules that define the business corporation's role in our political life—very likely short-circuits public deliberation. So also does a legislature in which aggregation of interests is the dominant mode of lawmaking.[40] Indeed, the present workings of the separation of powers is not doing much to facilitate the kind of complex deliberation that republican government requires.

Finally, there is the question of the condition of the middle class and the possibility of its serving as the pivot of republican politics.[41] We can best start with the economic condition of that class. Those at the present median level of family income, who are certainly middle class, cannot save much for their retirement. To be sure, they may not be on the economic ropes, for middle-class households typically own at least one car and many of the accoutrements of modern consumption-oriented living. But they also have a very small financial cushion, are very likely to be uneasy about any major expense, and dread the prospect of unemployment.[42]

A class significantly composed of people with this sort of experience of economic insecurity[43] is not likely to feel particularly generous to those who are even worse off, especially if they have to pay for their generosity out of their own pockets; they also tend to suspect that the quality of the public services available to them is poorer because of those less well-off. In short, families living at or near the median family income—which includes a substantial portion of middle-class Americans—are not secure financially, and neither is the quality of their lives much enhanced by the quality of the public services available to them. The economy that made the last decades of the twentieth century a cornucopia for the asset-controlling class was not economically kind to the middle class.[44] Similarly, the cultural shifts promoting much more personal expression, a wider array of publicly displayed sexual choices, and a general "liberation" of the culture are probably, on balance, a gain for the economically secure. They can now give fuller rein to self-expression without fear of great disapproval by the media, their neighbors, or the law. Moreover, the economically well-off have the resources to deal with many of the unpleasant consequences of sex, drugs, and rock and roll. They can pay for therapists, absorb lost work days and send their children to special schools. For most of the middle class, such costs are much harder to absorb.

Then there is the matter that many middle-class people have concluded that the culture is moving in a direction that undercuts what they hold most dear—a stable family with settled and respectful relations between parents and children. Many middle-class adults undoubtedly no longer feel confident that they can raise their children in ways that reflect the standard set of middle-class virtues. There are too many features of the larger society, many believe, that make the task very difficult, popular culture being the obvious culprit. It doesn't help that the media regularly report behavior by public officials and leading business people—those whom parents might hold up as examples of successful lives—that undercut these same virtues.

Economy and culture together provide substantial incentives for middle-class disengagement from the politics of anything more than the attempt to keep their economic and cultural ship from foundering. The rise of home schooling is but the latest indication of a desire to protect one's own from the larger society. A class with such an outlook is unlikely to wish or be able to play the leading role in the political life of a republican regime.

It is thus a long way from where we are at present to a politics with the middle class as political pivot. One sign of the distance is the regular effort by those who speak for the asset-controlling class to convince the middle class that the have-littles are dangerous, greedy, and deserve little in the way of governmental aid to improve their condition. These same opinion shapers also argue the corollary: that any attractive future for the middle class depends on a business class that receives very large material rewards for its role in the economy and a highly privileged political position. The difficulties for class alliances that serve the public interest are compounded by a party system whose leaders seem surprised by the thought that a republican regime requires vigorous government (the Republicans) and that a commercial republic must give the concerns of large-scale business particular attention (the Democrats).

In light of what constitutes a flourishing commercial republic, enough has been said about our present state of affairs to hazard a conclusion. We are in a parlous but not desperate state. Our lawmaking is very likely moving us away from securing the institutional politics that will constitute us as a fully realized commercial republic. We are unlikely, however, to be so far down the road of indifference or even hostility to the effort to secure and maintain republican institutions that a turn to a vibrant politics of the public interest and its accompanying class politics is out of reach. We may yet show the world how to combine free, popular, limited government with an enterprise-based market system. We are not, then, in a "crisis" if by that is meant that we are without hope of realizing our aspirations. The foundation of our working constitution remains, loosely at least, in popular consent; our lawmaking still significantly occurs in public assembly; and it is still widely believed that government should be limited. Similarly, the principles that lie behind these practices and concerns are still alive and thus so is the idea of republican government.

Still, the indifference of American political science to most of the questions at the center of a theory of republican constitution is not very encouraging for friends of the commercial republic. While much of what political scientists write is irrelevant for the future of republican government, unfortunately they do teach the next generation of citizens. The situation in the law schools is not much better. There are other possible sources of constitutional thinking, but there have been few recent reports of constitutional life from journals of opinion and the mass media. The importance of such derelictions is readily seen as soon as we recognize that an important source of our shortcomings is intellectual—that is, the sources are not just in the institutional workings and broader politics of the present society. We are thus well advised to consider the reasons for the paucity of constitutional teachers and the weakness of political science.

The usual suspects are probably the right ones: Hobbesian instrumental reason, modern natural science, and the Nietzschean critique of transcendental value. These have helped create an intellectual culture in which the idea of good regimes and the task of developing a body of thought directed at how best to achieve them is considered the province of those who indeed live in the provinces. The implication is that they have not received the latest news from the capital about what sophisticated people are saying about such matters. The "public philosophies" we do have, the two most prominent being New Deal liberalism and free-market conservatism, do not help matters. New Deal liberalism, like social democracy to which it is a close first cousin, is deeply centralist in its orientation. It views local political life mostly as a problem—the place of backward looking, inegalitarian thinking, and administrative incompetence. So much for the sources of republican citizenship! Free-market conservatism, when its adherents feel compelled to countenance government and politics at all, is uneasy with the idea of the public interest. The discussions of such conservatives offer a barren soil for those who understand that the republican public interest is aimed at securing republican institutions, and that no invisible hand can do the job.

If we cannot bring ourselves to take seriously that a commercial republic requires the legislature to engage in deliberative lawmaking; if we cannot find ways to foster a citizenry capable of judging whether its lawmakers are disposed to work on giving the public interest concrete meaning; if we cannot promote a secure and confident middle class that owns productive assets; and if we cannot create a political class capable of organizing movement between the various modes of lawmaking in a republic, then our choices are not very attractive. We might look to the high court to secure basic rights and consign the rest of our collective life to the clash of political armies on a darkling plain, which is pluralism's dubious contribution to political theory. Or we can hope that future events present us with the possibility of some sort of strong democracy, where even more is asked of the citizenry than in a commercial republic. There may be yet other alternatives—including even the social democratic form of a party-corporatist regime. But all of them ask even more of us than republican government does or are foreign imports that have little hold on our affections.

CONSTITUTIONAL THEORY AND HUMAN MOTIVES

It is useful to pause here and consider the roots of the kind of constitutional theory presented. As the account of the political constitution of the commercial republic has unfolded, I have given a central place to what might be called "morally ambiguous" motives. A well-ordered commercial republic relies on self-interest, ambition, pride, greed, and a kind of uneasiness with authority. A commercial republican regime not only controls such often unattractive, even dangerous motives, but also relies on them for producing the good that is republican government.[45]

Machiavelli is the great teacher of the ambiguity of good and bad in political life.[46] He makes us ask whether morally unattractive motives are an inevitable feature of political life—part of the necessity of which political action must take account, constraining and relying on them if it is to succeed.[47] A deeper concern in Machiavelli's thought is whether political good can be produced at all without morally ambiguous or unattractive actions, and thus whether it is right to think of these actions as simply immoral.[48] Machiavelli goes even further and invites us to consider whether the language of morality is misplaced, or worse, when we seek to understand and evaluate political life. Pierre Manent suggests one possibility when he comments that "Machiavelli did not erase the distinction between good and evil. On the contrary, he preserved it—and he had to, if he wanted to establish the scandalous proposition that 'good' is founded by 'evil.'" Manent earlier says that, according to Machiavelli, "the 'good' happens and is maintained only through the 'bad.'"[49]

After the twentieth century we may suspect that Machiavelli goes too far. But he does teach us that we must look at the political whole if we are to understand and act with effect in politics. To look at this whole is to take account of the full range of human motives at work in politics. It is to see how these motives must be harnessed to effective political action in the form of creating political institutions and the politics in which they are embedded. These can be fitted together to constitute the same whole but in another version—as a political regime, which is a coming together in a regularized fashion of these motives. To think about the political whole is to think about the human whole. Machiavelli tries to strengthen us, to get us to cease averting our eyes from examining the bad, and to see that some portion of it is essential to achieving the good. What looks to be bad from the standpoint of morality can be good from the point of view of political theory and action if it helps humankind to live freely. If we cannot face the bad and make use of it, then we risk allowing it to do its work, thereby making good regimes impossible to create and destroying those in existence.

That we seemingly must rely on morally ambiguous motives to serve the justice promised by a commercial republican and all other good regimes suggests, once more, that this justice can only be partial, not ideal. As Harvey Mansfield writes, in commenting on Machiavelli, "Every regime . . . has a self-definition that is partisan." A regime is "the organizing form that gives the virtues a partisan bent as they appear in politics." The rulers of a regime are "partisan creatures."[50] As we must have political regimes to achieve any measure of justice or good, all of our efforts to do so will be partisan, unless, of course, we are somehow able to create a universal, and by that, presumably, an ideal regime. The same point emerges when we realize that only politics can limit politics: the politics that limit the use of political power to subvert the public interest is itself a creation of mixed motives.

The subject of political theory is humankind in motion, men and women propelled by self-interest, eros, rationality, spiritedness, and so forth. As Machiavelli argues, "all things of men are in motion, and cannot stay steady."[51] We may surmise that he means that political theory must be practical, and that we should follow Aristotle in avoiding "the philosopher's mistake of despising what is practicable."[52]

THE ATTRACTIONS OF CONSTITUTIONAL THEORY

A theory of political constitution invites us to take seriously that the gravest political problems in the contemporary United States concern how we have organized ourselves to cope with a conflictual and uncertain world. We may also have policy problems—failures in this or that sector of the society—but these do not seriously threaten the realization of our aspirations. However, we may now have reached the point where an avid interest in policy alternatives is a substitute for and a diversion from deeper constitutive questions. But it must be puzzling sometimes for those who ply the policy trade that, with all the brain power being harnessed, all the late nights, and all the trades and bargains, much of what is attempted has little effect on the problems that prompted all the effort in the first place. Isn't this a clue that something deeper is wrong—that the ordinary workings of the political economy, the things that go on without policy interventions, are the source of the problem? The beast of society goes marching by, and public policy is there to clean up its mess.

Granted, it is disconcerting to consider whether our constitutive institutions and their politics can be taken as fixed. Nevertheless, there is good reason to think that we cannot continue to take these institutional workings as the unproblematic medium within which we debate policy alternatives and attempt to carry out the ones that emerge. It seems to be difficult to resist thinking that the problem of political-economic reform is fundamentally a matter of good policy, even though many of our policy problems are largely the result of failings in the manner in which our constitutive institutions work. Or, even more unsettling, they often seem to be the result of institutions that work—in the sense that their routines run smoothly, and those who work in them feel that they are doing a good job—but whose smooth working presents the larger society with grave difficulties.

In the end, however, the value of the kind of constitutional thinking I have been commending is best seen not by comparing it to policy analysis, but to other theories of similar ambition. Thus, I have already suggested why those who look to arguments about the proper extent of government are on the wrong track—whether they are defending active and strong government or criticizing it as breaching the appropriate limits on the exercise of political power. Republican government must and can be all three: strong, active, and limited. It does not act on anything that takes its fancy; nor is it so passive and weak that it has neither the ability nor the inclination to act when necessary.[53] It is, in short, moderate government.

By contrast, those who look to the state of the family and the culture— the stock-in-trade of contemporary conservatives—are on to something. A republican regime does require a certain sort of character in its citizens. But until we understand just what that character is—what is needed from citizens, for example, if deliberative lawmaking is to succeed—we cannot know what we want from families and the organs of culture. Nor, indeed, do we know whether they can provide it. The theory of republican constitution I have sketched points to the kinds of questions we must pose here. Without them our search for answers can only be haphazard.

The list of those who would be helped by thinking constitutionally could be extended to include, for example, civic republicans, communitarians, and various stripes of strong democrats. Despite some significant differences, they all argue for a highly participatory politics. Roughly speaking, the more citizen participation there is, the better. They also agree that political equality should obtain in all domains of lawmaking. Many of those encompassed by these labels, however, seem unwilling to face the fact that in our world—the world of significant private ownership of productive assets, a world that is not likely to disappear any time soon—those who control these assets will, must, and ought to have a politically privileged position. A theory of constitution of the commercial republic at least has the advantage that it is also a theory of political economy. Similarly, it is worth noting that if we think through the constitutive design of a commercial republican regime, we are unlikely to find the dispute between liberals and communitarians very riveting. This dispute, as it is most often portrayed, revolves around communitarians accusing liberals of being unable to see that any good regime must have a substantial role for community.[54] But the kind of liberal commercial republic I have been commending here requires public-spirited citizens, that is, the same sort of citizens on whose backs communitarian theorists would like to ride to intellectual glory.

But enough. The point is easily made. Without a theory of the constitution of the whole regime to which we aspire, we are unlikely to be acute judges of our collective problems. Both pluralists—those who pin their faith on the clash of interest groups—and libertarians—those who look to the free market as the best means to deal with our collective business—are object lessons in what happens when we mistake the part for the whole. Both are entranced by the idea of self-regulating systems. Both fail to see that these systems can only exist when conscious effort is expended in securing them, and that this requires a design for governmental authorities that promises that a sustained effort will, in fact, be made.

A theory of political constitution of the kind I propose stands far enough beyond where we are to be useful as a measure of our condition. But it is not so far away that it cannot provide a diagnosis of our present state or indicate ways to remedy its failings. It is not utopian, pointing to something obviously beyond our reach. A theory of political constitution stands between what is and what might be, and its face is set against what should never be.

My arguments in the preceding chapters suggest that constitutional thinking, particularly in the form of a theory of the political constitution of good regimes, is an attractive focus for political science. Instead of the sterile conflict between normative analysis (political philosophy) and empirical investigation (political science), we have a political theory that accommodates both, indeed requires both. If the habit of thinking constitutionally takes hold, it might even come to pass that the writings of political scientists will be of interest to citizens, who would then find in them discussion of such matters as whether they live in a good regime, whether it is flourishing or declining, and whether there is anything to be done to promote the former and reverse the latter.

If, as I have argued, our political failings include significant problems with our constitutive institutions, and were we simply to leave matters as they are, the American republic would be one more partial failure in humankind's effort to discover a way for the people to govern themselves. We need not, and indeed cannot, address constitutive matters every day. But not to address them at all—now a distinct possibility—would not only leave us at the mercy of fortune, but would increase the odds of our drifting toward a state of affairs from which friends of republican government will find it difficult to organize an escape.

There are some who doubt that the complex mix of normative and empirical analysis that makes up constitutional thinking is possible. Our reasoning capacities are too limited they say.[55] But we need not and, in fact, cannot start from scratch. This is true both theoretically and practically. We, as Americans, inevitably will build on the legacy of Madison and his successors. And we already have some version of the institutions needed for a well-ordered commercial republic. Thus we do not need to consider all pieces of the regime simultaneously, and deliver ourselves of a detailed account of what to do about every piece and how to do it. Instead we can try to improve on what we already have. Moreover, the kinds of political judgments that comprise a theory of republican political constitution mean these judgments must be collective, a pooling of the efforts of many people. No one person need to attempt them unaided.

For those who find the enterprise of rethinking the theory of the political constitution of the American regime unreasonably onerous, even dangerous, some comfort might be found in the words of John Pym in launching the impeachment of Manwaring in 1628:

Therefore it is observed by the best writers upon this subject that those commonwealths have been most durable and perpetual which have often reformed and recomposed themselves according to their first institution and ordinance; for by this they repair the breaches and counterwork the ordinary and natural efforts of time.[56]

To think constitutionally means resisting the temptation to see politics as a second-rate activity, one inferior to law, markets, private cooperation, aggregative institutions operating as automatic adding machines, or judges acting as philosophers. We have no alternative but to live by politics, and those who avert their eyes in its presence only succeed in demoralizing us and making us cynical because, in the nature of the case, we cannot act as they wish us to. Equally unfortunate, we are meanwhile not attending to securing and maintaining the institutional politics that control the misuse of power and that allow us to achieve a full measure of our purposes. The fruit of constitutional thinking is a set of workable, durable, and attractive modes of association.

A theory of political constitution in a democratic age such as ours is directed to the people who will be its constituent sovereign.[57] Just as important, it is directed to those—friends of the regime—who devote themselves to seeing that a regime of popular self-government is realized. If there is a written constitution, the theory of political constitution should inform it. It need not be a single document called a "constitution." Nor, as noted, need it be, and probably cannot be, a complete account of a theory of political constitution. However, one important part of a written constitution is a delineation of the frame of government—the principal institutions and their powers. In setting this out in words, the people as constituent sovereign intend to set in motion actions to produce the institutions defined on the page. It is difficult to set out in a short document (and it should be short if it is to be authoritative) the full range of constitutive questions and the answers to them. But the basic structure and powers can be forcefully and clearly defined, so that those in and out of government have at least a starting point for the inevitable disputes about who can do what.

Constitutional theorists are friends of the regime they hope to bring about. Their ambition is to help create an attractive and durable political regime for a particular people situated in a particular place with their own history, virtues, and vices. In talking with those they hope to encourage to join them in that journey, constitutional theorists invoke ideals where these are shared, point to the lessons of failures, and generally comment on the adequacy of steps that have been or might yet be taken. Not being social engineers, or for that matter prophets, this is the best constitutional theorists can do. But it is no small task. This, in any event, is a democratic age, and no one person or small group will be permitted to claim much more than that they are part of the efforts of the people to construct their own framework for political living. Theorists of republican political constitution, then, are colleagues of their more work-a-day fellow citizens who have not been vouchsafed the modest pleasures of sustained reflection on how good and good-enough political regimes may be brought into being.

Indeed, if we are to be a free and equal people actively engaged in self-government, we must ourselves make the necessary constitutive judgments or rely on those whom we have deputized to make them for us. In this fashion we give the law to ourselves and thus limit ourselves. We cannot, moreover, suppose that the answer to this problem of practical reasoning is a set of people able and willing to devote themselves in a more or less selfless manner to its solution. We must instead build for the most part on the work of ordinary men and women with middling powers of practical reasoning who have ordinary inclinations toward a comfortable life and the serving of their own narrow but useful political interests. The problem is how to get people like us—ordinary men and women—to do the necessary work.

Liberal regimes are for ordinary people who spend their days doing ordinary things. The justification for one of its forms, a commercial republic, lies in the characteristic liberal argument that political life should aim to secure liberty of mind and body, to make us responsible for the quality of our own lives, and to give us bodily comfort. Liberalism is not very elevating to some. But to those who live out their lives without liberty, self-government, and bodily comfort, it can seem a very elevated ideal indeed. Liberal regimes may well depend at critical junctures on the exertions of some whose talents and concerns set them apart from their fellows, but it is not a regime that can give public pride of place to great deeds and thoughts. That is its attraction—its concerns are mundane, shared by most of us. But for that reason, they fall short of what many have claimed is our due and is considerably less than we are capable of. But if all or nearly all of us are allowed to engage in such common and commonplace matters, something of extraordinary value will have been realized. Commercial republican government, resting as it does on moderate motives, is a modern project in its aim for moderate liberty and moderate well-being.

Still, we may wonder whether all this moderation is sufficient to secure a republican regime over any significant length of time. Yes, such a regime must rest on the myriad efforts of ordinary people, but there are occasions when there appears to be no substitute for statesmanship, when, because of external threat or internal turmoil, the regime must in effect be refounded. This was true, of course, at the founding of the American Republic, when Madison and his colleagues in an act of statesmanship attempted to create a form of popular self-government in which statesmanship would not be needed. That we needed Abraham Lincoln suggests that the effort was not entirely successful and that statesmanship continued and continues to be needed. Because the politics of a republic is, at bottom, the politics of opinion, republican statesmanship must largely take the form of opinion leadership, and all, even most, of its practitioners need not hold public office. But they must be able to think constitutionally. Quite apart from whether there are now very many of our fellow citizens with democratic skills and a concern for constitutive matters, it would help if our political culture itself encouraged abiding constitutive concerns. For, even if statesmen are needed, most of them will not simply spring forth unaided, with a full grasp of constitutive matters. Some will do so, but most will be leaders who need help in judging in what direction to shape opinion and how to do so. Contemporary political science, and political thinking more generally, offers too little to such apprentice leaders. While it is not possible to build a political constitution of popular rule around the regular availability of statesmen, it is possible to increase the odds that such persons of broad and penetrating vision will appear. That, of course, is one of the purposes of republican constitutional thinking.

However, the charms of rethinking the theory of the constitution of the American Republic are hard to underestimate.[58] A political constitution is an abstract conception. Many also think that we need to attend to more proximate and material worries. And many of those who suspect that thinking constitutionally is badly needed are uneasy in the face of so large a task. This is a poor position to be in for a regime that must ask so much of its citizens, political leaders, and thinkers. Without efforts like the one offered here—that is, without disciplined ways of thinking about the fundamental features of a commercial republican regime and what is required to secure and maintain it—we can only count on luck to keep us pointed in the right direction. But counting on luck is only sensible for people who can make their own.

10

A Modest Program for Republicans (with a small "r")

To SERVE liberal justice is to create and maintain a certain kind of political regime that has as a defining feature the politics of self-limitation. The people limit themselves, constraining their rule by serving the public interest. The constitution of such a regime or political way of life makes it possible for ordinary men and women to practice the virtues taught them by their religions and moral codes, and it is the central concern of republican constitutional theory. For contemporary Americans, this means realizing further the commercial republic to which our aspirations commit us. In turn, this requires that we rely not only on higher motives but on less attractive ones: to serve justice requires injustice.

Republican reform for Americans, then, consists of a further realization of a constitutive politics, in both its public interest and broad class-interest forms. My discussion of these political forms has to this point focused on what *could* work and why it is plausible to think that lawmakers and citizens can behave in the necessary ways. My task in this final chapter is to say something about what can bring such a politics into being—to turn what *could be* into what *is*.

SOME PRELIMINARIES

For a constitutional theory to be compelling, it must not only point to the paths reform must take, but also tell us which proposals will stand in the way of realizing the kind of regime to which we are committed. An instructive example in this regard is the path of reform suggested by Bruce Ackerman's powerfully argued version of the constitutional theory of the American republic.[1]

Ackerman's constitutional theory aims to combine several features of governmental design that are widely approved of by politically attentive Americans: (1) the people are to rule, democracy is to be taken seriously; (2) day-to-day politics is to be bound by some form of principled restraints; (3) the Supreme Court is to play an important role in binding or limiting day-to-day politics; and (4) the whole political-legal system should economize on virtue, not asking from ordinary citizens more than they are able or wish to give. Ackerman attempts to pull these strands together with what he calls "dualist" theory. The theory rests on a distinction between two kinds of politics, one ordinary, the other special in that it is about the largest matters, what we might call constitutive questions. The first he refers to as normal politics, the second as higher-law politics.[2]

In Ackerman's account, normal politics is dominated by private interest. Voting decisions are typically not based on much reflection, and the force of private interest in these choices is said to be strong. There are, according to Ackerman, some impulses in normal politics to look beyond private and narrow interests, to take notice of the public good. At some junctures he allows that these impulses must be strengthened, but elsewhere he indicates that we must economize on such virtues because they are not likely to be strong to begin with. The overall impression that Ackerman leaves is that higher-law politics allows ordinary politics to carry on pretty much as usual with all its narrowness, shortsightedness, and self-interestedness.

In Ackerman's view, constitutive-level politics is the politics of We the People arguing about the basic rules that will govern us. Here, says Ackerman, the People at their best act in a principled fashion—binding themselves by setting out the higher law that will constrain the popular organs of government through which the citizens pursue their own interests. When the citizens so act, they rewrite the Constitution, which is the document that sets out in general fashion what We the People have said. The Supreme Court, then, codifies the new higher law by converting its generalities into concrete legal decisions.

At the heart of higher law politics is a set of procedural norms requiring that public deliberation on the new higher law be widespread and broadly informed—and that those who carry the day in these deliberations be able to do so not just once but twice—first at the proposal stage and second at the deliberative stage. These norms are meant to ensure that higher law-making is reasoned, not the result simply of the exercise of political power. Ackerman's higher-law politics functions in much the same way as Madison's rights and the permanent interests of the community. That is, it is supposed to limit what the people can do through ordinary politics. Ackerman's is a thoughtful attempt to use one kind of politics to bind another. To this degree, it is consistent with the constitutional theory set out here.

However, the reforms to which Ackerman's constitutional theory point are not likely to help us more fully realize a commercial republic, and they may even impede the effort. Thus, one possibility[3] is that Ackerman would urge us to concentrate our reform efforts on strengthening higher-law politics. The difficulty is that such an episodic politics[4] can do relatively little to serve the public interest. We need the kind of continuous attention that normal lawmaking at its best can give; constitutive institutions can only flourish if they are maintained and strengthened on an on-going basis. Moreover, since maintaining and strengthening the constitutional politics of the regime and the constitutive institutions at its center is to serve the public interest, Ackerman's theory leaves us without an effective way to realize further the political way of life to which we are committed. Nor can the theory be saved by devising a less episodic process, since that runs up against the argument Madison made (which he directed at Jefferson) that regular large-scale remaking of the constitutional design would unsettle the citizenry's affection for the American regime.[5]

But even if it were desirable to construct a more or less continuous higher-law politics, how would the citizenry learn to operate such a demanding process? Insofar as it would be a version of normal politics, contemporary American politics tells us what we may expect: our day-to-day politics fosters a citizenry that is, at least in significant part, concerned to secure its own particular interests. There is little in our ordinary politics that promotes a concern for the diffuse and long-term benefits that securing the constitutive foundations of republican government confers. It is, therefore, unlikely that there would be much public-regarding behavior in Ackerman's normal politics—nor, more generally, would many citizens be inclined to rise to the regular demands of a higher-law politics. A dualist constitution designed to produce a higher lawmaking that attends to constitutive questions is more likely to work if the citizenry had some practice in thinking about such matters. It is, after all, the same People that are acting in normal and higher-law politics. But if we were to direct our efforts to reforming normal politics by fostering a public-spirited citizenry, we would be abandoning dualist theory.

We may think of Ackerman's constitutional theory as an alternative account to the one offered here of how best to constitute a commercial republic. For republican constitutional theory to be compelling, it must also enable us to assess what, if anything, can be imported from other kinds of republican regimes. An obvious possibility is social democracy; its strong egalitarianism, disciplined political parties, and significant controls on the political behavior of business are likely to seem attractive to many citizens of the American commercial republic.[6] But what works in one kind of regime may not work in another; indeed, it might make things worse. For this reason, efforts to use the power of the state to redistribute wealth and income on a large scale would almost certainly have to reach into the middle class through taxation and other means. Such actions would make it less likely that this class can play the pivotal political role that is necessary for a fully realized commercial republic. Similarly, I have noted that strongly disciplined ideological parties would impede deliberative lawmaking, which is a constitutive feature of a commercial republic. The same general point can be made in reverse: introducing institutional reforms to make social democratic legislatures more deliberative would almost certainly impede the bargaining among government leaders and peak business and labor organizations that is the source of many of the social democratic policies that are found so appealing. Social democracies may be very attractive republican regimes, but political importing, unlike its economic counterpart, may not increase the well-being of the countries involved.

Finally, it is important to note that republican lawmaking is reflexive since it is aimed at serving the public interest. That is, we can view constitutional theory as advice to lawmakers concerning how to serve the public interest. Or we can see it as an account of how to constitute the politics of the regime so that it revolves around deliberative ways of lawmaking and the appropriate kind of class political activity.[7] For most purposes, that is, we can say that these are two ways of talking about the same thing: to serve the public interest *means* to create and maintain the set of institutions and the politics that give them life and that together constitute the regime. If we succeed in creating such institutions and their accompanying politics, we will have served the public interest. Nor should this be surprising: the metaphor of constitutional theory as shipbuilding[8] indicates that what might be thought of as the political relations among the shipbuilders and the purposes their decisionmaking should serve are two versions of the same thing.

In what follows, I focus for the most part on reforms designed to increase the likelihood that the kind of politics a republican regime requires— namely, one that serves the public interest—is at work. This is partly because it is all too easy to give advice to lawmakers and neglect to consider what, in the first place, will make them interested in considering the public interest. Said differently, my principal task is not to work out a design for a new republic; it is rather to get our present constitutive institutions to work as they should. This is not to say, however, that our current lawmakers will be relieved when they see the list of particulars for reform set out here. They are being asked to reform significantly the very politics that has made them lawmakers.

A REPUBLICAN REFORM PROGRAM

I have already touched on some of the reforms that are needed if we are to have the constitutional politics that will realize more fully a commercial republic. We have seen that the interests of controllers of productive assets must be broadened, and considered how this might be done. I have talked about some of the ways local political life should be reformed, and discussed the need to make the middle class more secure and confident, noting some steps that might be taken in this direction. All of these reform ideas, arising as a matter of course in the discussion of how both a deliberative politics and a broad class politics will operate, suggest a general point. If my account of these two types of politics is compelling, most readers could on their own construct a list of reforms to help strengthen them. Thus, the four major areas in which reform is needed follow directly from the republican constitutional theory set out in the preceding chapters: (1) the political outlook of the citizenry must be altered to some degree in order to make it more capable of operating a republican regime; (2) some features of our major constitutive institutions need to be changed; (3) our class politics requires reshaping so that it regularly revolves around broad societal interests; and (4) republican political leadership must be promoted. The outlines of the specific reforms that are required also follow more or less directly from the substance of the constitutional theory.[9] Hence, discussion of reform, both for readers and for me, can be modest—which, in any case, is a good thing at the close of a long book.

ALTERING THE POLITICAL OUTLOOK OF THE CITIZENRY
Reforming Local Political Life

Crucial to forming a public-spirited citizenry is an institutional context in which citizen judgments about the public interest can be created and refined. A fundamental feature of creating such a context is an increase in the present powers of local governments, which in turn helps to free local politics from the alliance between land interests and public officials. We need, then, to consider which legal powers are required if local governments are to pursue strategies to make them less dependent on mobile capital.

In addition to altering the terms under which businesses can move in and out of a locality, there are at least three broad strategies for promoting local prosperity, none of which relies primarily on attracting or holding mobile capital: community-based economic development; entrepreneurial mercantilism; and municipal enterprise.[10] A community-based economic approach revolves around employing devices such as land trusts and community development corporations, and investing in local human resources through educational and training programs. An entrepreneurial mercantilist strategy centers on local government's intervention in the local marketplace to promote the growth of selected firms and economic sectors: it is a kind of local industrial policy. A municipal enterprise strategy is built around municipal ownership of various kinds of local enterprises including, for example, utilities and mass transit.[11]

In some cases, municipalities already have the necessary powers—and the problem is largely one of fostering a local politics that, unlike the present pattern, supports the exercise of these powers.[12] Thus local governments have the power to create development corporations and training programs. In other cases, notably for municipalization but also for some varieties of mercantilism, it is less clear that they have the necessary powers. As for shaping the terms under which capital can move in and out of localities, local governments have some of the necessary powers and lack others. The most important of those they lack are the power to exact from departing businesses repayment for local public investment on their behalf, and the power of eminent domain to acquire, at market value, the departing company. In general, it is difficult to be precise about the powers municipalities actually have because the courts have not pursued a consistent line in their decisions about the legal capabilities of local governments.[13] A crucial step in a program for republican reform, therefore, is to ensure that municipalities have the necessary powers.[14] Central to that effort must be overturning Dillon's rule, which has broadly guided courts in ruling on local government actions and which says that the only powers they have are the ones specifically granted to them by state decision.

With regard to attracting new businesses, the problem is different in kind. Here localities do not so much need new legal powers as some reduction in the pressures to promote local prosperity through local efforts. The key is national policy—and, in particular, a policy of full employment, which means that localities would be under much less pressure than presently to generate new jobs and new sources of revenue and would have a stronger tax base.

All of these proposals aim to alter the interest-driven politics centered on the alliance between land interests and local politicians that characterizes much of local political life. Adding to the array of municipal powers would help. But the pursuit of mobile capital and the rearrangement of land use patterns are not just directed toward securing local prosperity. They are also important means by which local officials build and maintain political followings. Unless ways can be found to wean them from such political strategies, localities cannot employ new powers or use the ones they already have. Few officials will be so devoted to their locality's prosperity as to risk seriously their hold on public office by pursuing policies that weaken their political base.

What can be done to promote a politics that will support a wide variety of ways to secure local prosperity? Part of the answer is that the new policies and strategies will themselves generate incentives that can be used to build political followings. This should not be surprising. Given the authority and the expectation that they accomplish things, enterprising public officials will quickly discover ways to turn the use of these powers to political advantage. More specifically, fiscally prudent citizens will likely be attracted by a policy of exacting repayment from departing businesses that have received municipal subventions aimed at keeping them from moving. Politically adept local officials should be able to convince those worried about local taxes and the like that the departing malefactors have been made to cough up every penny they owe. Similarly, local officials should not find it difficult to convince the have-littles that their economic prospects have improved dramatically because municipal powers have been used to create innovative education and training programs. Again, those committed to local economic growth are likely to find themselves drawn to the support of public officials who prove themselves effective in using community development and other local investment strategies. Communitarian-minded citizens, moreover, are likely to find officials who pursue municipal ownership policies attractive, given the citizens' view that important community resources should not be subject to the measuring rod of the market. Finally, municipal ownership and investment strategies can provide the opportunity for adept officials to politically attract a wide range of local citizens if they are able to create a way for the benefits of such ownership and investment to accrue directly to the citizenry. For example, all local citizens could be given shares in municipal funds that provide capital for local investment. Each of these political strategies, moreover, can be used not only to attract citizen favor; they can also be used to attract political operatives whose base of support is in the various citizen target groups.

Increased municipal powers thus open up a wide range of political strategies rooted in both material and ideological benefactions. Astute political leaders can be relied on to vary the mix as their political situation requires. Such political strategies at least create the possibility for sustaining the kind of legislative and participative politics that is the foundation for local political life as a school of republican citizenship.

A republican local politics requires something more. Its friends must be skeptical of policies that make it easy for—indeed invite—citizens to opt out of local political life. Reducing local autonomy reduces the stakes of local politics,[15] which in turn is destructive of public-spiritedness because such policies remove from public choice the reasons that draw rational people to attend to local political matters. Thus, efforts to balkanize local politics—through special districts, separate school boards, and the like—will hinder the development of public-spiritedness. For much the same reasons, any significant subsidizing by local governments of private schooling should be resisted. Such subsidies will allow even those of moderate means to remove their children from the public school system, giving them substantially less reason to pay attention to local political life.[16] Additionally, if local political life is balkanized by special districts, privatizing local government services, or similar devices, it will be exceedingly difficult for citizens and those who speak for them to consider the full range of concrete matters relevant to the public interest.

Just as many conservative, free-market-oriented reforms that aim to commodify local service provision will undercut the possibility of a republican local political life, so will some proposed by the liberal Left. In the pursuit of equality, for example, there have been those who argue that we should aim to equalize expenditures across local governments by mandating an end to property taxes as the principal municipal revenue source. Thus, the New Jersey Supreme Court has ruled that local school districts must not only equalize their spending per pupil, but see that the "special needs" of various districts are dealt with, meaning in effect that the state must also worry about equalizing the outcomes of schooling.[17] The logic of such decisions is that localities cannot legitimately vary by the amount of local funds they spend on various services: all local governments are to look pretty much alike. Unless local governments can to some major degree decide on their own expenditures, participating in local politics will not be worth the effort.

School vouchers are a possible and important exception to all this. So long as local governments have something like the present set of responsibilities for curriculum and other major aspects of learning, vouchers will not undercut the importance of local political life. Parents will only be able to choose among various schools within the boundaries set by local school authorities. There will still be much at stake to draw parents into local political life. Vouchers, however, can undercut the kind of local politics a republican regime needs if it is possible for parents to supplement their value. This will enable even moderately well-off parents to piggyback on the vouchers and spend less money than is now required to place their children in schools that charge high tuition. This, even more than at present, will balkanize local politics in another way—namely, by class segregation. In doing so, it will weaken the prospects that citizens are inclined to deliberate with one another: they will not share the crucial and common experience of shaping public school policy. On the other hand, to the degree that a voucher system improves school performance—a subject of much dispute at present—the prospects for a public-spirited citizenry may be modestly improved.

The question of social segregation suggests another element of reform. There are good reasons to invoke the powers of courts and the national government in a design for a republican local politics. They have historically been the guarantors of civil liberties and the protector of racial minorities. In order for local polities not to be balkanized by race and class both within and between them, as they are today to a significant degree, central government action and intervention by the courts is required. Such a role, in part, rests on the powerful argument that small polities are more likely to be factional than larger ones. A strong role for courts and the national government, of course, pulls in the opposite direction from the reforms just considered. The dilemma is this: while a relatively autonomous local politics is necessary if there is to be a citizenry capable of making deliberative lawmaking work, one of the other elements of the public interest is institutions that are able to secure rights. No amount of political or institutional contrivance can make such a tension disappear, although a possible way to reduce it is to make provision in the design of a republican local politics for the protection of civil liberties and the reduction of racial segregation. But that is simply to name a possibility, not to elaborate a proposal. Moreover, the path of reform would be considerably easier if friends of republican government could simply concentrate on protecting racial minorities and improving their life chances, or on protecting civil liberties. The burden of constitutional thinking is that such simple choices are not available to us if we care about republican government.

Finally, it is worth noting here that if what might be called strong republican communities are at work, then the legislative burden on the central government ought to decline. Many more socio-economic questions than at present would plausibly be resolved locally. Consequently, national lawmakers would be less distracted from focusing on the public interest, assuming they are so inclined to begin with.

All this leaves us with a question we have already noted in chapter 7: given the rise of the global economy, how effective would it be to grant localities additional powers to secure local prosperity? Many will argue that the increased powers will not be effective. Capital, even more than in the past, is simply too mobile to be shaped by the regulations of municipalities, they might say, and investment will not be made in places where there are laws and regulations that significantly restrict the discretion property holders expect. However, Paul Krugman, a leading expert on international trade, says that "reports of the death of national autonomy are greatly exaggerated."[18] An increasingly small portion of the workforce is involved in the manufacturing sector, whose markets are more nearly worldwide: only about 11 percent of the U.S. workforce in 2003 was involved in manufacturing. It is also the case, as already noted, that about 60 percent of American economic activity is locally oriented. In short, it is possible for localities to have a significant effect on their economic fortunes. Krugman's summary judgment is pertinent here: "When you look at the economics of modern cities what you see is a process of localization: a steadily rising share of the workforce produces services that are sold only within the same metropolitan area."[19]

Adding Deliberative Elements outside Formal Institutions

Choosing lawmakers through election is fundamental to republican government. It is then that citizens can judge whether lawmakers are capable of deliberation on the public interest. But elections are blunt instruments. They are a one-time up or down judgment. What is needed is a more continuous process of judging that regularly prods lawmakers to engage in deliberation. Similarly, the ultimate sanction of elections can work well only if citizens develop the judgment they need to pick out the hacks and their compatriots in failed lawmaking. A republican local politics is necessary here, but it is unlikely to be sufficient.

An additional way to nurture judgment of the sort required here is through a variety of institutional contrivances that bring into being groups of citizens who, between elections, can stand in for the citizenry as a whole. There is a range of possibilities, from constituting a mini-populus[20] to deliberative opinion polls,[21] civic forums,[22] and citizen juries.[23] What these have in common is the selection of a group—in some versions, notably the deliberative poll, the group is a statistical sample of the citizenry—that is provided with extensive information about a public matter. The group then deliberates, and their resulting judgment is interpreted as what the citizenry as a whole would say if it had the time and information to think through the matter at issue. If a large enough number of citizens are involved in a full complement of such mini-citizenries, and the citizenry is well on the way to being public-spirited in the manner I have described, the result would be the more continuous process of judgment that republican government needs.

If national lawmakers themselves were involved in the operation of these mini-citizenries—for example, briefing participants, engaging before them in debate with one another, and responding to citizen questions—the citizenry would be even better able to assess its lawmakers. For example, if those lawmakers who participate in the mini-citizenries acquit themselves in reasonable style, the citizens would likely say that what some lawmakers can do, all should be able to do. Such proceedings would thus reinforce what citizens learn through a republican political life. Moreover, if the judgments reached by the mini-citizenries differ from what lawmakers decide, the latter would feel compelled to explain their reasoning. Thus, a two-way discussion could occur, again strengthening the incentives lawmakers will have to give the public interest concrete meaning.

Other Reforms

There are several other areas that need attention if there is to be a fully developed republican citizenry. Little more can be done here than to mention them. The republican school of local political life rests in part on the qualities citizens bring to it. Given this, stable families should be fostered that are able to teach that we have obligations to people outside our family circle, including to the citizenry at large. Whatever else is needed to achieve this, a policy of full employment at no less than modestly remunerative wages will be necessary: the best family policy is a full employment policy. With slight exaggeration we can say that in the absence of steady work, steady families are unlikely. Similarly, a sense of proud independence can be strengthened by increasing economic security. The benefits, moreover, are twofold: not only are the prospects for a strong measure of public-spiritedness improved, proud independence is important in its own right.[24] Again, local politics as a school of citizenship also requires neighborhoods that have some modest powers: otherwise, local politics in larger cities will be unable to provide the kind of political participation a republican school requires.[25] Finally, the decline of interest groups with a full range of policy interests suggests that something should be done to reverse the trend. Part of the job is broadening the interests of large-scale asset-controllers, which we have already discussed. Such broadening, we may reasonably assume, would strengthen business organizations with encompassing interests. Reversing the decline of organized labor is the other obvious need, but just how to do this is far from clear, especially with the substantial reduction that has occurred in the size of the industrial workforce.[26]

Reforming Major Constitutive Institutions
Improving the Separation of Powers

INCREASING DELIBERATION IN THE LEGISLATURE. We should start with the obvious problem: deliberation takes a good deal of time, which is precisely what legislators lack. Consider the account given by Warren Rudman, the former senator from New Hampshire, of a typical day. It starts at 6:00 A.M. with breakfast with constituents who are worried about an editorial in the state's most important newspaper saying that the senator is promoting atheism by voting against school prayer. At 8:00 A.M. the senator meets with his staff to discuss the day's calendar and to sift through the mail from constituents. From 9:00 A.M. to noon the senator moves between three

simultaneous hearings held by committees on which he sits. On breaks in
the hearings, he deals with other matters such as talking to reporters. At
12:15 P.M. he has lunch with a prominent businessman in the state that lasts
until one o'clock, at which time bells start ringing announcing floor votes,
most of which are on bills that cannot pass but about which many members
want to make speeches for the newspapers back home. During the after-
noon, Senator Rudman moves between votes on the floor and trips to his
party's campaign office to make calls to people who might give money to
his election coffers. The calls must be made from the party headquarters
because it is illegal to solicit campaign contributions from one's office. At
6:00 P.M. the senator goes to two fund-raisers for colleagues. At 8:00 P.M. he
is back on the floor for a major debate on the federal budget. At 1:00 A.M.
the majority leader gives up trying to find a compromise on the budget that
could gain wide support. And so it goes, one day after another, into which
are mixed trips back to his home state and the approximately twenty-eight
seconds he gives to his daughter's schoolwork.[27]

Given schedules such as this, no one should be surprised that contemporary lawmakers have little time to smell the roses, much less engage
in extensive deliberation with their colleagues. Another sense of the time
pressures legislators face is given by Michael Malbin, who estimated that
in 1977, which we might suppose were relatively palmy days with regard to
the press of legislative business, members spent an average of eleven min-
utes a day on legislative research and reading.[28] If one adds up the length of
the legislative agenda, the great demands of constituency service—whose
claims on lawmakers' time have grown as the involvement of the federal
government in the lives of the citizenry has increased—and the chase for
political money, there simply isn't much time for a serious exchange of
views among lawmakers.[29] Indeed, many legislative questions end up being effectively settled by a few members of subcommittees and committee
staffs.[30]

What can be done about time pressures? An obvious possibility is to reduce the amount of legislation being considered. But isn't the large number
of bills introduced in any session simply the natural result of a complex society and economy that generates many problems with which government
must deal? If so, even if the press of business is a serious problem for deliberation, little can be done about it under present conditions. However,
the extent of legislative business is, in part, a reflection of the fact that contemporary legislative leaders and ordinary lawmakers do not have a strong
grasp of the elements of the public interest. If they did, they would make
less law and not respond to every passing wave of citizen concern. They
would instead concentrate on legislation that serves the public interest. Of
course, lawmakers would still have to engage in aggregative lawmaking,

where there are few standards that can keep at least some proposals off the legislative agenda. Still, if there were a sustained attempt to give concrete meaning to the public interest, lawmakers would be inclined to ration the attention they give to bills that are the product of the pulling and hauling of aggregative lawmaking.

Another step in controlling the number of bills seriously considered—one more nearly within our grasp—is to reduce the number of committees and subcommittees on which lawmakers may sit. Such a step would directly facilitate deliberation insofar as legislators would have an opportunity to develop policy expertise in specific areas. This, in turn, would bolster their efforts to think concretely about the public interest. Moreover, if a norm of deference were also at work,[31] lawmakers who do not sit on a committee would tend to defer to those who do on matters within the committee's purview. The propensity, therefore, for lawmakers to introduce bills that do not arise out of their own committees' concerns would be reduced.

Also relevant here is how committee chairs are chosen. Two such methods are unlikely to be very helpful: the chairs of committees and subcommittees are chosen by the leader of the majority party without consultation with other prominent lawmakers; or the party caucus chooses them through voting. If the leader alone chooses them, many chairs will simply be his or her creature and lack the standing to bring other members into a process of deliberative lawmaking. If the caucus chooses them, chairs will likely be too independent-minded to work as part of the legislative leadership needed to run the legislature as a school of deliberative lawmaking.

In considering all such legislative reforms, the consequences of term limits should be kept in mind. Practical reasoning about the public interest requires judgment tutored by long acquaintance with efforts to give concrete meaning to its elements. Yet term limits will produce legislative leaders and lawmakers who are unlikely to have ever thought systematically about such matters. Moreover, successful legislating on such matters generally requires the "train of measures" that revisits a problem, correcting and extending initial efforts. This is a job for experienced (and reflective) lawmakers. Additionally, since there is every possibility that high court and legislature will not always agree on such matters, and that there will therefore be lengthy dialogues between the two, a constant turnover of legislative leaders and ordinary lawmakers weakens the legislature's ability to play a constructive role in such public discussion.

To argue for term limits, in reality, is a counsel of despair. It means, in effect, to give up on the legislature as a crucial component of a fully realized republican regime and to say that there is no prospect of having a lawmaking body that can play the essential role of reasoning about the limits of popular rule. Term limits will leave in the hands of the Supreme

Court the problem of giving concrete meaning to the appropriate scope of popular government—that is, it will be left to a branch of government that is likely to concern itself with only parts of the problem and that will weigh up what it does consider without vigorous commentary from those who have a greater sense of the citizenry's views.

The shape of the political culture also influences whether we should expect extensive legislative deliberation. A large number of lawmakers and citizens appear to agree with the proposition that the president is "the only elected official that represents the country."[32] After all, it will be said, if one wants results, the executive is the appropriate agent. Why get bogged down in all that talking, and, worst of all, have to do it in public. Presidents can act, the commentator might continue, while Congress can only talk. In the contemporary world, where the pressures to act are, in fact, great, it will require legislative leaders of considerable sophistication concerning the principles of republican government to defend the proposition that, while energy and unity of view is a good thing, it is not everything. Not only that, the defense might continue, too much energy and unity, and rather less discussion of how to reconcile diverse views on the specifics of the public interest, is undesirable. In this vein, William Safire, a man given to few illusions about the current state of American politics, comments that a symbiosis has grown up between the media and its listener-readers that "has transmogrified all leadership—even genuine leadership—into mere celebrity. We never cover what leaders think—but always cover what sort of people they are."[33]

Yet another obstacle to extensive legislative deliberation is the development of new techniques of interest group lobbying, which increase the pressure on lawmakers to attend to group interests. We now have "grass-roots" organizations that wouldn't know a blade of grass if they stepped on one—being, as they are, wholly the creation of a small coterie of people in Washington with a mailing list of those who might be sympathetic to their cause. Organizations with greater claims to reflecting some widely held view, like the American Association of Retired Persons (AARP), actually have members. But too often their membership consists largely of those who wish for discounts on cars and hotel rooms. The most egregious organizations are the products of lobbying firms whose employees invent the organization and telephone citizens in an attempt to induce them to call or fax their lawmakers in the name of what is no more than a box of stationery (if it is even that). The firm's employees will even offer to patch citizens through to lawmakers' offices, saving the citizenry the expense and trouble of actually taking any action.[34] Instead, then, of interest groups with broad views whose concerns are brought to members of Congress by lobbyists with a long record of dealing with lawmakers, representatives and senators now have phones ringing off the hook and red-hot fax machines. Even those lawmakers who can smell the smoke given off by the manufacturing process are apt to feel a tensing of the muscles when they disregard interest group bombardment. The anxiety is hardly conducive to giving serious consideration to the public interest.

There is plainly a good deal more to consider by way of promoting legislative deliberation. It is not easy to curtail the growth of narrow interest groups, whether real or fictitious, not least because republican government is designed to protect and even facilitate private interest. Moreover, the growth of interest groups reflects the growth of government, and it is not easy to throw the engine into reverse. About the political culture, particularly, it is difficult to know what to say. If ordinary citizens persist in believing that the president is the appropriate center for lawmaking, then the incentive on the part of the politically active to maintain the legislature as a school of the public interest is weakened. It is hard work, and why should they bother if the citizenry evidences little interest? Much the same thing can be said about the very idea of the public interest. It is easy to say that the political culture needs changing because it increasingly undercuts belief in anything more than me and mine. But it is hard to know how to achieve such change, especially given that, under republican government, the reforms proposed cannot take the form of a direct inculcation of values, certainly not by agents of the state. There would also need to be limits on what religious organizations can do in this regard, including preventing them from erecting virtually unscalable walls between children and the wider society. But just how to draw the line is far from clear.

CONSTITUENCIES AND THE SEPARATION OF POWERS. Two points are worth noting here. First, the separation of powers, when combined with a variety of exclusionary devices, including gerrymandering and various means of discouraging voting, can lead not to deliberation but to factional government or something approaching it. This historically has been the case with the exclusion of black Americans from the political process. The mention of gerrymandering and political exclusion suggests a more general observation, which is the second point. The separation of powers can only do its job of promoting deliberation if most of the constituencies from which members of the House are elected are relatively heterogeneous. Otherwise, representatives have little incentive to change their positions or even engage with fellow lawmakers. We may soon arrive at such a state of affairs—unless something is done to prevent a further decline in the number of electoral districts that reflect the diversity of the interests of the citizenry at large. The large number of safe congressional seats is an indication of how large the problem presently is.[35]

Because a source of the increasing homogeneity of electoral districts is, in fact, gerrymandering, one possible reform is to take the decision concerning the boundaries of election districts out of the hands of state politicians and put it into the hands of nonpartisan commissions.[36] However, if the present trend continues toward disciplined ideological parties at the national level, and national leaders are able, partly as a result of this discipline, to exercise considerable influence at the state level, then the move toward homogeneous districts is likely to accelerate, making reform harder to achieve. Still, it is possible to go too far toward heterogeneous and thus more competitive electoral districts: representatives constantly worried about reelection are unlikely to see the virtue of bracing arguments over the concrete meaning of the public interest.

A COUNCIL OF REVISION. A considerably more radical possibility is to remove the Supreme Court as the principal authority on constitutional matters. Other countries, among them France, do so by establishing outside the ordinary judicial system a body that, following Madison, we might call a "council of revision." Judges on such a council might serve for less than lifetime terms, and their decisions might be reversible through legislative action requiring either a supermajority or successive votes. Moreover, there is no reason why all or even most of those sitting on such a council need to be lawyers. After all, as is true of the Supreme Court now, many of the decisions that would come before such a council of review would not in any obvious sense be legal matters. The detailed design of such a council is, of course, crucial, but most important here is the realization that other political orders treat the problem of how to review legislative action differently than we do and very likely do not fare any worse.[37]

STRENGTHENING MAJORITARIAN FEATURES OF THE LEGISLATURE. The separation of powers does not require that minorities in either branch of the legislature can effectively veto legislation. To the degree that this occurs, rule by civic majorities is made more difficult. This has happened consistently over the history of the Congress, as has its evil twin, minority factional rule. We only have to remember the history of racial domination and the manner in which minorities in the legislature prevented anything of significance being done about it for over a century after Emancipation. In general, friends of republican government should be skeptical of devices that significantly impede legislative majorities and, in particular, they should resist legislative rules that, in effect, require spending bills to pass by a supermajority. They should similarly argue against a constitutional amendment that requires a balanced budget: a civic majority might see the need for budget deficits, and even ordinary majorities might have good reasons to increase expenditures over revenues.

A Real Civil Service

The question of reform here can be put in the form of a conjecture or question. Suppose there existed an American civil service whose senior members were understood to be not only devoted to the public interest but also a source of disinterested expertise on a wide range of policy questions. Would its introduction—in effect, a fourth branch of government—directly into lawmaking increase the odds that deliberative lawmaking would occur? In order for this to be the effect, it seems likely that the advice tendered by high-ranking civil servants would have to have the force of public opinion behind it. The question then is whether, if the separation of powers were reconfigured to introduce another major constitutive element into lawmaking, the public interest would more likely be served. Herbert Storing, a careful student of the matter, thought it would be. He commented that "the civil service is one of the few institutions we have for bringing the accumulated wisdom of the past to bear upon political decisions."[38]

Improving the Socio-political Balance

The term "socio-political balance" refers to the need in republican government to prevent any major social interest from using the powers of the state to dominate other interests. There are several aspects of an effort to improve the balance in the present state of affairs.

Controlling Faction

Madison principally dealt with the problem of social balance by constructing a constitutional design that would control faction. In chapter 3 we saw that employing his design has brought only partial success. The successes of the radical wing of the Republican party since September 11, 2001 suggest that our failures in this respect are still with us. Consider, for example, the radical Republican claim that the president has, in national security matters, plenary authority—including the power to detain American citizens indefinitely and without trial, and to prevent them from communicating with anybody outside their place of detention. And my account of the political behavior of large-scale controllers of productive assets also indicates that the failures in controlling faction are not just a historical blemish.

What can be done to improve matters? Part of the answer has already been given: a well-developed public interest politics will itself help retard faction. Lawmakers who are committed to serving the public interest are less likely to listen to the blandishments of factions. To this we may add a point long ago made by Robert Dahl.[39] Crucial to more effective control of faction, he implies, is the outlook of elites. We may say that Madison, the reluctant democrat, looked to the citizenry at large as the final guarantor for the control of faction, while Dahl, the strong democrat, looks to elites. This suggests the need for both sorts of controls. But while it is relatively easy to think through how best to foster public-spiritedness in the citizenry, it is more difficult to do so for elites. Here I can only comment that it seems entirely likely that it is to the political culture that we must turn, but, again, just how to nudge that in the right direction is far from clear.

Dahl's conception of how republican governments manage to limit the purposes they pursue to ones consistent with robust self-government is helpful in another respect. He shows the importance of organizational pluralism. His point, which is both powerful and simple, is that unless a republican regime is constituted so that there are centers of power independent of the state, the control of faction is unlikely to succeed.[40] Power would be concentrated and those able to deploy it would be in possession of the whole political field. If the manner in which the independent centers are constituted also fosters internal deliberation, and the working constitution encourages negotiations among the centers, republican government gains an additional advantage: deliberative lawmaking is facilitated by social interests.[41] To the degree this happens, the likelihood of factional rule is further diminished. In general, we can say that reform should aim at strengthening what might be termed a "compound republic."[42] For example, hobbling the union movement any further would be a step in the wrong direction; indeed, strengthening it is desirable. Concomitantly, developing forums where business and labor leaders can negotiate over major policy questions serves republican government. By contrast, and in the manner of the present Republican majority in Congress, allowing business interests to write legislation for congressional sponsors, and pushing it through the Congress without any outside scrutiny, undercuts republican government.

It is worth adding here that following Madison's lead and working to multiply societal interests even further than at present will not help in the control of faction. We already have a wild and luxuriant array of interests, and still further growth will make deliberative lawmaking that much more difficult.

A Wider Distribution of Capital

Probably the most important reform for securing socio-political balance is a wider distribution of capital, a proposal already touched on in chapter 8's discussion of how to broaden the interests of capital.[43] It is worth expanding that discussion to consider how such a wider distribution would make the class coalitions, which will be a central feature of republican politics, more likely to serve the public interest. In the earlier discussion, I focused on directly affecting the interests of capital by changing who owns it. Here my concern is with what might be termed an "indirect strategy": if capital is more widely distributed, classes other than the principal controllers of large-scale assets would have greater resources and be more economically secure. In consequence, their political outlook would be broadened and they would be in a better position to join in coalition with one another (the have-littles would be more attractive allies). Even more important, they would be more formidable bargainers in negotiation with large asset-controllers on the terms of coalition. Both of these consequences would work to broaden the interests of capital, if not permanently, at least for the duration of the relevant coalitions.

Two kinds of proposals are worth mentioning here. In one, individuals are the direct recipients of what in chapter 8 I called life grants,[44] while in the second they are given ownership of capital more narrowly understood. The key to these redistributive proposals is that *individuals* own capital, not the state or its agents. The proposals aim at a genuine property-owning democracy—not a regime in which there is plenty of property and a measure of democracy but somehow the two don't overlap much. The difference between these kinds of schemes and the ones proposed by those on the political Right is that in these proposals *all citizens* would have a significant amount of capital.

A modest form of the proposal starts by noting that the federal government now provides large incentives for accumulating wealth to middle- and upper-income people. Thus, there are tax deductions for home ownership—which is the principal repository of wealth for most middle-class people—and for IRAs and 401(k) plans. We might expand the logic of using the federal government in this fashion by building wealth directly. In one version of the idea, which overlaps with the idea of life grants, all citizens at birth are given $1,000 and an additional $500 every year for five years with the funds being invested. This proposal—called "KidSave"—was offered by Bob Kerrey when he was senator from Nebraska and has been endorsed by a variety of people both on the Left and Right. By the time the child reaches twenty-one, $20,000 would be available for education or other forms of investment. The amounts, of course, could be increased. The idea, as with life grants, is to make more nearly equal everyone's starting point in life.[45]

The second class of proposals is more radical in attacking the problem of inequality of wealth. Two of the most elaborately worked out ones involve some form of worker ownership and the distribution of capital ownership through what are, in effect, enormous mutual funds. Such proposals are self-generating: once the economic rules are changed, the logic of the new forms of ownership as they work themselves out over time simply means more economic equality. Here the contrast to liberal and social democratic redistributive strategies is particularly clear. These latter strategies keep the state involved more or less indefinitely, and the hand of the state in equalizing wealth is thus visible. By contrast, the self-generating proposals under consideration here employ the invisible hand of the market supplemented by the hiding hand of government (see below).

The details of each type of proposal, while of the greatest importance, are too complex to be dealt with here.[46] The fundamental point, however, is that the "commercial" part of the commercial republic is a potential engine of great power in helping to realize the "republican" part. As things stand now, in important ways the market and private ownership work against republican government. Since they are also fundamental to its working, we cannot dispense with them. But once we more widely distribute wealth, the wonders of compound interest and all the other wealth-magnifying devices of an enterprise-based market system start to work in favor of republican government.

The heart of these proposals is that they concentrate on wealth as opposed to income. In doing so, they highlight the fact that the principal distinction between the comfortable (and those above them on the economic ladder) and the rest of society is that the former do not have to work for all of the income they receive. Their wealth works for them, and it also provides a cushion against disasters of many kinds that is unavailable to those who live from paycheck to paycheck.

In short, if we want to change the economic position of the majority of Americans, we would do better to look toward reforms that continue to pay off throughout the life of the individual. By contrast, most twentieth-century proposals for reducing the extent of economic inequality are designed to operate after the fact: the power of the central government is used to moderate the inequality produced by the workings of capitalism. This is usually attempted through a strongly progressive income tax and cash or in-kind subsidies in the manner of European social democracy and its cousin, American liberalism. The idea is to claw back from capitalism's winners enough income to create a moderate level of equality in the citizenry at large. The difficulty with such a strategy—the obvious political one aside if the strategy is strongly pursued—is that it leaves intact the structural arrangements that generate the inequality in the first place. Wealth-building strategies attempt to do something about the starting point for each citizen, understood either as the beginning of life or the onset of adulthood. In doing so, the idea is to modify the effects of these structural arrangements from the beginning.

Turning back specifically to broadening the interests of capital, there is another obvious reform possibility, one which involves curtailing the political ability of large-scale capital controllers to serve narrowly defined interests. While it is too much to hope that controllers of productive assets can be turned into stalwarts of the public interest, an obvious step here is some kind of campaign finance reform. A wide variety of such proposals exist, including ones now enshrined in law, and there is a variety of excellent treatments of the subject.[47]

The grounds for controlling campaign finance is the fundamental reform question. As many critics point out, controlling who can give money and how much, and who can spend it raises free speech questions. While money is not speech, the ability to disseminate one's views widely requires it. Still, controlling both campaign contributions and expenditures does not just affect individual rights; it also is relevant to securing the political regime on which those rights depend. Constitutional thinking, as I have elaborated it here, makes clear that it is deeply misleading to talk about protecting rights in an abstract way severed from the political regime that gives them life. And once we see that we must talk about the political constitution of the whole regime when we are considering which rights to enforce and how to do so, the case for campaign finance legislation emerges: we wish to regulate campaign contributions because we need to control the propensity of capital controllers for factional rule, a propensity made even more dangerous by the privileged political position they enjoy. Similarly, we need to control expenditures if we are to have the politics of broad class interest that is necessary for the public interest to be served.

With the case for control of political money established in this fashion, the details of particular proposals can usefully be assessed. One very arresting possibility is to make campaign contributions anonymous. If contributors truly wish to see that a particular point of view gets heard in the political process or that a particular candidate gets elected, then it should not matter whether the recipient of the money knows its source. The reason why donors want the receiver to know the source of the funds is, of course, so that the donor can ask for something more than good public policy or good people in office. Similarly, it is equally flawed to argue that any complex political system needs a good deal of money to run, and that this is why any serious restriction on campaign contributions is wrongheaded. If donors want to see the political system work, they can simply send the money without attaching their name to it.

We need only add here by way of additional emphasis that a wide distribution of the ownership of capital would make the middle class more secure and confident, and thus better able to play its role as the political pivot of the politics of broad class interest. A wider distribution would also transform the have-littles into have-somes, making them more attractive allies for the middle class. In this context it is worth noting that one of the most effective devices for providing the have-littles with higher *incomes* is to expand the Earned Income Tax Credit. As Milton Friedman argued long ago, the negative income tax is a powerful anti-poverty device.[48] To which we can repeat that it would help the have-littles become more effective political actors if there were full employment with at least modestly remunerative wages. This is an old dream of American liberalism, one not made less relevant by the fact that it has rarely been achieved.[49] We might say that a commercial republic that cannot manage even this is a political order at war with itself.

A Secure and Confident Middle Class

Even recognizing, as we did in chapter 8, the need for significant limits on what government should directly do to foster a secure and confident middle class, those who wish for a fuller realization of a commercial republic must look to policies over and above a wider distribution of capital. That is necessary but is unlikely to be sufficient. Not the least of the reasons, as we have already seen, is that socio-economic trends are not moving in the right direction. Two pieces of data further suggest the economic dimension of the problem. The University of Michigan's Panel Study of Income Dynamics, which generates some of the most reliable data on the distribution of income, has tracked the same American families since 1968. It found that, although 65 percent of white American men who turned twenty-one before 1980 had reached middle-class earnings[50] by the age of thirty, only 47 percent of those who turned twenty-one after 1980 managed to do so. The percentages for blacks were respectively 29 percent and 19 percent. The study also found that before 1980 more than a third of low-income families joined the middle class, while after 1980 only a quarter did.[51]

Economic insecurity, and otherwise feeling beleaguered, is to some degree an inevitable feature of middle-class life—at least in broadly democratic regimes where the economic top and bottom both press on the middle class.[52] Moreover, aspirations for a good life are high among middle-class citizens, while income is not high enough to produce a feeling of confidence that trouble can be absorbed and most obstacles overcome. In an increasingly prosperous society, the middle class is in the unenviable position of finding that the majority of the goods that traditionally distinguished it from those lower in the economic hierarchy bring in their trail an inevitable degree of dissatisfaction. Possessing them may even produce a sensation of being cheated. Thus higher education and home ownership in a good neighborhood are both intrinsically scarce goods: the very definition of their goodness requires that not everyone have them. The worth of higher education in an instrumental sense depends on how few people have it, just as quiet neighborhoods cannot be so if any and everyone could move in or could create unquiet neighborhoods on the next block.[53] If access to higher education and the economic means to own a home expand, the social value of these goods declines—and, at some level, many middle-class people sense that this has now occurred. More speculatively, we might say that the rise of the welfare state itself has increased middle-class insecurity because some of the goods whose possession distinguished the middle class from the have-littles are now open to all, since they are provided or subsidized by the state. The whole situation becomes that much more difficult for middle-class people when their incomes stagnate, as they have in recent years.[54]

Recent changes in the tax laws engineered by the Bush administration have not improved matters for the middle class. The Congressional Budget Office (CBO) has estimated that, as a result of these changes, the share of taxes paid by the top 20 percent went down while the share of the next two quintiles went up. Taking a different view of the same matter, the CBO estimates that the middle quintile (average income $57,000) has had its after-tax income boosted by 2.3 percent as a result of the changes. By contrast, those in the top quintile (average income $204,000) have had their income increased by 5.2 percent and those in the top 1 percent (average income $1,171,000) have had theirs boosted by 10.1 percent.[55] There seems little doubt that the recent tax changes are moving us in the wrong direction if we wish to realize more fully a commercial republic. A more progressive income tax than the one we have is thus crucial to republican reform. And so is the reinstatement of the estate tax. A political system that cannot see that the creation of a hereditary aristocracy of wealth is no road to republican government is one that has come loose from its aspirational moorings.

It is also worth noting in this context that improving the quality of public services will increase the middle class's sense of confidence and security. Unlike for large-scale asset-controllers, the quality of middle-class lives depends heavily on good public services. Schools that work, streets that are safe, health care that is reliable and affordable, all make for a decent quality of life for them—and thus promote the sense that one is doing fine and is relatively secure. Middle-class people do not have the resources to insulate themselves from a poorly run public sector.

Race, Religion, and Social Balance

In the American case, the problem of social balance is complicated by the prominent role of race and religion in our political life. The manner in which race, partly by intention, has made a politics of broad class interest more difficult to mount has been widely noted.[56] While it seems likely that race will continue to be a factor for some time, its effect in this respect is unlikely to grow, indeed, it has been receding. Still, it is probable that a politics of broad class interest will be achieved only to the degree that the association of race and class at the bottom of the economic pile is significantly weakened: racial innuendo will be harder to use by opponents of coalitions with the have-littles.

The situation is reversed with regard to religion, which seems to be growing in political importance. The political role of religion has been with us from the beginning of the Republic. Observers of American politics since at least the time of Tocqueville have noted that religion plays a greater role in our collective life compared with other countries shaped by the liberal enlightenment. I earlier pointed out that religious beliefs play some part in fostering public-spiritedness, and they generally shape the lives of a very large number of Americans. Therefore, friends of the commercial republic cannot ally themselves with those who decry the role of religion in politics. However, should religion succeed in overwhelming class as the fundamental political axis, then to that degree it will be more difficult to realize fully a commercial republic. In such a republic, a division by class is to be preferred: it serves as a rough and ready way to organize a politics of self-interest that overlaps with the public interest. Any proposal that promises to replace class by some other form of division must be scrutinized carefully.

Thus, one not very attractive state of affairs for friends of the republic would be a division, on one side, between the middle class and have-littles— both strongly attracted to an evangelical and fundamentalist Christianity— and, on the other, the controllers of productive assets and their allies in the professional middle class attached to an aggressive secularism. If such a division between believers—especially those attracted to using politics to advance their faith—and secularists threatens to displace class, the prospects for doing anything significant about it are slim. This is one of those Madisonian instances where the cure is likely to be as bad as the disease. A politics built around the care of souls will end up destroying republican government, but, in a citizenry where religious belief is widespread, so will an aggressive secularism that employs the power of the state. However, it seems plausible that a secure and confident middle class will be able to harbor a wide variety of religious beliefs, including secular criticisms of religion itself. This in itself will keep religion within republican bounds and by republican means. Similarly, if secularists restrain their enthusiasm for pointing out to believers the error of their ways, the prospects for republican government improve. As a package of reforms, however, this will fail to dazzle. But once we realize that we are attempting to shape the mores of a people, the difficulties become obvious. Just how are we to turn the hearts of the citizenry away from the conviction that the beliefs that guide their lives should also guide the political order?

IMPROVING THE PROSPECTS FOR REPUBLICAN
POLITICAL LEADERSHIP
Political Parties and Political Leadership

In addition to fostering a certain set of mores or culture, promoting the kind of political leadership that a commercial republic needs presents the greatest difficulty for political practice. Indeed, the two are related since the character of political leadership is itself affected by the culture. Still, there is one relatively concrete step to take: fostering the kind of political parties that facilitate republican government.

I made the fundamental points earlier: a republican regime needs political parties that are composed of broad coalitions representing people with interests, rather than interests attached to people. If the latter is the case, it will be difficult for parties to facilitate the kinds of class coalitions a commercial republic needs. Also, highly disciplined parties will make it considerably more difficult for the legislature to engage in deliberative ways of lawmaking. There are other similar obstacles to republican government. If the majority party in the legislature is disciplined and also controls the presidency, and the president is a strong party leader, the possibility of factional government increases significantly. The American system of separation of powers gives the executive a substantial grant of independent authority. Thus, when the legislature cannot act as political counterweight and engage in serious oversight of the executive, the president is in a position to do much as he pleases. Not the least among the things he may do is to weaken civil liberties: public officials are usually not cheered by opposition to their policies. Moreover, should the party which the president heads be one that provides a home for major business interests, he may also work to see that large-scale asset-holders manage to keep a great deal more than is necessary of the economic rewards an enterprise-based market system provides. The result would be to undercut other parts of the public interest, notably, political and economic equality.

How can we foster the kinds of parties that republican government needs? There is a long and complicated literature on the subject going back a half-century or more, with the success of reform efforts themselves being decidedly mixed.[57] One thing at least is suggested by this history: the more political money flows to organizations other than the national political parties, the harder it will be for political leaders to create a legislative school and organize broad class coalitions. Crucial resources will lie in the hands of people who want neither. Said differently, weak political parties are no good for republican government either. The recent set of campaign

finance reforms—which provide strong incentives for giving large amounts
of political money to independent issue organizations (the so-called 527
organizations) rather than to the political parties—is a step in the wrong
direction. The basic character of republican political parties is relatively
easy to specify: they must have resources large enough that their leaders in
the legislature and in the country can reach beyond core party supporters
when crafting legislation and building political coalitions.

The Allure of Wealth and Executive Power

Two other aspects of a republican reform program are worth mentioning
here. First, the job of republican leaders will be made easier if large numbers of Americans no longer find it necessary to amass as much wealth as
possible—particularly in building coalitions that restrain the more narrow
interests of asset controllers and in promoting legislation in the public interest. It will also help if there are opinion leaders who try to convince the
citizenry that a life of "graceful simplicity" is to be preferred to the tiring
and usually unsuccessful effort to amass "enough" wealth.[58] If a significant
number of citizens could be persuaded to adopt such a view, business privilege and the size of the inducements offered to secure large-scale investment
could be reduced. Economic growth would be less important to ordinary
citizens and, as a result, so would the economic decisions of controllers
of large-scale productive assets. The need for political leaders to convince
voters that they are doing everything possible to secure economic growth
would then be reduced, and it might even come to pass that business leaders would actually have to knock on the door before telling public officials
what they require. But one should not be optimistic about the charms of
the simple life being felt by ordinary Americans. Over two hundred years
of a commercial society has left its mark.

Second, the existing form of opinion leadership that focuses on the president as the primary branch of government must be challenged. The marriage of opinion leadership and the executive was created by the New Deal
and there is little doubt that it has achieved great things in realizing more
fully a commercial republic. But unless there are opinion leaders who can
resist the allure of executive power and who see the fundamental importance of deliberative lawmaking anchored by the legislature, we will likely
not get much farther down the commercial republican road. It would also
help if there were a political science—which is, after all, a kind of opinion
leadership—that taught the value of moving toward a self-limiting popular
sovereign capable of deliberative ways of lawmaking. It would be especially
useful, moreover, if the arguments it offered were part of the study of the
constitution of political regimes. Alas, contemporary political science has
more or less repudiated its Aristotelian origins and it has little more than
a passing interest in the teachings of Montesquieu and Tocqueville. And

what it might have learned from Madison is mostly filed away under the category of American political thought, which turns out to occupy a small space at the back of the file cabinet.

IF FRIENDS of republican government must choose where first to direct their efforts, as they undoubtedly must if they are to have any effect, then the place to start is probably with the wider distribution of the ownership of capital. This would probably have the most pervasive effects—especially if it is joined to a full employment policy aimed at providing at least modest remuneration for all. Both social balance and the political outlook of the citizenry would be strongly affected, with a lesser but real effect on the ability of political figures to act as republican political leaders. In short, the prospects for serving the public interest would rise significantly—in addition to the direct effects that a wider distribution of wealth would have. The reform next in order is strengthening the middle class. Republican government cannot succeed without a stratum between wealth-holders and labor-providers that is confident and secure enough to play the role of political pivot. Finally, the reform of local political life is also fundamental. There is no other arena where the citizenry can learn what it needs to know if it is to choose its governors wisely and be interested in limiting its own rule.

I want to emphasize that these fundamental reforms are not institutional in the manner often called for by constitutional theory. Such institutional matters are important, as the discussion above indicates. But, if I am correct, the most important reforms are in the areas of work, property, mores, and local political life. This should not be surprising: Locke and Tocqueville are, after all, two of the greatest theorists of republican government.

It only remains to add here that a reform program for republican government must be reflexive, directed both at increasing the odds that lawmaking serve the public interest and providing lawmakers with an account of its substance. But a program of reform must also face the problem that Rousseau defined long ago:

> For a nascent people to be capable of appreciating sound maxims of politics and of following the fundamental rules of reason of state, the effect would have to become the cause, the social spirit which is to be the work of the institution would have to preside over the institution itself, and men would have to be prior to laws what they ought to become by means of them.[59]

CONCLUSION

Because the success of a republican program of reform depends on the very things reform is to bring about, it will be self-reinforcing. Thus, once the middle class is politically secure and confident, the prospects for a wider distribution of wealth improve. More generally, lawmakers who legislate in the public interest will find themselves operating in a political environment in which there are greater incentives for them to do so. Everything depends on everything else, which is after all the point of talking about regimes in the first place. Still, given the uncertain character of reform, there is always the possibility of tragedy, irony, and farce. It might be farce—that is, ludicrous—for a people to act as its own classical Legislator. It might also be a tragedy: noble deeds brought low due to a fatal flaw. Or it might be a matter for irony: something worth doing, but which sophisticates view with amused detachment.

A republican reform program is also janus-faced: it looks to both the political Left and the political Right, but in doing so is aligned with neither. Friends of the American commercial republic might be described as radical conservatives. They must be radical in their reform proposals if they are to secure a commercial republican regime that rests on the frame of government they have inherited.

Republican regimes are neither social democratic nor libertarian. For republicans, as opposed to libertarians, government is *desirable*, not a grudging necessity. They are not only concerned with preventing factional rule, but also with serving the public interest. Advocates of a republican regime also understand that law, that is, government, creates liberty: if we cannot carry on our lives with purposive intelligence and without fear, we cannot be free. Liberty is a gift of a government energetic enough to say what the law is and to implement it. Those who live without such government understand all too clearly how its absence eviscerates liberty. Thus government must not only be energetic if the promise of liberty is to apply equally to all. It must also be strong and active enough to make equal protection of the law a reality. Government—properly designed—occupies a secure place in the affections of republicans. This becomes all the clearer when we notice that republican government promises not only to create a free people, but one that is also equal and engaged in governing itself.

Nevertheless, republican government is limited government. While its public interest contains egalitarian elements, it is not in the open-ended service of equality of the kind contemplated in social democracy. Nor can republicans accept the concentration of governmental power that a fully realized social democracy requires. Republicans, after all, hope to foster a people engaged in self-government, and the place that liberty holds in their affections makes them chary of open-ended grants of authority. We might capture the republican path between statist and minimalist government by saying that republicans believe not only that there is such a path, but that energetic government in the service of well-defined purposes, that is, strong government, can gain and keep the affections of a people free to consider the merits of the political way of life of which they are a part.

In a well-ordered commercial republic the burdens on government would be less than they presently are because a republican citizenry is inclined to meet some significant portion of its collective difficulties through its own devices. In this it will be well served by a public interest that seeks to promote a strong civil society, a set of rights that are given real content by government action, a government so designed that the factional tendencies of the controllers of productive assets are curbed, an economy that generates something less than the present level of inequality, and a set of governmental and economic institutions so ordered that at least modestly remunerative work is available. In a well-ordered republican regime, government will not have to constantly sweep up the regular messes generated by society and economy, with the attendant pressures for government to take on yet larger burdens. Its promise is that, by focusing on crucial features of the economy and society, it can enable citizens to conduct their own lives in a fashion they find attractive; it will also foster their ability to choose lawmakers who understand that securing such an economy and society is their job. A well-ordered commercial republic will not be indifferent either to the kind of economy that generates very large differences in income and wealth among its citizens, or to the failures of its local communities. To this degree, it will depart from current American practice. But neither will a realized commercial republic think its job is to secure its citizens against all of the risks attendant on living in a complex society. This will also be a departure from recent practice. Instead of seeking directly to provide the good society, it will help provide the means by which the citizenry can build its own— community by community, workplace by workplace, and family by family.

Furthermore, the republican belief in a public interest gives life to the idea that we are not social atoms; the shape of our lives depends heavily on others. It is in the interest of each of us as adherents of republican government that others support and participate in the effort to secure a flourishing commercial republic. To act on this interest means to look to government as the only agent capable of increasing the odds that all will find it possible to engage in this common effort.

Republican constitutional theory is an effort to find the connections between the broad purposes of the regime and a politics that offers a reasonable promise of giving them life. There is, however, always the possibility that no politics can serve our aspirations to realize a commercial republic and the justice it promises. Attractive forms of political life are undoubtedly more various and more possible of realization than is regularly claimed by people of conservative temperament and political persuasion. Americans are not prisoners of the politics of the early twenty-first century. Still, it seems likely that there are limits to the attractive forms politics can take. (As for other kinds of politics, we know just about anything is possible.) Thus, the constitutional theory outlined here, like any theory of political practice, must be tested against whether the behavior it calls for is possible of realization without enormous cost. If it is not, that theory must be discarded. It is worth trying to think through this question of behavior because the political constitution of a well-ordered republican regime promises to create a working whole out of two highly attractive but seemingly irreconcilable political ideas: (1) that a republican regime is a good regime because it aims at a defensible conception of justice, and its claims on us are thus independent of our consent; and (2) that the people are the constituent sovereign of republican government and only they can limit themselves.

A program of reform for republicans is a constitutive program. Its underlying concern is with political practices as they together constitute a more fully realized commercial republic. Since the practices are interconnected, friends of the regime cannot just focus their energies on securing a particular element of the political constitution they wish for. Thus, if they focus on making Congress more open in its lawmaking so that citizens can judge the qualities of their lawmakers, but fail to ensure that the citizenry has the inclination to do so, the result may well be a legislature even less likely than the present one to make law in the service of the public interest.

The present historical juncture may be the last time it is plausible to assert that Americans really do aspire to be a commercial republic. Many American intellectuals may no longer believe that this is the business we should be in, although it is unlikely that the rot has spread very far beyond them. Still, it is unwise for friends of the commercial republic to simply wait for something to turn up that would lead to a fuller realization of the commercial republic than we now have. What is most likely to turn up, as the Micawbers of this world sometimes learn, is not an inheritance left by a rich aunt, but the appearance of her wretched nephew determined to move into our household with many of his even less attractive companions. Still, republican friends ought not forget that the central concerns and devices that make up the commercial republic are an inheritance from an earlier era, and that to attempt in the early twenty-first century to give this regime full life is an exercise in leaning into the wind.

Regimes, however, cannot be changed like socks or imported like automobiles. Thus our real choices at present—barring working toward the creation of a new regime that might be born well beyond the horizon—lie in the extent we feel ourselves able to more fully realize a commercial republic. We could, of course, do little or nothing—and concentrate, instead, on making our executive-centered working constitution perform better by harnessing the executive and the administrative apparatus to the engine of social justice, in the manner of New Deal liberalism. Or, perhaps we might follow the conservative vision of making the presidency the avatar of a regnant American democracy abroad and the vehicle through which the reach of the state is sharply curtailed at home (but keeping it as a means to strengthen the moral indoctrination of the young in the traditional pieties). For liberals, the executive branch would then work to protect the vulnerable, while for conservatives it would protect national security and secure the values that are said to have made America great. There is also the possibility—a more politically neutral, technocratic one—in which the president and the bureaucracy are agents of scientific or, in any case, neutral expertise, as apparently President Carter hoped for. Or, yet again, we might instead concede that the political arms of government are beyond reforming as agents of a principled view of political life, and repair to the redoubt of the courts—in the Left version to promote political and other forms of equality, in the Right version to secure individual liberty and economic efficiency. Or, once more, we might look to revivify the party system. In the view of some, political parties are what have made the constitution work, as they have knitted together state, local, and national politics, connected the citizenry to national politics, and enabled coordination to occur between the branches. Their decline, adherents of this argument say, has only made governing the United States that much more difficult. Here we encounter the old dream of responsible political parties as the key to popular self-government.[60]

None of these possible measures is without merit for friends of the commercial republic, though each is just as greatly flawed. As a representative of the people, the president and the presidency offer energy but not great complexity of view; a republic is not a vast law court; and political parties must be very coherent and far-seeing indeed to carry the burden advocates of responsible parties lay out for them. Moreover, saying that some slightly modified version of what we presently have as a working constitution is the best we can do is to consign ourselves to be a nation of tinkerers. Even if we are content to merely tinker, however, we will still need a theory of political constitution: some tinkering causes explosions.

Republican regimes give due regard to the healthy fear that government evokes in the governed, but without being mesmerized by the supposed virtues of severely constrained government that can do little for the collective dilemmas of those it is meant to serve. Republican regimes ask of the mass of citizens more than many of them can easily give, but nothing that requires greatness of soul or the capacity for deep reflection. Republican government, I have said, is a modern project in its aim for moderate liberty and moderate well-being. Its promise is that the large mass of ordinary citizens will have a reasonable chance of a life free of immoderate arbitrariness inflicted by the powerful, and enough bodily and economic security to allow them to resist the blandishments and threats of those who wish to rule rather than govern.

NOTES

Chapter One

1. Leo Strauss interprets Machiavelli as believing that "a true analysis of political 'facts' is not possible without the light supplied by knowledge of what constitutes a well-ordered commonwealth." *Thoughts on Machiavelli*, 234. But whether by "commonwealth" Machiavelli meant a political regime is not easy to say. Cf. Mansfield, *Machiavelli's New Modes and Orders*, 207.

2. Below I will talk about our aspiration to be a fully realized commercial republic, and it is that political-economic regime that I have in mind here.

3. For those who are not so committed, they too will need a theory of political constitution, but not of a commercial republic. See Elkin and Soltan, eds., *A New Constitutionalism*; Soltan and Elkin, eds., *The Constitution of Good Societies.*

4. Quoted in Stourzh, "*Constitution:* Changing Meanings of the Term," 43.

5. "Let us look at what sorts of things preserve and destroy cities, and what sorts do so for each sort of constitution and for what reasons some are governed well and others are the reverse. For when these sorts of things have been examined, perhaps we might also have more insight into what sort of constitution is best, and how each sort is best arranged, and by using what laws and customs." *Nicomachean Ethics*, 1181b, 16–23.

6. See Nichols, *Citizens and Statesmen*, chap. 3.

7. See the discussion in chapter 2.

8. Other important constitutional theorists of republican government include, notably, Tocqueville and Mill (who was strongly influenced by his great predecessor). In his essay considering Coleridge's "Theory of the Constitution," Mill refers to the "the science of political institutions." *Mill on Bentham and Coleridge*, 155.

9. For a fuller discussion, see Elkin, *City and Regime*, passim, esp. 120.

10. Lippmann, *Principles of the Good Society*, 247–48, 250. For a particularly acute discussion of self-limitation, see Nedelsky, *Private Property*, esp. chaps. 1, 5–6.

11. Mansfield, *Taming the Prince*, 254.

12. Consider here book 1 of Machiavelli's *Discourses*.

13. See Barber, *On What the Constitution Means*; Cropsey, "United States as Regime"; Elkin, *City and Regime*, chap. 6.

14. See Walzer, *Interpretation and Social Criticism*.

15. In the following pages I draw freely from my "Constitutional Theory of the Commercial Republic."

16. I make clear, especially in chapters 3 and 10, my belief that we fall significantly short of fully realizing commercial republican government. It is enough here to set out the case for a particular view of American aspirations, and to simply state that no people ever fully realizes its aspirations, however they are formulated.

17. "All along, the War [the English Civil War] had been fought to restrain the abuses of government, but until now they had been abuses of the monarch. During the course of the summer the Army discovered that parliamentary tyranny was equally dangerous." Kishlansky, *Monarchy Transformed*, 174–75.

The American desire for limited government does not make us less than fully paid-up democrats. In contrast to what they sometimes imply, even strong democrats do not believe that anything the people will they should get. Rousseau distinguished the general will from the will of all, which is by way of saying what "the people" is. More recently, for Benjamin Barber, "political talk" of a certain kind is the legitimate mode through which the people speak. See Barber, *Strong Democracy*. Robert Dahl, another prominent strong democrat, at various points makes clear that the people cannot legitimately abrogate their own primary political rights. See Dahl, *Preface to Economic Democracy*, chaps. 1–2.

It is also worth noting in this context that social democratic regimes of the kind found, for example, in Scandinavia, are less concerned with limits on government. They are, not coincidentally, more strongly majoritarian than republican regimes, and more egalitarian in their policies than republics are likely to be. This book may thus be understood as an inquiry into the political constitution of one type of popular self-government, a republican regime. A similar book could be written about social democracies.

18. In this attachment to private ownership of productive assets, we differ from Western Europeans who give much less emphasis to property rights and the like as essential to a good regime.

19. For some evidence about our aspirations, see Lane, "Market Justice, Political Justice," 383–402; McClosky and Zaller, *The American Ethos*; Conover et al., "Duty Is a Four Letter Word." For powerful evocations of our aspirations, see Wills, *Lincoln at Gettysburg*; Beer, *To Make a Nation*.

20. Cf. Abraham Lincoln's "Address to Cooper Institute," February 27, 1860, in *Lincoln: Speeches and Writings 1859–1865*. Cf. also Rousseau's comment that "the individuals to whom I owe my life, who gave me what I needed, who cultivated my soul, who communicated their talents to me, may no longer exist, yet the laws that protected my childhood live on." Quoted in Starobinski, "Letter from Rousseau," 31–32.

21. Cf. Philip Pettit's comment concerning one account of "rightness" in moral theory that "what constitutes an option as right is that no one could reasonably object to it . . . where it is a matter of common knowledge that people are seeking agreement

with one another about matters of rightness." "Consequentialist Perspective," 121–22. Those who are able and willing to so reason are the heirs of Bacon, who thought that a "wholly new politics of liberty was possible if the appetite for 'perfecting oneself' were harnessed to commercial and manufacturing instruments for increasing prosperity." Quoted in Caton, *Politics of Progress*, 48.

22. It has sometimes been argued that not *all* aspects of the founders' thought should guide us, not least because many of them were slaveholders. But it is not their thought as such that ought and does have a hold on us, but only that part of it that has withstood this exchange over time among those willing and able to give reasons for their views. My argument here is not that we are obliged to accept whatever the founders said—a kind of originalism with a vengeance. Rather, their views and our aspirations are to be and have indeed been subjected to reasoned argument. It is that which gives the founders' views on the essentials of republican government a claim on us, while others of their views ought to have no such hold. On this argument, it does not matter that Madison or any of the other founders may have been racists or misogynists, or indeed anything else we have come to believe is wrong. All that needs to be accepted is that it is plausible to believe that Americans are committed to realizing a republican form of government married to a system of private property in productive assets. If indeed we are, I contend that this is in major part because of the kind of political order the founders helped put into motion.

23. For an account of Madison's and Jefferson's views on this subject, see McCoy, *Last of the Fathers*, 53–60. For an excellent modern discussion, to which I am greatly obliged, see Barber, *What the Constitution Means*, esp. the introduction and chap. 1. It is worth contemplating here how many originalist defenses of the Constitution as supreme law would now exist if the original unamended Constitution was still said to be the law of the land.

24. Since my concern here is with the theory behind the Constitution—that which provides its rationale—I do not consider the arguments concerning how, if at all, the text of the Constitution binds us and how we are to interpret it. I have, however, already noted one relevant consideration: does the Constitution adequately embody that underlying theory? A few additional comments are useful. If it is accepted that the Constitution is best understood as a necessarily partial statement of how we hope to realize our aspiration to be a commercial republic, it can hardly be the case that we are bound by provisions in it that make it impossible or even very difficult to realize this desired outcome. It does not follow, however, that anyone who believes that features of the Constitution do get in the way of realizing our aspirations must then resist its provisions any way they can. Prudence will probably suggest otherwise, as might the prospects for amending it to make it more consistent with efforts to realize a commercial republic.

25. See again Barber, *What the Constitution Means*; see also White, *When Words Lose Their Meaning*. For a lengthier statement, see Elkin, *City and Regime*, esp. chap. 6. Cf. Rawls, *Political Liberalism*, lectures 1 and 4.

26. Is this aspirational account of how our aspirations are formed democratic enough in a democratic age? It must be—in much the same way that the case for democracy cannot itself be democratic.

27. Judith Shklar makes the essential point. "Who are the 'we' of whom I seem to talk so confidently?" And she answers by saying that "we" are the people "who are familiar with the political practices of the United States and who show their adherence to them by discussing them critically, indeed relentlessly." *Ordinary Vices*, 226–27. Cf. Michael Walzer's comment that "we discuss the complaint, therefore we are." *Company of Critics*, 3. We are, in short, allegiants who thus take an internal point of view in considering our present political practices.

28. Aspirations thus need not be held by even a majority—although I believe that there is substantial agreement on the kind of regime the United States should be.

29. On this idea, see the parallel discussion in Dworkin, *Law's Empire*, chaps. 2–3, 6–7. See also the description of a modified form of the game "Twenty Questions" in my *City and Regime*, chaps. 2, 6–7.

30. See the discussion later in this chapter.

31. Consider here Leo Strauss's comment that, in a "politically relevant" sense, evaluative distinctions "cannot be 'demonstrated'" and so classical political philosophers addressed "men who, because of their natural inclinations as well as their upbringing, took those distinctions for granted." "On Classical Political Philosophy," in Strauss, *Rebirth of Classical Political Rationalism*, 58.

32. Edmund Burke, who thought about this matter a good deal, commented that "[p]eople will not look forward to posterity who never look backward to their ancestors." *Reflections on the Revolution in France*, 119.

33. See Bromwich, *Choice of Inheritance*, 43–78.

34. The argument here parallels that by Rawls who talks of a "political conception...that [has] some hope of gaining the support of an overlapping consensus." Rawls defines the latter as a consensus that will be "affirmed by the opposing...doctrines likely to thrive over generations in a more or less just constitutional democracy." The focus of a political conception of justice is the "framework of basic institutions" that Rawls further specifies as needing to "fit together into one unified scheme of social cooperation...and the principles, standards and precepts that apply to them, as well as how these norms are expressed in the character and attitudes of the members of society who realize its ideals." "The Idea of an Overlapping Consensus," 1, 3. In chapter 9, I indicate the manner in which I disagree with Rawls, but this disagreement does not affect the point being made here.

35. The latter would include those who are presently attempting to develop civic republicanism as a guide to political practice.

36. This is not to say that the Anti-Federalists, like their successors, had no doubts about the value of commerce. They had reservations about where it might lead, but they still thought some version of it was essential if republican government was to succeed. See Storing, *What the Anti Federalists Were For*.

37. Cf. J. H. Hexter's comment that "in the constitutional mode we can retain our concern for nature and reason and justice and order in our social cosmos without binding ourselves to an impossible quest for final and definitive solutions." In this mode, men and women seek "to maintain living and effective contact between the realm of justice and reason and nature and order on the one hand and the sphere of [their] daily doing[s] in an actual political society on the other." *Vision of Politics on Eve of the Reformation*, 230.

38. Cf. Montesquieu's comment that "[i]t is better to say that the government most in conformity with nature is the one whose particular arrangement best relates to the disposition of the people for whom it is established." *Spirit of the Laws*, 8. Even those who think there is a better regime than a commercial republic may be said, if not to aspire to the realization of such a republic, at least to approve of the effort to bring it to fruition. Since we may presume that they feel obliged to defend the good against the bad, they ought to defend a good regime so long as that regime will not prevent them from trying to convince their fellow citizens that there is a better regime available. The only people who will not then share in this enlarged sense of our aspirations to realize a commercial republic are those who think that such a regime will work to prevent any serious consideration of alternative regimes, and those who aspire to a regime worse than a commercial republic.

39. Cf. Rawls's comment that "the aims of political philosophy depend on the society it addresses." "Idea of an Overlapping Consensus," 1.

Given the discussion here, it will come as no surprise that I do not think that arguments from social contracts, consent, original positions, or any view that attempts to reconstruct what rational individuals somehow understood would agree to, have much normative force. One line of objection is to inquire into why consent or agreement in and of itself is to have much weight. If the answer is that it is not mere consent that is doing the work, but reasoned consent of some kind, then it is hard to see what essential work the apparatus of contract or the veil of ignorance is doing. The need here is to be clear about why reason has moral force. I am not, of course, claiming to have fully provided the answer here. I would only say that this is the right question for contract theorists, just as it is for me. I agree that the apparatus of social contracts, veils of ignorance, consent, and the like are important ways for determining whether arguments established on other grounds are likely to make sense to people who are instrumentally rational. But in the hands of many practitioners of such thought experiments, this is not how they are presented. I suspect, in particular, that some theorists who deploy arguments from consent merely want to make the point that a government that purports to be popular needs to be rooted in widespread acceptance of its broad character if it is, in fact, going to act like a popular government—that is, not rely on systematic and widespread use of force. As Hume indicated, as a practical matter all government rests on opinion. This is a prudential conclusion, and it may be a necessary one; but it does not in itself confer moral-political worth on a regime. See the additional discussion of Rawls's arguments in chapter 9.

I have similar doubts about whether what rational individuals find themselves agreeing on by way of actual practices—conventions if you will—have the moral force sometimes attributed to them. See, e.g., Hardin, *Liberalism, Constitutionalism, and Democracy*. It is not easy in such arguments to separate what has been agreed on because it is somehow rational from the ability of the powerful to contrive a situation where the less powerful do their bidding. Unless the less powerful are plainly in a situation where coercion is unlikely now or in the future, I do not see how we can give much normative weight to what they seem to agree to.

The discussion of "our aspirations," while hardly free from difficulties at least has the merit of asserting that the kind of reasoning human beings are actually capable of in the face of all the temptations to be evil, feckless, and self-interested has some bearing on the content of political value. It may not be Aristotle or Kant; but then it also doesn't look like the contrivance of a closet-scribbler trying to take political struggle out of politics.

40. As such, our motto, now perhaps a little out of date, might be "Neither Marx nor Toyota."

41. For evidence that many Americans have, historically, not valued some of the features of a commercial republic, see the impressive book by Rogers M. Smith, *Civic Ideals*. It is important to emphasize here that my contention is not that most Americans have held the aspirations I describe, only those willing and able to exchange reasons, and not even all of them at every juncture. I am, however, not unmindful of the difficulties of defending such an argument: a great deal will depend on what I mean by "willing," "able," and "reasons," especially as the latter, as I have said, points to more universal standards.

42. See Walzer, *Spheres of Justice*, 9. See also Thompson, *Whigs and Hunters*, 265; Galston, "Community, Democracy, Philosophy," 124. We might say that the theory of political constitution offered here is from an internal point of view. See Soltan, *Causal Theory of Justice*; Dworkin, *Law's Empire*, esp. chap. 1; Elkin, *City and Regime*, esp. chap. 6.

43. For Americans, the best statement of these liberal principles is to be found in the Declaration of Independence. Cf. Wills, *Lincoln at Gettysburg*. Given the arguments here, it is instructive that the authoritative statement of liberal principles is found in the Declaration, not in the Constitution.

For a range of arguments that support liberty as an element of liberal justice, see Hayek, *Constitution of Liberty*; *The Federalist* (Madison, Jay, and Hamilton); Mill, *On Liberty*; and Shklar, "Liberalism of Fear." For equality, see Rawls, *Theory of Justice*; Dworkin, "Why Liberals Should Care about Equality," in *Matter of Principle*; Dahl, *Preface to Economic Democracy*. And for self-government, see Dahl, *Democracy and Its Critics*; Dewey, *Public and Its Problems*.

44. But see chapter 4.

45. Cf. Montesquieu's comment that freedom consists of the "tranquility of spirit which comes from the opinion each one has of his security." *Spirit of the Laws*, 157.

46. *On Liberty and Other Essays*, 72. In succeeding paragraphs, I suggest some limits on our liberty, at least if we wish to live well. More importantly for the present context, we cannot live any way we please if that requires that the people can rule any way they please.

47. Kymlicka, *Contemporary Political Philosophy*, 204.

48. *Utilitarianism*, 199.

49. On this, see Shklar, "The Liberalism of Fear"; Rawls, *Political Liberalism*.

50. Cf. Stephen Salkever's argument that "democracy here is to be understood neither as morally neutral nor as morally ideal but as morally indefinite—a term covering a range of moral possibilities." *Finding the Mean*, 208.

51. Cf. Steven J. Lenzner's characterization of Burke's views: for Burke, he says, though the end or purpose of the "best constitution" is not constructed by man, "the manner of its production is." "Strauss's Three Burkes," 371.

52. *The Federalist* No. 1.

53. But the matter can only be settled by extensive empirical investigation.

54. See, in order, Shklar, "Liberalism of Fear"; Macpherson, *Life and Times of Liberal Democracy*; Smith, *Liberalism and American Constitutional Law*; Dworkin, "What Rights Do We Have," in *Taking Rights Seriously*.

Chapter Two

1. Those uncomfortable with my focus on *The Federalist* might consider that my concern here is not with Madison's thought as such but with the most sustained and powerful theory of limited republican government that we have—and that is to be found in Madison's essays in *The Federalist*. It is in those writings that his most characteristic concerns are set out and the links among them considered. Moreover, it is likely that an effort to assemble a theory from the whole corpus of his writings will result in a theory that either bears a strong resemblance to the one he sets out in *The Federalist* or is not more compelling than the one presented there. Additionally, if the rest of his thinking on limited popular government sharply differs from what he says in *The Federalist*, this would mean that any theory constructed from the whole of his writings must be incoherent, riven as it would be with contradictory premises. I do not believe this to be the case, and so it is possible to supplement my interpretation of Madison's thought in *The Federalist* by looking to other of his writings, and this I do. Even so, I do not undertake a complete account of Madison's thought. There are, however, several comprehensive interpretations of his political thought that grapple with the apparent contradictions in it. See especially Banning, *Sacred Fire*; Matthews, *If Men Were Angels*; McCoy, *Last of the Fathers*; Rosen, *American Compact*.

2. This point applies not only to founders of republican regimes. Lenin may be said to have understood quite well what distinguished the Bolshevik regime from its predecessors and what was needed for it to succeed. A powerful expression of living reality, of what was being attempted in the new American Republic as it struck one thoughtful participant, is given by Hamilton in *The Federalist* No. 1: "[I]t seems to have been reserved to the people of this country, by their conduct and example, to decide the important question, whether societies of men are really capable of establishing good government from reflection and choice, or whether they are forever destined to depend, for their political constitutions, on accident and force."

3. Cf. Edmund S. Morgan's comment that "Madison wrote not only the United States Constitution, or at least most of it, but also the most searching commentary on it that has ever appeared." "The Fixers," 25. Similarly, Jennifer Nedelsky says that "James Madison not only established the agenda for the Constitutional Convention of 1787; he provided the formulation of the problems our Constitution was designed to solve." *Private Property*, 16. Lance Banning says Madison was "preeminent among the men who shaped, explained and won an overwhelming mandate for the nation's fundamental law." *Sacred Fire*, 1. See also Ketcham, *From Colony to Country*; Rakove, *Original Meanings*.

Ackerman, *We the People*, 314, has a useful discussion of just why many Americans now would have trouble seeing Madison as the great theorist of the commercial republic: he had slaves; he did not advocate suffrage for women; and he did little to prevent Indians from being killed and pushed off their ancestral lands. Moreover, he was an aristocrat of sorts. Ackerman (314–16) goes on to argue that, because our working constitution has departed in significant ways from the one Madison was instrumental in setting up—we are no longer ruled by a faction of white men but live in a political order that is committed to racial and gender equality—there is, from the point of view of women, black, brown, and Native Americans reason to try to reduce the defects that remain. It would be different, if we had not made the changes. Thus, even those whose predecessors suffered under the Madisonian constitution have reason to think it has merit.

4. In my understanding of Madison, I have been helped by the many excellent discussions of his thought, particularly that by Jennifer Nedelsky. In *Private Property and the Limits of American Constitutionalism*, she explores the relationship between the propertied and the Madisonian design with great subtlety and sophistication. I have also found very useful the discussions of Herbert Storing, Martin Diamond, Cass Sunstein, Samuel Beer, Gary Wills, David Epstein, Joseph Bessette, Drew McCoy, Lance Banning, and Marc Plattner. A recent comprehensive and thoughtful overview of Madison's thought can be found in Banning, *Sacred Fire*.

5. See the discussion in chapter 4.

6. Nedelsky, *Private Property*, 156. See *The Federalist* No. 39.

7. Madison to John Adams, 22 May 1817, quoted in McCoy, *Last of the Fathers*, 65.

8. Madison to Jefferson, 27 June 1823, quoted in McCoy, *Last of the Fathers*, 71.

9. Lippmann, *Principles of the Good Society*, 250.

10. When Madison talks of the people as a citizenry, he is, of course, referring to one composed of white men, and not indeed all of them. This was the extent of political inclusion at the time. However, Madison's formulations can without difficulty be expanded to include all adults—as I do here and as we have, in fact, done in practice. It is one of the prime indicators of the power of his thought that such an expansion seems wholly natural. See also note 3.

11. *The Federalist* No. 10.

12. For a longer list of features that provides additional detail, see Matthews, *If Men Were Angels*, 190.

13. In setting out my account of Madison's theory, as it appears in *The Federalist* No. 10, I have attempted to make explicit what he sometimes left implicit. In doing so, I have run the danger that a comprehensive account of his thought would reveal that he was explicit elsewhere or that some of my inferences are wrong. I have attempted to guard against the problem by checking my discussion against the account of Madison's thought given by its most acute students. For those students, see note 4. While they do not all agree with one another, there is substantial support in this literature for the propositions I set out here. I am also aware that some students of Madison's thought believe that he changed his mind on crucial matters and, for example, shifted from being a strong advocate of the national government

to lending aid to those who argued the case for strong states' rights. I am, however, convinced by Banning's argument that what changed was not Madison's theory, but political circumstances. See *Sacred Fire*, passim.

14. See, most notably, Pocock, *The Machiavellian Moment*, esp. pt. 3.

15. Cf. Epstein, *Political Theory of the Federalist*, 7.

16. *The Federalist* No. 10. It is worth pointing out that while Madison sometimes wrote as if he included political parties under the heading of faction, it is unlikely that he thought they were the crucial problem. Since Madison thought there could be nonfactious majorities (see below), this alone suggests that political parties need not be factious. Moreover, if a principal concern of parties is patronage and other forms of material largesse, to this degree they are not factions but distributive-minded coalitions. It is true, however, that if parties simply see the state as a repository of potential plunder, they might well be counted as factions on the ground that they aim to subvert the permanent interests of the community.

17. *The Federalist* No. 10. It is worth noting here that Dahl's widely discussed critique of Madison in 1956 (*Preface to Democratic Theory*) is no longer tenable, as he himself admits. See *Democracy and Its Critics*, 169–73 and chaps. 20–21. Dahl's reluctance to face difficult normative questions in 1956 has been a continuing weakness in his writings since then. See, e.g., how he treats rights in *A Preface to Economic Democracy*.

18. *The Federalist* No. 10.

19. Madison to James Monroe, 5 October 1786, in *Writings* 2:273. See also his letter to Jefferson, 17 October 1788, quoted in Banning, *Sacred Fire*, 131.

20. *The Federalist* No. 51.

21. See *The Federalist* No. 55. Jack Rakove, a careful student of Madison's thought, says that "[f]or most 18th century liberals, the problem of rights was to protect the whole people against the coercive power of monarchy. Madison was the first to realize that this formula was irrelevant to the American republic, where real power lay with popular majorities, who would use legislative power to burden whichever minorities they disliked." "A Nation Still Learning." Cf. Jefferson, *Notes on the State of Virginia*, 120.

22. *On Liberty*, 62.

23. *The Federalist* No. 51.

24. *The Federalist* No. 10.

25. See Madison's speech on suffrage to the Constitutional Convention, in Farrand, ed., *Records of the Federal Convention*, 3:450–51. With the benefit of hindsight, we can see that this is too optimistic a view. Outside the United States, at least, the propertied have regularly created and supported governments that systematically subvert civil and political rights. See generally Banning, *Sacred Fire*, pt. 2. Moreover, in the United States, the propertied have not been notable for their stalwart support of extensions of civil and political rights to all adults.

26. *The Federalist* No. 10. Cf. Nedelsky, *Private Property*, 5 and passim. Madison believed that factions of "interest" were more long-lived that those of "passion." In particular, factions rooted in the ownership of property or lack thereof sprang more directly from nature, since they stem from the "unequal faculties of acquiring

it" (*The Federalist* No. 10). As Ackerman argues in *We the People*, 186–88, factions of interest for Madison were thus more dangerous. Ideological zeal wanes and leaders who elicit strong passions die or move on to some other endeavor.

27. See the discussion in chapters 4 and 8; see also Nedelsky, *Private Property*, chaps. 3 and 6.

28. *The Federalist* No 10.

29. Madison, *Notes of Debates*, 194. See also ibid., 403–4; Madison's speech on suffrage, in Farrand, ed., *Records of the Federal Convention*, 3:451.

30. "Allow the right [of suffrage] exclusively to property, and the rights of persons may be oppressed." Nedelsky, *Private Property*, 18, quoting Madison in a letter to John Brown, October 1788. The letter itself is reprinted in Madison, *Mind of the Founder*, 58. See also Madison's speech on suffrage to the Constitutional Convention, in Farrand, ed., *Records of the Federal Convention*, 3:450–55. Madison said quite emphatically that "confining the right of suffrage to freeholders . . . violates the vital principle of free government that those who are bound by laws, ought to have a voice in making them" (453). Here he also revealed a widespread uneasiness about the effects on property rights of extending suffrage "equally to all" (450). Still, popular self-government is one of the foundations on which Madison's constitutional theory rests. For an especially strong argument on this count, see Banning, *Sacred Fire*, chap. 3, 252.

31. See Parenti, "The Constitution as an Elitist Document"; Greenberg, "Class Rule and the Constitution."

32. I take up this matter again later in this chapter.

33. See Nedelsky, *Private Property*, chap. 2.

34. See the essays by Plattner and others in Goldwin and Schambra, ed., *How Capitalistic Is the Constitution?*; Nedelsky, *Private Property*, 23–24.

35. Quoted in Morgan, "The Fixers," 25. The quote is from a letter to Jefferson. For the correspondence between the two, see the superb volumes edited by James Morton Smith, *The Correspondence between Jefferson and Madison*.

36. *The Federalist* No. 10.

37. Ibid.

38. *The Federalist* No. 51. Lengthy discussion of these precautions can be found in the works of the authors cited in note 4.

39. *The Federalist* No. 10.

40. Ibid.

41. Ibid.

42. *The Federalist* No. 51.

43. Ibid.

44. *The Federalist* No. 48.

45. Although Madison did not argue the point at length, it is consistent with his thought on the relation between size and faction: small republics were less attractive because, in the absence of a more or less complete homogeneity of opinion and interest, the minority would be even more vulnerable to the factional schemes of the majority than in a large republic. In the former, it is likely that there would be only one line of cleavage, and, with that, the minority would be a permanent minority with all this entails about its rights being vulnerable.

46. *The Federalist* No. 51.

47. *The Federalist* No. 10.

48. Ibid.

49. Martin Diamond, "Democracy and *The Federalist*." Cf. Judith Best's comment that the "promotion of commerce will foster heterogeneity. This axiom is implicit in Madison's recognition that this protection [of diverse talents] results in 'different degrees and *kinds* of property.'" Best is quoting *The Federalist* No. 10 in "Fundamental Rights and the Structure of Government," 43.

50. *The Federalist* No. 51.

51. See the discussion later in this chapter on the public interest and promoting deliberation.

52. See *The Federalist* No. 55. But see also the discussion of public-spiritedness later in this chapter. Cf. Hamilton's comment: "This supposition of universal venality in human nature is little less an error in political reasoning than the supposition of universal rectitude. The institution of delegated power implies that there is a portion of virtue and honor among mankind, which may be a reasonable foundation of confidence." *The Federalist* No. 76. Cf. also Samuel Johnson's comment: "I know, Madam, how unwillingly conviction is admitted when interest opposes it." Quoted in Morley, ed., *Everybody's Boswell*, 74. Perhaps the safest thing to say here is that Madison put a great deal of faith in ambition and self-interest but also hoped that public-regarding motives would be at work. Indeed, he knew they must be if republican government was to succeed.

53. *The Federalist* No. 10. For a prominent example of disregarding the permanent and aggregate interests of the community in discussing faction, see Dahl, *Preface to Democratic Theory*, chap. 1.

54. For the community's aggregate interests, see chapter 8.

55. As did Madison on occasion: one charge made against the proposed House of Representatives was that "so small a number of representatives will be an unsafe depositary of the public interests." *The Federalist* No. 55. Jacob Cooke attributes the essay to Madison, noting that Hamilton in a rather loose way claimed authorship of this and several other essays that Cooke assigns to Madison. Cooke argues that it is "a question not of veracity but of memory." See Cooke's introduction to *The Federalist*, xxx. In any event, Madison uses phrases such as "the common good" that parallel in content the idea of the public interest.

56. It follows, further, that those feckless lawmakers who cannot be bothered to exert themselves in the service of the public interest are not preventing big government, as many, including themselves, suppose; they are the deadweight of a stricken republican regime, and, if the disease is widespread enough, are, if not quite its murderers, actively employed in the country's funeral parlors. See chapters 5–10.

57. *The Federalist* No. 37.

58. For additional consideration of active government, see the discussion below on deliberation and the discussion in chapter 5.

59. Walzer, "Liberalism and the Art of Separation," 315–30.

60. *The Federalist* No. 10.

61. See also Samuel Beer's comment (*To Make a Nation*, 283) that Madison did not view the separation of powers as creating "separate centers of power" simply to

serve the end of "limitation." The quoted words are Madison's from the *National Gazette*, February 4, 1792. See Madison, *Papers of James Madison*, 14:217.

62. Quoted in Beer, "Federalism and the Nation-State."

63. Later in his career Madison began to see the dangers of minority faction, or so one astute commentator on Madison argues, and the appreciation of this problem made him more inclined to value political parties as vehicles for expressing majority will. See Milkis, *Political Parties and Constitutional Government*, 190. See also Banning's very helpful discussion in *Sacred Fire*, 183, 342–43.

64. See chapter 3.

65. *The Federalist* No. 57. Cf. Dicey, *Law of the Constitution*, chap. 8. Consider also Michael Oakeshott's comment that the rule of law is government "by means of the enforcement by prescribed methods of settled rules binding alike on governors and governed." "Fortunes of Scepticism," 15. Also consider John Trenchard and Thomas Gordon's comment in 1721 that

> when the deputies thus act for their own interest, by acting for the interest of their principals; when they can make no laws but what they themselves, and their posterity must be subject to; when they can give no money, but what they must pay their share of; when they can do no mischief but what falls upon their own heads in common with their countrymen; their principals may then expect good laws, little mischief and much frugality.

Cato's Letters, quoted in Hayek, *Political Order*, 20–21.

66. Cf. Justice Jackson's comment that self-government requires that "the Executive be under the law, and that the law be made by parliamentary deliberations." *Youngstown Sheet and Tube Co. v. Sawyer*, 343 U.S. 579, 655 (1952) (Jackson, J., concurring). See also chapter 6 where Jackson is again invoked.

67. Except when the people, acting as constituent sovereign, create the regime itself. See Beer, *To Make a Nation*; Ackerman, *We the People*, esp. chaps. 1–3, 10–11. Even during the amendment process, the people are bound by constitutional rules. But see Locke on prerogative, *Two Treatises on Government*, chap. 14; Mansfield, *Taming the Prince*, passim.

68. *The Federalist* No. 57.

69. In chapter 5, I return to the rule of law, emphasizing that the content of the law must be principled. I mean that account, when added to the need to control faction, to encompass Madison's arguments on the rule of law.

70. *The Federalist* No. 63.

71. Cf. Robert J. Morgan's comment that "Madison's theory that the stability of the American republic would depend upon a constitutional superstructure of representation to modify the social power of conflicting interests bears little resemblance to the pluralists' political universe." "Madison's Theory of Representation," 882.

72. *The Federalist* No. 10.

73. "Parties," in Madison, *James Madison: Writings*, 505.

74. See Madison to Washington, 16 April 1787, quoted in Nedelsky, *Private Property*, 49; McCoy, *Last of the Fathers*, 41. Cf. Burke's comment that "[p]ublic life

is a situation of power and energy: he trespasses against his duty who sleeps upon his watch." *Thoughts on Our Present Discontents,* in Burke, *Selections,* 59.

75. *The Federalist* No. 45. As Drew McCoy puts it concerning the existence of a permanent public good: "[T]hese ends were not always promoted by—and certainly ought never to be automatically equated with—the apparent will of 'the people.'" *The Last of the Fathers,* 41. See also Beer, *To Make a Nation,* 261–64. It is striking that Madison used the phrase "the permanent... interests of the community" in one of the two important *Federalist* papers (Nos. 10 and 51) in which he spells out the basic ideas underlying his constitutional design. See also Madison, "Vices of the Political System of the U.S."

76. Jennifer Nedelsky argues that Madison assumed little needed to be said since the essential features of the public interest were well understood. See *Private Property,* chap. 2. Cf. Madison's comment, on the relation between the Constitution and particular laws, that it would be imprudent to provide in the document "a complete digest of laws on every subject to which the Constitution relates" and a corollary account of "all the possible changes which futurity may produce." Madison's whole discussion in *The Federalist* No. 44 is instructive on the relation between general purposes and particular acts.

77. *The Federalist* No. 10.

78. See Madison's letters to Jefferson dated 24 October and 1 November 1787, in Smith, *The Republic of Letters,* esp. 501. See also *The Federalist* No. 51. For a very helpful discussion of this point, see Beer, *To Make a Nation,* 261–64. Modern discussion tends to see rights and the public interest as in tension. See, e.g., Dworkin, *Taking Rights Seriously,* esp. chap. 7. In chapter 5, I present additional arguments about why the securing of rights should be understood as part of the public interest, not something in tension with it. Madison, however, often distinguished the two, but not as things adverse to one another. See, e.g., the language in *The Federalist* No. 10. But if I am correct that Madison understood that rights must be secured and that this would often require government action, especially if there were to be equal rights for all, then it is natural to see such exertions as part of the overall effort of government to serve the public interest.

79. *The Federalist* No. 37. See also Storing, "The Constitution and the Bill of Rights."

80. *The Federalist* Nos. 11–12, 30–31. See the discussion in Banning, *Sacred Fire,* 56, 62–63. It should be said that, while Madison favored a commercial society and advocated a role for government in promoting it, he was uneasy about manufacturing as the basis for economic prosperity. He favored a vibrant commercial society but envisioned it, if at all possible, as a population of freeholders. Still, manufacturing might well be acceptable. For the twists and turns in Madison's thoughts on these matters, see McCoy, *Last of the Fathers,* 175–77, 182–83, 186–89, 192–93.

81. Williams, *Contours of American History,* 145, quoting Madison.

82. Beer, *To Make a Nation,* 352, quoting Madison, "Vices of the Political System." Cf. Madison's comment that "it is not just government... where arbitrary restrictions, exemptions and monopolies deny to part of its citizens that free use of their faculties, and free choice of their occupations which... are the means of

acquiring property strictly so called." "Property," in Madison, *James Madison: Writings*, 516.

83. See Madison, *The Mind of the Founder*, pt. 4. For arguments about why we should be cautious in treating Madison as if he were Hamilton, see Banning, *Sacred Fire*, 212.

84. "Public Opinion," *National Gazette*, December 19, 1791, in Madison, *James Madison: Writings*, 500–501. See also Nedelsky, *Private Property*, 177–82; McCoy, *Last of the Fathers*, 127. As noted, Madison, as against Hamilton, did have some worries about manufacturing as a source of national wealth. He worried, for example, that a citizenry composed of wage earners would be too dependent economically to be stalwart in the defense of their liberty. See, e.g., Appleby, *Capitalism and a New Social Order*, 93. See also Banning, *Sacred Fire*, 297–99. As I indicate shortly, Madison also worried that commerce, and particularly manufacturing, would intensify the conflict between the propertied and the propertyless, and thus would weaken republican government.

85. "Parties," 504. See also Pole, *The Pursuit of Equality in American History*, who comments that Madison would probably have not thought that the problem of economic inequality would require the action of government "before the Hamiltonian programme began" (122).

86. *The Federalist* No. 62. Cf. Shklar, *American Citizenship*, chap. 2.

87. "Remarks on Mr. Jefferson's Draught of a Constitution," October 1788, in Madison, *Mind of the Founder*, 37. See also Madison's remarks added to his record of speeches at the Convention on the rights of suffrage, in Farrand, ed., *Records of the Federal Convention*, 3:450–55.

88. Madison to Rev. F. C. Schaeffer, 8 January 1820, quoted in McCoy, *Last of the Fathers*, 203.

89. See note 116.

90. Siegan, "The Constitution and the Protection of Capitalism."

91. See Parenti, "The Constitution as an Elitist Document"; Greenberg, "Class Rule and the Constitution." See Macpherson, *The Life and Times of Liberal Democracy*.

92. Tocqueville, *Democracy in America*, vol. 1, pt. 2, chaps. 4 and 9; vol. 2, pt. 2, chaps. 4–7.

93. See Haefele, "What Constitutes the American Republic?"; Haefele, "Problems of Democratic Social Choice."

94. *The Federalist* No. 10.

95. Ibid. William Leggett, a passionate commentator on American politics in the Jacksonian period, makes a similar point. See his remarks quoted in chapter 6 in the discussion of the character of a republican legislature.

96. Taylor, *An Inquiry into the Principles and Policy of the Government of the United States*, 51.

97. *The Federalist* No. 10. See also Elkin, "Madison and After." In his *Notes*, Madison wrote that "he was an advocate for the policy of refining the popular appointments by successive filtrations, but thought it might be pushed too far" (40).

98. *The Federalist* No. 62. Cf. Hamilton's discussion in *The Federalist* No. 60. See also *The Federalist* Nos. 63, 71.

99. *The Federalist* No. 10.

100. See *The Federalist* No. 63.

101. For Madison's view of political parties, see Milkis, *Political Parties and Constitutional Government*, chap. 1. Growing out of the conflict with Hamilton about the shape of the new polity, Madison came to have a more positive view of political parties, calling them "instrument[s] of democratic choice." Quoted in Banning, *Sacred Fire*, 4; Elkins and McKitrick, *The Age of Federalism*, 267, contend that political parties for Madison are "a necessary evil" and over time the emphasis came to fall on the "necessary" part of the formulation.

102. Cf. Beer's comment in *To Make a Nation* (283–64): "In each instance, an institutional structure of representative government enhances rational deliberation."

103. Each branch is to have "a partial agency in . . . the acts of the others." *The Federalist* No. 47.

104. See generally Adair, *Fame and the Founding Fathers*.

105. *The Federalist* No. 57. Hamilton agrees. In *The Federalist* No. 71, he says that the "republican principle demands, that the deliberate sense of the community should govern the conduct of those to whom they intrust the management of their affairs."

106. Madison's remarks to the Virginia ratifying convention on June 20, 1788. See Madison, *Papers of James Madison*, 11:163. Also reprinted in Elliot, ed., *Debates, Resolutions*, 536–37. Cf. Diamond, "Decent Though Democratic"; Lerner, "The Supreme Court as Republican School Master," in *The Thinking Revolutionary*. See also Storing, *What the Anti-Federalists Were For*, 72; Banning, "Second Thoughts on Virtue and the Course of Revolutionary Thinking," 247, where the full quote is given. Cf. Banning, *Sacred Fire*, 354–55. In addition, see *The Federalist* No. 55; Hamilton's remarks in *The Federalist* No. 76; Madison's comments in the "Government of the United States," in Madison, *James Madison: Writings*, 509; Madison's comment in *The Federalist* No. 49 that "it is the reason of the public alone that ought to control or regulate the government."

107. "Vices of the Political System," 77; *The Federalist* No. 10.

108. *The Federalist* No. 10. Cf. Mansfield, *Taming the Prince*, 264–74.

109. See Banning's discussion, esp. at 83, in *Sacred Fire*.

110. See *The Federalist* No. 10.

111. See the discussion in the following section on the social basis of the regime.

112. *The Federalist* Nos. 40, 55, and 57. Cf. Hamilton's remarks in *The Federalist* No. 60. Cf. Michael Schudson's account of Jefferson's views on the matter: "Citizens were to be democratic clinicians who could spot a rash of ambition before it became a full-grown tyranny. They would turn back the ambitious and self-seeking at the polls." "Social Construction of the 'Informed Citizen.'" 31. Cf. Tushnet, "Thomas Jefferson on Nature and Natural Rights."

113. *The Federalist* No. 10. Cf. *The Federalist* No. 57; Tushnet, "Thomas Jefferson on Nature and Rights"; Nedelsky, *Private Property*, chap. 2.

114. Cf. Beer, "Federalism and the Nation-State."

115. Mansfield, *Taming the Prince*, 271.

116. Madison estimated that, by 1929, the United States would have 192 million people and that this would end the nation's "precious advantage" of widely

distributed property and the general hope of acquiring it. It would be a society increasingly polarized between "wealthy capitalists and indigent laborers." Adair, "Experience Must Be Our Only Guide," in *Fame and the Founding Fathers*, 118. Adair is here quoting and discussing Madison's comments in "Notes on Suffrage [1829]," in Madison, *Letters and Other Writings*, 4:21–30.

117. *The Federalist* No. 10.

118. Of the six crucial features that were to characterize the American political order, this is the one that most rests on inferences drawn from the arguments Madison made in *The Federalist*. I here seek to make sense of what many, including Charles Beard (*Economic Interpretation of the Constitution*), Jennifer Nedelsky (*Private Property*), Richard Matthews (*If Men Were Angels*), and others have argued—namely, that Madison sought to ensure that people like himself, men of property and standing, would play a prominent role in the new government.

119. For more discussion on this point, see chapter 4.

120. Cf. Nedelsky, *Private Property*, esp. chaps. 2 and 6; Banning, *Sacred Fire*, 83–84. Hamilton (*The Federalist* No. 35) said that "the representative body, with too few exceptions to have any influence on the spirit of the government, will be composed of landholders, merchants, and men of the learned professions."

121. See *The Federalist* No. 10. Madison in a speech on suffrage to the Constitutional Convention said that "large districts are manifestly favorable to the election of persons of general respectability, and of probable attachments to the rights of property." Farrand, ed., *Records of the Federal Convention*, 3:454.

122. Madison understood that the propertied class also included those employed in commerce and manufacturing. Over time, the balance, he thought, would shift toward these two forms of economic activity. If that were to occur, and if my analysis here is correct, the sociological basis of the regime would, at some point, be significantly weakened. That is, indeed, what has occurred. See chapter 3. For a useful discussion here, see Morgan, "Madison's Theory of Representation in the Tenth Federalist," 874–75. Consider here Burke's comment that comfortable Whig families "stand upon such elevated ground as to be enabled to take a large view of the widespread and infinitely diversified combinations of men and affairs in a large society." "An Appeal from the New to the Old Whigs," in Burke, *Works*, 3:85–86. Consider also the comment of a modern political thinker: "Universalism is the natural ideology of the bourgeoisie since, as long as people living in the same society are thought to have some 'general,' 'common,' or 'public' economic interests, capitalists as a class represent these interests." Przeworski, *Capitalism and Social Democracy*, 21.

123. Madison thus did not look to those who would be inclined to move on when they did not get a satisfactory return on their investment, nor to land speculators, who are another kind of capitalist.

124. Madison, it would seem, was less sanguine about the political proclivities of financial types—stock-jobbers, for instance. I have already indicated that he was worried about the effects of the growth of manufacturing on political life. See Banning, *Sacred Fire*, chap. 10. I return to this point about the effects of a full-blown capitalism on the Madisonian design in chapters 3 and 8.

125. *The Federalist* No. 51.

126. Banning, *Sacred Fire*, passim.

127. A nice question is whether Madison, at bottom, viewed men of property as merely useful to the new regime. If it were possible and necessary, could their services be dispensed with? If so, he valued the rights of property more than the propertied.

128. Consider here—and more generally with regard to Madison's thought—Kant's remarks on republican government:

> The republican constitution is the only entirely fitted to the rights of man, but is the most difficult to establish and even harder to preserve, so that many say a republic would have to be a nation of angels, because men with their selfish inclinations are not capable of a constitution of such a sublime form. But [this is an error: republican government] is only a question of a good organization of the state, whereby the powers of each individual are so arranged in opposition that one moderates or destroys the other. . . . Man is forced to be a good citizen even if he is morally not a good person. The problem of organizing a state, however hard it may seem, can be even for a race of devils, if only they are intelligent.

On History, 111–12.

129. Cf. Beer's comment that Madison's "institutional ordering, however, was not simply restrictive, a set of restraints designed merely to prevent disorder. . . . They were primarily incentives" to promote "greater understanding of the public interest." *To Make a Nation*, 383. Herbert Storing comments that "the Federalists, moreover, reminded Americans that the true principle of the Revolution was not hostility to government but hostility to tyrannical government." *What the Anti-Federalist Were For*, 71. See also Wills, *Explaining America*, chap. 5.

130. For parallel views of Madison, see Wills, *Explaining America;* Sunstein, "The Enduring Legacy of Republicanism," in Elkin and Soltan, eds., *New Constitutionalism;* Bessette, *Mild Voice of Reason*. For earlier statements of my own on this question, see Elkin, *City and Regime*, chaps. 7–9; Elkin, "Constitutionalism's Successor," in Elkin and Soltan, eds., *New Constitutionalism;* Elkin, "Constitution of a Good Society," in Elkin and Soltan, eds., *Constitution of Good Societies*.

131. As Vardana Sinha, an undergraduate at the University of Maryland, puts it in an unpublished paper (on file with the author), "Madison's fundamental belief was in a strong government based on relatively unchanging institutions which guide lawmakers into a direction best suited to serve the public interest."

132. Beard, *Economic Interpretation*, 157.

133. Nedelsky, *Private Property*, 42.

134. Matthew Arnold, "Dover Beach," stanza 4. I owe to Ed Haefele the citation to Arnold as the source of the image of a "darkling plain."

135. In Elliot, ed., *Debates, Resolutions*, 3:37, cited in Storing, *What the Anti-Federalists Were For*.

136. Latham, *Group Basis of Politics*.

137. Dennis Mueller, *Public Choice; Public Choice II.*

138. Bessette, *Mild Voice of Reason.*

139. Diamond, *Founding of the American Republic.*

140. Bork, *Tempting of America.*

141. Wood, *Creation of the American Republic;* Pocock, *Machiavellian Moment;* Storing, *What the Anti-Federalists Were For;* Banning, *Sacred Fire.*

142. Cf. Tocqueville's comment that "if it is admitted that a man possessing absolute power may misuse that power by wronging his adversaries, why should not a majority be liable to the same reproach.... The power to do everything which I should refuse to any one of my equals, I will never grant to any number of them." *Democracy in America,* 240.

143. Cf. John Adam's assertion that a republic is "an empire of laws, not of men." *Thoughts on Government,* 83. Cf. Jonathan Boucher's comment that the "primary aim, therefore, of all well-framed Constitutions is, to place man, as it were, out of reach of his power, and also out of the power of others as weak as himself, but placing him under the power of law." *View of the Causes and Consequences of the American Revolution,* quoted in Reid, *Concept of Liberty,* 9.

144. Cf. Judith Shklar's comment that "it is clear that arbitrariness is the cardinal sin from which law must be kept at all costs." *Legalism,* 34. See also Burke's comment that "[l]aw and arbitrary power are at eternal hostility." Quoted in Reid, *Concept of Liberty,* 60.

145. For useful discussions of the relation between constitutional and limited government, see Friedrich, *Constitutional Government and Democracy;* Mansfield, *America's Constitutional Soul.*

146. *The Federalist* No. 10.

147. See, most notably, Hayek, *The Road to Serfdom.*

148. See chapters 5 and 8.

149. See, among many examples, Wechsler, "Towards Neutral Principles of Constitutional Law"; Wellington, "Common Law Rules." See also the discussion of legalism in chapter 4.

150. Cf. Storing, "Constitution and the Bill of Rights."

151. Among others, this is the error many libertarians fall into. See chapter 9. Consider here S. E. Finer's comment that "if the powerholders exercise self-restraint, the written constitution is unnecessary and if they do not then no written constitution will check them." *Five Constitutions,* 16.

152. Kammen, *A Machine That Will Go of Itself.* This does not imply that most citizens have understood or will understand the value of the Madisonian constitutional design. They might, especially in a period like the one after the Revolution in which experience of an unattractive form of government was widespread. Citizens might then rise above narrow interests as a result of the public-spiritedness engendered by a constitutional revolution and have, as a result of experience under a weak government, an incentive to pay attention. Madison, for one, thought that was true in 1787. But he also did not doubt the importance of rhetoric in making a case for the value of the new design, especially to people who might not appreciate its deep attractions and who might otherwise be inattentive.

Chapter Three

1. Before considering the weaknesses in Madison's constitutional theory, it is worth noting one unalloyed practical success of his design—namely, securing the rule of law in the sense that those who make the laws are bound by them. In this regard, with some minor exceptions—Congress has not been enthusiastic in applying all of the laws regulating the workplace to its own staff—the design has generally worked well in practice. We thus have succeeded in avoiding a fundamental feature of tyranny. But then so have all well-established contemporary democracies.

2. However, according to Drew McCoy, Madison *did* think slavery was a terrible instance of majority tyranny. But he could never find a way to proceed practically to eliminate it. See McCoy, *Last of the Fathers*, 235, chaps. 6–7.

3. Whether any have ended racial subjugation earlier than we have is a difficult question to answer, not least because no other Western regime has had among its people a significant racial minority that was central to its economic life.

4. Montgomery, *The Fall of the House of Labor;* Tomlins, *The State and the Unions;* Halperin et al., *The Lawless State.*

5. Madison says that the principal and most destructive disease of republican government is majority faction. But this is because—as will become apparent—he was wrong about the effects of the republican principle of majority rule on controlling minority faction. Moreover, majority factional rule is at least rule by a majority.

6. People like Felix Rohaytan and Robert Rubin, both prominent leaders of the financial industry, are exceptions to the run of high-level corporate executives.

7. For an overview of the changes in "property," see Appleby, *Capitalism and the New Social Order,* and MacDonald, *We the People* on the economic history of the early Republic. It is important to emphasize here that in addition to large land-holders there were from the beginning other kinds of significant property hold-ers, notably different kinds of merchants. See *The Federalist* No. 60. It is therefore possible that the Madisonian design, in this regard at least, was flawed from its inception.

8. Marx was one of the first to see that capitalism had such economic potential. See Marx and Engels, *Communist Manifesto.*

9. Japan and Korea are other examples of particularly strong links between busi-ness and the state, although in these two cases the links take a rather different form. See Johnson, *MITI and the Japanese Miracle.* What Lindblom calls the "privileged political position of business" is at work in all systems of advanced capitalism but varies in the extent of privilege and the degree of its visibility. See note 10.

10. If significant political privilege had existed for controllers of productive assets in Madison's time, would he have thought it necessary to devise political advantages for them? For more extensive discussion of the whole matter, see Elkin, "Pluralism in Its Place"; Elkin, *City and Regime,* chap. 7; Elkin, "Theory of American Busi-ness"; Elkin, "Business–State Relations." For the term "privileged position," see Lindblom, *Politics and Markets,* chaps. 12–17.

11. Except in wartime.

12. The classic argument here is Friedrich Hayek's. See *Law, Legislation and Liberty*. A comprehensive version of the whole question can be found in the "calculation debate" involving, among others, Ludwig von Mises and Oskar Lange. For a comprehensive discussion, see Steele, *From Marx to Mises*. For a different version, see Dahl, *Dilemmas of Pluralist Democracy*, esp. chap. 6.

13. Harold Wilson, a British Prime Minister in the latter half of the twentieth century, said that "all political history shows that the standing of a government and its ability to hold the confidence of the electorate at a general election depend on the success of its economic policy." Quoted in Oreskes, "Washington Talk." Cf. Karl Polanyi's comment concerning the development of modern industrial capitalism: "The employers were the owners of the factories and mines and thus directly responsible for carrying on production in society (quite apart from their personal interest in property). In principle, they would have the backing of all in their endeavor to keep industry going." *Great Transformation*, 235.

14. Cf. the characterization by two *New York Times* reporters of the powerful political role of the Business Roundtable, a major business organization. Walsh and Deutsch, "Is True Reform Possible?"

15. Lindblom, *Politics and Markets*, chap. 15.

16. Quoted in Wolfe, *America's Impasse*, 67.

17. Quoted in Miller, *Democratic Dictatorship*, 185; originally quoted in Furnas, *Americans: A Social History*.

18. Galambos and Pratt, *Rise of the Corporate Commonwealth*, 103. Readers who wonder how far back such views of the relation between business and the state go might find the following comments informative. John Millar, a theorist of the Scottish Enlightenment, said that "[t]he voice of the mercantile interest never fails to command the attention of government." Quoted in Lehman, *John Millar of Glasgow*, 339. In their physiocratic text, *Philosophe Rurale*, Quesnay and Mirabeau stated that "[i]t would be useless for the authorities to try to force him [the merchant, the banker, etc.] to fulfill the duties of a subject: they are obliged to induce him to fit in with their plan, to treat him as a master, and to make it worth his while to contribute voluntarily to the public revenue." Quoted in Meek, *The Economics of Physiocracy*, 63. The degree of privilege in these earlier periods was probably considerably smaller than after large-scale industrialization. However, the outlines of the relation between controllers of capital and the state were already apparent. The relation can also be found in regimes where capital is not privately controlled and the state is not democratic. See Kaminski, *Collapse of State Socialism*.

19. See McDonald, *Novus Ordo Seclorum*, passim; Banning, *Sacred Fire*, chap. 10. For a general treatment of the question, see Ferguson, *Cash Nexus*.

20. See Reich, *Locked in the Cabinet*, passim, and esp. 64, 90, 136, 213–14.

21. Cf. Daniel Webster's remarks (quoted in Beard, *Economic Basis of Politics*, 19, 21–23), in a speech to the Constitutional Convention of Massachusetts in 1820: "If the nature of our institutions be to found government on property, and that it should look to those who hold property for its protection, it is entirely just that property should have its due weight and consideration in political arrangements." Webster also said, according to Beard, that "the principle of representing property . . . was well

established by writers of the greatest authority." To be sure, Webster did not think that we then had or *should* have substantial economic inequality; to the contrary, he thought there was "great equality of condition" (23), but his overall view of the relation between property and political power is telling: the propertied must be given a political position commensurate with their holdings. His view parallels the position of Gouverneur Morris: if there *is* a concentration of property, and if the large-scale propertied aren't given a privileged role, they will subvert the regime. See Nedelsky, *Private Property*, chap. 3.

22. "Triangles" because there are three parties: interest groups, administrative agencies, and congressional subcommittees. "Iron" because they strongly resist outside influence. See Freeman, *Political Process*; Lowi, *End of Liberalism*. For changes from "triangles" to "networks," see Heclo, "Issue Networks and the Executive Establishment."

23. For additional discussion of this aspect of the permanent or public interest, see chapter 5.

24. For an account of why, see Dahl, *Preface to Economic Democracy*, chap. 2, and the discussion in chapter 5 of this book.

25. See chapters 5 and 7.

26. Again, see the discussion in chapter 5.

27. Smith, *Wealth of Nations*, 250. See also Miller, "The Constitution and the Spirit of Commerce," 155.

28. *The Federalist* No. 10.

29. See note 30. It is worth noting in this connection that James Wilson did discuss the matter. See Nedelsky's account of his views in *Private Property*, chap. 4; cf. Beer, *To Make a Nation*, chap. 11.

30. That the hole is not small is suggested by Madison's lack of sustained discussion concerning how to reconcile his propositions that under republican government the citizenry would be strongly prone to faction and that it would have "sufficient virtue" to accomplish its tasks. The two can be reconciled if it is recognized that public-spiritedness must be increased and thus the balance between factional propensity and this public-regarding outlook shifted toward the latter. This is the road down which Madison was reluctant to travel. For my effort at reconciliation, see chapters 6–8.

31. *The Federalist* No. 51.

32. See chapter 2.

33. See my assessment of the pertinent literature in "Business–State Relations," 115–39.

34. The canonical text is probably Stigler, *Citizen and the State*. See also the broad survey by Peter H. Aranson and Peter C. Ordeshook, "Public Interest, Private Interest."

35. *The Federalist* No. 51.

36. Home ownership, for example, is now approaching 70 percent. U.S. Bureau of the Census, "Reports on Residential Vacancies and Home Ownership."

37. As noted, such a privileged position will characterize *any* advanced industrial society, whether it is democratic or not. Consider, for example, the comments

of a highly regarded student of the Soviet economy that "the center of power [of the'Communist establishment'] seems to revolve around the directors of big industry." Aslund, "Moscow's New Power Center."

38. It will be otherwise when it comes to the aggregate interests of the community. See chapter 5.

39. Madison, *Notes of Debates in the Federal Convention*, 233. Later on, Madison reports, Morris wondered whether the "mechanics and manufactures who will receive their bread from their employers" will "be the secure and faithful Guardians of Liberty?" Ibid., 402. See also Nedelsky, *Private Property*, esp. 80, where she quotes Morris to the same effect.

40. Quoted in Storing, *What the Anti-Federalists Were For*, 57–58.

41. Taylor, who made this remark in 1814, is quoted in Aldrich, *Old Money*, 202.

42. And later on, apparently understood. See Banning, *Sacred Fire*, 348–67, 374.

43. For a similar assessment, see Nedelsky, *Private Property*, chaps. 2, 5.

44. Cf. Lance Banning's discussion in chapters 11 and 12 of *Sacred Fire*.

Chapter Four

1. I here follow J. L. Mackie: "[An] institution is constituted by many people behaving in fairly regular ways, with relations between them which transmit and encourage and . . . enforce those ways of behaving." *Ethics*, 80.

2. Van Parijs, "Social Justice as Real Freedom for All," 42.

3. Freeden, *Rights*, 66. Cf. Harvey Mansfield's comment that "Aristotle . . . seems to avoid the philosopher's mistake of despising what is practicable, because that mistake arises from or leads to irresponsibility in both citizenship and science." *Taming the Prince*, 47.

4. Bernard Williams says, apropos of philosophers like John Rawls who have been shaped by it, that "analytic philosophy has been much taken up with defining things." "The Reluctant Philosopher," 18.

5. Van Parijs, *Real Freedom for All*, 42.

6. "Means and Ends," 62. Cf. C. West Churchman and Ian Mitroff's argument that knowledge cannot be separated from the process of its implementation. "Management of Science."

7. Cf. Michael Novak's comment that "the notion that an unworkable ideal is a morally acceptable ideal, however, troubled me. If an ideal doesn't work, isn't that evidence that it is out of touch with reality? Isn't that a sign that it is a *false* ideal?" *Spirit of Democratic Capitalism*, 198. Consider also Lon Fuller's comment that "no abstractly conceived end ever remains the same after it has been given flesh and blood through some specific form of social implementation." "Means and Ends," 55. The whole of Fuller's essay is crucial for the argument I am making here.

8. Cf. Unger, *False Necessity*, 20–21: "For if the real meaning of an ideal depends upon its tacit institutional background, a shift in the latter is sure to disturb the former."

9. Consider the implications of G. A. Cohen's proposal in "Society with a State-imposed Egalitarian Income Distribution," discussed in Nagel, "Getting Personal,"

5. My point here is part of a larger argument that "ought" implies "can," but I am pointing to a particular kind of "can"—the prospects for creating viable institutions at reasonable cost—as being of central importance.

10. See Sandel, *Democracy's Discontent;* MacIntyre, *After Virtue.*

11. Surely, moreover, all political theories contain contradictions of some kind. If political life were simple enough to be captured within a limited number of logically entailed propositions, political theory would be an exercise for school children. It is unlikely that logical analysis can be used for much more than discarding grossly inadequate political and moral theories.

12. And which of us is free from contradictions in our character?

13. In general, there are always contradictions in our practices—if by that is meant that we try to pursue two or more purposes, the pursuit of any one interfering with the pursuit of the others. This is our condition as human beings—and we have evolved a variety of ways to deal with it. As Bernard Crick once said about contradictions in another context, the bourgeois state contains inner contradictions and that is what it is all about. Below I will suggest that there are limits to contradictions among practices. Political regimes, whose overall character is an institutional expression of a form of political rule, cannot tolerate just any sort of contradiction, or at least unlimited contradiction.

14. Cf. Bernard Williams's comment that "it seems . . . to be assumed that the virtues of an intellectual theory, such as economy and simplicity, translate into a desirable rationality of social practice." "Auto-da-fe," 36.

15. See Kymlicka, *Contemporary Political Philosophy.*

16. Cf. Charles Larmore's comment that most philosophers do not see as central to their enterprise "that the world is peopled not by one mind but many minds, each with its own point of view. . . . Questions arising from the manyness of minds and having to do with the relation in which persons stand to one another . . . are admitted to be important, but they play a minor role." "Lifting the Veil," 32.

17. See Elkin, "Economic and Political Rationality," and the references cited there.

18. Friedrich Hayek is more sophisticated than his colleagues in this regard, seeing that liberty is a product of law and thus of a certain kind of government. See the discussion just below. Many classical liberals, Hayek included, seem to suggest that something like the public interest or common good is essential to free government, but none of them pursue the matter, possibly because to do so would open up difficult questions concerning the links between individual liberty and that collective good.

19. See Hayek, *Road to Serfdom.*

20. *Law, Legislation and Liberty,* vol. 1, *Rules and Order,* 144.

21. Ibid., chap. 2. For a parallel distinction, see Michael Oakeshott's discussion of the civil condition versus the enterprise association in *On Human Conduct,* chap. 2.

22. *Law, Legislation and Liberty,* vol. 1, *Rules and Order,* 71.

23. For a view parallel to Hayek's in this respect, again see Oakeshott, *On Human Conduct,* esp. pts. 1–2. All legal theorists are probably formalists to some degree if

they believe, with A. V. Dicey, that there must be only one law that applies equally to officials and ordinary citizens. See Dicey, *Law of the Constitution*. A typical concern of formalists—one that probably has its roots in this concern that law should apply equally to governed as well as governors—is that for declarations to be law they must be general, not refer to known persons or groups. For a useful critique of this view of law, see Epstein, "Beyond the Rule of Law." In general, there are a variety of views concerning what the rule of law actually entails. They have in common the idea that government cannot do as it pleases, simply announcing its intentions and calling them law. The limits variously come from whether the appropriate procedures are followed in deciding on these intentions; whether the intentions must be general, applying to all equally; or whether certain procedures are followed in applying the intentions. Hayek's account is a combination of the first two, with the second predominating.

24. There are other criticisms to be made of Hayekian formalism that bear less directly on the question of how to think constitutionally. See Jones, "The Welfare State and the Rule of Law," 143–56.

25. *Constitution of Liberty*, 205.

26. Peter Levine says in a communication to the author that, in this context, it might be worth citing Hayek's idealization of eighteenth-century England (see, e.g., *Constitution of Liberty*, 171–75). According to Hayek, Levine indicates, it was during this period that the rule of law found its most ardent and sophisticated expression in theory and in legal decisions. But Hayek fails to acknowledge the high frequency of corrupt and arbitrary legislation that occurred during the same period. The Second Enclosure Movement was accomplished by means of many private bills that simply seized particular common lands and turned them over to the powerful local landowners (who were often Members of Parliament themselves). So the high point for the rule of law in court decisions and speeches coincided with one of its low points in practice—surely a problem for Hayek's approach.

27. Even though Hayek does set out an explicit institutional design in *Law, Legislation and Liberty*, vol. 3, *The Political Order of a Free People*, chap. 17, it is largely a blueprint, an inert set of definitions of institutional competences with very little consideration of what will motivate those who operate these institutions to do what is required of them.

28. *El Mercurio*, April 12, 1981, quoted in O'Brien, "Monetarism in Chile," 77–78.

29. *Road to Serfdom*, 7.

30. See especially *Principles of a Free Society*.

31. See the discussion of the public interest in chapter 5.

32. See Friedman, *Capitalism and Freedom*; Buchanan and Tullock, *Calculus of Consent*.

33. Not a few revolutionaries have thought that the people are not worthy of their efforts. It is the people that need to be replaced, they think, if the revolution is to succeed.

34. As most people in the lecturing trade surely know. What trade I am in is a reasonable enough question. The answer, of course, is the same one as Epstein, or indeed any political theorist who believes that political life as it is practiced can

be better. But it matters what the content of the lecture is. To encourage the right institutional design, as I do here, promises that there will be forces at work stronger than simply words to promote citizen restraint. Also, political theory and rhetoric are closer relatives than is often supposed today. And the mention of rhetoric raises the question as to whom the lectures of political theorists are directed. Surely, if the cause is some form of popular self-government, the citizenry is one audience. But is it the only audience, even the most important one?

35. Glover, *Humanity*, 6.

36. But not by all social choice theorists. See, e.g., Haefele, *Representative Government*; List and Goodwin, "Epistemic Democracy"; List and Dryzek, "Social Choice Theory"; List and Pettit, "Aggregation of Reason."

37. For both an account and criticisms of such aggregative views, see Elkin, "Economic and Political Rationality"; Elkin, *City and Regime*, chap. 10; Elkin, "Constitutionalism's Successor," in Elkin and Soltan, *A New Constitutionalism.*

38. A particularly clear example of this style of thinking can be found in Stokey and Zeckhauser, *Primer of Policy Analysis.*

39. A good example of an aggregative view of political institutions is Becker, "Competition and Democracy." The development of such arguments can be traced in Dennis Mueller's editions of *Public Choice.*

40. The question is almost certainly more complex to the degree that there are, as I think there must be, institutions not only designed to aggregate preferences but ones that are designed for such other purposes as fostering certain qualities among citizens and securing political equality. The discussion in the following chapters should make this clear.

41. Coleridge asks: "[W]hat is organization, but the connection of parts to a whole, so that each part is at once end and means?" Quoted in Holmes, *Coleridge,* 321.

42. In what follows, I do not present a sustained argument that this is so. I proceed mostly by what might be called "persuasive definition"—employing a terminology that invites the conclusion that the world operates in the fashion I am suggesting. If the definition of a regime combines, in a compelling way, a wide variety of crucial aspects of political life, we have warrant to think that the political world can indeed be understood as containing packages of institutions, and that, in our efforts at political understanding and reform, we need to take this as central in reaching judgments about how to proceed in our constitutional thinking and practice.

43. See Elkin, "Markets and Politics," 720–32; Elkin, "Economic and Political Rationality"; Elkin, "Political Institutions and Political Practice."

44. "By 'order' we shall describe a state of affairs in which a multiplicity of elements of various kinds are so related to each other that we may learn from our acquaintance with some spatial or temporal part of the whole to form correct expectations concerning the rest, at least expectations which have a good chance of being correct." Hayek, *Law, Legislation and Liberty,* vol. 1, *Rules and Order,* 36.

45. Ibid., 59.

46. See the discussion above in the section "Values and Institutions."

47. The widespread talk about trade-offs reflects the success that economists have had in shaping our thinking about the public world. Economists teach that

all problems of choice are ones of economizing—how much of what we value we must give up in order to get more of what we value. This is as true of apples and pears as it is of major political institutions. The apparent difference in importance and complexity, many economists believe, is just that, apparent. And the sooner we see that everything can be weighed in terms of preference satisfaction, utility, or money—all of which enable us to think about what use of our resources is efficient and thus allow us to judge the worth of something compared to something else— then the more rational will be our public life. There are lots of sarcastic replies to be made to such hubris—including such choice oldies as "Here is a man who knows the price of everything and the value of nothing." But the most telling comment is the one made by Amartya Sen that a society can be Pareto optimal (for present purposes meaning it can be efficient) and be perfectly disgusting. Sen, "Rational Fools." For my own rather less pithy view of the matter, see "Economic and Political Rationality."

48. Aristotle defined a regime as "an arrangement in cities connected with the office[s] [establishing] the manner in which they have been distributed, what the authoritative element of the regime is, and what the end of the partnership is in each case." *Politics* 1289a. In *Nicomachean Ethics* (181b15–20) he wrote that political science studies "what sorts of influences preserve and destroy cities, and what sorts do so for each sort of constitution." See also Ceaser, *Liberal Democracy and Political Science*; Salkever, *Finding the Mean*; Elkin, *City and Regime*, esp. chaps. 6–10. See also the discussion in chapter 1 of this book of our aspirations.

49. See Tocqueville, *Democracy in America*, vol. 1, chaps. 5–6; vol. 2, pt. 2, chap. 1; vol. 2, pt. 3, passim.

50. For example, see Arendt, *Origins of Totalitarianism*; Friedrich and Brzezinksi, *Totalitarian Dictatorship*.

51. See the discussion in chapters 7–8.

52. See chapters 3 and 8.

53. In the following section of this chapter, I consider on what grounds we can so call them.

54. See Walzer, *Spheres of Justice*, chap. 1.

55. There is thus a tension between the universalist claims for a particular conception of rule and the justice at which it aims, and the fact that all regimes have ruling classes. See the discussion in chapters 8–9.

56. Strongly egalitarian regimes are corrupted when the political stratum arrogates to itself special privileges, and argues that its privileges are needed if equality is to be served: cupidity masked by piety. Such regimes fail when the elite no longer believes in its own justifications, and, possibly, when few other people do.

57. I earlier said that behaviors that pull in opposing directions can co-exist. The point here is that there are limits to such "contradictions," and, to return to the earlier point, the critics of liberalism have not established that a liberal regime will somehow prevent the co-existence of particular combinations of, say, rights- and community-enhancing institutions.

58. Can forms of justice be ranked, one judged better than another? In what terms or on what scale can that judging take place?

59. Cf. here Haakonssen, *Natural Law*, esp. the summary in chap. 1 of how the term "natural law" has been used.

60. Are theocracies good regimes? They may be if they have principles that guide how political power may be used in the service of their theological purposes.

61. Cf. Raymond Aron's comment that "a regime without a principle is not a regime." "On Arendt and Totalitarianism," 109.

62. To say any more here means moving into the deeper reaches of political philosophy. I will only say that my view of how to distinguish between good and bad regimes draws on that strand of classical political philosophy that looks to the kind of beings we are. Defensible conceptions of justice are rooted in defensible conceptions of human nature—what goods or ends or virtues we can say are necessary to human well-being and what states of affairs, purposes, and vices we should guard against. For an excellent argument along these lines, see Salkever, *Finding the Mean.* Here is where we need political and moral philosophy—on the question of what it means to say something is good and on what basis we can say it.

63. Cf. Montesquieu, *Spirit of the Laws;* Tocqueville, *Democracy in America;* Almond and Verba, *Civic Culture;* Putnam, *Making Democracy Work.*

64. In chapter 5, I elaborate the conception of limits on government and center it on a conception of the public interest, much as Madison did when talking about the permanent interests of the community.

65. In chapter 5, I add to this formulation that a regime has a conception of the public interest.

66. Graham Walker says that a "constitution is a polity's normative architecture; it is that ensemble of standards, aspirations, and practices that forms a people's identity and is authoritative for their common life and institutions." "The Constitutional Good," 92.

67. See Oakeshott, *Human Conduct,* pt. 2, "On the Civil Condition."

68. See Maddox, "Note on the Meaning of Constitution," 806–7; Cicero, *De Re Publica,* bk. 1.

69. *The Federalist* No. 10.

70. See Shklar, *Legalism.*

71. Adams, *Thoughts on Government,* 83.

72. Very helpful overviews of the central issues here can be found in Shklar, *Legalism;* Unger, *Law in Modern Society;* Sunstein, *Legal Reasoning;* Posner, *Problems of Jurisprudence.*

73. Wechsler, "Towards Neutral Principles of Constitutional Law," 15–16. This article is one of the most widely cited in legal and constitutional theory. See Cass Sunstein's "Neutrality in Constitutional Law," 5.

74. "Mr. Liberty," 17–22. It is worth noting here that Dworkin's essay is, in part, written as a commentary on Learned Hand's argument that "a nation is sick when its most important collective moral decisions are reserved for specialists who decide in isolation and furnish the public with only Delphic verdicts" (Dworkin's phrasing, at 21). Below, I comment directly on Dworkin's mix of legal reasoning and moral philosophy. Here I am only interested in his juxtaposition of politics and law.

75. See, e.g., Ely, *Democracy and Distrust*, esp. chaps. 4–6.

76. Among those who hold this view, just what to do with the fact that the Constitution and its remaking were acts of democratic will—see Bruce Ackerman's *We the People*—has occasioned a good deal of anguished writing. For two serious efforts, see Burt, *Constitution in Conflict*; Bickel, *Least Dangerous Branch*.

77. See Nedelsky, *Private Property*.

78. "What were the concerns that created a virtual obsession with separating public law from private law, both conceptually and practically during the nineteenth century? Above all was the effort of orthodox judges and jurists to create a legal science that would sharply separate law from politics." Horwitz, "History of the Public/Private Distinction," 1423. See also Kennedy, "Stages of the Decline of the Public/Private Distinction."

79. Nedelsky, *Private Property*, 190. See also her discussion at 197–202.

80. West, "Rethinking the Rule of Law." West cites, among others, Fiss, "Objectivity and Interpretation"; Scalia, "The Rule of Law as a Law of Rules."

81. Snowiss, *Judicial Review*, 5. Cf. Shannon Stimson's comment that in Madison's view a Council of Revision made up of those who would rule on whether a law was outside of the spirit of the Constitution was necessary, but that he "never conceived of it as a judicial body but as a political alternative to one." *American Revolution in Law*, 117. Also relevant here is Martin Shapiro's comment that in France the review of the constitutionality of legislation is "not decided by normal jurisprudential techniques." "Judicial Review in France," 5.

82. There was no need to spell out a specific set of rights because nothing in the new Constitution suggested that people did not have these rights, and by listing them it might be implied that the rights on the list were the only ones the people had—which is, of course, what has happened. Consider here the controversy over whether there is a right to privacy.

83. On Madison and the Bill of Rights, see Storing, "Constitution and the Bill of Rights"; Banning, *Sacred Fire*, chap. 9.

84. William Simon says that "the [legal] culture's premise [is] that the organization of productive relations is not a matter of 'public' concern." That is, the legislature should not concern itself with such matters—which is a political judgment if ever there was one. "Social Republican Property," 1335.

85. The obvious high points of such discussion would include Locke, Madison, and Mill.

86. See Dahl, *Preface to Economic Democracy*, 21–31.

87. See Shklar, "Liberalism of Fear."

88. "Natural Law Revisited," 165.

89. The phrase is Dworkin's, quoted in Seller, "Forming a More Perfect Union," a review of Dworkin, *Freedom's Law*.

90. Charles Fried comments that "there is something peculiar, to say the least, about asking courts to be engines of philosophical analysis and development." "Artificial Reason of the Law," 37.

91. Bickel, *Least Dangerous Branch*, 183–98, passim.

92. Ely, *Democracy and Distrust*.

93. "Does law have special forms of logic? Does it offer a distinctive form of reasoning? To both questions, the simplest answer is no." Sunstein, *Legal Reasoning*, 13. Cf. Richard Posner's comment that "there is no such thing as 'legal reasoning.'" *Problems of Jurisprudence*, 459. Consider also Sanford Levinson's characterization of Oliver Wendell Holmes's view that "there is no autonomous technique of 'thinking like a lawyer.'" "Strolling Down the Path of the Law," 1229.

94. As is true in France. See Shapiro, "Judicial Review in France."

95. See the discussion in chapter 5.

96. See, e.g., Hayek, *Law, Legislation and Liberty*, vol. 1, *Rules and Order*, chaps. 5–6.

97. See also the discussion in chapter 6 of a republican high court. For an excellent discussion of the character of this sort of reasoning—and an accompanying argument about its limits when it comes to the constitutive matters that are our concern here—see Sunstein, *Legal Reasoning and Political Conflict*.

98. Cf. James Stoner's comment that Coke gave "precedence to prudence over jurisprudence." *Common Law and Liberal Theory*, 66.

99. Quoted in Banning, *Sacred Fire*, 278–79, from a speech by Madison, June 17, 1789; Madison, *Papers of James Madison*, 12:232.

100. I should here emphasize the relation between my argument and that of the group of legal theorists who travel under the banner of "Critical Legal Studies." As I understand that movement, one of its central claims is that courts are essentially political bodies. With this I agree. But if it is part of the movement's argument that there is no room for the exercise of reasoned argument in deciding constitutive matters, then I part company. My view is that while there is no special sort of legal reasoning with regard to constitutive matters, there can be political reasoning—in contrast to the brute exercise of political power.

101. With suitable adjustments the same metaphor works for any good regime. All good regimes need to make room for the exercise of practical reason in the service of giving concrete meaning to broadly defined purposes.

102. Or more precisely, ship–*re*builders, since if they are already at sea they must be already sailing in something. That they are already in a boat emphasizes the point made in chapter 1 that the activity of political constitution rarely, if ever, starts *de novo*: there is an institutional inheritance. On the shipbuilding image, see the early formulation by Otto Neurath: "We are like sailors who have to rebuild their ship on the high seas without ever being able to take it apart in a dock and reconstruct it out of the best parts." "Protokollsatze." Quoted in Blumenberg, *Shipwreck with Spectator*, 77. Note also that Neurath suggests another reason why what I have called the "rationalism of the machine shop" is an unattractive way to think about institutions: we have no political dry dock.

103. Cf. my discussion earlier in this chapter of political institutions as modes of association.

104. A powerful statement of this last view can be found in Oakshott, *On Human Conduct*.

105. For a longer statement, see Elkin, "Economic and Political Rationality"; Elkin, *City and Regime*, chap. 10.

106. "Means and Ends," 54.

107. For a parallel discussion with a particular concern for ethics, see Annas, *Morality of Happiness*. Annas comments that "many modern ethical theories have as their ideal the model of derivation, from a set of favored primitive terms or theses" (442). She contrasts this with ancient theories that look to "a practical skill."

108. Madison said that his approach to thinking through various features of the new constitution was frequently "if...not the language of reason...that of republicanism." "Parties," 504.

109. Cf. Machiavelli, *The Prince*, and his discussion of fortune, necessity, virtue, and acquisition.

110. *Law, Legislation and Liberty*, vol. 1, *Rules and Order*, 17.

Chapter Five

1. Madison's twentieth- and twenty-first century successors also offer accounts of the appropriate limits on popular rule, but they are no more convincing than was Madison. Theodore Lowi in *The End of Liberalism* looks to "good law" but ends up with a kind of proceduralism that he elsewhere criticizes. Bruce Ackerman in *We the People* looks to a higher law politics for the substance of the limits on popular rule, but is unconvincing on whether it is robust enough to do the job. Robert Dahl's democratic proceduralism, which he has developed in the course of his many works, starting with *A Preface to Democratic Theory*, leaves him deeply ambivalent about whether there should be any substantive limits on popular rule. The result is an uneasy account of their substance, and a tendency to rely too heavily on the more noble side of human nature. Each of Madison's successors is struggling to define the limits on what the people may do without relying on transpolitical standards (Dahl and Lowi) or only mildly so (Ackerman). Each offers a possible approach. But we should be uneasy about following in any of their paths, at least if we intend to do so at full gallop. For more on these theorists, see chapters 9–10.

2. See Sen, "Rational Fools." See also Sen, *Collective Choice*, chaps. 1–6; Sen, "Utilitarianism and Welfarism."

3. And I agree. See chapter 7.

4. See Wechsler, "Towards Neutral Principles of Constitutional Law." See also Horwitz, "Public/Private," 1425.

5. Very helpful discussions, on which I have relied heavily, can be found in Sunstein, "Neutrality in Constitutional Law"; Nedelsky, *Private Property*; Fisher, Horwitz, and Reed, eds., *American Legal Realism*, esp. sec. 4.

6. See Horwitz, "Public/Private"; Freeman and Mensch, "Public/Private Distinction."

7. Horwitz, "Public/Private," 1426.

8. Sunstein, "Neutrality in Constitutional Law."

9. But see the discussion of self-limitation below and in the succeeding chapters.

10. Nedelsky, *Private Property*, chap. 6. See also Radin, "Liberal Conception of Property."

11. It may turn out that the current Supreme Court is attempting to provide such standards, but the recent record is mixed. See note 18.

12. Nedelsky, *Private Property*, 254 ff.

13. Michelman, "Takings 1987," 1621. See Sterk, "Federalist Dimension" for the later period.

14. Nedelsky, *Private Property*, 225. Cf. Laurence Tribe's comment that regulation of property would be judicially sustained if "any state of affairs either known or reasonably inferable afforded support for the legislative judgment." *American Constitutional Law*, 450. See also Nedelsky, *Private Property*, 231–40. None of this means that there is no right to property. Plausibly there is; see the discussion below on rights. Even if there is such a right, however, it does not provide judges or lawmakers generally with clear and general guidelines about the appropriate reach of public power and thus how to demarcate the boundary between the public and private spheres.

15. This was said at a pretrial hearing and later cited by the U.S. Court of Appeals for the Sixth Circuit in *Local 1330, United Steelworkers of America v. United States Steel Corporation*, 631 F.2d 1264, 1280 (6th Cir. 1980). The appellate court also quoted the lower court's observation that "[u]nfortunately, the mechanism ... to recognize this new property right, is not now in existence in the code of laws of our nation" (631 F.2d at 1266, quoting 492 F. Supp. 1, 10 (N.D. Ohio 1980)).

16. Nedelsky, *Private Property*, 231.

17. Locke, *Two Treatises of Government*, 305–6. Locke argued that the invention of money allows us to get around the limits on accumulation. Whether he is convincing is another matter. Also open to discussion is whether Locke's argument for a regime built around property ownership is meant to rest on a right to private property rooted in labor. See also the discussion by Dahl, *Preface to Economic Democracy*, 73–83.

18. The Supreme Court in a recent decision on "takings" has shown some inclination to return to a stronger view of property rights. See *Dolan v. City of Tigard*, 512 U.S. 374 (1994).

19. For one version of this argument, see Alexander, "Public/Private Distinction."

20. See the U.S. Supreme Court case *San Antonio Indep. Sch. Dist. v. Rodriguez*, 411 U.S. 1 (1973).

21. Recall that in chapter 4, I considered the question of whether, if there is something called legal reasoning, it can help with the constitutional design of regimes. Here my concern is whether it can tell us what the limits are on public authority.

22. A nice, clear statement of the claim can be found in Wechsler, "Towards Neutral Principles of Constitutional Law," esp. 15.

23. As the state of Alaska does.

24. See chapter 6.

25. The most wide-ranging and compelling discussion of these and related matters is in the work of Samuel Bowles and Herbert Gintis. See esp. *Democracy and Capitalism*.

26. See ibid., chap. 3.

27. "Humanist Liberalism," in Rosenblum, ed., *Liberalism and the Moral Life*, 43.

28. See Josephson, *Gender, Family, and the State*.

29. Although I criticize legal reasoning here and in my discussion of the kind of reasoning needed for thinking about republican political constitution, this does not

commit me to doubting that legal theory, courts, and lawyers have something of great significance to contribute to republican government. See chapter 6. To further forestall needless worry, my argument here is that, whether or not legal reasoning exists, and whether it is useful in matters other than ones I discuss, it does not much help in the matters with which I am concerned in this book.

30. As well as a proposal by Ackerman that we will consider in chapter 9. See also Lowi, *End of Liberalism*.

31. *The Federalist* No. 10.

32. *The Federalist* No. 51.

33. *The Federalist* Nos. 63 and 71.

34. *The Federalist* No. 10.

35. On Thatcher's comment, see her interview in *Women's Own*, 3 October 1987, and Barry's discussion of her remark in *Does Society Exist*. On the existence of the public interest, see Barry, *Political Argument*, chaps. 12–13; Goodin, "Institutionalizing the Public Interest"; Flathman, *The Public Interest*.

36. For some recent examples of theories of democratic deliberation, see Bohman, *Public Deliberation*; Elster, ed., *Deliberative Democracy*; Gutmann and Thompson, *Democracy and Disagreement*. My first attempt at an account of the public interest in *City and Regime* was largely proceduralist and as a result was flawed in the ways indicated. As is apparent, I now believe that more of a substantive nature can and must be said about the public interest.

37. See, e.g., *Preface to Democratic Theory*, esp. chap. 1.

38. See *Democracy and Its Critics*, esp. chap. 21.

39. For an explicit statement by Dahl that this is the public interest, see ibid., 306–8.

40. See the discussion later in this chapter on whether something can be the interests of someone even if they themselves do not recognize this.

41. See, most notably, Braybrooke and Lindblom, *Strategy of Decision*; Lindblom, *Politics and Markets*; Hayek, *Road to Serfdom*, and *Law, Legislation and Liberty*, vol. 2, *Mirage of Social Justice*, 1–100.

42. But it rests on substantive commitments, as we shall see.

43. See Ackerman, *Social Justice*; Rawls, *Political Liberalism*.

44. *Political Order of Changing Societies*, 24.

45. *In Defense of Politics*, 177. By making decisions "politically" Crick means employing a form of nonviolent political rule in societies where a large variety of wills must be accommodated. See additionally Robert Dahl's discussion of the public interest in *Democracy and Its Critics*, chap. 21. Also relevant here is Bobbio, *Future of Democracy*.

46. *Natural Law and Natural Rights*, 155.

47. There are three prerequisites for serving the public interest. Any theory of republican political constitution presupposes that there will be civil peace, governmental stability, and security against foreign threat. Without them, any account of the public interest is largely beside the point if we are concerned with political practice. Thus, John Jay said (in *Federalist* No. 3): "Among the many objects to which a wise and free people find it necessary to direct their attention, that of providing for

their *safety* seems to be first." Consider also Hobbes's *Leviathan*, where it is argued that civil peace, governmental stability, and security against foreign threat are the reasons that people enter into a governmental compact. See as well the preamble to the U.S. Constitution, which specifies that among the purposes for the which the Union was formed are to "insure domestic tranquility" and "provide for the common defense." As Madison himself said, the first task in designing a constitution is to "enable the government to control the governed; and in the next place to oblige it to control itself" (*The Federalist* No. 51). It is also an elementary point of all statecraft that if foreign threats are not resisted, any government will be prevented from choosing the purposes it shall pursue, no less serving the public interest. The question of international security raises difficult questions about the organization of lawmaking and executive power. The focus here is on what may be called the "domestic political constitution." A comprehensive theory of political constitution would need to attend to both concerns. Justice Jackson, in *Terminiello v. Chicago*, 337 U.S. 1, 37 (1949) (Jackson, J., dissenting), stated the general point when he commented that a constitution is not a suicide pact. See chapter 9, note 20.

What about ecological sustainability? It depends on whether it must be attended to before anything else other than the prerequisites just noted. If it must—that is, if it is a foundation of any political order intended for the long haul—it too is a prerequisite of serving the public interest. At present, this is far from clear.

48. *The Federalist* No. 10.

49. Dahl, *Preface to Economic Democracy*, chap. 1.

50. In the context of discussions about "inequality of property," Madison talked about "political equality among all." See Pole, *Pursuit of Equality*, 122. See generally Sen, *Development as Freedom*.

51. *Message to Congress on the State of the Union*, January 11, 1944, in *Public Papers and Addresses*, vol. 13, 40–42. For a very helpful discussion of the relation between work and citizenship, see Shklar, *American Citizenship*, where she comments that "earning and spending are hardly private in the sense that prayer and love might be" (63).

52. For additional discussion of this argument, see chapter 7.

53. See chapter 2; Sunstein, "Beyond the Republican Revival."

54. "Liberalism in its origins is an ideology of work," observes Isaac Kramnick in *Republicanism and Bourgeois Radicalism*, at 1. Robert Kennedy said that the solution to poverty is "dignified employment at decent pay." Quoted in Sandel, *Democracy's Discontent*, 303.

55. Commercial republican economic equality will also require a wider distribution of the ownership of capital. However, this is too complicated a matter to discuss here, but see the brief discussion in chapter 10. For some useful ideas, see Kelso and Adler, *Capitalist Manifesto*; Stauber, *New Program for Democratic Socialism*; Dahl, *Preface to Economic Democracy*; Meade, *Liberty, Equality and Efficiency*; Ackerman and Alstott, *Stakeholder Society*. Consider in this context the comments of Daniel Webster: "In my judgment...a republican form of government rests, not more on" "political Constitution than on these laws which regulate the descent and transmission of property." Webster went on to say that the pattern of property

distribution "fixed the . . . frame and form of government." From a speech given to the Massachusetts Constitutional Convention in 1820, quoted by Lustig, *Liberal Corporatism*, 279 n.34, citing Baker and Mason, eds., *Free Government in the Making*.

56. Lindblom, *Politics and Markets*, chaps. 12–17; Elkin, "Markets and Politics."

57. Tocqueville, *Democracy in America*, 280. Nancy Rosenblum says that "government should insure background conditions that make forming, joining and leaving groups practicable." *Membership and Morals*, 350.

58. A very useful discussion of this point is by Hayek in *Law, Legislation and Liberty*, vol. 1, *Rules and Order*, chap. 4.

59. Cf. Hayek's comment that "the fathers of the American Constitution would probably have been horrified if it had been suggested that their handiwork was intended to be superior to the rules of just conduct as embodied in the common law." Ibid., 178.

60. Cf. Michael Walzer's comment that "[t]he central issue for political theory is not the constitution of the self but the connection of constituted selves, the pattern of social relations." "Communitarian Critique of Liberalism," 21.

61. Cf. Harvey Mansfield's comment on Montesquieu that "he shows how liberty *emerges* in a whole which mixes the law with what we would call its conditioning factors in a series of 'relations.'" *Taming the Prince*, 221.

62. *The Federalist* No. 10.

63. There is a dilemma here. To rest the definition of faction on aims or intentions will sometimes make it difficult to determine whether we are dealing with a faction. This is especially true if the organization or group says that they value some elements of the public interest. On the other hand, if we look to actual behavior, it may be too late. The factional damage is already done.

64. Compare here two of Robert Dahl's comments on the public interest. In *Dilemmas of Pluralist Democracy* (chap. 7), he dismisses the idea of a public interest, at least one that requires any amount of abstract reasoning on the part of the citizenry. In *Democracy and Its Critics* (chap. 21), he presents a view of the public interest as being rooted in what it takes to maintain democratic political institutions.

65. See chapters 6–8.

66. May we say, then, that an objective public interest is an aristocratic element in a regime of popular self-government? Cf. Mansfield, *Taming the Prince*, 56–57.

67. That the roots of the public interest are in the day-to-day life of the society indicates why many are unlikely to disagree. Moreover, the fact of disagreement does not mean that the public interest is not in the interests of the dissenting citizens. In fact, it will be in their interests to the degree that these citizens aspire to have a fully realized commercial republic. Whether at any given moment a citizen makes the connection between serving the public interest and the realization of a commercial republic is another—albeit important—matter. This is, of course, the old problem of "real" versus "apparent" interests, although no less important for being old. It also brings to mind Tocqueville's formulation of "self-interest rightly understood." *Democracy in America*, vol. 2, pt. 2, chap. 9.

68. Cf. David Held's question whether the participants in a thought experiment of a Rawlsian kind would "not define their good or interest in terms of a common

structure of political action, which would shape and bind all forms of public power, and which would create the basis for an association of equally free persons?" *Democracy and the Global Order*, 169–70. Consider also Robert Dahl's comment that the public interest is what the citizenry "would choose if they possessed the fullest attainable understanding" of the matter, and if they were free of bias. *Democracy and Its Critics*, 308. They would also need to be free of coercive relations. See Held, *Democracy and the Global Order*, 162, for details of the experiment.

Held later talks about the public interest—his term is "democratic public law"—and says "it specifies the conditions necessary for members of a political community to be free and equal in a process of self-determination" (200). He talks about these conditions as "the democratic good" (205).

69. "To 'Ought' from 'Is,'" 26.

70. Regimes are to be judged by their manner of rule, I have said.

71. The public interest of other good regimes may also include the securing of rights.

72. For a different sort of argument assimilating rights to the public interest, see Finnis, *Natural Law*, chap. 8.

73. Cf. Oakeshott's view of rights in "Political Economy of Freedom," in *Rationalism in Politics*, and *On Human Conduct*, pt. 2. Michael Ignatieff simply says that "we need to stop thinking of human rights as trumps and begin thinking of them as part of a language that creates the basis for deliberation." "Attack on Human Rights," 116. Cf. John Hart Ely's comment that "freedoms are more secure to the extent they find foundation in the theory that supports our entire government, rather than gaining protection because the judge deciding the case thinks they're important." *Democracy and Mistrust*, 102.

74. The *justification* for rights may concern individuals, but that is another matter.

75. See Dworkin, *Taking Rights Seriously*.

76. For example, Galston, *Liberal Purposes*.

77. "Human Rights," 60. We might add here that human beings must not be treated as "meat"—that is to say, cruelly—and deprived of the liberty to think as they wish, because if there is value to be found in the world, it can only be broadly known and understood by people who are free to think and talk about it. God may speak, and people hanging on meathooks may hear Him, but they are unlikely to understand Him very well or work out the implications of His message without liberty. Talk about rights is one way to make this point.

78. Even if I am wrong on both counts—about the transconventional value of good regimes and rights—the language of rights can still be exceedingly useful. It points to transpolitical (as oppposed to transconventional) standards or values, that is, to values that are not conventions of the politics of the day, but are the normative inheritance of our political way of life. The justification for rights would not then transcend all politics and is not then transconventional, but the value of rights gains our assent as the distillation of long-standing practices that promise a substantial measure of human good. We may not be able to go much further in our effort at justification but nor are we, as a result, obliged to give up our belief in rights. Thus, it is probably widely agreed that people should not be treated as

instruments of the will of others, that we cannot flourish as human beings if we are treated arbitrarily and told what to do without reasons being offered, and be subject, without warning, to changes in the rules. The language of rights is the one we, the makers and inheritors of a republican political way of life, have worked out to talk about these matters. In this we are acting on a history of observations and generalizations about what allows human beings to live their lives with a modicum of hope and satisfaction.

79. Among contemporary theorists, the most notable is Ronald Dworkin. See *Taking Rights Seriously,* chaps. 6–7, 12.

80. This, nevertheless, seems to be Robert Nozick's view. See *Anarchy, State, and Utopia,* chap. 1.

81. Cf. Robert Dahl's comment that "tested by mental experiments in the realm of hypothetical cases, it appears impossible to discover any right that can reasonably be justified in utter disregard for its consequences for the well-being of persons affected by the exercise of that right." *Dilemmas of Pluralist Democracy,* 97. See also William Galston's comment: "As Griffin, Nagel, Scanlon, Flathmen, and Sen (among others) have argued, it runs contrary to the most basic facts and judgments of our experience to assert that there is a good such that even the slightest loss cannot be counterbalanced by even tremendous gains along other dimensions. Amounts matter." Galston, *Liberal Purposes,* 172, where the citations to the works of the authors mentioned are given.

82. Although even here, those with a turn of mind for such things can no doubt come up with a story in which forcing people to do this is the price for avoiding the nuclear destruction of a significant part of the human race.

83. There will be other kinds of lawmaking in a fully realized republican regime, notably that concerned with the aggregation of interests. See chapter 8.

84. Since lawmaking built around a class politics can also serve the public interest, a full theory of republican political constitution must set out the incentives that promote the appropriate version of it. See chapter 8.

85. Not all lawmaking will confront such tensions or contradictions, but it is probable that these will be present in the most important lawmaking efforts because they cut deep into what constitutes the regime.

86. Consider in this context Hayek's comment that "it is the character rather than the volume of governmental activity that is important." *Constitution of Liberty,* 22.

87. Cf. Madison's discussion in *The Federalist* No. 37.

88. See Galston, *Liberal Purposes.*

Chapter Six

1. To demonstrate this requires more extensive discussion than I can present here. However, I have said much of relevance in the preceding chapters, especially chapters 2 and 3, and I will say more in the remaining chapters. For additional discussion, see Elkin, *City and Regime;* Elkin, "Citizen and City"; Elkin, "Constitutional Theory of the Commercial Republic."

2. The constitutional theory I am presenting here is not, therefore, comprehensive. There are three substantial omissions: the constitutional politics for the conduct of foreign affairs, whose absence I have already noted; the politics of the federal system (for there are good reasons to suppose that this is a valuable feature of a republican constitutional design); and, although I have touched on the subject, the role of courts as custodians of "a common law for the age of statutes." See Calabresi, *Common Law for the Age of Statutes*. The focus here is on national political institutions in their guise as lawmakers for domestic matters.

3. *Drift and Mastery*, 18.

4. *The Federalist* No. 22.

5. See chapter 5.

6. Apart from the necessity of such lawmaking for securing the public interest, deliberative ways of lawmaking are valuable for a more or less separate reason: they encourage us, or more precisely those who speak for us, to speak about public matters in the elevated language of the public interest even as less noble motives are at work. What we sometimes call "hypocrisy" or "cynicism" is the price vice pays to virtue. Imagine, by contrast, lawmaking where the currency of speech is a parading of narrow and self-interested motives and interests. On what grounds might this be supposed to be better? That it is more frank? But so is the sausage factory's detailed account of how it makes sausage. There may be occasions in which we wish to know all the gruesome details, but they probably come much less often than the votives of frankness suppose.

7. "Philadelphia Revisited," 1085.

8. *The Federalist* No. 78.

9. The quote is from Justice Ginsburg's James Madison Lecture at New York University Law School, March 1993, quoted in Lewis, "How Not to Choose." Cf. Robert Post's comment after the Supreme Court upheld the new campaign finance law that "the Court gave Congress space to breathe" because the "tension was too high," that Justice O'Connor "understood that the rhythm of the Court's relationship with the Congress had to be attended to." Quoted in Greenhouse, "A Court Infused with Pragmatism." Stephen Griffin's discussion of how the separation of powers actually works is very helpful in this context. He argues that the Court "enforces the Constitution" but "only with the permission or acceptance of the political branches." He further argues that the political branches play the central role "in American constitutionalism as a whole." "Constitutional Theory Transformed," 305–6. See also Eisgruber, *Constitutional Self-Government*, 3–5, and see generally chaps. 1–3, 6.

10. Montesquieu said of the separation of powers: "The form of these three powers...should be rest or inaction. But as they are constrained to move by the necessary motion of things, they will be forced to move in concert." *Spirit of the Laws*, pt. 1, chap. 6, p. 164.

11. "Philosophie politique: de la souveraineté." Quoted in Manent, *Intellectual History of Liberalism*, 101.

12. See generally Beer, *To Make a Nation*. Party-corporatist regimes deal with the complexity of the public interest by having an "informal" division of powers

between cabinet, party organizations, and the civil service, with the parliament and the courts in the background ready to wheel themselves in if something startling and outrageous is being attempted. In the case of republican regimes like the American one, the separation is formal, built into the constitutional design. For us, formality is key.

13. Hamilton said, after his comment in *The Federalist* No. 78 cited above, that not only does the Constitution not suppose a superiority of the judicial to the legislative power, "it only supposes that the power of the people is superior to both." When Hamilton noted that where legislation "stands in opposition to that of the people declared in the Constitution the judges ought to be governed by the latter," he may be understood as saying that the Supreme Court has the power of judicial review; it is not exercising, nor does it have, the power of judicial supremacy. Cf. Murphy, Fleming, and Barber, *American Constitutional Interpretation*, 264–68. Said differently, Hamilton enjoined the high court to look to the Constitution when judging the law that lies behind the cases that come before it. However, if the legislature contends that the relevant law is constitutional, the Supreme Court's view is not supreme. The people's is.

14. Cf. Locke, *Two Treatises* (on the sovereignty of the people and that disputes between executive and legislature can only be settled by them). See also Zuckert, "Hobbes, Locke and the Problem of the Rule of Law," in *Launching Liberalism;* Ackerman, *We the People*, pt. 2. Although Ackerman's distinction between normal and higher law politics faces grave difficulties (see chapter 10), he is very helpful for understanding just how the kind of impasse I have laid out might be resolved in a fashion consistent with my proposal for a republican political constitution. Also relevant here is the theory of critical elections, which claims that certain elections set in motion and then confirm major changes in public policy. The seminal works are Key, "Theory of Critical Elections," and Burnham, *Critical Elections.*

15. Robert Dahl, in his discussion of the separation of powers, misses this point. See *Preface to Democratic Theory*, 136. See also note 13 above.

16. *The Federalist* No. 51.

17. Kammen, *Machine That Would Go of Itself.*

18. Richard Posner, a federal appeals court judge, says, however, that there is considerably less deliberation in the Supreme Court than there used to be. "The People's Court."

19. Cf. Robert McCloskey's comment that "judicial review in its peculiar American form exists because America set up popular sovereignty and fundamental law as twin ideals and left the logical conflict between them unresolved." *American Supreme Court*, 247. He also says that "the Court learned to be a political institution." Ibid.

20. Consider here Harold Berman's argument that the rule of law is the result of the political achievement of creating an independent legal profession. *Law and Revolution*, pt. 2. It is worth noting here that Congress can and indeed has played a significant role in protecting rights. Witness voting rights, civil rights, and disability rights legislation. See Griffin, *American Constitutionalism*, 116 ff.

21. It will help here to remember that lawmaking in the public interest is reflexive.

22. See chapters 2 and 3. See also the discussion in chapter 7.

23. Tocqueville comments "that in a society in which lawyers occupy without dispute the elevated position that naturally belongs to them, their spirit will be eminently conservative." *Democracy in America*, 253.

24. Richard Posner, who in addition to being a sitting federal appeals court judge is a legal theorist, says that the "Supreme Court is a political court. The discretion that the judges exercise can fairly be described as legislative in character." "The Anti-Hero," 30. Cf. Martin Shapiro's comment that "the American pretense that constitutional questions are technical legal questions with single, objective, neutral, correct answers is always confronted with the reality that such questions are actually public policy questions.... If we see constitutional questions as essentially political questions, and the choices of constitutional interpretation that are inevitable as choices for the people then the French arrangement avoids the American problem." "Judicial Review in France," 16–17. Consider also the comment by Andrew Kleinfeld, a judge sitting on the Ninth Circuit: "That a question is important does not imply that it is constitutional. The Founding Fathers did not establish the United States as a democratic republic so that elected officials would decide trivia, while all great questions would be decided by the judiciary." Quoted in *Washington Post*, April 12, 1996.

25. According to Tocqueville: "One can even say that [the Supreme Court's] prerogatives are almost entirely political although its constitution is entirely judicial." *Democracy in America*, 141. Cf. Richard Posner's comment that "most of the issues that are sufficiently novel to get all the way to the Supreme Court are political." He goes on to say that a plausible view of the Court's role is that "judges are entitled (indeed required) to apply their Constitutional views to the cases before them. The important point is that they are no more entitled to do so than other branches." "The People's Court," 34.

26. Cf. Paul Brest's comment that "proper constitutional adjudication closely resembles common-law adjudication. Both consist of reasoning from principles rooted in conventional morality and elaborated through judicial doctrine." "Fundamental Rights Controversy," 1068, characterizing the view of Wellington, "Common Law Rules."

27. For a recent statement, see Kramer, *The People Themselves*.

28. Cf. Lerner, *The Thinking Revolutionary*.

29. Goldstein, *The Intelligible Constitution*.

30. "Moral Reading of the Constitution," 49.

31. Ibid.

32. For a lucid, deeply thoughtful account of the executive in republican government, see Mansfield, *Taming the Prince*. Mansfield shows that "execution" is fundamental to republican government—indeed its essence, he says, is in its constitutionalizing execution. Taking Mansfield as a starting point would likely lead to a somewhat different account of commercial republican political constitution than is offered here. Not the least of the questions he raises is how the operations of judging and deliberating that are at the center of republican government can be held together. One possible answer is by the executive.

33. *Spirit of the Laws*, pt. 2, bk. 11, chap. 6, 164.

34. Richard Nixon said at one point that "when the president does it, that means it is not illegal." Quoted in Glennon, "Can the President Do No Wrong?" 923. George W. Bush's claim that if the president declares that an American citizen is "an enemy combatant" he may be taken to a secret place and held *incommunicado* indefinitely also comes out of the presidential "I am the law" school of republican political theory. Cf. Saddam Hussein's reply, after his capture, to an Iraqi official: "Were these laws [under] which I am accused written under Saddam Hussein?" And when the answer was given that they were, Saddam replied, "So what entitles you to use them against the President who signed them?" Hussein is quoted in the *Independent* (London), July 2, 2004.

35. *Youngstown Sheet and Tube Co. v. Sawyer*, 343 U.S. 579, 655 (1952) (Jackson, J., concurring). See the discussion in chapter 2 on preventing faction. Cf. Haefele, "What Constitutes the American Republic."

36. In principle, there is nothing preventing the Supreme Court from doing so, or at least publishing opinions that ordinary people can understand. But the historical development of judicial independence, tied as it is to the growth in power of the legal profession, more or less guarantees that courts will speak in the power-generating mystifications of legal discourse. Again, see Goldstein, *The Intelligible Constitution.*

37. Increasingly, many Republicans in Congress seem to prefer the role of faithful member of a party battalion that on command marches through the lobby. See the discussion of political parties later in this chapter.

38. Locke, *Two Treatises*, chap. 19, para. 212, 407.

39. Madison simply commented that "in republican government the legislative authority necessarily predominates." *The Federalist* No. 51. Cf. Theodore Lowi's comment that "the Civil Rights Act of 1964 still stands as a reminder to anyone who cares to reflect upon it that the Congress can, under proper conditions, be the center of government." *End of Liberalism*, 311. Consider also here the sophisticated account that Joseph Bessette in *The Mild Voice of Reason* gives of the record and capabilities of Congress as a deliberative body.

40. Blau, ed., *Social Theories of Jacksonian Democracy*, 87.

41. *Congress and the Common Good*, 18–19.

42. See the discussion by Karol Soltan where he characterizes the process being described here as one in which resources are "attached" to alternatives, not to actors. In short, collective decisionmaking will be shaped not by the resources that the parties to the choice can bring to bear but by the various kinds of "reasonableness" displayed by the alternatives. See Soltan, "Generic Constitutionalism."

43. "Liberal Virtues," 1284. Cf. James Fishkin's analysis of what is the case when deliberation is not at work: "[A]n alternative is not contrasted effectively with its rivals,…arguments are not answered, and…decisionmakers have little competence or factual information to evaluate the proposals offered to them." *Democracy and Deliberation*, 38. Cf. also J. H. Hexter's contrast between an "erudite experienced alertness" and "analytical deductive efficiency." "Thomas Hobbes and the Law," 485. If we leave off the erudition part, legislative reasoning will be more like "experienced alertness" than "deductive efficiency."

44. Cf. Rawls's remark that "the exchange of opinion with others checks our partiality and widens our perspective; we are made to see things from their standpoint and the limits of our vision are brought home to us." *Theory of Justice*, 358.

45. *Law, Legislation and Liberty*, vol. 1, *Rules and Order*, 118.

46. *The Federalist* No. 63.

47. *Politics and Markets*, chap. 19.

48. *Law, Legislation and Liberty*, vol. 1, *Rules and Order*.

49. See Haefele, "Toward a New Civic Calculus"; Haefele, "What Constitutes the American Republic."

50. Nedelsky, *Private Property*, chap. 6.

51. Cf. Tocqueville's comment that "whenever at the head of some great undertaking you see the government in France or a man of rank in England, in the United States you will be sure to find an association." *Democracy in America*, 489.

52. Cf. Dahl, *Dilemmas of Pluralist Democracy*, passim.

53. See Przeworski, "Democracy as a Contingent Outcome of Conflicts."

54. *Preface to Economic Democracy*, chap. 1.

55. This, of course, leaves open the question of how rights and civic organizations were created in the first place. However, as my present concern is with further realizing a commercial republic that already exists, this very important question need not be dealt with here.

56. Are there likely to be any forces presently at work that will prompt citizens to favor lawmakers who give some weight to economic equality? Probably the closest to such a force is a widespread but not intense preference that all citizens earn their own keep and thus have access to steady work. Insofar as there is also a widespread sentiment that all jobs must pay a reasonable wage, we are on our way to a conception of rather modest but real economic equality. Both historically minded theorists and those concerned with the present have argued that liberalism is a political theory that has work at its center. See Kramnick, *Republicanism and Bourgeois Radicalism* on republicanism, and Shklar, *American Citizenship* on work as a component of full citizenship.

57. The origins of this argument can be found in Montesquieu, for which see Mansfield, *Taming the Prince*, chap. 9.

58. Dahl, *Dilemmas of Pluralist Democracy*, chap. 7; Dahl, *Democracy and Its Critics*, chaps. 20–21.

59. Cf. Locke's comment that "Esteem and Disgrace are, of all others, the most powerful Incentive of Mind, when once it is brought to Relish them." *Some Thoughts Concerning Education*, sec. 56.

60. For a classic account of such motives, as they applied to the framers of the Constitution, see Adair, "Fame and the Founding Fathers," in *Fame and the Founding Fathers*.

61. Rep. Benjamin Cardin as quoted in *New York Times*, May 8, 1994.

62. Quoted in Madison, *Notes of Debates*, 323.

63. See the marvelous discussion by William Muir in *Legislature*.

64. *On Liberty and Other Essays*, 417.

65. As some of the legislative reforms over the last several decades seem to have done. See, e.g., Zelizer, *On Capitol Hill*; Sinclair, *Legislators, Leaders, and Lawmaking*.

66. This all assumes, of course, that *being* a great legislative leader will in fact garner some measure of fame. Should the citizenry always prefer legislative loud-mouths to quieter architects of good law, then the odds go down significantly that a deliberatively minded legislature is possible to create and sustain.

67. Consider here the House of Commons: fun to watch, but no one supposes much lawmaking is actually going on.

68. Note Haefele's reference to Jefferson's comment that a bill "will be amended by its friends." "Toward a New Civic Calculus," 274.

69. See *The Federalist* No. 10.

70. On the other hand, highly disciplined parties—on the British model—will turn legislators into party battalions who march through the lobbies at their leader's command. This will only serve to undercut deliberation. How to navigate between parties strong enough to provide leadership and ones so strong as to make delibera-tion impossible is a central problem in constitutional design. See also the discussion in chapters 8 and 10.

71. There is a large literature on the impact of electoral systems. For a good overview see Rae, *Political Consequences of Electoral Laws.*

72. See Haefele, "What Constitutes the American Public." I am also indebted to conversations with Haefele for the point about the electoral college.

73. But see Marty Cohen et al., "Beating Reform." Paper delivered to the annual meeting of the American Political Science Association, 2001. On file with author.

74. On this whole question, see Mansbridge, "A Deliberate Theory of Interest Representation."

75. Noted by David Broder and Spencer Rich in the *Washington Post*, September 19, 1993.

76. See chapter 10 for additional discussion.

77. Berns, "Does the Constitution 'Secure These Rights?'"

Chapter Seven

1. Cf. William Galston's comment that among "the greatest vices of popular government [is] the propensity to gratify short-term desires at the expense of long-term interests." "Liberal Virtues," 1283.

2. Ralph Lerner argues that a nation of private calculators with short memories will forget the consequences of not tending to the public business. See *Revolutions Revisited*, esp. the final chapter titled "Revival through Recollection." Much of this was well understood by the early theorists of the commercial republic. Even Adam Smith, a strong advocate of the value of *private* interest, believed that a commer-cial republic could not work only through the aggregation of private interests: the same Adam Smith who wrote *The Wealth of Nations* also wrote *The Theory of Moral Sentiments.*

3. *The Federalist* No. 62.

4. Jefferson to John Adams, quoted in Mason, *Free Government in the Making,* 385.

5. *On Liberty,* 181.

6. *Democracy in America*, 56–57. Cf. Elkin, *City and Regime*, chaps. 6–9.

7. *Democracy in America*, 65.

8. It is possible that civic education by schools can ease the burden on local politics by increasing political knowledge and encouraging political participation. But there is no substitute for actual participation. Political knowledge and action of the kind being discussed here can only take deep hold through the relevant political experience.

9. In this regard, see the beautifully presented argument by Robert Kraynack, "Tocqueville's Constitutionalism."

10. In the preceding paragraph I have drawn freely on my *City and Regime in the American Republic*, chap. 8. In this regard, Henry Simons simply said that "modern democracy rests upon free, responsible local government and will never be stronger than that foundation." *Economic Policy for a Free Society*, 13.

11. Participating in the exercise of public authority also reinforces a kind of proud independence. See the discussion in the next section of this chapter. To feel a sense of responsibility, to learn to weigh interests and concerns that are not our own, is humbling; but, in being so, it provides a realistic foundation for believing that we can participate intelligently in such important matters. Pride in the quality of our judgment is a plausible conclusion to draw from such experiences. Again, local government is the only place where large numbers of citizens can learn this lesson.

12. *Democracy in America*, 66.

13. Cf. Norton Long's characterization of the views of John Dewey that "only in the local community could the public discover itself and in doing so realize its shared common purposes that alone make possible real democracy." "Dewey's Conception of the Public Interest." In *Public and Its Problems*, Dewey said that true democracy required broad public participation and face-to-face discussions about concrete problems. He wanted people to govern themselves in local units, for, "unless local communal life can be restored, the public cannot adequately resolve its most urgent problem: to find and identify itself." The "home" of democracy, he thought, was "the neighborly community." Dewey concluded his book by noting: "We lie, Emerson said, in the lap of an immense intelligence. But that intelligence is dormant and its communications are broken, inarticulate and faint until it possesses the local community as its medium." I owe these quotes and the surrounding language to Peter Levine.

14. In the following paragraphs, I draw freely on my "Citizen and City."

15. For an object lesson in the form of a highly colored portrait of a group of people whose understanding of their obligations reaches little beyond their immediate circle, see Banfield, *Moral Basis of a Backward Society*. An overview of aspects of this whole problem is in Putnam, *Bowling Alone*.

16. Cf. Tocqueville's comment that "religion, which among Americans never mixes directly in the government of society, should therefore be considered as the first of their political institutions." *Democracy in America*, 280.

17. It seems likely that religion plays a key role here. We not only learn to connect our own well-being to that of others by participating in a particular religious congregation but also through direct religious teaching.

18. Cf. James Q. Wilson's remark that there are "understandings that arise spontaneously out of, and necessarily govern, human relationships: the need to show some concern for the well-being of others, treat others with minimal fairness, and honor obligations." "The Moral Sense," 8. Consider also Aristotle's comment that it is "in the household first [that] we have the sources and springs of friendship, of political organization, and of justice." *Eudemian Ethics*, 1242 b1. For very different kinds of arguments and evidence that supports this position, see Frank, *Passions within Reason;* Frohlich and Oppenheimer, *Choosing Justice.*

19. For the classic discussion, see Tocqueville, *Democracy in America*, 63–70, 512–13, 525–30.

20. I am here only concerned with the manner in which proud independence affects public-spiritedness in the context of local political life. Proud independence has other effects. For example, it is needed if citizens are to be careful guardians of their private interests.

21. Cf. Thomas Pangle's comment that republican citizens need a "combination of pride and humility." *Ennobling Democracy*, 177. See also Tocqueville, *Democracy in America*, 95, and vol. 1, pt. 2, chaps. 9–10.

22. The effects of the organization of work on human character were well understood by Adam Smith who, at the dawn of the industrial revolution, argued that dull repetitive work can only undercut the self-respect that is at the core of the capacity for independent judgment. See also Marshall, *Principles of Economics*, esp. 1–2.

23. See Lane, *Market Experience*, 198–99. Relevant here as well is the effect of hierarchy in the workplace.

24. See ibid., chaps. 9–10.

25. See Moon, "Moral Basis of the Welfare State"; Shklar, *American Citizenship;* Walzer, *Spheres of Justice;* Avinieri, *Hegel's Theory of the State*, chap. 7, esp. 244–48.

26. Cf. Louis Brandeis's comment that "[f]or good or for ill, [government] teaches the whole people by its example." *Olmstead v. United States*, 277 U.S. 438, 485 (1928) (Brandeis, J., dissenting).

27. Cf. Key, *Responsible Electorate*, chap. 1. The media have and will likely continue to have impacts on the citizenry's independence. Again, if journalists treat citizens as fools, a concern for the public interest is unlikely to flourish among the public.

28. On trust, see Banfield, *Moral Basis of a Backward Society;* Putnam, *Making Democracy Work;* Fukyama, *Trust;* Wilson, *Moral Sense;* Uslaner, *Moral Foundations of Trust.*

29. Which, even with high crime rates, most of us are not.

30. See Lane, *Market Experience*, esp. chap. 7.

31. *Wealth of Nations*, 734. Thus, the poor are doubly handicapped. They neither have complex, demanding work if they have any work at all, and their participation in the marketplace is in other respects also limited: money is the passport to market participation and this of course is what the poor lack.

32. Nancy Rosenblum says that "democracy is defined by political philosophers as a regime of 'reciprocal recognition among equals.' Mutual respect is its essence." *Membership and Morals*, 352. These matters are sometimes discussed under the

heading of "political equality," and my discussion should be read as assuming that all citizens have at least formal-legal equality.

33. See Judith Shklar's discussion of Rousseau in this respect in *Men and Citizens*, 19.

34. But see the Federalist(!) Noah Webster's comment that "an equality of property, with a necessity of alienation, constantly operating to destroy combinations of powerful families, is the very *soul of a republic* . . . . An equal distribution of property is the *foundation* of a republic." "Examination into the Leading Principles of the Federal Constitution."

35. U.S. Bureau of the Census, "Median Income of Families by Selected Characteristics, Race, and Hispanic Origin of Householder: 2000, 1999 and 1998.

36. U.S. Bureau of the Census, "Mean Income Received by Each Fifth and Top 5 Percent of Households (All Races): 1967 to 2001." See Krugman, *Peddling Prosperity*, 135, who indicates that the economic distance between the bottom quintile and the top 1 percent is massive; it is greater today than when he wrote.

37. In 2001, almost two hundred thousand Americans reported incomes of $1 million or more and there were 2.4 million with incomes from $200,000 to $1 million. Reported in Samuelson, "Nothing Exceeds Like Excess."

38. U.S. Bureau of the Census, "Household Income Limits by Percentile: 1967 to 2001."

39. Cf. Anderson, *Pragmatic Liberalism*, chap. 7.

40. See chapter 10. "Too much" economic equality is no good either because it would likely undercut proud independence: very great equality can probably only be achieved by wholesale government transfers. And those who receive them would almost certainly have undercut a sense of pride in their accomplishments if the principal way in which most people earn their living is through paid work. Wholesale transfers probably won't do much either for the proud independence of those from whom the transfers are taken.

41. See Lane, *Market Experience*, pt. 7.

42. From remarks delivered to Congress in support of an inheritance tax, June 19, 1935. Quoted in Aldrich, *Old Money*, 235.

43. See the discussion in Elkin, *City and Regime*, chap. 8, esp. 153–55.

44. See ibid., chaps. 8–9, and the discussion below.

45. What about people who don't work? If they are retired there is no problem: they will have worked. But what about the ill and infirm, the long-term unemployed, and those who never intend to enter the labor market? There is no easy way around the point that, in a commercial republic, employment is crucial to republican citizenship and not just for the reasons I have been considering here. See the very useful discussion by Judith Shklar in *American Citizenship*.

46. Quoted in Shattuck, "The Reddening of America," 5.

47. *Principles of the Good Society*, 263.

48. Pitkin, "Justice," 347. The reference is to Tussman, *Obligation and the Body Politic*.

49. Think of the small town Rotarian who enters local political life in order to advance his business and soon finds himself worrying about the state of the schools

and local health care, neither of which (the school being part of a regional system) have much effect on his local taxes. Cf. Jon Elster's comment that "over time one will become swayed by considerations about the common good. One cannot indefinitely praise the common good *du bout des levres*, for . . . one will end up having preferences which initially one was faking." *Sour Grapes*, 36.

50. For a sophisticated version of local political life as an exercise in executive government, see Peterson, *City Limits*.

51. Elsewhere I have spelled out some of the institutional details of such a deliberative and participative local political life. See *City and Regime*, chaps. 8–9, esp. 171ff. See also the discussion below and in chapter 10.

52. *Politics and the Public Interest*, 139–40.

53. See the classic discussion in Olson, *Logic of Collective Action*.

54. Quoted in Diggins, *Lost Soul of American Politics*, 245–46.

55. See Tocqueville, *Democracy in America*, esp. vol. 2, pt. 1, chap. 2, "On the Principal Source of Beliefs among Democratic Peoples."

56. In answering, it is easiest to move back and forth between how a reformed local political life can foster a concern for the institutional elements themselves and for the values they embody. This is partly a matter of ease of exposition. But it is also the case that all that a reformed local politics can sometimes do is foster a concern for the values. If, however, citizens develop a regard for such values, they will likely elect lawmakers interested in securing the institutions that constitute a commercial republican regime. Or, to be more precise, throughout this and the preceding chapter, I am making the reasonable assumption that sometimes lawmakers will discuss the public interest directly in institutional terms, at other times they will first consider values and only then turn to institutions, and most likely of all, that they will move back and forth between the two.

57. See Elkin, *City and Regime*, chaps. 2–5. Although the arguments unfolded here have their origins in observations about cities, whether large or small, and work best in that context, they are meant to apply to suburbs as well. The politics of older suburbs are also strongly shaped by land-use questions as are newer suburbs looking for a strong tax base. Only well-to-do homogeneous suburbs with a strong tax base have a politics that differs substantially from that sketched here. Otherwise said, virtually all local political orders can, with the necessary reforms, provide a school of republican citizenship.

58. The pull mobile capital has on local politics is less than some accounts indicate, but it is still significant. It has been estimated that some 60 percent of all economic activity is local. It is also worth noting the percentage of the work force in manufacturing—an industry where locational choices are very important—has declined to about 11 percent. See chapter 10, particularly the arguments drawn from Alperovitz, *America beyond Capitalism*.

59. In this discussion of the powers and politics of localities and their effects on a local politics of the public interest, I draw freely on chapters 8 and 9 of my *City and Regime*.

60. See the discussion in Siena, ed., *Antitrust and Local Government*. Dillon's rule establishes that municipal governments are not sovereign bodies; their powers are

limited to those specifically granted to them by state governments. This has been the view of the courts since the early twentieth century. The constitutional law on these matters, however, is not as clear as it might be. See *Community Communications, Inc. v. City of Boulder, Colorado*, 455 U.S. 40 (1982); *Garcia v. San Antonio Metropolitan Transit Authority*, 469 U.S. 528 (1985); *Hawaii Housing Authority v. Midkiff*, 467 U.S. 229 (1984); *Town of Hallie v. City of Eau Claire*, 471 U.S. 34 (1985); *Fisher v. City of Berkeley, California*, 475 U.S. 260 (1986).

61. See, e.g., Ackerman, *Private Property and the Constitution*.

62. Cf. the remark by the district attorney of Galesburg, Illinois after the Maytag Company decided in 2004 to close its plant after a decade of tax breaks: he said that he wished to sue the company to recoup excess tax breaks and other incentives to stay. Cf. also the comments of a Putnam County, New York commissioner who said that future tax breaks should be tied to "the length of stay and the number of jobs." "Towns That Handed Out Tax Breaks Cry Foul as Jobs Leave Anyway," *New York Times*, October 20, 2004.

63. For additional discussion of the likely changes in politics, see chapter 10.

64. See the discussion in chapter 3.

65. "After initially cheering their prosecutor [the district attorney of Galesburg, Illinois] for trying to regain some of the money used to keep Maytag, some people say they are afraid that they may scare off future employers." "Towns That Handed Out Tax Breaks Cry Foul as Jobs Leave Anyway," *New York Times*, October 20, 2004.

66. Because not all lawmakers can be equally competent across all areas of public concern, the implication is that in a well-functioning republican regime, those running for high office ought not try to fake having a deep interest in a policy area. They will be branded hacks. Better to say something general about the public interest with the firm implication that one needs to know a great deal more about the matter at hand.

67. Must it be said that republican regimes, like other regimes, also require political theorists to point out how its constitutive politics must operate and for what purposes? One would not think so, but it is apparently the case that some students of political theory, especially those with strong democratic inclinations, are made uneasy by the fact that some people claim special knowledge. It smacks of "privileging" certain kinds of knowledge and of "guardianship," so it is said. It may be a bad idea for large numbers of citizens to go around saying that they have a privileged view of the public interest. But is it really possible to have *any* flourishing regime no matter how democratic and worthy without some idea about how it must work if it is to be sustained? What, after all, is political theory for? For a view apparently to the contrary, see Dahl, *Dilemmas of Pluralist Democracy*, chap. 7.

68. Those who say that public-spiritedness of the kind I have been describing is impossible on a significant scale might want to reflect on just how it came about that, in their professions and communities, they have come to be seen as exemplary persons—for I assume that that they are nothing less and that their merit is widely recognized.

69. Because this will not be easy for most people, opinion leaders must play a crucial role. Unfortunately, they can make the task much more difficult for citizens

by obscuring the difference between public and private interests, and even confounding them. I turn to this question below and in chapter 8.

70. Cf. Hanna Pitkin's comment that "diversity is a source of strength" for a deliberative process. *Fortune Is a Woman*, 300–304.

71. To paraphrase a comment of William James, one of the secrets of popular government is to ensure that common habits are carried into public life.

72. Cf. Shelley Burtt's comment that, in commercial republican regimes, citizens will not "engage in politics for abstractly public reasons." "Virtue Transformed: Republican Argument in Eighteenth Century England," chap. 7, 21. See also Burtt, "Politics of Virtue Today."

73. There are other features of local and national political life that will further increase the odds. See the discussion below and chapters 9–10.

74. *Spirit of the Laws*, chaps. 11–12. See generally Hartz, *Liberal Tradition in America*; Macpherson, *Political Theory of Possessive Individualism*; Kramnick, *Republicanism and Bourgeois Radicalism*.

75. Quoted in Arkes, *First Things*, 46.

76. The term is Samuel Beer's. See *To Make a Nation*. Cf. Tocqueville's comment that "[w]hat one calls a republic in the United States is the tranquil reign of the majority. The majority, after it has had the time to recognize itself and to certify its existence, is the common source of powers. But the majority itself is not all-powerful. Above it in the moral world are humanity, justice, and reason; in the political world, acquired rights. The majority recognizes these two barriers." *Democracy in America*, 379–80.

77. Others, however, did see the vital role of a middle stratum in a republic— Tocqueville, for example.

78. See Schattschneider, *Semi-Sovereign People*, chaps. 2–3.

79. Can the kinds of political parties I have been sketching—which must have a measure of discipline and be national in orientation—flourish in a regime with the kind of autonomous local politics I have described? The question makes clear the importance of an account of federalism for a full theory of republican constitution. A republican regime needs both a vital local political life and a national-level politics capable of focusing on the public interest. How are these two—which pull in different directions—to be kept in balance? In the history of the American republic the answer has been political parties rooted in local political life but also with some measure of national focus. Federalism, along with national security and international relations, are two of the big silences in the account of the political constitution presented here.

80. See the concluding sections of chapter 8.

81. Two obvious figures in this regard are Lincoln and Franklin Roosevelt. Consider Hamilton's comment in *The Federalist* No. 72 that those who believe in taking risks, whose ruling passion is love of fame, are the "noblest minds."

82. See Mansfield, *Machiavelli's Virtue*, chap. 1.

83. "Geographic Mobility: Population Characteristics, March 1999 to March 2000." *Current Population Reports*, U.S. Census Bureau.

84. *The Federalist* No. 27.

85. Increasing local powers may also increase the degree of local corruption. More powers means more opportunities for grafters.

86. For additional discussion, see chapter 10.

87. Marx and Engels, *Communist Manifesto*, 19.

Chapter Eight

1. Whether this is possible is another matter, for it is far from clear whether there are motives associated with such outlooks that are reliable enough to build a politics around.

2. "Self-interest well understood is a doctrine not very lofty, but clear and sure." Tocqueville, *Democracy in America*, 502.

3. Cf. Tocqueville's comment that "societies, like organized bodies, follow certain fixed rules in their formation from which they cannot deviate. They are composed of certain elements that one finds everywhere and at all times. Ideally, it will always be easy to divide each people into three classes." *Democracy in America*, 200.

4. A state strong enough to enforce a stringent conception of equality will be a danger to civil liberties and to political rights more broadly.

5. If we are to understand fully the class politics of the regime, we would also need to consider the outlook and political role of the professionals and managers, what some have called the "new class." These are people who do not themselves control significant productive property, but many of them work for those who do. Joining them might be what used to be called the independent professions, which to a greater degree than in the past, are able to construct very comfortable lives. Are these disparate parts being formed into an upper-middle or new class? See also the discussion below.

6. A privileged voice should not only be contrasted to the political equality that aggregative lawmaking should have, but also to the equality of rights that republican government entails. Equal rights need not—indeed, should not and probably cannot—require that every individual should have equal weight in determining the content of the law. *All* types of democratic capitalism, including a commercial republic, must deal with the following facts:

a. the state cannot comprehensively command the behavior of asset controllers;

b. citizens will press public officials to increase their economic well-being, which means that officials will need the cooperation of asset controllers, with the result that large-scale businessmen will have a privileged political position;

c. left to their own devices, businessmen will have a narrow view of their own interests, thereby endangering the public interest.

It is unlikely, therefore, that forms of democratic capitalism other than a commercial republic can avoid the problems that arise from these facts. Moreover, it is doubtful whether any other form of democratic capitalism can do a significantly better job than a fully realized commercial republic of preventing the political actions of controllers of productive assets from undercutting the public interest. This includes social democracies.

7. For the original proposal, see Kelso and Adler, *Capitalist Manifesto*. ESOPs are employee ownership plans in which stock in a company is distributed to those who work in it in return for various advantages given to the firm by federal law.

8. This was the intention of Kelso and Adler's original argument for broadening stock ownership. See *Capitalist Manifesto*.

9. See Wolff, *Top Heavy*, chaps. 3–5.

10. See Berle and Means, *Modern Corporation and Private Property*.

11. See Simon, "Social Republican Property."

12. See Roemer, *Equal Shares*.

13. Dahl, *Preface to Economic Democracy*, 100.

14. Below I also argue that wider distribution of capital is one of the ways, possibly the crucial way, to enlarge the middle class. See also chapter 10.

15. See Parijs, *Real Freedom for All*; and, again, the discussion in chapter 10.

16. Robert Dahl is doubtful that a separation of powers is important for popular self-government. See *Preface to Democratic Theory*, 136. But we have inherited it and almost certainly must live with it, and we can, as chapter 6 indicates, improve its workings. Moreover, as Dahl fails to see clearly enough, all free governments have some dispersal of powers at work. It need not be done formally, in the constitutional design of institutions, as we have done. But it must be done if representative or free government is to succeed. The real problem, then, is not that the separation of powers impedes democratic government, as Dahl argues, but whether formally dividing power through constitutional means is a particularly costly way of proceeding given the American aspiration to constitute a commercial republic. In deciding the matter—again as Dahl does not seem to appreciate—there are advantages to a formal separation, not least of which is that public officials must carry out in public some of their negotiations on important public matters. See the discussion in chapter 6.

17. To forestall some likely worries here, I am not arguing that the interests of the middle class as I describe them will be at work in the present political economy. They will be to some degree, not least because their interests are shaped by their position in the economy. Relevant here is the long-standing discussion of "objective" and "subjective" class interests. The assumption here is that if there are classes, there must be some measure of objective interests that characterize them.

18. Some middle-class people will own productive assets in the form of small businesses, which presumably will make them, as compared to other middle-class people, even more attached to property rights and to a vibrant commercial society.

19. It is likely that their views of inequality of wealth will be similar.

20. See Verba, Kelman, et al., *Elites and the Idea of Equality*; Verba and Orren, *Equality in America*. Also see McCloskey and Zaller, *American Ethos*.

21. See Shklar, *American Citizenship*, 81–82.

22. Many asset controllers in fact argue something like this and one result is that we certainly do not have reasonable wages for all who are employed: it is still not uncommon in the United States for people to work full-time and have a family income below the poverty line. We do not, moreover, have full employment if we include in the unemployed those who no longer are seeking work and those working part-time who wish to work full-time. A reasonable estimate of the total of the working poor and the unemployed in this broader definition certainly has in the recent past approached one out five people of working age.

23. Mary Nichols, in discussing Aristotle's political theory, says that "the middle-class regime, which is 'best for most cities and most human beings,' is the best way in Aristotle's view of combining oligarchy and democracy to produce a polity." *Citizens and Statesmen*, 97, quoting Aristotle, *Politics* 1295a25–26. Nichols's comment also reinforces the point made in previous chapters that the ruling stratum's conception of justice will be partial, that is to say, it will to some degree be partisan. Nichols's formulation also suggests that a good political regime will have a mix of class elements. See the discussion of the mixed regime at the end of this chapter.

24. See the sophisticated discussion in Przeworski, *Capitalism and Social Democracy*.

25. See Herbert Gans, *The Levittowners*, and *Middle American Individualism*.

26. Robert Eden, in a private communication, comments that Woodrow Wilson "sought to elevate the educated middle-class and to keep them in a leading role nationally; keeping deliberative politics and its norms at the center and apex of government was crucial to this synthesis.... The middle-class can only maintain hegemony if deliberation is sovereign." Most members of the middle class are also likely to see the importance of the civic organizations that are a central feature of civil society. They are after all joiners, people for whom civic work through church, workplace, and community is a mainstay of their lives.

27. See Mansfield, "Hobbes and the Science of Indirect Government," 97–110.

28. Cf. Harvey Mansfield's comment that "[t]he replacement of statesmanship by party is an attempt to avoid dependence on great men." *Statesmanship and Party Government*, 17.

29. For an account of why a two-party system is crucial for republican government, see Haefele, "What Constitutes the American Republic?"

30. There is a case to be made that we now have one and a half parties of liberty but, alas, no party of equality.

31. There is some reason to think that at least one of the two main contemporary parties—the Republicans—is moving down the ideological path, or so many thoughtful observers have concluded. See, e.g., Dionne, "New Rules of Politics."

32. See Haefele, "What Constitutes the American Republic?"; Key, *Politics, Parties and Pressure Groups*; Agar, *Price of Union*.

33. See Burns, *Deadlock of Democracy*; Schattschneider, *Party Government*; American Political Science Association, "Towards a More Responsible Two-Party System."

34. See Dahl, *Preface to Economic Democracy*, chap. 1.

35. On aggregative politics, see the discussion in the next section of this chapter. There will also be a third type. Again, see the next section.

36. *The Federalist* No. 10. Madison probably did not mean by this term precisely the meaning I give to it here. Regardless, he did mean that republican politics would need to concern itself with an aggregative measure of citizen well-being.

37. For different versions of the specifics of such political processes and their benefits, see Banfield, *Political Influence*; Haefele, *Representative Government and Environmental Management*; Lindblom, *Intelligence of Democracy*; Dahl, *Who Governs?*

38. See Ely, *Democracy and Distrust*, chaps. 4–5.

39. Four, if we add moral politics.

40. For various versions of the point, see Schlesinger, *Cycles;* Hirschman, *Exit, Voice and Loyalty;* Ackerman, *We the People.*

41. For an example of the overwhelming by a narrow group politics of a broad class and public interest politics, consider the recent (2004) tax bill. It is a 633 page behemoth that was covered by the *New York Times* under such headings as "How Tax Bill Gave Business More and More." *New York Times,* October 13, 2004.

42. Of course, the problem is found in all regimes, or at least all of the ones humankind will find itself living in.

43. See Madison's remarks to the Virginia ratifying convention, June 20, 1788, in *Papers of James Madison,* 11:163.

44. See Page, *Who Gets What from Government.*

45. *Machiavelli's Virtue,* 236.

46. Ibid., passim.

47. Early discussions of this class labeled it the "new" class. See Kristol, *Two Cheers for Democracy;* Gouldner, *Future of Intellectuals.*

48. See Elkin, "Pluralism in its Place."

49. Cf. Beer, *To Make a Nation,* pts. 2–3; Ackerman, *We the People,* chap. 1.

50. *The Federalist* No. 1.

51. Dahl says there is a third alternative, rule by minorities. But, as he recognizes, this is only attractive if the same minorities do not rule much or all of the time. The danger that this will occur is greater than Dahl seems to realize. Minorities' rule may be more attractive than minority rule, but whether it is more attractive than majority rule is far from clear. Moreover, it certainly is not easier to constitute a regime with minorities' rule at its center than to constitute one with majority rule. See Dahl, *Preface to Democratic Theory.*

52. Cf. Beer, *To Make a Nation,* esp. 384, where Beer argues that the American constitutional design is meant to provide a system of regularized incentives for the protection and promotion of rational deliberation by a government of the many.

53. Cf. Mansfield, *Machiavelli's New Modes and Orders,* where he discusses how the contents of political modes and orders can change and be changed.

54. *Democracy in America,* vol. 2, pt. 2, chap. 20.

55. See, e.g., ibid., vol. 1, pt. 2, chap. 8; Mansfield, *The Spirit of Liberalism,* passim.

56. Cf. Madison's comment in *The Federalist* No. 10 that "to secure the public good and private rights . . . and at the same time preserve the spirit and the form of popular government, is then the great object to which our inquiries are directed."

57. See the parallel argument in Barber, *On What the Constitution Means,* esp. chaps. 1, 6.

Chapter Nine

1. Harvey Mansfield comments that it has been said that "the secret dream of liberalism . . . [is] to do away with politics altogether." *Spirit of Liberalism,* 95.

2. Cf. John Gray's comment that the subject of "English-speaking political philosophy" with its concern to "state the principles of an ideal liberal constitution . . . was not political. It was law." "Autonomy Is Not the Only Good," 30. See

also his comment that "political philosophy has come to be seen as a branch of jurisprudence, whose central task is the design of an ideal constitution according to the principles of a 'theory of justice,'" "The Light of Other Minds," 112. Consider also Newey, "How Do We Find Out What He Meant?" 29, where he comments that "the major project in modern liberalism is to use ethics to contain the political." Relevant as well is Judith Shklar's comment that, in what she terms "legalism," "politics is regarded not only as something apart from law, but inferior to law." *Legalism*, 111. Simon Blackburn has, in various venues, termed what is at work here the "mandarin style" of philosophy.

3. *Ages of American Law*, 111.

4. See the discussion in chapter 4.

5. Philip Pettit says this effort at ideal theory is one in which Rawls and similarly inclined philosophers "have preferred to spend ... their time reflecting on the meaning of consent, or the nature of justice, or the basis of political obligation." *Republicanism*, 240.

6. Carter, "Critique of Freedom as Non-domination," 43. Cf. Jeremy Waldron's view that the question Rawls poses is "what would institutions look like if they were designed by people who were already agreed on a set of principles of justice?" Quoted in Mount, "Against Smoothness," reviewing Waldron, *Dignity of Legislation*. Mount goes on to say that Waldron "argues fiercely ... that this isn't an interesting question. If such an agreement existed already or could come after exhaustive deliberation, then political institutions would soon become fairly unimportant," dealing as they would with only minor or technical matters.

7. *Justice as Fairness*, 13.

8. *Theory of Justice*, 9.

9. Ibid., 8.

10. Ibid., 8–9. Whether this can be "assumed" is, in effect, the subject under discussion here. It is worth emphasizing that in *Political Liberalism*, the book that followed *A Theory of Justice*, Rawls is still pursuing ideal theory. It is easy to mistake his intention in *Political Liberalism* (see, e.g., his comment that the theory of justice in his earlier book was unrealistic [xvii]) because one of his starting points is that people in a society like the United States will not share a comprehensive philosophical doctrine that leads to a particular conception of justice. A society like ours will be pluralistic, argues Rawls, with a variety of comprehensive but reasonable religious, philosophical, and moral doctrines. Rawls's discussion in *Political Liberalism* is, however, not meant to be empirical in the sense of considering, in light of what we know about political behavior, what conception of justice will prove workable. Rather, he is engaged in the same exercise as he was in *A Theory of Justice*, namely, how would a society look if all its citizens were committed to a particular conception of justice. In *Political Liberalism*, Rawls complicates the problem by stipulating the fact of moral and philosophical pluralism. If it can be shown that it is possible for a conception of justice much like justice as fairness to emerge in "the best of forseeable conditions" (xvii), we can still go on to ask what the institutions of the society would look like if they were designed by people committed to this conception of justice. Rawls's realism is not the realism of someone wondering whether and how it is possible to create a just society, given people as they are or might plausibly become. The

realism, if that is what it is, consists of demonstrating that it is, in principle, possible for a certain conception of justice to be held, given the ineluctable and thus realistic feature of modern democratic societies—their pluralism. There is no claim that people will in fact hold that conception, nor is it clear that they can.

The way Rawls proceeds in *Political Liberalism* lands him in the same kind of trouble that I am arguing is endemic to his whole enterprise, namely, a kind of unsteady mix of ideal and practical theory. (See, e.g., his comments at 142 and 158 in *Political Liberalism* that he wishes to do more than avoid "futility" and that his theory is not "utopian.") This can lead us down some unattractive practical paths. Thus, in this second book there is the strong implication that the more a political order is organized around the exercise of public reason, the better it is. Theorists like Amy Guttman and Dennis Thompson (*Democracy and Disagreement*) seem to have drawn just this conclusion. Perhaps Rawls is right. But Madison, for one, argued otherwise—that of at least equal importance is the prevention of faction. One is tempted here to say that, Rawls's having looked at the world and having noted the existence of value pluralism, should have looked at it more comprehensively. Similarly, why stop at "accept[ing] the facts of commonsense political sociology" (*Political Liberalism*, 193) as they bear on whether liberal regimes can be neutral with regard to conceptions of the good. Why *those* facts and not the "facts of political sociology" as they bear on what is necessary to actually secure a regime in which the exercise of public reason is a crucial component of its workings. Indeed, why not the facts of commonsense political sociology all across the board? Of course, to take these into account would call into question whether ideal theory is really useful, or whether we must have some sort of mix of normative and empirical analysis. Moreover, if a theory of justice would take account of all the commonsense facts of political sociology, why wouldn't we want to take it as a guide to practice? Such a theory would be able to meet the kind of objections to Rawls's theory that I have been canvassing. But by then the theory is unlikely to be *Rawls's*, at least as that is presently set out. On all this, see Elkin, "Thinking Constitutionally."

11. "May" because there might be no way to bridge the gap between where we are and progress along a path marked out by the utopia. On whether we should take such a path, see the discussion below.

12. The aim of utopias is "to picture the awful distance between the possible and the probable by showing in great detail how men *could* live, even though they *always* refuse to do so.... For the fault [of our refusing] is not in God, fate or nature but in ourselves—where it will remain.... If one thinks that the only purpose of political philosophy is to provide serviceable guides to action for politicians and political groups, then indeed utopia [is] a useless enterprise. If critical understanding and judgment, however, are also real ends, then the construction of such models is not only justifiable, it is a perfect instrument." Shklar, *Men and Citizens*, 1–2.

13. As ideal theory, the argument also leaves something to be desired. How much in the way of Shklar's "critical understanding and judgment" that utopian thinking can bring may be gained from a theory that invites endless discussion of whether the etiolated, instrumentally rational human beings at the heart of Rawls's theory would indeed choose his two principles of justice. Cf. Colin McGinn's comment

about a social contract argument that parallels Rawls's: "[W]hat is the point of unity with purely hypothetical others." "Reasons and Unreasons," 37.

14. *Theory of Justice*, 126–30.

15. Rawls, *Political Liberalism*, xvii. They are, however, realistic in a way that Rawls's "circumstances of justice" are not, in spite of his claim to the contrary. The circumstances are too broadly defined to be so. We need not only know that there will be conflict, but what kinds of conflict. Similarly with scarcity. Are all valued things equally scarce?

16. Again, consider here Madison's comment that government must first control the people, and only then itself.

17. *The Federalist* No. 51.

18. The road down which the citizenry of a well-ordered regime travels, according to Rawls, is defined by a constitutional convention that is "guided by the two principles of justice." *Theory of Justice*, 357. Consider, by contrast, Stanley Rosen's comment that "[i]t is not enough to say that we advocate the noble as opposed to the base.... In politics, whether world-historical or local, it is always necessary to specify the particular case." *Ancients and the Moderns*, 11. Cf. Burke's comment that "the circumstances are what render every civil and political scheme beneficial or noxious to mankind." *Reflections on the Revolution in France*, 283.

19. Lipsey and Lancaster, "General Theory of the Second Best."

20. Cf. Justice Jackson's comment—noted earlier in chapter 5 at note 47—that a constitution is not a suicide pact: "[I]f the court does not temper its doctrinaire logic with a little practical wisdom, it will convert the constitutional Bill of Rights into a suicide pact." *Terminiello v. City of Chicago*, 337 U.S. 1, 37 (1949) (Jackson, J., dissenting). See also Justice Goldberg's remarks in *Kennedy v. Mendoza-Martinez*, 372 U.S. 144, 160 (1963).

21. See the excellent discussion of minimax and maximax decision principles in Nozick, *Anarchy, State and Utopia*, 298. I am arguing here that Rawls's intellectual strategy falls under the rubric of maximax about which Nozick says that it is "an insufficiently prudent principle which one would be silly to use in designing institutions."

22. "The philosopher in Montesquieu's conception does not legislate for legislators by laying down the principles of their laws in a natural law, but rather causes the 'spirit' of their laws to emerge by considering each set of laws as a whole." Mansfield, *Taming the Prince*, 215.

23. David Schaeffer says it well: "One can say that Rawls' conception of political philosophy is the mirror image of modern, positivistic social science: whereas the latter aspires to be value-free, the former is fact free." *Justice or Tyranny*, 85.

24. Cf. Robert McCloskey's comment that James Wilson, one of the founders of the American republic, sought to reconcile "the venerable Western idea of a binding higher law with the relatively new idea of the will of the people." McCloskey, "Introduction" to Wilson, *Works*, 38.

25. In the design of *any* good regime, a central place must be given to the exercise of practical political reason. Thus not only republics must have a place for it but so must kingships and aristocracies, to use the classical classification. They too

must provide forums for judging the relative importance of the ends they wish to pursue given the choices to be made. Kings have counselors, and aristocrats have institutions in which they discuss their common business. In short, good regimes are defined not only by their mode of rule and the accompanying conception of justice, but also by the presence of forums for the exercise of practical political reason.

26. On all this, see the powerful and compact essay by Bernard Crick, *In Defense of Politics*.

27. Cf. Walter Lippmann's comment that "if the people do rule, they must rule in a particular way." *Principles of the Good Society*, 263. He prefaces this conclusion by arguing that "instead of recognizing that the will of the people must prevail, and that the function of a constitution is to refine that will, [late-nineteenth- and early-twentieth-century classical liberals] sought to set up judicial dogma which inhibited popular will. . . . But after the industrial revolution and the political and social revolutions which it caused, the only conceivable source of authority is the power of the people and the only hope of good government is the progressive refinement of the people's will." Ibid., 259–60, 263.

28. Consider here the controversy between two of the most prominent legal theorists of the twentieth century, Lon Fuller and H. L. A. Hart. While they appear to have differed on just about everything else, when it came to considering the content of natural law both had very modest and general notions. Fuller spoke of the "internal morality of law," but when he considered what value or values this morality would serve, he talked in generalities about a satisfactory life. See chapter 6. Moreover, while it precludes a variety of ways that political authorities might exercise their powers, Fuller's internal morality still leaves largely open the purposes to which those powers might be directed. See his *The Morality of Law*, esp. chap. 4. As for Hart, the very name he gives to his account of natural law—he calls it a "minimum content"—is suggestive. See *Concept of Law*, chap. 9.

29. This is sometimes argued. Pope John Paul's encyclical letter "Evangelium Vitae" (Gospel of Life) issued March 31, 1995 states: "Democracy cannot be idolized to the point of making it a substitute for morality or a panacea for immorality. Fundamentally, democracy is 'system' and as such is a means not an end. Its 'moral' value is not automatic, but depends on conformity to the moral law to which it, like every form of human behavior, must be subject; in other words, its morality depends on the morality of the ends which it pursues and of the means which it employs." Quoted in "The Vatican's Doctrine," *New York Times*, March 31, 1995. Cf. Finnis, *Natural Law and Natural Rights*, esp. chaps. 7–8. But consider also Thomas Aquinas, whose thinking on these matters is understood by Harvey Mansfield (*Taming the Prince*, 93) to include the following: "Rather than determining human law, natural law must be determined (in the sense of specified) by human law, and these determinations are made by prudence, not by the fixed rules or methods of an art." Aquinas himself said that civil laws are derived from natural laws "by the mode of particular determination according to which each city determines for itself what is fitting." Quoted in ibid., 9.

30. *Natural Right and History*, 162. On whether this is Strauss's own view, note should be taken of Stanley Rosen's comment that "we have to understand that

Strauss' public persona as a conservative spokesman for classical natural right was intended by him as a salutary but exoteric doctrine." *Hermeneutics as Politics*, 125. The view of natural law I am setting out here is suggested by Nahum Glatzer's comment that only the election of the people of Israel came from God, but that all the details of the Law came from man alone. A similar view may be what George Werzel, a distinguished Catholic thinker, has in mind when, in Michael Sean Winters's phrasing, he argues that "[n]atural law allows a polity to argue reasonably to the common good." "Balthasar's Feast," 40.

Consider here Lloyd Weinreb's comment that "no principal of justice or a just social order transcends the circumstances in which it arises or some other basis in convention, because only conventional understandings enable us to overlook the incoherence of the idea itself. In a sense, therefore, convention replaces nature as the source of normative order." *Natural Law and Justice*, 11. Cf. Berel Lang's remark that "there is nothing surprising or problematic in the claim that we come to know what moral principle is…by encountering it first in history." *Act and Idea in the Nazi Genocide*, 29.

Also consider here Ronald Dworkin's comment that natural law should be understood to mean that "abstract or vague or otherwise unclear laws…should be interpreted so far as their language permits, to conform to the objective moral rights the natural law doctrine assumes people to have." "Justice for Clarence Thomas," 44. To the extent that Dworkin means that "objective moral rights" are to be weighted by the exercise of practical reason in the context of the other valued ends that compose the public interest, then his view is consistent with the one I argue for. Dworkin's "interpretation" is my "practical political reason." But Dworkin sometimes sounds as if rights always trump the public interest.

Finally, consider Jeremy Waldron's comment that "we do not in any interesting sense *begin* with natural law principles. We have to reason to them every bit as much as we reason to their application." *Dignity of Legislation*, 68.

31. *Finding the Mean*, 142, 239. Salkever also comments that "[t]heorizing about virtue can inform practical thinking about actions but cannot replace it." Ibid., 239. In these remarks and in the book generally, Salkever provides an Aristotelian view of political judgment with which he agrees.

32. Cf. Gadamer's comment that "[t]he idea of natural law has for Aristotle, only a critical function. No dogmatic use can be made of it, i.e., we cannot invest particular laws with the dignity and inviolability of natural law." *Truth and Method*, 285. Although this is not the place to pursue the point, it seems likely that the medieval view of natural law, as standards that are just somehow out there, is less easy to sustain than the Aristotelian view that it is facts about us as human beings that are crucial for any view of what ends we should pursue and how we should pursue them. Aristotle's account seems much closer to the nature of practical choice with all its contingent messiness than at least some other versions of natural thinking. For the medieval view, see Gierke, *Political Theories*, 73–87, esp. n.256.

33. Kolb, *Critique of Pure Modernity*, 96.

34. "Human Functioning and Social Justice," 212–13.

35. There are data that suggest that it will be far from easy to alter significantly these distributions. According to Richard Harwood, in 1939, 30 percent of Americans favored a cap on personal incomes; in 1992 only 17 percent did. Two-thirds of Americans in 1992 thought it was "good for Americans" to have a class of wealthy people; and in 1992, 71 percent rejected the idea that the country is divided between the "haves and the have-nots." Harwood, "The Anger Isn't Out There." A study in the 1980s showed the United States as having the lowest percentage of people who believed that it is the responsibility of government to reduce the differences in income between those with high and low income. Twenty-nine percent of Americans agreed with this proposition, while at least 60 percent of the citizens of six West European countries did so. See Dionne, "Loss of Faith in Egalitarianism Alters U.S. Vision." See also the analysis in Verba et al., *Elites and the Idea of Equality.*

36. How much public-spiritedness is there presently? It will come as no great surprise to those who follow research trends in the social sciences that there is very little good research on what, by any accounting, is a fundamental question. Benjamin Page and Roger Shapiro do report ("The Rational Public and Beyond") that "often majorities support policies that will cost them money." They also indicate that "more than is often acknowledged, too, Americans are willing to sacrifice for the collective good" (109). Based on in-depth exploration of the matter, Richard Harwood concludes that at least the citizens he talked to had a concern for the public interest but did not necessarily call it that, thinking rather in terms of getting involved in civic life, which they distinguished from "politics." *Citizens and Politics.* On balance, then, the problem is not that we are entirely self-interested. Probably the only people who believe that are paid to believe it—notably economists and others who appear to explain everybody else's behavior in this fashion. Still, it is doubtful that there is anything like enough public-spiritedness to provide a secure foundation for republican lawmaking.

37. For some evidence and argument that supports the characterization of local political life in this and the next paragraph, see chapter 10 and Elkin, "Citizen and City," as well as *City and Regime*, chaps. 8–9.

38. Here and in the succeeding paragraphs, I draw freely on my "Citizen and City."

39. East St. Louis has a per capita income of $11,169 versus the national average of $21,587 according to the U.S. Census. Approximately 22.7 percent of families in the city live on incomes below $10,000 and as of 1999, 35.1 percent of all individuals in East St. Louis lived below the poverty line. U.S. Bureau of the Census 2000 Summary File (SF-3)—Sample Data for East St. Louis City.

40. It is difficult to be certain how much deliberative lawmaking there is. See the very useful discussion in Bessette, *Mild Voice of Reason.* One important difficulty is that while there may be a good deal of deliberation about the broad outlines of particular pieces of legislation, the details that define its actual impact—that, in fact, *are* the legislation—can be the result more of bargaining than of reasoned discussion. In such cases, deliberation may well be window dressing. The essential question is whether the general framework that arises out of deliberation in fact sharply constrains the bargaining over details. If so, we can talk about deliberative

ways of lawmaking being at work. Given this distinction, a plausible estimate of how much the Congress engages in deliberation is that there is a lot of window dressing and not enough sharp constraint.

Then there is the recent rise of more ideologically coherent parties—especially among the Republicans—which might seem to point to a fair amount of deliberation in the legislative arena. In addition to what I have already said about ideological parties (see chapter 7), we may ask, with Philip Selznick, "Do decisions driven by ideology or belief qualify as deliberation?" He goes on to answer that "if critical judgment is the key, the answer may often be no." "Defining Democracy Up." Theodore Lowi sums up the case that there is too little deliberation by arguing that what happened during the "Second Republic," that is, the one at work since the New Deal, is that "Congress was redefined as a useful collection of minorities." *End of Liberalism*, 275. In addition to Besette, on this whole question, see Maass, *Congress and the Common Good*; Kelman, *Making Public Policy*; Mayhew, *Electoral Connection*. The exception that proves the rule is to be found in the congressional debate on the impending Gulf War. One long-time and thoughtful observer of the Congress, David Broder, said that "never in 35 years have I seen more lawmakers talking seriously with each other about the choice they were about to make." "Bravo Congress." The implication is that the sight of Congress rising to principle is as edifying as it is unexpected.

41. For useful, more elaborate discussions of the middle class, see Strobel, *Upward Dreams, Downward Mobility*; Greenberg, *Middle-Class Dreams*; Ehrenreich, *Fear of Falling*; Phillips, *Boiling Point*.

42. Data reported by the *New York Times* in a nationwide telephone poll show that 34 percent of the respondents or someone in their household had been laid off from a job since 1980. Of those who reported that no one in their household had been laid off, 58 percent said that they knew of a neighbor or relative who had been laid off since 1980. See *New York Times*, March 7, 1996. If this data is at all representative—and it is worth noting that the poll was taken in the middle of an enormous economic boom—it is highly plausible that a large section of the contemporary middle class knows intimately the fear of losing a job. This conclusion is strengthened by data that indicate that in an average month between March 1996 and November 1999, approximately 2.1 million people lost their jobs. U.S. Federal Government, "Dynamics of Economic Well-Being: Labor Force Turnover, 1996–1999."

Other, more recent data strengthen the point. The percent of people making between half and double the median family income fell from 71.2 percent in 1969 to 60.7 percent in 2002. "As Income Gap Widens, Uncertainty Spreads," *Washington Post*, September 20, 2004, reporting data from the U.S. Census Bureau. Similarly, the percentage of households with income between $25,000 and $75,000, adjusted for inflation, fell from 51.9 percent to 44.9 percent during 1980 to 2003. "Economic Squeeze Plaguing Middle Class Families," *New York Times*, August 28, 2004, reporting U.S. Census Bureau data. And one analyst reports that "family incomes have become two to three times more unstable in the past three decades, even for well-educated workers and two-earner families." Hacker, "Middle-Class Tightrope."

43. Consider that one in five full-time workers now do not have health insurance. *Washington Post*, December 31, 2004.

44. See Wolff, "Stagnating Fortunes of the Middle Class."

45. Republican government makes sometimes dangerous motives such as ambition safe for popular self-government. This is one of the effects of a well-ordered separation of powers.

46. See *The Prince* and the *Discourses on Livy*. For extraordinarily helpful accounts of Machiavelli's thought, see Mansfield, *Machiavelli's Virtue; Taming the Prince*, chap. 6; *Machiavelli's New Modes and Orders*. See also Shklar, "Bad Characters for Good Liberals," in *Ordinary Vices*.

47. Harvey Mansfield (*Taming the Prince*, 277) remarks that according to Machiavelli, "men may choose, but the only prudent choice is anticipation of necessity."

48. Leo Strauss characterizes Machiavelli's view this way: "Morality is possible only within a context which cannot be created by morality, for morality cannot create itself. The context within which morality is possible is created by immorality. Morality rests on immorality, justice rests on injustice. . . . One must define virtue in terms of the common good." *What Is Political Philosophy*, 41–42.

49. *Intellectual History of Liberalism*, 14. If we were to replace the language of morality as applied to politics, what would we replace it with? The language of prudence? Of virtue?

50. Mansfield, "Machiavelli and the Idea of Progress," in *Machiavelli's Virtue*, 112; Mansfield, "Machiavelli's Virtue," in ibid., 22.

51. *Discourses on Livy*, 23.

52. Mansfield, *Taming the Prince*, 47.

53. As Samuel Beer says, "Constitutionalism in America, in short, is not a barrier to, but an instrument of, democracy." *To Make a Nation*, 340.

54. For two of the many useful discussions, see Herzog, "Six Impossible Things before Breakfast"; Walzer, "Communitarian Critique of Liberalism."

55. See especially the work of Hayek considered in chapter 4.

56. As quoted in J. P. Kenyon, *The Stuart Constitution 1603–1688*, p. 15.

57. See the Declaration of Independence where it is announced that governments derive "their just powers from the consent of the governed." Cf. Beer, *To Make a Nation*.

58. Cf. the comment of Harvey Mansfield and Nathan Tarcov that "neither those eager for rewards nor those desiring to be let alone will be partisan friends of a republic." Machiavelli, *Discourses on Livy*, xiv.

Chapter Ten

1. Ackerman, *We the People*.

2. Ackerman presents dualist theory not as the best theory possible of how we might organize our political order, but as the best account and defense of how the American political order now operates. The fact that dualist theory is offered as a defense of what is, rather than what might be, makes it awkward to criticize Ackerman's arguments. He might well agree with any criticisms offered and simply

say, "Well, this is not what *I* would want; it is simply the best defense of what we have." For ease of exposition, I posit that dualist theory is thought by Ackerman to be not only the best defense of our practices, but also an attractive theory of the political constitution of the American regime. This is consistent with the tone of the book. Moreover, it would be a very odd project indeed to present a defense of current American political practice while believing that it is fundamentally unattractive. See ibid., 319–23.

3. Ackerman does not spend much time explicitly talking about reform, so we must to some degree infer his views.

4. Ackerman says that there have been three and a half efforts at higher-lawmaking in American history.

5. *The Federalist* No. 49.

6. See chapter 1.

7. As well, of course, about how to constitute an aggregative politics and what to do about moral politics.

8. See chapter 4.

9. The details of the reforms are another matter. They require sophisticated analyses that cannot be undertaken here. See, e.g., Roemer, *Equal Shares;* Bowles and Gintis, *Recasting Egalitarianism.* Both are volumes in a project—Real Utopias—directed by Erik Wright.

10. See Imbroscio, "Reconstructing City Politics."

11. For an extensive discussion, see ibid., chap. 3. These strategies are not mutually exclusive and within each there is a wide range of possibilities.

12. See chapter 7 above and the discussion below.

13. See Elkin, *City and Regime,* chap. 9, and chapter 7 above.

14. For very useful discussions, see Frug, "The City as a Legal Concept."

15. A rough measure of local autonomy would include the degree to which officials are elected by the local citizenry or are appointed by those who are; the extent to which local government revenues are raised through local taxation; and the degree to which local powers can be exercised over significant features of local life without approval from more inclusive governments. For a helpful discussion, see Derthick, "How Many Committees?"

16. But see the discussion below. Private schooling cannot be prohibited in a republican regime. The question, then, is whether public resources should be used to make it more attractive than it presently is for the vast majority of citizens.

17. See *New York Times,* July 13, 1994.

18. "We Are Not the World," *New York Times,* February 13, 1997.

19. Quoted in Alperovitz, *America beyond Capitalism,* 126. The data are also to be found in ibid., chap. 12 ("Is Local Democracy Possible in the Global Era?"). I have followed Alperovitz's analysis closely in this discussion of globalization.

20. Dahl, *Democracy and Its Critics,* chap. 23.

21. Fishkin, *The Voice of the People;* Kay, *Locating Consensus for Democracy.*

22. Barber, "American Civic Forum."

23. See Crosby, "National Coalition for Dialogue and Deliberation," available at http://www.thataway.org.

24. Increased economic security accompanied by greater economic equality—which a full employment policy at least moderately remunerative wages will promote—will also directly serve the public interest. It will do so indirectly as well by fostering the mutual respect needed among the citizenry if there is to be deliberative lawmaking.

25. There are difficulties to be overcome here. See Elkin, *City and Regime*, 171–74.

26. Mancur Olson argues in *The Rise and Decline of Nations* that what he calls "encompassing groups" are also necessary for high rates of economic growth.

27. The estimates were given in an informal talk by Senator Rudman in 1996 before an audience of citizens concerned with the state of contemporary American politics.

28. Malbin, *Unelected Representatives*, 243.

29. See Mansbridge, "Congress: Representation and Deliberation."

30. Malbin, *Unelected Representatives*, 243.

31. See Bessette, *Mild Voice of Reason*, 147.

32. Blumenthal, "Rendezvous with Destiny," 40.

33. *New York Times*, August 26, 1993.

34. See the description of such activities by lobbying firms in the *New York Times*, March 17, 1993, and November 1, 1993.

35. In the 2004 elections, seven House incumbents lost; in 2002, eight did. According to the Center on Voting and Democracy, in 2004, 83 percent of the House contests were decided by a margin of at least 20 percent; 95 percent were decided by a margin of 10 percent or more. The data are quoted in the *Washington Post*, November 4, 2004. I owe this point to Clarence Stone, who has taught me much about the ways in which the separation of powers can also undercut republican government.

36. However, there is some evidence that the increase in the number of safe seats is a result of a kind of geographic sorting in which people gravitate to localities that conform to their partisan outlook. As a result we get the blue state/red state phenomenon with the concentration of blue staters on the two coasts and red staters in the middle of the country.

37. See Posner, "People's Court."

38. "Political Parties and the Bureaucracy," 155. See also Cook, *Bureaucracy and Self-Government*; Rohr, *To Run a Constitution*.

39. Dahl, *Who Governs?* chaps. 27–28.

40. Dahl, *Dilemmas of Pluralist Democracy*, chaps. 1–3.

41. See Mansbridge, "Deliberative Perspective on Neo-Corporatism."

42. See Vincent Ostrom's parallel but different use of this phrase of Madison's in *The Political Theory of the Compound Republic*. See also Schmitter, "Still the Century of Corporatism?"; Cohen and Rogers, "Secondary Associations."

43. See also chapter 3.

44. In one version of the proposal developed by Bruce Ackerman and Anne Alstott, each person on reaching adulthood would be given $80,000 to use as they see fit. *Stakeholder Society*. For why $80,000, see their discussion at 58–60.

45. See Alperovitz, *American beyond Capitalism*, esp. chap. 1. I have learned much on these matters from teaching a seminar with Gar Alperovitz on the possibilities for a new democratic political economy. For his views on the matter, see ibid. In this paragraph of the text and the ones immediately following I draw heavily on his discussion in chapter 1 of the book.

46. In addition to the very clear discussion by Alperovitz, see Bowles and Gintis, *Recasting Egalitarianism*; Dahl, *Preface to Economic Democracy*; Stauber, *New Program for Democratic Socialism*; Roemer, *Equal Shares*.

47. See, e.g., Levine, *New Progressive Era*, chap. 4.

48. *Capitalism and Freedom*, chap. 12.

49. For one set of very interesting proposals to achieve this, see Weitzman, *Share Economy*.

50. Defined as twice the poverty level—which is no great amount of money.

51. For this and other data, see the table "Money Matters" in *Economist*, February 24, 1996.

52. For a view that middle-class insecurity is growing, see Hacker, "False Positive," 14–17.

53. Cf. Fred Hirsch's comment that a suburb's "relevant features are to a substantial extent derivative. In this sense, suburban living of given quality characteristics is a positional good, limited in absolute availability by the context of surrounding conditions and influence." *Social Limits to Growth*, 38.

54. See Wolff, "Stagnating Fortunes of the Middle Class"; Greenberg, *Middle Class Dreams*; Levy, *New Dollars and Dreams*.

55. Cited in Friedman, "Bush and Kerry." See also Johnston, "The Richest Are Leaving Even the Richer Far Behind"; Cassidy, "Tax Code."

56. See Hochschild, *Facing Up to the American Dream*.

57. See, most recently, Zelizer, *Capitol Hill*.

58. For an account of a life of graceful simplicity and the prospects of its gaining a hold on Americans, see Segal, *Graceful Simplicity*.

59. Rousseau, *Social Contract*, 71.

60. See American Political Science Association, "More Responsible Two-Party System."

BIBLIOGRAPHY

Ackerman, Bruce. *Private Property and the Constitution.* New Haven: Yale University Press, 1977.
———. *Social Justice in the Liberal State.* New Haven: Yale University Press, 1980.
———. "The Storrs Lectures: Discovering the Constitution." *Yale Law Journal* 93 (1984): 1013–72.
———. *We the People.* Cambridge: Harvard University Press, Belknap Press, 1991.
Ackerman, Bruce, and Anne Alstott. *The Stakeholder Society.* New Haven: Yale University Press, 1999.
Adair, Douglas. *Fame and the Founding Fathers: Essays.* Edited by Trevor Colbourn, with a personal memoir by Caroline Robbins and a bibliographical essay by Robert E. Shalhope. New York: Published for the Institute of Early American History and Culture at Williamsburg, Va., by Norton, 1974.
Adams, John. *Thoughts on Government* [1776]. In *The Political Writings of John Adams,* ed. George A. Peek. New York: Liberal Arts Press, 1954.
Agar, Herbert. *The Price of Union.* Boston: Houghton Mifflin, 1950.
Aldrich, Nelson Jr. *Old Money: The Mythology of Wealth in America.* New York: Knopf, 1988.
Alexander, Larry. "The Public/Private Distinction and Constitutional Limits on Private Power." *Constitutional Commentary* 10: 361–78.
Almond, Gabriel Abraham, and Sidney Verba. *The Civic Culture: Political Attitudes and Democracy in Five Nations, an Analytic Study.* Boston: Little, Brown, 1965.
Alperovitz, Gar. *America beyond Capitalism.* Hoboken, N.J.: Wiley, 2005.
Amar, Akhil Reed. "Philadelphia Revisited: Amending the Constitution Outside Article V." *University of Chicago Law Review* 55(4) (Fall 1988): 1043–1104.
American Political Science Association. "Toward a More Responsible Two-Party System: A Report of the Committee on Political Parties." *American Political Science Review* 44(3), pt. 2 (1950): supplement.
Anderson, Charles. *Pragmatic Liberalism.* Chicago: University of Chicago Press, 1990.

Annas, Julia. *The Morality of Happiness.* New York: Oxford University Press, 1993.

Appleby, Joyce Oldham. *Capitalism and a New Social Order: The Republican Vision of the 1790s.* New York: New York University Press, 1984.

Aranson, Peter H., and Peter C. Ordeshook. "Public Interest, Private Interest, and the Democratic Polity." In *The Democratic State,* ed. Roger Benjamin and Stephen L. Elkin. Lawrence, Kan.: University Press of Kansas, 1985.

Arendt, Hannah. *The Origins of Totalitarianism.* New York: Harcourt Brace Jovanovich, 1973.

Aristotle. *Eudemian Ethics.* In *The Complete Works of Aristotle,* ed. Jonathan Barnes. Princeton: Princeton University Press, 1984.

———. *Nicomachean Ethics.* Edited by Joe Sachs. Newburyport, Mass.: Focus Publishing, 2002.

———. *Politics.* Translated and with an introduction, notes, and glossary by Carnes Lord. Chicago: University of Chicago Press, 1985.

Arkes, Hadley. *First Things: An Inquiry into the First Principles of Morals and Justice.* Princeton: Princeton University Press, 1986.

Arnold, Matthew. "Dover Beach." In *Matthew Arnold,* ed. Miriam Allot and Robert H. Super. New York: Oxford University Press, 1986.

Aron, Raymond. "On Arendt and Totalitarianism." In *In Defense of Reasons: Essays by Raymond Aron.* Lanham, Md.: Rowman and Littlefield, 1994.

Aslund, Anders. "Moscow's New Power Center." *New York Times,* April 19, 1991.

Avinieri, Shlomo. *Hegel's Theory of the State.* Cambridge: Cambridge University Press, 1972.

Ball, Terence, and J. G. A. Pocock, eds. *Conceptual Change and the Constitution.* Lawrence, Kan.: University Press of Kansas, 1988.

Baker, Gordon E., and Alpheus Mason. *Free Government in the Making: Readings in American Political Thought.* New York: Oxford University Press, 1985.

Banfield, Edward C. *The Moral Basis of a Backward Society.* New York: Free Press, 1967 [1958].

———. *Political Influence.* Glencoe, Ill.: Free Press, 1961.

Banning, Lance. *The Sacred Fire of Liberty: James Madison and the Founding of the Federal Republic.* Ithaca: Cornell University Press, 1995.

———. "Second Thoughts on Virtue and the Course of Revolutionary Thinking." In *Conceptual Change and the Constitution,* ed. Terrence Ball and J. G. A. Pocock. Lawrence, Kan.: University Press of Kansas, 1988.

Barber, Benjamin. "An American Civic Forum." *The Good Society* 5(2) (1995): 10–14.

———. *Strong Democracy: Participatory Politics for a New Age.* Berkeley: University of California Press, 1984.

Barber, Sotirios. *On What the Constitution Means.* Baltimore: Johns Hopkins University Press, 1984.

Baron, Marcia, Philip Pettit, and Michael Slote, eds. *Three Methods of Ethics.* Malden, Mass.: Blackwell, 1997.

Barry, Brian M. *Does Society Exist?: The Case for Socialism.* London: Fabian Society, 1989.

———. *Political Argument.* London: Routledge and Kegan Paul, 1965.

Beard, Charles Austin. *The Economic Basis of Politics*. New York: Knopf, 1945.

———. *An Economic Interpretation of the Constitution of the United States*. New York: Free Press, 1965 [1935].

Becker, Gary. "Competition and Democracy." *Journal of Law and Economics* 1 (1958).

Beer, Samuel Hutchison. "Federalism and the Nation-State." In *Rethinking Federalism*, ed. Karen Knop et al. Vancouver: University of British Columbia Press, 1995.

———. *To Make a Nation: The Rediscovery of American Federalism*. Cambridge: Harvard University Press, Belknap Press, 1993.

Benjamin, Roger, and Stephen L. Elkin, eds. *The Democratic State*. Lawrence, Kan.: University Press of Kansas, 1985.

Berle, Adolf, and Gardiner C. Means. *The Modern Corporation and Private Property*. New York: Harcourt, Brace, 1968.

Berman, Harold Joseph. *Law and Revolution: The Formation of the Western Legal Tradition*. Cambridge: Harvard University Press, 1983.

Berns, Walter. "Does the Constitution 'Secure These Rights?'" In *How Democratic Is the Constitution?*, ed. Robert Godwin and William Schambra. Washington, D.C.: American Enterprise Institute, 1980.

Bernstein, Richard. "Books of the Times: A Clinton Adviser's Not-Always-Happy Memories." *New York Times*, April 30, 1997.

Bessette, Joseph M. *The Mild Voice of Reason: Deliberative Democracy and American National Government*. Chicago: University of Chicago Press, 1994.

Best, Judith. "Fundamental Rights and the Structure of Government." In *The Framers and Fundamental Rights*, ed. Robert A. Licht. Washington, D.C.: American Enterprise Institute, 1992.

Bickel, Alexander M. *The Least Dangerous Branch; the Supreme Court at the Bar of Politics*. Indianapolis: Bobbs-Merrill, 1962.

Blau, Joseph L., ed. *Social Theories of Jacksonian Democracy: Representative Writings of the Period 1825–1850*. Indianapolis: Bobbs-Merrill, 1954.

Blumenberg, Hans. *Shipwreck with Spectator: Paradigm of a Metaphor for Existence*. Translated by Steven Rendall. Cambridge: MIT Press, 1997.

Blumenthal, Sidney. "Rendezvous with Destiny." *New Yorker*, March 8, 1993, 30–44.

Bobbio, Norberto. *The Future of Democracy: A Defence of the Rules of the Game*. Cambridge: Polity, 1987.

Bohman, James. *Public Deliberation*. Cambridge: MIT Press, 1996.

Bork, Robert H. *The Tempting of America: The Political Seduction of the Law*. New York: Free Press, 1990.

Boswell, James. *Everybody's Boswell*. Edited by Frank Morely. London: Bell and Hyman, 1980.

Boucher, Jonathan. *A View of the Causes and Consequences of the American Revolution; in Thirteen Discourses, Preached in North America between the Years 1763 and 1775*. London: printed for G. G. & J. Robinson, 1797.

Bowles, Samuel, and Herbert Gintis. *Democracy and Capitalism: Property, Community, and the Contradictions of Modern Social Thought*. New York: Basic Books, 1986.

———. *Recasting Egalitarianism*. Edited by Erik Olin Wright. London: Verso, 1998.

Braybrooke, David, and Charles E. Lindblom. *A Strategy of Decision: Policy Evaluation as a Social Process*. New York: Free Press, 1963.

Brest, Paul. "The Fundamental Rights Controversy: The Essential Contradictions of Normative Constitutional Scholarship." *Yale Law Journal* 90 (1981): 1063–1109.

Broder, David. "Bravo Congress." *Washington Post*, January 15, 1991.

Bromwich, David. *A Choice of Inheritance: Self and Community from Edmund Burke to Robert Frost*. Cambridge: Harvard University Press, 1989.

Buchanan, James M. *The Economics and the Ethics of Constitutional Order*. Ann Arbor: University of Michigan Press, 1991.

Buchanan, James M., and Gordon Tullock. *The Calculus of Consent: Logical Foundations of Constitutional Democracy*. Ann Arbor: University of Michigan Press, 1962.

Burke, Edmund. *Edmund Burke: Selections*. Edited by A. M. D. Hughes. Oxford: Oxford University Press, 1930.

———. *The Portable Edmund Burke*. Edited with an introduction by Isaac Kramnick. New York: Penguin Books, 1999.

———. *Reflections on the Revolution in France and the Proceedings in Certain Societies in London Relative to That Event*. In *Works*, vol. 2. London: Bohn, 1855.

———. *The Works of the Right Honourable Edmund Burke*. London: Oxford University Press, 1907–34.

Burnham, Walter Dean, *Critical Elections and the Mainsprings of American Politics* New York: Norton, 1970.

Burns, James MacGregor. *The Deadlock of Democracy: Four-Party Politics in America*. Englewood Cliffs, N.J.: Prentice-Hall, 1963.

Burt, Robert. *The Constitution in Conflict*. Cambridge: Harvard University Press, 1992.

Burtt, Shelley. "The Politics of Virtue Today: A Critique and a Proposal." *American Political Science Review* 87(2) (June 1993): 360–68.

———. "Virtue Transformed: Republican Argument in Eighteenth Century England." Unpublished ms. Yale University, n.d. on file with author.

Calabresi, Guido. *A Common Law for the Age of Statutes*. Cambridge: Harvard University Press, 1982.

Carter, Ian. "A Critique of Freedom as Non-Domination." *The Good Society* 9(3) (2000): 43–46.

Cassidy, John. "Tax Code." *New Yorker*, September 6, 2004.

Caton, Hiram. *The Politics of Progress: The Origins and Development of the Commercial Republic*. Gainesville: University of Florida Press, 1988 [1986].

Ceaser, James. *Liberal Democracy and Political Science*. Baltimore: Johns Hopkins Press, 1992.

Churchman C. West, and Ian I. Mitroff. "The Management of Science and the Mismanagement of the World." In *The Experimenting Society: Essays in Honor of Donald T. Campbell*, ed. W. Dunn, 103–24. New Brunswick, N.J.: Transaction Publishers, 1998.

Cicero. *De Re Publica*. Translated by C. W. Keyes. Cambridge: Harvard University Press, 1928.

Cohen, Joshua, and Joel Rogers, "Secondary Associations and Democratic Governance." *Politics and Society* 20(4) (1992): 393–472.

Community Communications Co., Inc. v. City of Boulder, Colorado, 455 U.S. 40 (1981).

Conover, Pamela Johnson, et al. "Duty Is a Four-Letter Word: Democratic Leadership in a Liberal Polity." Unpublished paper on file with author.

Cook, Brian. *Bureaucracy and Self-Government*. Baltimore: Johns Hopkins University Press, 1996.

Crick, Bernard R. *In Defence of Politics*. Chicago: University of Chicago Press, 1993.

Cropsey, Joseph. "The United States as Regime." In *The Moral Foundations of the American Republic*, ed. Robert Horwitz. Charlottesville: University Press of Virginia, 1977.

Dahl, Robert. *After the Revolution?: Authority in a Good Society*. New Haven: Yale University Press, 1990.

———. "Decision-Making in a Democracy: The Supreme Court as a National Policy-Maker." *Journal of Public Law* 6(2) (1958): 279–95.

———. *Democracy and Its Critics*. New Haven: Yale University Press, 1989.

———. *Dilemmas of Pluralist Democracy: Autonomy vs. Control*. New Haven: Yale University Press, 1982.

———. *On Democracy*. New Haven: Yale University Press, 1998.

———. *A Preface to Democratic Theory*. Chicago: University of Chicago Press, 1956.

———. *A Preface to Economic Democracy*. Berkeley: University of California Press, 1985.

———. *Who Governs? Democracy and Power in an American City*. New Haven: Yale University Press, 1961.

Derthick, Martha. "How Many Communities? The Evolution of American Federalism." In *Dilemmas of Scale in America's Federal Democracy*, ed. Martha Derthick. New York: Woodrow Wilson Center Press, Cambridge University Press, 1999.

Dewey, John. *The Public and Its Problems*. Athens, Ohio: Swallow Press, Ohio University Press, 1985 [1954].

Diamond, Ann. "Decent Though Democratic." In *How Democratic Is the Constitution?*, ed. Robert A. Goldwin and William Schambra. Washington, D.C.: American Enterprise Institute, 1982.

Diamond, Martin. "Democracy and *The Federalist:* A Reconsideration of the Framers' Intent." *American Political Science Review* 53(1) (March 1959): 52–68.

———. *The Founding of the Democratic Republic*. Itasca, Ill.: F. E. Peacock Publishers, 1981.

Dicey, A. V. *Introduction to the Study of the Law of the Constitution*. London: Macmillan, 1959.

Diggins, John P. *The Lost Soul of American Politics: Virtue, Self-Interest, and the Foundations of Liberalism*. New York: Basic Books, 1984.

Dionne, E. J., Jr. "Loss of Faith in Egalitarianism Alters U.S. Vision." *Washington Post*, April 30, 1990.

———. "The New Rules of Politics." *Washington Post*, May 30, 2003.

Dworkin, Ronald. "Justice for Clarence Thomas." *New York Review of Books* 38(18) (November 7, 1991): 41–45.

————. *Law's Empire*. Cambridge: Harvard University Press, Belknap Press, 1986.

————. *A Matter of Principle*. Cambridge: Harvard University Press, 1985.

————. "The Moral Reading of the Constitution." *New York Review of Books*, March 21, 1996, 46–50.

————. "Mr. Liberty." Review of Gerald Gunther, *Learned Hand: The Man and the Judge. New York Review of Books* 41(14) (August 11, 1994): 17–22.

————. "Natural Law Revisited." *University of Florida Law Review* 34(2) (Winter 1982): 165–88.

————. *Taking Rights Seriously*. Cambridge: Harvard University Press, 1978.

Ehrenreich, Barbara. *Fear of Falling: The Inner Life of the Middle Class*. New York: Pantheon Books, 1989.

Eisgruber, Christopher L. *Constitutional Self-Government*. Cambridge: Harvard University Press, 2001.

Elkin, Stephen L. "Business–State Relations in the Commercial Republic." *Journal of Political Philosophy* 2(2) (June 1994): 115–39.

————. "Citizen and City." In *Dilemmas of Scale in America's Federal Democracy*, ed. Martha Derthick. New York: Woodrow Wilson Center Press, Cambridge University Press, 1999.

————. *City and Regime in the American Republic*. Chicago: University of Chicago Press, 1987.

————. "The Constitutional Theory of the Commercial Republic." *Fordham Law Review* 69(5) (2001): 1933–68.

————. "Economic and Political Rationality." *Polity* 18(2) (Winter 1985): 253–71.

————. "Madison and After: The American Model of Political Constitution." *Political Studies* 44(3) (1996): 592–604.

————. "Markets and Politics in Liberal Democracy." *Ethics* 92(4) (July 1982): 720–32.

————. "Pluralism in Its Place: State and Regime in Liberal Democracy." In *The Democratic State*, ed. Roger Benjamin and Stephen L. Elkin. Lawrence, Kan.: University Press of Kansas, 1985.

————. "Political Institutions and Political Practice." In *Handbook of Political Theory and Policy Science*, ed. Edward Portis and Michael Levy. Westport, Conn.: Greenwood, 1987.

————. "The Theory of American Business." *Business in the Contemporary World* 1(3) (Spring 1989): 25–37.

————. "Thinking Constitutionally: The Problem of Deliberative Democracy." *Social Philosophy and Policy* 21(1) (2004): 39–75.

Elkin, Stephen, and Karol Soltan, eds. *Citizen Competence and Democratic Institutions*. University Park, Penn.: Pennsylvania State University Press, 1999.

————, eds. *A New Constitutionalism: Designing Political Institutions for a Good Society*. Chicago: University of Chicago Press, 1993.

Elkins, Stanley, and Eric McKitrick. *The Age of Federalism*. New York: Oxford University Press, 1993.

Elliot, Jonathan, ed. *The Debates, Resolutions, and Other Proceedings, in Convention, on the Adoption of the Federal Constitution, as Recommended by the General Convention at Philadelphia, on the 17th of September, 1787: with the Yeas and Nays on the Decision of the Main Question*. Collected and revised, from contemporary publications, by Jonathan Elliot. Washington: printed by and for the editor, 1827–30.

Elster, Jon, ed. *Deliberative Democracy*. New York: Cambridge University Press, 1998.

———. *Sour Grapes: Studies in the Subversion of Rationality*. New York: Cambridge University Press; Paris: Editions de la Maison des sciences de l'homme, 1983.

Ely, John Hart. *Democracy and Distrust: A Theory of Judicial Review*. Cambridge: Harvard University Press, 1980.

Epstein, David F. *The Political Theory of* The Federalist. Chicago: University of Chicago Press, 1984.

Epstein, Richard Allen. "Beyond the Rule of Law: Civic Virtue and Constitutional Structure," *George Washington Law Review* 56(1) (November 1987): 149–71.

———. *Principles for a Free Society: Reconciling Individual Liberty with the Common Good*. Reading, Mass.: Perseus Books, 1998.

Erlanger, Steven. "Rally in Belgrade Protests Early Closing of Serbian Universities." *New York Times*, May 27, 2000.

Farrand, Max, ed. *The Records of the Federal Convention of 1787*. New Haven: Yale University Press, 1911.

———. *The Federalist* (James Madison, John Jay, and Alexander Hamilton). Edited by Jacob E. Cooke. Middletown, Conn.: Wesleyan University Press, 1961.

Ferguson, Niall. *The Cash Nexus: Money and Power in the Modern World*. New York: Basic Books, 2001.

Finer, S. E., ed. *Five Constitutions*. Harmondsworth, UK: Penguin Books, 1979.

Finnis, John. *Natural Law and Natural Rights*. Oxford: Clarendon Press, 1980.

Fisher v. City of Berkeley, California, 475 U.S. 260 (1985).

Fisher, William W., Morton J. Horwitz, and Thomas Reed, eds. *American Legal Realism*. New York: Oxford University Press, 1993.

Fishkin, James S. *Democracy and Deliberation: New Directions for Democratic Reform*. New Haven: Yale University Press, 1991.

Fishkin, James S. *The Voice of the People*. New Haven: Yale University Press, 1995.

Fiss, Owen. "Objectivity and Interpretation." *Stanford Law Review* 34 (1982): 739–63.

Flathman, Richard E. *The Public Interest: An Essay Concerning the Normative Discourse of Politics*. New York: Wiley, 1966.

Frank, Robert H. *Passions within Reason*. New York: Norton, 1988.

Freeman, Alan, and Elizabeth Mensch. "The Public/Private Distinction in American Law and Life." *Buffalo Law Review* 36 (1986): 237–57.

Freeman, J. Leiper. *The Political Process*. New York: Random House, 1965.

Freeden, Michael. *Rights*. Minneapolis: University of Minnesota Press, 1991.

Fried, Charles. "The Artificial Reason of the Law—Or: What Lawyers Know." *Texas Law Review* 60 (1981): 35–58.

Friedman, Benjamin. "Bush and Kerry: A Big Divide." *New York Review of Books*, October 2, 2004, 27–29.

Friedman, Milton. *Capitalism and Freedom*. Chicago: University of Chicago Press, 2002.

Friedrich, Carl J. *Constitutional Government and Democracy: Theory and Practice in Europe and America*. Boston: Ginn, 1950.

Friedrich, Carl J., and Zbigniew K. Brzezinksi. *Totalitarian Dictatorship and Autocracy.* New York: Praeger, 1966 [1965].

Frohlich, Norman, and Joe Oppenheimer. *Choosing Justice: An Experimental Approach to Ethical Theory.* Berkeley: University of California Press, 1992.

Frug, Gerald. "The City as a Legal Concept." *Harvard Law Review* 93 (1980): 1057–1154.

Fukuyama, Francis. *Trust: The Social Virtues and the Creation of Prosperity.* New York: Free Press, 1995.

Fuller, Lon L. "Means and Ends." In *The Principles of Social Order: Selected Essays of Lon L. Fuller,* ed. Kenneth I. Winston. Durham: Duke University Press, 1981.

———. *The Morality of Law.* New Haven: Yale University Press, 1977 [1969].

Furnas, J. C. *The Americans, A Social History of the United States: 1587–1914.* New York: Putnam, 1969.

Gadamer, Hans Georg. *Truth and Method.* Translation edited by Garrett Barden and John Cumming. New York: Seabury Press, 1975.

Galambos, Louis, and Joseph Pratt. *The Rise of the Corporate Commonwealth: U.S. Business and Public Policy in the Twentieth Century.* New York: Basic Books, 1988.

Galston, William A. "Community, Democracy, Philosophy: The Political Thought of Michael Walzer." *Political Theory* 17(1) (February 1989): 119–30.

———. *Liberal Purposes: Goods, Virtues, and Diversity in the Liberal State.* Cambridge: Cambridge University Press, 1991.

———. "Liberal Virtues." *American Political Science Review* 82(4) (December 1988): 1277–90.

Gans, Herbert J. *The Levittowners: Ways of Life and Politics in a New Suburban Community.* New York, Pantheon Books, 1967.

———. *Middle American Individualism.* New York: Oxford University Press, 1988.

Garcia v. San Antonio Metropolitan Transit Authority, 469 U.S. 528 (1984).

Gierke, Otto. *Political Theories of the Middle Ages.* Translated by F. W. Maitland. Cambridge: Cambridge University Press, 1987.

Gilmore, Grant. *The Ages of American Law.* New Haven: Yale University Press, 1977.

Glennon, Michael. "Can the President Do No Wrong?" *American Journal of International Law* 80 (1986): 923–30.

Glover, Jonathan. *Humanity: A Moral History of the Twentieth Century.* New Haven: Yale University Press, 2000.

Goldstein, Joseph. *The Intelligible Constitution: The Supreme Court's Obligation to Maintain the Constitution as Something We the People Can Understand.* New York: Oxford University Press, 1992.

Goldwin, Robert A., and William Schambra, eds. *How Capitalistic Is the Constitution?* Washington, D.C.: American Enterprise Institute, 1982.

———. *How Democratic Is the Constitution?* Washington, D.C.: American Enterprise Institute, 1980.

———. *How Does the Constitution Secure Rights?* Washington: American Enterprise Institute, 1985.

Goodin, Robert E. "Institutionalizing the Public Interest: The Defense of Deadlock and Beyond." *American Political Science Review* 90(2) (June 1996): 331–43.

Gouldner, Alvin Ward. *The Future of Intellectuals and the Rise of the New Class: A Frame of Reference, Theses, Conjectures, Arguments, and an Historical Perspective on the Role of Intellectuals and Intelligentsia in the International Class Contest of the Modern Era.* New York: Seabury Press, 1979.

Gray, John. "Autonomy Is Not the Only Good." *Times Literary Supplement,* June 13, 1999, 230.

———. *Liberalism.* Minneapolis: University of Minnesota Press, 1995.

———. "The Light of Other Minds." *Times Literary Supplement,* February 11, 2000, 12–13.

Greenberg, Edward. "Class Rule and the Constitution." In *How Democratic Is the Constitution?,* ed. Robert Goldwin and William Schambra. Washington, D.C.: American Enterprise Institute, 1982.

Greenberg, Stanley B. *Middle Class Dreams: The Politics and Power of the New American Majority.* New Haven: Yale University Press, 1996.

Greenhouse, Linda. "A Court Infused with Pragmatism." *Washington Post,* December 12, 2003.

Griffin, Stephen M. *American Constitutionalism: From Theory to Politics.* Princeton: Princeton University Press, 1996.

———. "Constitutional Theory Transformed." In *Constitutional Culture and Democratic Rule,* ed. John Ferejohn, Jack N. Rakove, and Jonathan Riley. Cambridge: Cambridge University Press, 2001.

Gunn, J. A. W. *Politics and the Public Interest in the Seventeenth Century.* London: Routledge and Kegan Paul, 1969.

Gutmann, Amy, and Dennis Thompson. *Democracy and Disagreement.* Cambridge: Harvard University Press, Belknap Press, 1996.

Haakonssen, Knud. *Natural Law and Moral Philosophy: From Grotius to the Scottish Enlightenment.* Cambridge: Cambridge University Press, 1996.

Hacker, Jacob S. "False Positive." *New Republic,* August 16 and 23, 2004.

———. "Middle-Class Tightrope." *Washington Post,* August 10, 2004.

Haefele, Edwin T. "Problems of Democratic Social Choice." Unpublished paper on file with author.

———. *Representative Government and Environmental Management.* Baltimore: Published for Resources for the Future by Johns Hopkins University Press, 1973.

———. "Toward a New Civic Calculus." Paper delivered to the Conference on Public Policy and the Quality of Life in Urban Areas. New Orleans, January 1975. Paper on file with author.

———. "What Constitutes the American Republic?" In *A New Constitutionalism: Designing Political Institutions for a Good Society,* ed. Stephen L. Elkin and Karol Soltan. Chicago: University of Chicago Press, 1993.

Halperin, Morton, et al. *The Lawless State.* New York: Penguin, 1976.

Hardin, Russell. *Liberalism, Constitutionalism, and Democracy.* New York: Oxford University Press, 1999.

Hart, H. L. A. *The Concept of Law.* Oxford: Oxford University Press, 1961.

Hartog, Henrik. "The Constitution of Aspiration and 'The Rights that Belong to Us All.'" *Journal of American History* 74(3) (1987): 1013–34.

Hartz, Louis. *The Liberal Tradition in America: An Interpretation of American Political Thought since the Revolution.* New York: Harcourt, Brace, 1955.

Harwood, Richard. "The Anger Isn't Out There." *Washington Post,* May 30, 1995.

———. *Citizens and Politics: A View from Main Street America.* Dayton, Ohio: The Foundation, 1991.

Hawaii Housing Authority v. Midkiff, 467 U.S. 229 (1984).

Hayek, Friedrich A. von. *The Constitution of Liberty.* Chicago: Regnery, 1972 [1960].

———. *Law, Legislation and Liberty: A New Statement of the Liberal Principles of Justice and Political Economy.* Vol. 1, *Rules and Order.* Chicago: University of Chicago Press, 1973.

———. *Law, Legislation and Liberty: A New Statement of the Liberal Principles of Justice and Political Economy.* Vol. 3, *The Political Order of a Free People.* Chicago: University of Chicago Press, 1979.

———. *The Road to Serfdom.* Chicago: University of Chicago Press, 1945.

Heclo, Hugh. "Issue Networks and the Executive Established." In *The New American Political System,* ed. Anthony King. Washington D.C.: American Enterprise Institute, 1978.

Held, David. *Democracy and the Global Order: From the Modern State to Cosmopolitan Governance.* Stanford: Stanford University Press, 1995.

Held, David, ed. *Political Theory Today.* Stanford: Stanford University Press, 1991.

Herzog, Don. "As Many as Six Impossible Things before Breakfast." *California Law Review* 75 (March 1987): 609–29.

Hexter, J. H. "Thomas Hobbes and the Law." *Cornell University Law Review* 65(4) (April 1980): 471–90.

———. *The Vision of Politics on the Eve of the Reformation: More, Machiavelli, and Seyssel.* New York: Basic Books, 1973.

Hirsch, Fred. *The Social Limits to Growth.* Cambridge: Harvard University Press, 1976.

Hirschman, Albert. *Exit, Voice and Loyalty.* Cambridge: Harvard University Press, 1970.

Hobbes, Thomas. *Leviathan.* Harmondsworth, UK: Penguin Books, 1968.

Hochschild, Jennifer. *Facing Up to the American Dream: Race, Class and the Soul of the Nation.* Princeton: Princeton University Press, 1995.

Holmes, Richard. *Coleridge: Darker Reflections.* New York: Pantheon Books, 1999.

Horwitz, Morton. "The History of the Public/Private Distinction." *University of Pennsylvania Law Review* 130 (1982): 1423–28.

Huntington, Samuel P. *Political Order in Changing Societies.* New Haven: Yale University Press, 1968.

Ignatieff, Michael. "The Attack on Human Rights." *Foreign Affairs* 80(6) (November/December 2001): 102–16.

———. "Human Rights: The Midlife Crisis." Review of Paul Gordon Lauren, *The Evolution of International Human Rights: Visions Seen. New York Review of Books* 46(9) (May 20, 1999): 58–62.

Imbroscio, David. Reconstructing City Politics: Alternative Local Economic Strategies and Urban Regimes. Ph.D. diss., University of Maryland, 1993.

Jaffa, Harry V. *Crisis of the House Divided: An Interpretation of the Issues in the Lincoln-Douglas Debates.* Chicago: University of Chicago Press, 1982.

Jefferson, Thomas. *Notes on the State of Virginia.* Edited with an introduction and notes by William Peden. New York: Norton, 1972 [1955].

———. *The Republic of Letters: The Correspondence between Thomas Jefferson and James Madison.* Edited by James Morton Smith. New York: Norton, 1995.

Johnson, Chalmers. *MITI and the Japanese Miracle: The Growth of Industrial Policy 1925–1975.* Stanford: Stanford University Press, 1982.

Johnston, David. "The Richest Are Leaving Even the Rich Far Behind." *New York Times,* June 5, 2005.

Jones, Harry W. "The Welfare State and the Rule of Law." *Columbia Law Review* 58(2) (1958): 143–56.

Josephson, Jyl. *Gender, Families, and State: Child Support Policy in the United States.* Lanham, Md.: Rowman and Littlefield, 1997.

Kaminski, Bartlomiej. *The Collapse of State Socialism: The Case of Poland.* Princeton: Princeton University Press, 1991.

Kammen, Michael. *A Machine That Would Go of Itself.* New York: Vintage Books, 1986.

Kant, Immanuel. *On History.* Edited with an introduction by Lewis White Beck. Translated by Lewis White Beck, Robert E. Anchor, and Emil L. Fackenheim. Indianapolis: Bobbs-Merrill, 1963.

Kay, Alan. *Locating Consensus for Democracy.* St. Augustine, Fla.: Americans Talk Issues Foundation, 2000.

Kelman, Steven. *Making Public Policy: A Hopeful View of American Government.* New York: Basic Books, 1987.

Kelso, Louis O., and Mortimer Adler. *The Capitalist Manifesto.* New York: Random House, 1958.

Kendall, Willmore. "The Two Majorities." *Midwest Journal of Political Science* 4(4) (November 1960): 317–45.

Kennedy, Duncan. "The Stages of the Decline of the Public/Private Distinction." *University of Pennsylvania Law Review* 130 (1982): 1349–57.

Kennedy v. Mendoza-Martinez, 372 U.S. 144 (1963).

Kenyon, J. P., ed. *The Stuart Constitution, 1603–1688: Documents and Commentary.* Cambridge: Cambridge University Press, 1986.

Ketcham, Ralph Louis. *From Colony to Country: The Revolution in American Thought, 1750–1820.* New York: Macmillan, 1974.

Key, V. O. *Politics, Parties and Pressure Groups.* 4th ed. New York: Thomas Cowell, 1958.

———. *The Responsible Electorate; Rationality in Presidential Voting, 1936–1960.* Cambridge: Harvard University Press, Belknap Press, 1966.

———. "A Theory of Critical Elections," *Journal of Politics* 17 (February 1955): 3–18.

Kishlansky, Mark A. *A Monarchy Transformed: Britain, 1603–1714.* London: Allen Lane, 1996.

Knop, Karen, et al., eds. *Rethinking Federalism.* Vancouver, B.C.: University of British Columbia Press, 1995.

Kolb, David. *The Critique of Pure Modernity: Hegel, Heidegger, and After.* Chicago: University of Chicago Press, 1986.

Kramer, Larry. *The People Themselves: Popular Constitutionalism and Judicial Review.* New York: Oxford University Press, 2004.

Kramnick, Isaac. *Republicanism and Bourgeois Radicalism: Political Ideology in Late Eighteenth-Century England and America.* Ithaca: Cornell University Press, 1990.

Kraynak, Robert. "Tocqueville's Constitutionalism." *American Political Science Review* 81(4) (December 1987): 1175–95.

Kristol, Irving. *Two Cheers for Democracy.* Washington, D.C.: American Enterprise Institute, 1979.

Krugman, Paul. *Peddling Prosperity: Economic Sense and Nonsense in the Age of Diminished Expectations.* New York: Norton, 1994.

———. "We Are Not the World." *New York Times,* February 13, 1997.

Kymlicka, Will. *Contemporary Political Philosophy.* Oxford: Clarendon Press, 1990.

Lane, Robert. *The Market Experience.* Cambridge: Cambridge University Press, 1991.

———. "Market Justice, Political Justice." *American Political Science Review* 80 (June 1986): 383–402.

Lang, Berel. *Act and Idea in the Nazi Genocide.* Chicago: University of Chicago Press, 1990.

Larmore, Charles. "Lifting the Veil." *New Republic* 224(6) (February 5, 2001).

Latham, Earl. *The Group Basis of Politics.* New York: Octagon Press, 1965.

Lehmann, William C., ed. *John Millar of Glasgow, 1735–1801: His Life and Thought and His Contributions to Sociological Analysis.* Cambridge: Cambridge University Press, 1960.

Lenzner, Steven J. "Strauss's Three Burkes." *Political Theory* 19(3) (1991): 364–90.

Lerner, Ralph. *Revolutions Revisited.* Chapel Hill: University of North Carolina Press, 1994.

———. *The Thinking Revolutionary: Principle and Practice in the New Republic.* Ithaca: Cornell University Press, 1987.

Levine, Peter. *The New Progressive Era.* Lanham, Md.: Rowman and Littlefield, 2000.

Levinson, Sanford. "Strolling Down the Path of the Law (and towards Critical Legal Studies?): The Jurisprudence of Richard Posner." *Columbia Law Review* 91 (1991): 1221–52.

Levy, Frank. *The New Dollars and Dreams.* New York: Russell Sage Foundation, 1998.

Lewis, Anthony. "How Not to Choose." *New York Times,* May 10, 1993.

Lincoln, Abraham. *Abraham Lincoln: Speeches and Writings 1859–1865.* Edited by Don E. Fehrenbacher. New York: Library of America, distributed by Viking Press, 1989.

Lindblom, Charles E. *The Intelligence of Democracy; Decision Making through Mutual Adjustment.* New York: Free Press, 1965.

———. *Politics and Markets: The World's Political Economic Systems.* New York: Basic Books, 1977.

Lippmann, Walter. *Drift and Mastery: An Attempt to Diagnose the Current Unrest.* Englewood Cliffs, N.J.: Prentice-Hall, 1961.

————. *An Inquiry into the Principles of the Good Society.* Boston: Little, Brown, 1937.

Lipsey, Richard, and Kevin Lancaster, "The General Theory of the Second Best." *Review of Economic Studies* 24(1) (1956): 1–32.

List, Christian, and John S. Dryzek. "Social Choice Theory and Deliberative Democracy." Working Papers in Social and Political Theory. No. 2000-W6. Australian National University, June 2000.

List, Christian, and Robert Goodin. "Epistemic Democracy: Generalizing the Condorcet Jury Theorem." *Journal of Political Philosophy* 9(3) (2001): 277–306.

List, Christian, and Philip Pettit. "The Aggregation of Reason." Working Papers in Social and Political Theory. No. 2000-W8. Australian National University, June 2000.

Local 1330, United Steel Workers of America v. United States Steel Corporation, 631 F.2d 1264 (6th Cir. 1980).

Locke, John. *Some Thoughts Concerning Education; and, Of the Conduct of the Understanding.* Edited with introduction and notes by Ruth W. Grant and Nathan Tarcov. Indianapolis: Hackett, 1996.

————. *Two Treatises of Government.* Edited by Peter Laslett. Cambridge: Cambridge University Press, 1988.

Long, Norton. "Dewey's Conception of the Public Interest." Paper presented to Midwest Political Science Association, April 1980. Paper on file with the author.

Lowi, Theodore J. *The End of Liberalism: The Second Republic of the United States.* New York: Norton, 1979.

Lowi, Theodore J. *The End of the Republican Era.* Norman, Okla.: University of Oklahoma Press, 1995.

Maass, Arthur. *Congress and the Common Good.* New York: Basic Books, 1983.

MacCormick, Neil. "To 'Ought' from 'Is.'" *Times Literary Supplement,* September 11, 1998, 14–15.

Machiavelli, Niccolo. *Discourses on Livy.* Translated by Harvey C. Mansfield and Nathan Tarcov. Chicago: University of Chicago Press, 1996.

————. *The Prince,* translated and with an introduction by Harvey C. Mansfield. Chicago: University of Chicago Press, 1998.

MacIntyre, Alasdair C. *After Virtue: A Study in Moral Theory.* Notre Dame, Ind.: University of Notre Dame Press, 1984.

Mackie, J. L. *Ethics: Inventing Right and Wrong.* Harmondsworth, UK: Penguin, 1977.

Macpherson, C. B. *The Life and Times of Liberal Democracy.* New York: Oxford University Press, 1977.

————. *The Political Theory of Possessive Individualism: Hobbes to Locke.* Oxford: Clarendon Press, 1972 [1962].

Maddox, Graham. "A Note on the Meaning of 'Constitution.'" *American Political Science Review* 76(4) (December 1982): 805–9.

Madison, James. "Government of the United States." In *James Madison: Writings,* ed. Jack Rakove. New York: Library of America, 1999.

———. *Letters and Other Writings of James Madison*. Edited by William C. Rives and Philip R. Fendall. Published by order of Congress. New York: Worthington, 1884.

———. *The Mind of the Founder: Sources of the Political Thought of James Madison*. Edited by Marvin Meyers. Hanover, N.H.: published for Brandeis University Press by University Press of New England, 1981.

———. *Notes of Debates in the Federal Convention of 1787*. Introduction by Adrienne Koch. Athens: Ohio University Press, 1966.

———. *The Papers of James Madison*. Vols. 11 and 12. Edited by Robert A. Rutland, Charles F. Hobson, and William M. E. Rachal. Charlottesville, Va.: University Press of Virginia, 1977, 1979.

———. *The Papers of James Madison*. Vol. 14. Edited by Robert A. Rutland and Thomas A. Mason. Charlottesville, Va.: University Press of Virginia, 1983.

———. "Parties." In *James Madison: Writings*, ed. Jack Rakove. New York: Library of America, 1999.

———. "Property." In *James Madison: Writings*, ed. Jack Rakove. New York: Library of America, 1999.

———. "Vices of the Political System of the U.S." In *James Madison: Writings*, ed. Jack Rakove. New York: Library of America, 1999.

———. *The Writings of James Madison, Comprising His Public Papers and His Private Correspondence, Including Numerous Letters and Documents Now for the First Time Printed*. Edited by Gaillard Hunt. New York: Putnam, 1900–10.

Malbin, Michael. *Unelected Representatives: Congressional Staff and the Future of Representative Government*. New York: Basic Books, 1979.

Manent, Pierre. *An Intellectual History of Liberalism*. Translated by Rebecca Balinski with a foreword by Jerrold Seigel. Princeton: Princeton University Press, 1994.

Mansbridge, Jane. "Congress: Representation and Deliberation." In *Constitutionalism in America*. Vol. 2. Edited by Sarah Baumgartner Thurow. New York: University Press of America, 1988.

———. "A Deliberative Perspective on Neo-Corporatism." *Politics and Society* 20(4) (1992): 495–505.

———. "A Deliberative Theory of Interest Representation." In *The Politics of Interests: Interest Groups Transformed*, ed. Mark P. Petracca. Boulder: Westview Press, 1992.

Mansfield, Harvey C. *America's Constitutional Soul*. Baltimore: Johns Hopkins University Press, 1991.

———. "Hobbes and the Science of Indirect Government." *American Political Science Review* 65 (1971): 97–110.

———. *Machiavelli's New Modes and Orders: A Study of the Discourses on Livy*. Ithaca: Cornell University Press, 1979.

———. *Machiavelli's Virtue*. Chicago: University of Chicago Press, 1996.

———. *The Spirit of Liberalism*. Cambridge: Harvard University Press, 1978.

———. *Statesmanship and Party Government; A Study of Burke and Bolingbroke*. Chicago: University of Chicago Press, 1965.

————. *Taming the Prince: The Ambivalence of Modern Executive Power.* New York: Free Press, 1989.

Marshall, Alfred. *Principles of Economics: An Introductory Volume.* London: Macmillan, 1964.

Marx, Karl, and Friedrich Engels. *The Communist Manifesto.* Introduction by Leon Trotsky. New York: Pathfinder Press, 1998.

Mason, Alpheus Thomas. *Free Government in the Making: Readings in American Political Thought.* New York: Oxford University Press, 1965.

Matthews, Richard K. *If Men Were Angels: James Madison and the Heartless Empire of Reason.* Lawrence, Kan.: University Press of Kansas, 1995.

Mayhew, David R. *Congress: The Electoral Connection.* New Haven: Yale University Press, 1975 [1974].

McCloskey, Robert G. *The American Supreme Court.* Chicago: University of Chicago Press, 2005.

McClosky, Herbert, and John Zaller. *The American Ethos: Public Attitudes toward Capitalism and Democracy.* Cambridge: Harvard University Press, 1984.

McCoy, Drew. *The Last of the Fathers: James Madison and the Republican Legacy.* Cambridge: Cambridge University Press, 1991.

McDonald, Forrest. *Novus Ordo Seclorum: the Intellectual Origins of the Constitution.* Lawrence, Kan.: University Press of Kansas, 1985.

————. *We the People: the Economic Origins of the Constitution.* Chicago: University of Chicago Press, 1958.

McGinn, Colin. "Reasons and Unreasons." *New Republic,* May 24, 1999, 32–38.

Meade, James. *Liberty, Equality and Efficiency.* New York: New York University Press, 1993.

Meek, Ronald L. *The Economics of Physiocracy: Essays and Translations.* Cambridge: Harvard University Press, 1963 [1962].

Michelman, Frank I. "Takings 1987." *Columbia Law Review* 88(8) (1988): 1600–1629.

Milkis, Sidney M. *Political Parties and Constitutional Government: Remaking American Democracy.* Baltimore: Johns Hopkins University Press, 1999.

Mill, John Stuart. *Mill on Bentham and Coleridge.* With an introduction by F. R. Leavis. Cambridge: Cambridge University Press, 1980.

————. *On Liberty.* Edited with an introduction by Gertrude Himmelfarb. Harmondsworth, UK: Penguin, 1974.

————. *On Liberty and Other Essays.* Edited by John Gray. New York: Oxford University Press, 1998 [1991].

————. *Utilitarianism.* Edited with an introduction by George Sher. Indianapolis: Hackett, 2001.

Miller, Arthur Selwyn. *Democratic Dictatorship: The Emergent Constitution of Control.* Westport, Conn.: Greenwood Press, 1981.

Miller, Stephen. "The Constitution and the Spirit of Commerce." In *How Capitalistic Is the Constitution?,* ed. Robert A. Goldwin and William A. Schambra. Washington: American Enterprise Institute, 1982.

Mirabeau, Victor de Riquetti, marquis de and François Quesnay. *Philosophie Rurale.* Amsterdam: Chez les Libraires Associés, 1764.

Montesquieu, Charles de Secondat. *The Spirit of the Laws*. Edited and translated by Anne M. Cohler, Basia Carolyn Miller, and Harold Samuel Stone. Cambridge: Cambridge University Press, 1989.

Montgomery, David. *The Fall of the House of Labor*. Cambridge: Cambridge University Press, 1987.

Moon, Donald. "The Moral Basis of the Welfare State." In *Democracy and the Welfare State*, ed. Amy Gutmann. Princeton: Princeton University Press, 1988.

Morgan, Edmund S. "The Fixers." *New York Review of Books*, March 2, 1995, 25–27.

Morgan, Robert J. "Madison's Theory of Representation in the Tenth Federalist." *Journal of Politics* 36(4) (November 1974): 852–85.

Mount, Ferdinand. "Against Smoothness." *Times Literary Supplement*, September 24, 1999, 11–12.

Mueller, Dennis C. *Public Choice*. Cambridge: Cambridge University Press, 1979.

———. *Public Choice II*. Cambridge: Cambridge University Press, 1989.

Muir, William Ker. *Legislature: California's School for Politics*. Chicago: University of Chicago Press, 1982.

Murphy, Walter F., James E. Fleming, and Sotirios A. Barber. *American Constitutional Interpretation*. 2d ed. New York: Foundation Press, 1995.

Nagel, Thomas. "Getting Personal." *Times Literary Supplement*, June 23, 2000, 5–6.

Nedelsky, Jennifer. *Private Property and the Limits of American Constitutionalism: The Madisonian Framework and Its Legacy*. Chicago: University of Chicago Press, 1990.

Neurath, Otto. "Protokollsatze." *Erkenntnis* 3 (1932–33): 204–14.

Newey, Glen. "How Do We Find Out What He Meant?" *Times Literary Supplement*, June 26, 1998, 29.

Nichols, Mary P. *Citizens and Statesmen: A Study of Aristotle's Politics*. Lanham, Md.: Rowman and Littlefield, 1992.

Novak, Michael. *The Spirit of Democratic Capitalism*. New York: Simon and Schuster, 1982.

Nozick, Robert. *Anarchy, State, and Utopia*. New York: Basic Books, 1974.

Nussbaum, Martha C. "Human Functioning and Social Justice: In Defense of Aristotelian Essentialism (in Morality, Politics, and Human Beings." *Political Theory* 20(2) (May 1992): 202–46.

Oakeshott, Michael Joseph. "The Fortunes of Scepticism: Dispersal of Power and the Tradition of English Politics." *Times Literary Supplement*, March 15, 1996, 114–15.

———. *On Human Conduct*. Oxford: Clarendon Press, 1975.

———. *Rationalism in Politics and Other Essays*. Indianapolis: Liberty Press, 1991.

O'Brien, Philip. "Monetarism in Chile." *Socialist Review* 14 (1984): 77–78.

Offe, Claus, and Ulrich Preuss. "Democratic Institutions and Moral Resources." In *Political Theory Today*, ed. David Held. Stanford: Stanford University Press, 1991.

Olmstead v. United States, 277 U.S. 438 (1928).

Olson, Mancur. *The Logic of Collective Action; Public Goods and the Theory of Groups*. Cambridge: Harvard University Press, 1971.

———. *The Rise and Decline of Nations*. New Haven: Yale University Press, 1982.

Oreskes, Michael. "Washington Talk; Iraq Puts Election Truisms to Test." *New York Times*, August 10, 1990.

Ostrom, Vincent. *The Political Theory of the Compound Republic*. 2d ed. San Francisco: Institute for Contemporary Studies Press, 1987.

Page, Benjamin. *Who Gets What from Government*. Berkeley: University of California Press, 1983.

Page, Benjamin, and Roger Shapiro. "The Rational Republic and Beyond." In *Citizen Competence and Democratic Institutions*, ed. Stephen L. Elkin and Karol Soltan. University Park: Pennsylvania State University Press, 1999.

Pangle, Thomas L. *The Ennobling of Democracy: The Challenge of the Postmodern Era*. Baltimore: Johns Hopkins University Press, 1992.

Parenti, Michael. "The Constitution as an Elitist Document." In *How Democratic Is the Constitution?*, ed. Robert Goldwin and William Schambra. Washington, D.C.: American Enterprise Institute, 1982.

Parijs, Philippe van. *Real Freedom for All: What (If Anything) Can Justify Capitalism?* Oxford: Clarendon Press, 1995.

———. "Social Justice as Real Freedom for All: A Reply to Arneson, Fleurbaey, Melnyk and Selznick." *The Good Society* 7(1) (Winter 1997): 42–48.

Peterson, Paul E. *City Limits*. Chicago: University of Chicago Press, 1981.

Pettit, Philip. "The Consequentialist Perspective." In *Three Methods of Ethics: A Debate*, ed. Marcia W. Baron, Philip Pettit, and Michael Slote. Malden, Mass.: 1997.

———. *Republicanism: A Theory of Freedom and Government*. New York: Oxford University Press, 1997.

Phillips, Kevin P. *Boiling Point: Republicans, Democrats, and the Decline of Middle-Class Prosperity*. New York: Random House, 1993.

Pitkin, Hanna Fenichel. *Fortune Is a Woman: Gender and Politics in the Thought of Niccolò Machiavelli*. Berkeley: University of California Press, 1984.

———. "Justice: On Relating Private and Public." *Political Theory* 9(3) (August 1981): 327–52.

Plattner, Marc. "American Democracy and the Acquisitive Spirit." In *How Capitalistic Is the Constitution?*, ed. Robert Godwin and William Schambra. Washington, D.C.: American Enterprise Institute, 1982.

Pocock, J. G. A. *The Machiavellian Moment: Florentine Political Thought and the Atlantic Republican Tradition*. Princeton: Princeton University Press, 1975.

Polanyi, Karl. *The Great Transformation*. Boston: Beacon Press, 1957 [1944].

Pole, J. R. *The Pursuit of Equality in American History*. Berkeley: University of California Press, 1993.

Posner, Richard A. "The Anti-Hero." *New Republic* 228(7) (February 24, 2003): 27–30.

———. *The Problems of Jurisprudence*. Cambridge: Harvard University Press, 1990.

———. "The People's Court." *New Republic*, July 19, 2004: 32–36.

Przeworski, Adam. *Capitalism and Social Democracy*. Cambridge: Cambridge University Press; Paris: Editions de la Maison des sciences de l'homme, 1985.

———. "Democracy as a Contingent Outcome of Conflicts." In *Constitutionalism and Democracy*, ed. Jon Elster and Rune Slagstad. Cambridge: Cambridge University Press, 1988.

Putnam, Robert D. *Bowling Alone: The Collapse and Revival of American Community*. New York: Simon and Schuster, 2000.

———. *Making Democracy Work*. Princeton: Princeton University Press, 1993.

Radin, Margaret Jane. "The Liberal Conception of Property: Cross Currents in the Jurisprudence of Takings." *Columbia Law Review* 88 (1988): 1667–96.

Rae, Douglas W. *The Political Consequences of Electoral Laws*. New Haven: Yale University Press, 1971.

Rakove, Jack. "A Nation Still Learning What Madison Knew." *New York Times*, March 11, 2001.

———. *Original Meanings: Politics and Ideas in the Making of the Constitution*. New York: Knopf, 1996.

Rawls, John. "The Idea of an Overlapping Consensus." *Oxford Journal for Legal Studies* 7(1) (Spring 1987): 1–25.

———. *Justice as Fairness: A Restatement*. Edited by Erin Kelly. Cambridge: Harvard University Press, 2001.

———. *Political Liberalism*. New York: Columbia University Press, 1996.

———. *A Theory of Justice*. Cambridge: Harvard University Press, Belknap Press, 1999.

Reich, Robert B. *Locked in the Cabinet*. New York: Knopf, 1997.

———. *The Work of Nations: Preparing Ourselves for 21st-Century Capitalism*. New York: Knopf, 1991.

Reid, John Phillip. *The Concept of Liberty in the Age of the American Revolution*. Chicago: University of Chicago Press, 1988.

Roemer, John E. *Equal Shares: Making Market Socialism Work*. Edited by Erik Olin Wright. London: Verso, 1996.

Rohr, John. *To Run a Constitution: The Legitimacy of the Administrative State*. Lawrence, Kan.: University Press of Kansas, 1986.

Roosevelt, Franklin D. *The Public Papers and Addresses of Franklin D. Roosevelt*. New York: Random House, 1938–50.

Rosen, Gary. *American Compact: James Madison and the Problem of Founding*. Lawrence, Kan.: University Press of Kansas, 1999.

Rosen, Stanley. *The Ancients and the Moderns: Rethinking Modernity*. New Haven: Yale University Press, 1989.

———. *Hermeneutics as Politics*. New York : Oxford University Press, 1987.

Rosenberg, Gerald N. *The Hollow Hope: Can Courts Bring About Social Change?* Chicago: University of Chicago, 1991.

Rosenblum, Nancy L., ed. *Liberalism and the Moral Life*. Cambridge: Harvard University Press, 1989.

———. *Membership and Morals: The Personal Uses of Pluralism in America*. Princeton: Princeton University Press, 1998.

Rousseau, Jean-Jacques. *The Social Contract and Other Later Political Writings*. Edited and translated by Victor Gourevitch. Cambridge: Cambridge University Press, 1997.

Samuelson, Robert. "Nothing Exceeds Like Excess." *Washington Post*, November 5, 203.

Salkever, Stephen. *Finding the Mean.* Princeton: Princeton University Press, 1990.

San Antonio Independent School District v. Rodriguez, 411 U.S. 1 (1973).

Sandel, Michael J. *Democracy's Discontent: America in Search of a Public Philosophy.* Cambridge: Harvard University Press, Belknap Press, 1996.

Scalia, Antonin. "The Rule of Law as a Law of Rules." *University of Chicago Law Review* 56(4) (Fall 1989): 1175–88.

Schaefer, David Lewis. *Justice or Tyranny? A Critique of John Rawls's "Theory of Justice."* Port Washington, N.Y.: Kennikat Press, 1979.

Schattschneider, E. E. *Party Government.* Westport, Conn.: Greenwood Press, 1977 [1942].

———. *The Semisovereign People: A Realist's View of Democracy in America.* Reissued with an introduction by David Adamany. Fort Worth, Tex.: Harcourt Brace Jovanovich College Publishers, 1975.

Schlesinger, Arthur. *The Cycles of American History.* Boston: Houghton Mifflin, 1986.

Schmitter, Philippe. "Still the Century of Corporatism?" *Review of Politics* (Spring 1974): 85–130.

Schudson, Michael. *The Good Citizen: A History of American Civic Life.* New York: Martin Kessler, 1998.

———. "The Social Construction of the 'Informed Citizen.'" *The Good Society* 9(1) (1999): 30–35.

Segal, Jerome M. *Graceful Simplicity: Toward a Philosophy and Politics of Simple Living.* New York: Holt, 1999.

Seigan, Bernard. "The Constitution and the Protection of Capitalism." In *How Capitalistic Is the Constitution?,* ed. Robert Goldwin and William Schambra. Washington, D.C.: American Enterprise Institute, 1982.

Sellers, Mortimer. "Forming a More Perfect Union." *Washington Post,* May 12, 1996.

Selznick, Philip. "Defining Democracy Up." *Public Interest* (Spring 1995): 106–10.

Sen, Amartya Kumar. *Collective Choice and Social Welfare.* San Francisco: Holden-Day, 1970.

———. *Development as Freedom.* New York: Knopf, 1999.

———. "Rational Fools: A Critique of the Behavioral Foundations of Economic Theory." *Philosophy and Public Affairs* 6(4) (Summer 1977): 317–44.

———. "Utilitarianism and Welfarism." *Journal of Philosophy* 76 (September 1979): 463–80.

Shapiro, Martin. "Judicial Review in France." *Tocqueville Review* 12 (1990–91): 3–20.

Shattuck, Roger. "The Reddening of America." *New York Review of Books,* March 30, 1989, 3–5.

Shklar, Judith. *American Citizenship: The Quest for Inclusion.* Cambridge: Harvard University Press, 1991.

———. *Legalism.* Cambridge: Harvard University Press, 1964.

———. "The Liberalism of Fear." In *Liberalism and the Moral Life,* ed. Nancy L. Rosenblum. Cambridge: Harvard University Press, 1989.

———. *Men and Citizens: A Study of Rousseau's Social Theory.* Cambridge: Cambridge University Press, 1969.

———. *Ordinary Vices.* Cambridge: Harvard University Press, Belknap Press, 1984.

Siena, James V., ed. *Antitrust and Local Government: Perspectives on the Boulder Decision.* Cabin John, Md.: published for the National League of Cities by Seven Locks Press, 1982.

Simon, William. "Social Republican Property." *UCLA Law Review* 38 (1991): 1335–1413.

Simons, Henry Calvert. *Economic Policy for a Free Society.* Chicago: University of Chicago Press, 1948.

Sinclair, Barbara. *Legislators, Leaders and Lawmakers.* Baltimore: Johns Hopkins University Press, 1995.

Smith, Adam. *An Inquiry into the Nature and Causes of the Wealth of Nations.* Edited by Edwin Cannan. New York: Modern Library, 1937.

———. *The Theory of Moral Sentiments.* Edited by Knud Haakonssen. Cambridge: Cambridge University Press, 2002.

Smith, James Morton, ed. *The Republic of Letters: The Correspondence between Jefferson and Madison 1776–1826.* New York: Norton, 1995.

Smith, Rogers. *Civic Ideals: Conflicting Visions of Citizenship in U.S. History.* New Haven: Yale University Press, 1997.

———. *Liberalism and American Constitutional Law.* Cambridge: Harvard University Press, 1985.

Snowiss, Sylvia. *Judicial Review and the Law of the Constitution.* New Haven: Yale University Press, 1990.

Soltan, Karol Edward. *The Causal Theory of Justice.* Berkeley: University of California Press, 1987.

———. "Generic Constitutionalism." In *A New Constitutionalism: Designing Political Institutions for a Good Society,* ed. Stephen L. Elkin and Karol Soltan. Chicago: University of Chicago Press, 1993.

Soltan, Karol, and Stephen L. Elkin, *The Constitution of Good Societies.* University Park, Penn.: Pennsylvania State University Press, 1996.

Starobinski, Jean. "A Letter from Rousseau." *New York Review of Books,* May 5, 2003, 31.

Stauber, Leland. *A New Program for Democratic Socialism.* Carbondale, Ill.: Four Willows Press, 1987.

Steele, David Ramsay. *From Marx to Mises: Post-Capitalist Society and the Challenge of Economic Calculation.* La Salle, Ill.: Open Court, 1992.

Sterk, Stewart E. "The Federalist Dimension of Regulatory Takings Jurisprudence." *Yale Law Journal* 114(2) (2004): 203–71.

Stigler, George Joseph. *The Citizen and the State: Essays on Regulation.* Chicago: University of Chicago Press, 1975.

Stimson, Shannon C. *The American Revolution in the Law: Anglo-American Jurisprudence before John Marshall.* Princeton: Princeton University Press, 1990.

Stokey, Edith, and Richard Zeckhauser. *A Primer for Policy Analysis.* New York: Norton, 1978.

Stoner, James Reist. *Common Law and Liberal Theory: Coke, Hobbes, and the Origins of American Constitutionalism.* Lawrence, Kan.: University Press of Kansas, 1992.

Storing, Herbert J. "The Constitution and the Bill of Rights." In *How Does the Constitution Secure Rights?*, ed. Robert A. Goldwin and William A. Schambra. Washington, D.C.: American Enterprise Institute, 1985.

———. "Political Parties and the Bureaucracy." In *Political Parties USA*, ed. Robert Goldwin. Chicago: Rand McNally, 1961.

———. *What the Anti-Federalists Were For.* Chicago: University of Chicago Press, 1981.

Stourzh, Gerald. "*Constitution:* Changing Meanings of the Term from the Early Seventeenth to the Late Eighteenth Century." In *Conceptual Changes and the Constitution*, ed. Terrence Ball and J. A. G. Pocock. Lawrence, Kan.: University Press of Kansas, 1988.

Strauss, Leo. *Natural Right and History.* Chicago: University of Chicago Press, 1971 [1953].

———. *The Rebirth of Classical Political Rationalism: An Introduction to the Thought of Leo Strauss: Essays and Lectures.* Selected and introduced by Thomas L. Pangle. Chicago: University of Chicago Press, 1989.

———. *Thoughts on Machiavelli.* Chicago: University of Chicago Press, 1978.

———. *What Is Political Philosophy? and Other Studies.* Westport, Conn.: Greenwood Press, 1973 [1959].

Strobel, Frederick R. *Upward Dreams, Downward Mobility: The Economic Decline of the American Middle Class.* Lanham, Md.: Rowman and Littlefield Publishers, 1993.

Sunstein, Cass R. "Beyond the Republican Revival." *Yale Law Journal* 97 (1988): 1539–90.

———. *Legal Reasoning and Political Conflict.* New York: Oxford University Press, 1996.

———. "Neutrality in Constitutional Law (with Special Reference to Pornography, Abortion, and Surrogacy)." *Columbia Law Review* 92 (1992): 1–52.

Taylor, John. *An Inquiry into the Principles and Policy of the Government of the United States.* Fredericksburg, Va.: Green and Cady, 1814.

Terminiello v. Chicago, 337 U.S. 1 (1949).

Thompson, E. P. *Whigs and Hunters: The Origin of the Black Act.* New York: Pantheon Books, 1975.

Tocqueville, Alexis de. *Democracy in America.* Edited, translated, and with an introduction by Harvey C. Mansfield and Delba Winthrop. Chicago: University of Chicago Press, 2000.

Tomlins, Christopher L. *The State and the Unions.* Cambridge: Cambridge University Press, 1985.

Town of Hallie v. City of Eau Claire, 471 U.S. 34 (1985).

Trenchard, John, and Thomas Gordon. *Cato's Letters: Essays on Liberty, Civil and Religious, and Other Important Subjects.* New York: Da Capo Press, 1971.

Tribe, Laurence H. *American Constitutional Law.* Mineola, N.Y.: Foundation Press, 1988.

Tushnet, Mark. "Thomas Jefferson on Nature and Natural Rights." In *The Framers and Fundamental Rights*, ed. Robert A. Licht. Washington, D.C.: American Enterprise Institute, 1992.

Tussman, Joseph. *Obligation and the Body Politic*. New York: Oxford University Press, 1960.

Uchitelle, Louis. "Ideas and Trends: Recovery? Not in Your Paycheck." *New York Times*, January 8, 1995.

Unger, Roberto Mangabeira. *False Necessity: Anti-Necessitarian Social Theory in the Service of Radical Democracy: From Politics, a Work in Constructive Social Theory*. London: Verso, 2001.

———. *Law in Modern Society*. New York: Free Press, 1976.

U.S. Bureau of the Census. "Census 2000 Summary File 3 (SF 3)–Sample Data" for East St. Louis city, Illinois. Available at http://factfinder.census.gov/servlet/QTTable.

———. "Census Bureau Reports on Residential Vacancies and Homeownership." Available at www.census.gov/hhes/www/housing/hvs/qtr404/q404prss.pdf.

———. "Dynamics of Economic Well-Being: Labor Force Turnover, 1996–1999." Available at www.census.gov/prod/2004pubs/p70-96.pdf.

Uslaner, Eric M. *The Moral Foundations of Trust*. Cambridge: Cambridge University Press, 2002.

VandeHei, Jim, and Juliet Eilperin. "Political Caution in Zeal for Reform," *Washington Post*, July 13, 2002.

"Vatican's Doctrine." *New York Times*, March 31, 1995.

Verba, Sidney, Stephen Kelman, et al. *Elites and the Idea of Equality: A Comparison of Japan, Sweden, and the United States*. Cambridge: Harvard University Press, 1987.

Verba, Sidney, and Gary Orren. *Equality in America: The View from the Top*. Cambridge: Harvard University Press, 1985.

Waldron, Jeremy. *The Dignity of Legislation*. Cambridge: Cambridge University Press, 1999.

Walker, Graham. "The Constitutional Good: Constitutionalism's Equivocal Moral Imperative." *Polity* 25(1) (Fall 1993): 91–111.

Walsh, Mary Williams, and Claudia H. Deutsch. "Is True Reform Possible Here?" *New York Times*, July 14, 2002.

Walzer, Michael. "The Communitarian Critique of Liberalism." *Political Theory* 1 (February 1990): 6–23.

———. *The Company of Critics: Social Criticism and Political Commitment in the Twentieth Century*. New York: Basic Books, 1988.

———. *Interpretation and Social Criticism*. Cambridge: Harvard University Press, 1987.

———. "Liberalism and the Art of Separation." *Political Theory* 12(3) (August 1984): 315–30.

———. *Spheres of Justice: A Defense of Pluralism and Equality*. New York: Basic Books, 1983.

Webster, Noah. "Examination into the Leading Principles of the Federal Constitution." In *Pamphlets on the Constitution of the United States Published during Its Discussion by the People, 1787–88*, ed. Paul Leicester. Brooklyn, N.Y.: n.p., 1888.

Wechsler, Herbert. "Towards Neutral Principles of Constitutional Law." *Harvard Law Review* 73(1) (November 1959): 1–35.

Weinreb, Lloyd L. *Natural Law and Justice*. Cambridge: Harvard University Press, 1987.

Weitzman, Martin. *The Share Economy*. Cambridge: Harvard University Press, 1984.

Wellington, Harry H. "Common Law Rules and Constitutional Double Standards: Some Notes on Adjudication." *Yale Law Journal* 83 (1973): 221–311.

West, Robin. "Rethinking the Rule of Law." Paper presented to the Workshop of the Committee on Politics, Philosophy, and Public Policy. University of Maryland. October 12, 2001.

White, James Boyd. *When Words Lose Their Meaning: Constitutions and Reconstitutions of Language, Character, and Community*. Chicago: University of Chicago Press, 1984.

Williams, Bernard. "Auto-da-fe." *New York Review of Books*, April 28, 1983, 33–36.

———. "The Reluctant Philosopher." *Times Literary Supplement*, May 29, 1998, 18–19.

Williams, Raymond. *Keywords: A Vocabulary of Culture and Society*. New York: Oxford University Press, 1985 [1983].

Williams, William Appleman. *The Contours of American History*. New York: New Viewpoints, 1973 [1966].

Wills, Garry. *Explaining America: The Federalist*. Garden City, N.Y.: Doubleday, 1981.

———. *Lincoln at Gettysburg*. New York: Simon and Schuster, 1992.

Wilson, James. *The Works of James Wilson*. Edited by Robert Green McCloskey. Cambridge: Harvard University Press, Belknap Press, 1967.

Wilson, James Q. "The Moral Sense." *American Political Science Review* 87 (March 1993): 1–11.

———. *The Moral Sense*. New York: Free Press, 1993.

Wingo, Lowdon, and Alan Evans, eds. *Public Economics and the Quality of Life*. Baltimore: published for Resources for the Future and the Center for Environmental Studies by Johns Hopkins University Press, 1977.

Winters, Michael Sean. "Balthasar's Feast." *New Republic* 221(9) (August 30, 1999): 39–44.

Wolfe, Alan. *America's Impasse: The Rise and Fall of the Politics of Growth*. New York: Pantheon Books, 1981.

Wolff, Edward N. "The Stagnating Fortunes of the Middle Class." *Social Philosophy and Policy* 19(1) (Winter 2002): 55–83.

———. *Top Heavy: The Increasing Inequality of Wealth in America and What Can Be Done About It*. New York: New Press, 2002.

Woo-Cummings, Meredith, ed. *The Developmental State.* Ithaca: Cornell University Press, 1999.

Wood, Gordon. *The Creation of the American Republic 1776–1787.* Chapel Hill: University of North Carolina Press, 1969.

Youngstown Sheet and Tube Co. v. Sawyer, 343 U.S. 579 (1952).

Zelizer, Julian. *On Capitol Hill: The Struggle to Reform Congress and its Consequences, 1948–2000.* Cambridge: Cambridge University Press, 2004.

Zuckert, Michael P. *Launching Liberalism: On Lockean Political Philosophy.* Lawrence, Kan.: University Press of Kansas, 2002.

INDEX

AARP (American Association of Retired
  Persons), 288
abortion, 238
Ackerman, Bruce, 275–77, 313n3, 315n26,
  336n1, 344n14, 366n2, 368n44
active government: as characteristic of
  well-ordered commercial republic, 14;
  Madison on, 27, 43, 44, 47–48, 49; public
  interest and limits on, 144–46; republican
  government as, 86, 149, 246–47, 269, 302
Adams, John, 324n143
administrative state, 54, 59–60, 64, 220, 224
Africa, 93
agency, centrality to liberalism of, 13
aggregative politics: and amount of
  legislation, 286–87; versus class politics,
  236–37; in Congress, 264; as corruption
  of deliberation, 239; Madison on, 237,
  357n36; as necessary in complex society,
  133–34, 237; pluralism and, 133, 237,
  238; versus public interest politics,
  237–39. See also preference aggregation
aggregators, 86–88; constitutional thinking
  contrasted with, 96; as proceduralists,
  128; and society without conflict, 92. See
  also aggregative politics
agrarian society, 25
Alperovitz, Gar, 369n45
Alstott, Anne, 368n44
Amar, Akhil, 150
ambition: of legislators, 171; Madison on
  controlling faction through, 24, 25, 26,

36, 49; and public interest lawmaking,
  165–66; in separation of powers, 152
American aspirations: and basic character of
  commercial republic, 5–10, 94, 251,
  304–5; as giving content to public
  interest, 132; majority support for,
  310n28; normative force of, 8; starting
  with, 10–11, 311n39
American political order: constitutional
  theory and present political practice,
  261–67; modest reform program for,
  275–305; reconstructing, xii; sources of
  discontent with, 1–2; thinking
  constitutionally about, 251–74. See also
  Constitution of the United States
analytic philosophy, 76, 328n4
Annas, Julia, 110
Anti-Federalists, 9–10, 310n36
Aquinas, Thomas, 362n29
aristocracies, 297, 361n25
Aristotle: on class rule, 248; on
  constitutional thinking, 3–4, 307n5; on
  family and public-spiritedness, 350n18;
  on middle class, 4, 357n23; on mix of class
  outlooks, 248; on natural law, 260,
  363n32; as not despising the practical,
  268, 328n3; on political regimes, 74, 89;
  on political science, 3
Arnold, Matthew, 44
Aron, Raymond, 333n61
aspirations, American. See American
  aspirations